SECOND EDITION

FROM RUSSIA TO USSR AND BEYOND

Janet G. Vaillant
Harvard University
Cambridge, Massachusetts

John Richards II
Phillips Academy
Andover, Massachusetts

Longman

Union of Soviet Socialist Republics 1989

ARCTIC

NORWAY
SWEDEN
FINLAND

GERMANY
BALTIC SEA

POLAND
CZECH.
HUNGARY

★ Tallinn
ESTONIAN S.S.R.
Riga ● ★
LITHUANIAN LATVIAN
S.S.R.★ S.S.R.
Vilnius

● Murmansk

● Arkhangelsk

● Leningrad

★ Minsk
BELORUSSIAN
S.S.R.

ROMANIA
MOLDAVIAN S.S.R. ★ Kiev
Kishinev ★ UKRAINIAN
S.S.R.
BULGARIA
● Odessa

★ Moscow

● Gorki

RUSSIAN SOVIET FEDERATE

● Kharkov
● Dnepropetrovsk
● Donetsk
Yalta ●
● Volgograd
BLACK
SEA
● Sochi
TURKEY

● Kazan

● Perm

Kuibyshev ●

● Ufa

● Sverdlovsk

● Chelyabinsk
Magnitogorsk ●

● Omsk
Novosibirsk ●

GEORGIAN
Batumi ● S.S.R.
★ Tbilisi
Yerevan ● ★
ARMENIAN AZERBAIJAN
S.S.R. ★ S.S.R. ★ Baku

KAZAKH S.S.R.

● Karaganda

CASPIAN
SEA

TURKMEN S.S.R.

★ Ashkhabad

UZBEK
S.S.R.
Tashkent ●
★
Dushanbe ●★

Frunze ★ ★ Alma-Ata
KIRGHIZ
S.S.R.
TADZHIK
S.S.R.

IRAN

AFGHANISTAN

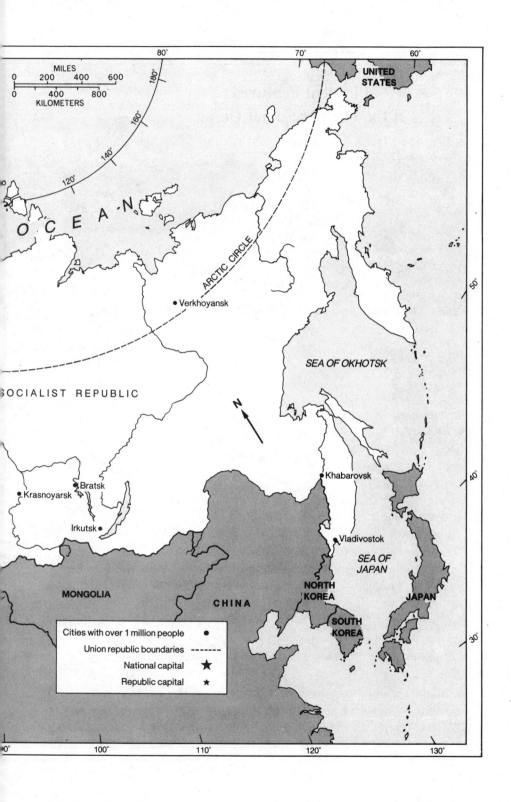

MILES
0 200 400 600

0 400 800
KILOMETERS

80°   70°   60°

180°
160°
140°
120°

O C E A N

UNITED
STATES

ARCTIC CIRCLE

• Verkhoyansk

SEA OF OKHOTSK

SOCIALIST REPUBLIC

50°

N

• Khabarovsk

40°

• Bratsk

• Krasnoyarsk

Irkutsk •

• Vladivostok

SEA OF
JAPAN

MONGOLIA

CHINA

NORTH
KOREA

JAPAN

SOUTH
KOREA

30°

Cities with over 1 million people   •
Union republic boundaries   - - - - - -
National capital   ★
Republic capital   ★

100°   110°   120°   130°

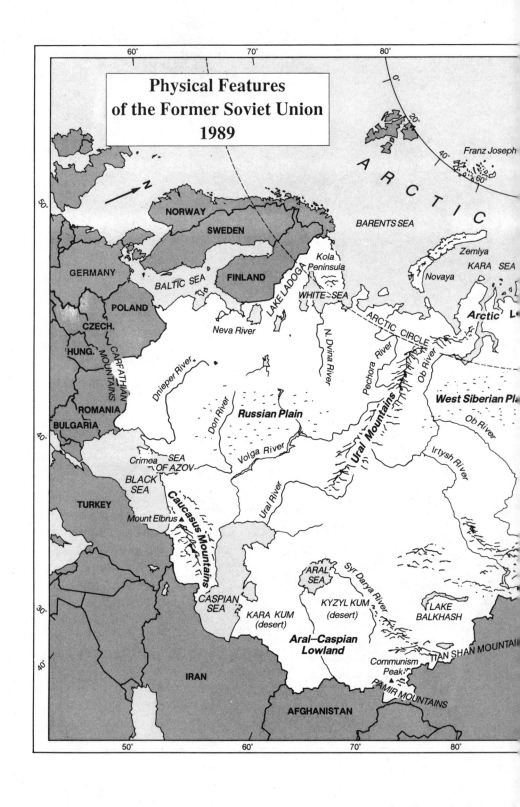

**Physical Features
of the Former Soviet Union
1989**

60° 70° 80°

0°
20°
40°
60°

Franz Joseph

ARCTIC

50°

NORWAY

BARENTS SEA

SWEDEN

Zemlya
KARA SEA

Kola
Peninsula

Novaya

FINLAND

GERMANY

BALTIC SEA

LAKE LADOGA

WHITE SEA

Arctic L

POLAND

Neva River

ARCTIC CIRCLE

CZECH.

N. Dvina River

Pechora River

Ob River

HUNG.

West Siberian Pl

CARPATHIAN MOUNTAINS

Dnieper River

Russian Plain

Ob River

ROMANIA

Don River

Ural Mountains

BULGARIA

40°

Volga River

Irtysh River

Crimea

SEA OF AZOV

BLACK SEA

Caucasus Mountains

Ural River

TURKEY

Mount Elbrus ▲

ARAL SEA

Syr Darya River

CASPIAN SEA

30°

KARA KUM
(desert)

KYZYL KUM
(desert)

LAKE BALKHASH

Aral–Caspian
Lowland

40°

Communism Peak ▲

TIAN SHAN MOUNTAI

IRAN

PAMIR MOUNTAINS

40°

AFGHANISTAN

50° 60° 70° 80°

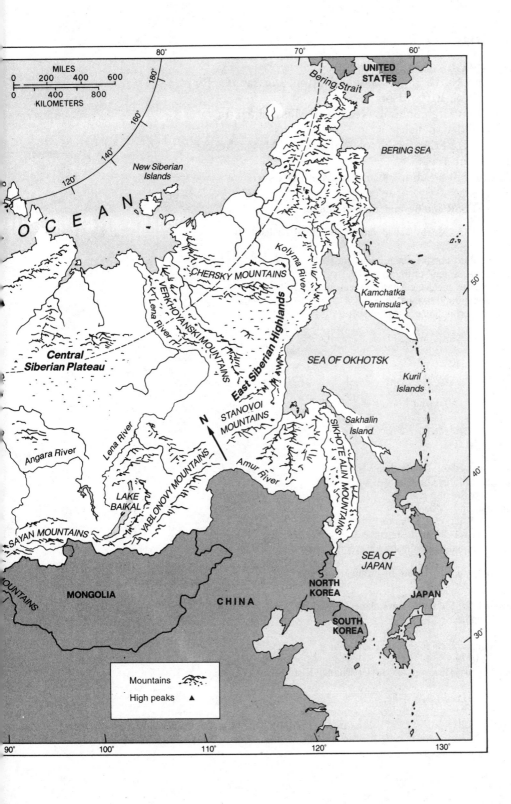

CONTRIBUTORS

Carol Horgan
Newton North High School, Newton, Massachusetts
Kendall Read Richardson
Needham High School, Needham, Massachusetts
Joan Sindall-Uspensky
Cambridge Friends School, Cambridge, Massachusetts
James J. Valin
Canton High School, Canton, Massachusetts

From Russia to USSR and Beyond, Second Edition

Longman, 10 Bank Street, White Plains, N.Y. 10606

Associated companies:
Longman Group Ltd., London
Longman Cheshire Pty., Melbourne
Longman Paul Pty., Auckland
Copp Clark Pitman, Toronto

To Our Children

Senior acquisitions editor: Lyn McLean
Production editor: Marcy Gray
Text design: Betty Sokol
Cover design: Susan J. Moore
Cover photo: AP/Wide World Photos
Production supervisor: Richard Bretan
Acknowledgments and photo/illustration credits appear on p. 404.

Library of Congress Cataloging-in-Publication Data

Vaillant, Janet G.
   From Russia to USSR and beyond / Janet G. Vaillant, John
Richards II. — 2nd ed.
        p.   cm.
   Includes bibliographical references and index.
   ISBN 0-8013-0779-1
   1. Soviet Union—History.   2. Soviet Union—History—
Sources.
I. Richards, John, Date   . II. Title.
DK41.V215   1992   92-4448
947.084—dc20   CIP

7 8 9 10 -ML- 99

CONTENTS

Chapter Four

RUSSIA IN REVOLUTION, 1917–1928 139

Chapter Eight

FROM RUSSIA TO USSR AND BEYOND   387

Appendix

Maps

PREFACE

The situation in the former Soviet Union is changing so rapidly that many teachers have wanted us to update this text. For the very same reason, however, it is with some hesitation that we set about doing so. An enormous struggle continues in all parts of that territory, the situation is unstable, and no one can foresee the future. The lesson for historians to ponder, and one that students can ponder as well, is how difficult it is to predict what will happen and how easy it will be some years from now to find reasons for why things turned out as they did. Hindsight is clear sight. Mikhail Gorbachev, and perhaps Boris Yeltsin, too, may be seen as transitional figures, but toward what, we cannot now be sure. We remain convinced that it is important for students to understand how the Stalin regime worked and the heavy legacy left by those difficult years. It is that system and its consequences with which leaders and peoples must now deal.

This edition contains an introduction on historiography. It is intended to encourage students to think about the hows and whys of the writing of history. Chapter 7 is also entirely new and has been written to complete the story up to the time of Gorbachev's resignation at the end of 1991. Both were written by Janet Vaillant. John Richards took primary responsibility for selecting and editing the chapters' readings. We have tried to identify the most important themes and general trends, but have not provided detail about institutions that may well prove transitory. There are also small revisions elsewhere in this edition. New facts brought to light by Soviet journalists and historians who are now able to speak more honestly about their past have been incorporated in places where they add precision to our account. We have deleted a few readings and added others, including two by Russian eyewitnesses of recent events that were written especially for this edition.

We would like to thank the students who read and commented on the text: Christopher Clay, Gregg S. Constantino, Annmarie Faiella, Tammy Jones, and Meghan McVay, as well as a Russian colleague, Anatoly I. Golovatenko, and several teachers, Lee Campbell, Robert A. Cole, and William S. Rogers, who read and commented on the new material. Thanks are also due to David O'Neil, Amanda Leness, and especially Rachel Graham for their reading and general support. Special thanks go to our editor at Longman, Lyn McLean, and her colleagues, Marcy Gray, Aerin Csigay, and Polly Kummel. Finally we are grateful to those students and teachers who have used this book and encouraged us to keep it current.

INTRODUCTION:
THE WRITING OF HISTORY

It has often been observed that "history is written by the victors." This was particularly true in the Soviet Union. The Communist party leaders who came to power after the revolution of 1917 believed that ideas were very important. They maintained strict control over what could be published, or even said aloud in public. Soviet historians and writers were expected to present a version of the Soviet past that justified the Communist party's rule and showed that all of the decisions that its leaders had made had been the right ones. Their work helped to provide the party with its legitimacy, that is, it provided justification for the party's rule over the country.

The enormous secrecy within the Soviet Union about what had happened there since the Revolution of 1917 also distorted what outsiders knew about Soviet history. Most American scholars and journalists who reported on the Soviet Union emphasized the brutality of Stalinism and reported on the repressions of the Brezhnev era. They could not fill in the details, however, and could only estimate how many people had been killed. When discussing the Soviet economy, they had to base their work on small bits of evidence and official Soviet statistics that were not always accurate. American scholars could not travel freely in the Soviet Union to investigate these matters. They had to get special permission to consult Soviet archives and records in order to confirm their ideas, and often that permission was not granted. Furthermore, many Western scholars were subtly influenced by the fear that if their writings were too critical of the Soviet Union, they might be denied permission to visit the USSR or to use any archives at all. These factors influenced what Western scholars thought and wrote about the USSR.

The politics of the Cold War, as the post-World War II competition between the USSR and the United States and its West European allies was called, also influenced what Americans read and thought about the Soviet Union. This period lasted from the end of World War II until the end of the 1980s, with only a few interludes of slightly better relations. During this time, American writers often used terms that indicated their hostility to the Soviet government, referring to the "godless communists" or the "totalitarian regime," a term that was often not carefully defined and became synonymous with "evil."

Even books written during this time that tried to avoid emotional and judgmental language usually emphasized the differences between the United States and the Soviet Union: differences in past experience, values, and present organization of the two societies. What was written was usually "true," but the part of the truth chosen, the way it was put together, and the language chosen—a word such as "regime" rather than "government" or descriptions such as "the faceless communist leadership"—emphasized the gap between "we" and "they," the freedom-loving, individualistic West and the oppressed, collectivist East. This general approach naturally spilled over into the history textbooks used in many schools. In the Soviet Union, even more than in the United States, history textbooks did not present a balanced picture and used language that helped portray the other side as an evil enemy.

One question students of the past need to think about is: "What is history anyway?" The word *history* is defined in a number of different ways. It refers to a branch of knowledge—knowledge of the past. It also includes the idea that history is a story. Like any story, it must have a narrator, a person who tells it, as well as an object, the events that have taken place in the past. Consider the people you know. They often tell simple stories about what happened to them yesterday or last year. Parents and grandparents tell about their youth. Most of us tell stories to friends about experiences we have had. If you listen to the stories people tell, you will notice that everyone chooses which stories to tell, what to emphasize in the story, and what to leave out. These choices may vary depending on the context in which the narrator finds himself.

If, for example, three people who were all present at the same incident tell what "really happened," their stories can be so different that it is hard to believe they are talking about the same event. Each will choose certain details to emphasize and will pick his or her own words in order to give the story what each considers to be the right emotional impact. The result is three stories about the same past event that differ because the narrators were different, and each of them had his or her own point of view about what was important and what it meant.

When we tell stories about ourselves, we are likely to become particularly selective. We shape our stories to fit our idea about ourselves, and what we want others to think about us. We do not point out that we dropped the ball in the second inning of the baseball game, but rather that we hit the single that moved the runner to third base in the fifth inning. We are not lying; we are recounting true facts. In a sense we are telling the truth, but it is a selected truth. Sometimes we do not even notice the way we have "rewritten the past." As our lives grow longer, and the events we are talking about grow farther away from the present, this tendency to rewrite the past affects what incidents and anecdotes we tell about ourselves, what part of our childhood we recall for others, and even what we honestly think happened. Sometimes a friend will recall an incident about us that we have forgotten, and if we like the story, and particularly if we like what it suggests about ourselves, we may add this new story to those we "remember." To this extent, we are all "historians," insofar as we all tell stories about the past. As we listen to the stories told by friends and acquaintances, it is easy to remember that there is a narrator as well as a set of facts about which the story is told. Sometimes this is more difficult to keep in mind when we are reading history books.

Professional historians differ from the casual storyteller. They undergo a long training period during which they learn techniques of investigation, how to work with historical records, how to evaluate sources, how to sift evidence and to bring order out of the many "facts" they discover. They distinguish between "primary sources," those written at the time by eyewitnesses, and "secondary sources," those written at a later date or by people with indirect knowledge of events. They learn, for example, to consider the motives and biases of a person who wrote or told about an event, and the differences between official documents and letters intended for use at the time, and memoirs written to place their author in a good light. Professional historians also develop skills for communicating to others what they have learned. Their published work is then evaluated by other historians who judge whether the author's methods meet professional standards and whether his or her conclusions take into account the discoveries of other historians working in the same field. Although historians often write about their own country or group, their subjects usually reach beyond their personal experience. Nonetheless, whatever place or time they choose to write about, it will have drawn their attention for some personal reason and because they think it important. Otherwise they would not put so much time and energy into trying to understand it and to present their knowledge to others. Good professional historians try to be conscious of personal motives that might influence their judgment. They think about general questions, such as whether or not anyone can ever find out or understand "what really happened." Their professional skill lies in their ability to build on the work of other historians, and their successful mastering of techniques for investigating, understanding, and communicating new knowledge about the past.

Professional historians usually begin their work with questions: "Why and how did the Puritans establish the first governments in New England," or "Why and how did Hispanic culture become so important in New Mexico?" They then begin research to understand what happened, how it happened, and why it happened. Historians often ask questions that are related to an important present concern. Ten years ago, many American historians asked questions about how the Communist party of the Soviet Union was able to establish and exercise its great power in the USSR. Perhaps this question can never be answered in a satisfactory way but many historians did research, wrote about what had happened, and suggested possible explanations. People then began to feel that they better understood what had happened.

Today, however, historians in both the former USSR and the United States are asking many new questions about the Russian and Soviet experience. Russians in particular are trying to find episodes in their history that illustrate their ability to develop a more open and democratic society. Historians interested in American history are also asking new questions. Twenty years ago, few historians investigated the role played by women at various times in the past, for example, nor was the role of African-Americans in the Civil War extensively researched. Today people are interested in the answers to these questions and historians have set to work on them.

The question that a historian asks at the beginning of an investigation is important because it directs his or her work. It helps determine which parts of the huge, complicated, and jumbled past are considered important and what should be emphasized in the final written account. For example, three historians of the Russian Revolution of 1917 and Civil War that followed—one of whom is asking questions about the participation of ethnic minorities, another of whom is interested in the role of women during that period, and a third who is fascinated by military strategy—will write quite different stories about these events. Later another historian may ask questions about general trends during this period, and draw on the work of his three colleagues in trying to answer his more general questions. In this way, historical knowledge is cumulative, but it is never complete. Changing times give rise to new questions, and suggest new approaches.

There is yet another issue to consider in thinking about historians and the past, particularly in relation to the work of Soviet historians, but it affects historians in other countries, too. This factor is particularly important in the teaching of history in schools. All citizens want their children to grow up to love their own country and to share the values of its "founding fathers," as we say in the United States. This is a completely natural and understandable desire. People prefer history that puts their country in a good light. Therefore, history textbooks are supposed to tell about the past in a brief, clear, balanced, and accurate fashion, but they are also intended to educate students to be loyal and good citizens of their own country.

In the Soviet Union, more obviously than in many countries, this second goal overshadowed the first. Soviet history textbooks simply left out unpleasant facts. They did not tell Soviet students about the millions of people killed by Stalin's purges, nor the millions who died during the campaign to collectivize agriculture, nor about the numbers of people put into psychiatric hospitals by the Brezhnev government because they had protested the unjust treatment of

Soviet minorities. The Soviet government maintained a strict censorship, and suppressed truth-telling when it might damage its claim to have always done everything in the best possible way.

Today, because of the policy of *glasnost*, journalists and historians are able to write more freely. They are investigating the facts about their own past and bringing a more complete knowledge about it to their peoples. They believe that without an honest knowledge of what has happened in their country, they cannot know how to build a better future.

The writing of good history remains a challenging task. Even professional historians who are not motivated primarily by political purposes, and who try to meet the standards of their colleagues, are not always accurate or just in their evaluation of the past. They may ignore an inconvenient fact that does not support their general theory about what happened, or be influenced by a point of view held before they began their research, or write in such a complicated and confusing way that readers misunderstand what they are trying to say.

The authors of this book have done their best to provide a clear, balanced, accurate, and fair account of Russian and Soviet history. To keep it short, we have had to leave many things out. We have been guided in our choice by the work of many professional historians, and by our own judgment as to which parts of the Russian and Soviet experience have had an enduring effect and seem most important for understanding the present. We have also included readings that present events from the point of view of people who lived through them. Nonetheless, all readers of this book should keep in mind that it, like all books of history, has a narrator as well as a subject, the Russian and Soviet past.

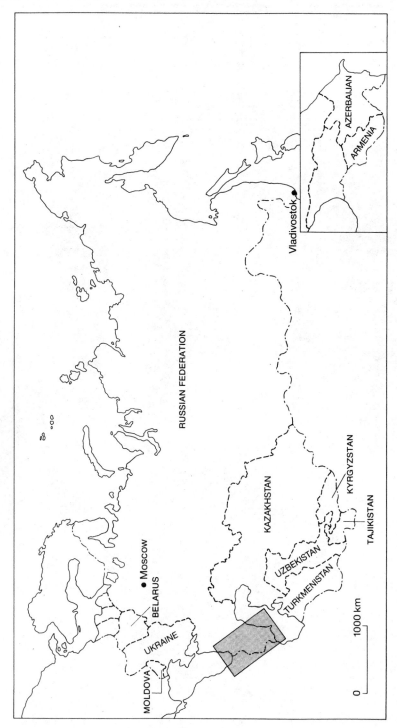

Commonwealth of Independent States, April 1992

Chapter One

GEOGRAPHY OF RUSSIA AND THE USSR

*T*he subject of this book is the history of Russia and the Soviet Union. To better understand that history, we should first examine the land these states have occupied—the vast territory between the heart of Europe and the Pacific Ocean. Because this territory includes parts of two continents, Europe and Asia, it often is referred to as Eurasia. In many respects, the geography of the Eurasian landmass is unique and dramatic and thus has provided an appropriate setting for a history that also is unique and dramatic.

Among the people who have lived in this land, the most numerous and the most powerful have been the Russians. Beginning in the sixteenth century, the Russians gradually built an empire by expanding throughout Eurasia and conquering neighboring peoples. In 1917, a revolution overthrew the Russian tsar, and in 1924 what had been the Russian Empire took a new name: the Union of Soviet Socialist Republics (USSR). While in theory a union of equal republics, in reality the country remained an empire, dominated by the Russians.

Now that huge empire has broken up, as the overseas European empires, such as the British and French, did. The fifteen republics that made up the Soviet Union have become independent states. Because this is a time of great change, it is difficult to know what to call the vast territory today. Eurasia remains, but the Russian Empire and the Soviet Union no longer exist as political entities. When describing current realities, we therefore will refer to "the former Soviet Union."

1

Among the many unique features of the Eurasian landmass, one is particularly obvious: its size.

SIZE

FACT: With 8.6 million square miles, the Soviet Union was larger than the United States and Canada combined. The Russian Republic alone, with 6.6 million square miles, is nearly as big as all of South America.

FACT: The USSR spanned eleven time zones, compared with just four in the continental United States. When it is 7 P.M. in Moscow, it is 6 A.M. the following day in Uelen, a village on the Bering Strait. As with the former British Empire, it was correct to say that the sun never set on the USSR. This remains true of the Russian Republic.

FACT: It is virtually the same distance from Moscow to Vladivostok as it is from Moscow to New York.

FACT: The borders of the former USSR were 37,250 miles in length, or one and one-half times the circumference of the earth. Nearly 27,000 miles were coastline, leaving more than 10,000 miles of frontier shared with twelve other countries.

Clearly, the territory occupied by the USSR was immense. For Russian and **Soviet** leaders, however, their country's size has been a mixed blessing. On the one hand, it has provided ample living space for a large and expanding population. It also increased the probability of having an abundance of natural resources to support that population. On the other hand, the vast distances confronted Russian and Soviet leaders with great challenges, such as giving diverse and scattered peoples the sense of belonging to one country. The breakup of the USSR in part reflected the failure of the Soviet leadership to meet this formidable challenge. A large country is hard to govern, communications within it become expensive, and its lengthy frontiers create staggering defense problems, in particular because the relationships of Russia and the Soviet Union with neighboring states were not always good. Nonetheless, the Soviet Union's status as a superpower rested, at least in part, on its great size. Even if the Russian Republic stands alone in the future, its size would mean it would be likely to have a strong voice in the future of the Eurasian world.

LOCATION

FACT: The westernmost point of the former USSR is farther west than Warsaw, Poland. Its easternmost point, Big Diomede Island in the Bering Strait, is a scant three and one-half miles from Little Diomede Island, which is part of the state of Alaska.

The Size of the USSR Compared with the U.S. (1989)

This fact illustrates a unique feature of the former USSR: It was the world's only state to occupy a sizable portion of two continents. The line geographers use to separate Europe from Asia is an invented one. From the Arctic Ocean it runs south along the Ural Mountains to the Caspian Sea, west to the Black Sea, and then southwest through the Bosporus and Dardanelles. Europe lies west of the Urals; Asia lies to the east.

This location posed a long-standing dilemma for Russian and Soviet thinkers and leaders. Their people have been adjacent to but not really a part of the great Chinese civilization to the east, the Islamic Middle East to the south, and Catholic and Protestant Europe to the west. In the course of their history, Russians have interacted with and borrowed from all three great cultures. Today's—and tomorrow's—Russian leaders must come to terms with the fact that theirs is a land that is both European and Asian, with vital interests in both areas.

Another important aspect of the geography of the Russian Republic, and therefore most of the land of the former USSR, is its northerly location.

FACT: Moscow, the Russian Republic's capital city of 8.5 million people, is on the same latitude as the southern end of Hudson Bay in Canada. The 3.5 million residents of St. Petersburg (formerly Leningrad) are at almost the same latitude as the residents of Skagway, Alaska.

FACT: Sochi, a favorite Russian resort on the Black Sea, is farther north than Boston.

Its extreme northern location has significant effects on the region's climate, as does the size of the Eurasian landmass.

CLIMATE: TEMPERATURE AND PRECIPITATION

FACT: The mean January temperature in Verkhoyansk, a small city in Siberia (the region east of the Urals), is −56°F. A temperature of −126°F was once recorded there.

FACT: Another, larger Siberian city, Yakutsk, has a mean January temperature of −46°F, and a mean July temperature of 66°F. Yakutsk has recorded temperatures as low as −84°F and as high as 102°F—a range of 186 degrees.

FACT: Eurasia has extremes of precipitation as well. The Black Sea coast of the Caucasus has an annual rainfall of about 100 inches, while there is less than 2 inches per year in parts of central Asia. European Russia averages 20 inches to 30 inches per year; this drops to 8 to 10 inches in eastern Siberia. On the whole, it is a relatively dry part of the world.

These facts have serious implications. They tell us a great deal about the impact geography and especially climate have on the people of an area and their economy. Much of Eurasia is subject to great ranges of temperature. Russia and the former Soviet Union have occupied a very extensive landmass with no large bodies of water to modify temperature extremes. Thus, much of Siberia can be blisteringly hot in the summer and frigidly cold in the winter. Eurasia has what geographers call a high latitude continental climate.

A location farther north on the globe than most of the United States means more than longer winters and shorter summers. It means that growing seasons are shorter as well. And that in turn means potentially serious problems in providing enough food for an expanding population.

A high latitude continental climate also means marginal amounts of rainfall for sustaining agriculture. This, too, affects food production and sometimes causes grain and meat shortages, a problem not only for the consumer but for economic planners. Under Soviet rule, the government saw to it that basic food prices were kept artificially low for the consumer, but subsidizing the consumer created a budgetary strain, which helped to produce the economic crisis that Mikhail Gorbachev inherited in 1985. The agricultural problems that plagued the Soviet Union were the result of inefficiency, mismanagement, and lack of incentive, to be sure, but it is also true that whatever the economic system, the country's location and climate will continue to challenge its ability to feed itself.

The climate has other effects as well. The Russians and some of their neighbors must devote great energy and resources to such elementary tasks as keeping warm and removing mountains of snow from their streets. Today, Americans are sensitive to the high cost of energy for heating and lighting homes and factories, and the same is certainly true for the Russians.

Finally, the bone-chilling temperatures point to yet another way in which the high latitude climate has made life difficult for the people who live there. The territory of the former Soviet Union, with nearly 27,000 miles of coastline, has remarkably few major ports. St. Petersburg, the second largest city, is one, but because it is so far north, it is icebound for most of the long winter. The same is true of Archangel, located even farther north on the White Sea, and of Vladivostok, the chief port in the Far East. Ironically, Murmansk, the farthest north of all the major ports, is ice-free year-round, thanks to the influence of the Gulf Stream. It is far from the country's industry and population centers, however. Ports on the Black Sea, such as Sebastopol and Odessa (both in Ukraine) are also largely ice-free, but do not have direct access to the major oceans, depending for access on Turkey, which controls the straits (Bosporus and Dardanelles) leading to the Mediterranean Sea.

TOPOGRAPHY

Examination of a physical map of Eurasia reveals its topography, including several significant mountain ranges. The entire area can be visualized as a gigantic amphitheater facing north toward the Arctic Ocean. The only high mountains are in the south, running in an arc from near the Bering Strait south and then west, eventually tapering off in the relatively low Carpathians of east central Europe. In the center of the arc, the peaks of the Altai, Tien Shan, and Pamir ranges are very high indeed, and close to the still higher peaks of Tibet, Nepal, and Kashmir. The eastern end of these mountains prevents moisture from the Pacific from penetrating the interior, and the high mountains of the south prevent warm air currents from the Indian Ocean from reaching the central Asian and Russian republics. The Urals are the only chain of mountains in the interior, and they are no barrier to the Arctic winds. Even if nature had turned them around by 90 degrees, they would not form much of a barrier; they are low mountains with an average elevation of only 2,000 to 2,500 feet.

FACT: The Pamir range in Tadzhikistan contains the highest peaks in the former USSR, with one greater than 24,500 feet—higher than any mountain in Europe, Africa, or the Americas. The highest mountain in the Caucasus range (and, incidentally, also the highest in Europe) is Mount Elbrus, at more than 18,400 feet.

FACT: To the east and west of the Ural Mountains lie two vast plains. On the east is the West Siberian Plain. At no point does this plain rise higher than one thousand feet above sea level. It is the world's largest area of level land.

The absence of natural boundaries, except in the south, created security problems for the Russians and Soviets, especially in the west. No river or mountain range separates them from their western neighbors, and over the vast plain that stretches from central Russia through Poland and Germany, tragedy has struck repeatedly: the Polish invasions in the sixteenth century, the Napoleonic invasion of 1812, and those of the Germans in 1915 and 1941. From the east came the devastating Mongol invasions of the thirteenth and fourteenth centuries. In times of national peril, the country's vast size and harsh winters ultimately became assets in thwarting enemies. In the era of nuclear weapons, all countries are vulnerable, of course, but the Russians and their neighbors have reason to continue to feel vulnerable to conventional weapons.

FACT: There are eleven rivers in the world whose lengths exceed 2,500 miles. Of these, four are in Russia. The longest is the Ob'-Irtysh at 3,360 miles.

FACT: Virtually all of Eurasia's rivers flow north-south or south-north. The Amur River in Siberia is a notable exception. Its course is generally west to east, and for much of its length it forms a boundary with China.

Eurasia is a land of rivers. It is estimated that there are more than 100,000 rivers in the former USSR. Traditionally, the rivers have been used for transportation, but they have two drawbacks. The first is that they are frozen

Log rafts on the Volga River.

for much of the year. (Passenger vessels plying the Volga traditionally begin their season on Lenin's birthday, April 22.) The other drawback is that with a primary need for transportation and communication that is east-west, rivers that flow south-north are only moderately useful.

SOIL AND VEGETATION

FACT: Forty-seven percent of the land of the former USSR is permanently frozen. It is called the permafrost zone because even in summer, only the top few inches thaw.

FACT: Forests cover 50 percent of its land area.

FACT: Swamps and marshes occupy 20 percent of the land area.

FACT: Seventeen percent of the land area consists of semiarid lands and deserts.

FACT: Only 10.7 percent of the land area is arable.

Note: These percentages do not total 100 percent because zones of topography and vegetation overlap. Some of the forest region is within the permafrost zone, while the swamps and marshes are part of the northern forest region.

Within the territory of the former USSR are several belts of vegetation, from **tundra** in the north to deserts in the south. But even in the areas that are frost-free for a sufficient number of days each year to permit crop cultivation, much of the land receives too little moisture to sustain good harvests. Where the forests have been partially cleared for cultivation, the soil is acidic and infertile. Such acidic soil is called *podzol*. In the **steppe** region of the southwest, the *chernozem*, or black earth, is exceedingly rich, but does not receive sufficient precipitation. Throughout Russian and Soviet history, there has been an average of one poor harvest in every three, causing shortages or famine. In the years from 1979 to 1982, the Soviet Union experienced four consecutive years of serious grain shortages, in large part due to drought. The droughts forced the importation of grain from Canada, Argentina, Australia, and the United States. Again in 1988 and 1989 poor harvests forced the Soviet government to increase grain imports by fifty percent, a trend that seems likely to continue in the near future.

NATURAL RESOURCES

FACT: The USSR was virtually self-sufficient in terms of raw materials. Two exceptions were rubber and quinine.

FACT: The USSR possessed the world's largest timber reserves.

FACT: In 1979, the Soviet Union led the world in the production of oil and coal. It regularly produced more than 20 percent of the world's petroleum and 25 percent of its natural gas.

FACT: Ninety percent of the former USSR's coal reserves are located east of the Urals, while 75 percent of the population and 80 percent of the industry are located west of these mountains.

Although the production and distribution of foodstuffs were serious problems for the USSR and remain so for the successor republics today, the Russian Republic itself is nearly self-sufficient in most raw materials, unquestionably a potential source of strength. For centuries, the Russians have depended on their abundant supply of timber for building and as a source of energy. Much of the timber comes from the extensive northern forest, known as the **taiga,** which consists largely of softwood trees such as spruce and fir.

In addition to its timber resources, the Russian Republic is in an enviable position as a leading producer of petroleum and the possessor of huge reserves of natural gas. Many of its natural resources are in inaccessible areas, however,

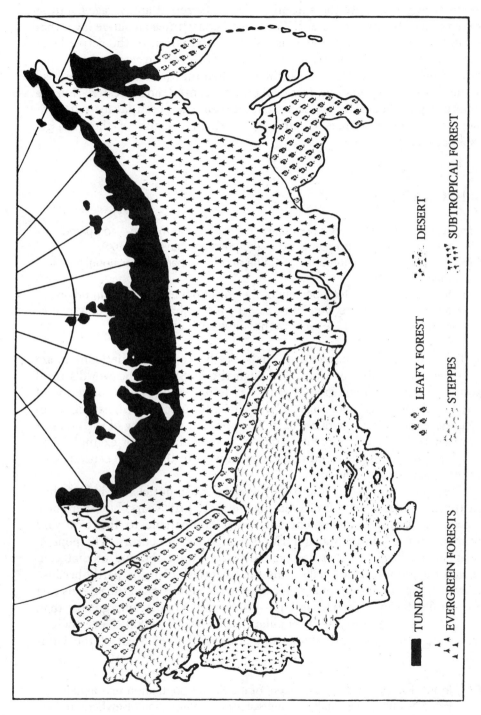

TUNDRA

EVERGREEN FORESTS

LEAFY FOREST

STEPPES

DESERT

SUBTROPICAL FOREST

Vegetation Zones of the Former Soviet Union

and are difficult to extract from the ground. This is especially true in the permafrost regions. There the subsoil is always frozen at an average depth of eighteen inches below the surface. The topsoil constitutes an active layer that is subject to thaw during warm seasons. The alternation of the active layer between frost and bog creates extremely severe challenges to miners and construction crews. Projects such as the Baikal-Amur Mainline (BAM) railroad and the natural gas pipeline from Siberia to central and Western Europe therefore require complex engineering solutions. The potential for self-sufficiency in natural resources is difficult to reach because of the climatic considerations.

DEMOGRAPHY

FACT: As of 1989, the USSR's population exceeded 286 million—compared with the 262 million registered in the previous census in 1979.

FACT: Only the People's Republic of China and India had greater populations than the USSR.

FACT: In 1926, only eighteen percent of the Soviet population lived in urban areas. In 1959 there were three Soviet cities with populations of a million or more. In 1989 there were twenty-three such cities.

The human resources of the lands of the former Soviet Union are interesting in a number of ways. Although the USSR had the world's third largest population, which grew steadily, it remained very low in terms of density, with immense stretches of land virtually unpopulated, especially in the Russian Republic's north and east. The population density of the lands of the former USSR is four percent of that of Massachusetts, for example. The areas of heaviest density are European Russia west of the Volga, central Asia, and the trans-Caucasus region.

The population is also shifting. Perhaps most noticeable is the shift from the countryside to the city during the past fifty years, but there also has been an eastward movement somewhat comparable to the westward movement in the United States during the nineteenth century. The population of Siberia began to increase dramatically toward the end of that century, and the growth continued during the twentieth century, partly because the Soviet leadership promoted the location of new industry in the regions east of the Urals. Today, Siberia has eight cities with populations greater than 500,000 and another forty with populations of over 100,000. Nevertheless, seventy-five percent of the Soviet population still lived west of the Urals in 1989.

FACT: In the 1989 census, 52.7 percent of the Soviet population was female. Females outnumber males by a greater percentage than elsewhere in the

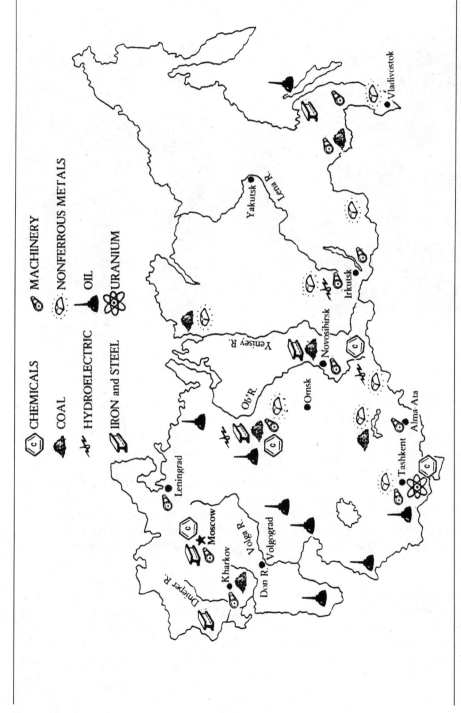

CHEMICALS

MACHINERY

NONFERROUS METALS

COAL

OIL

HYDROELECTRIC

URANIUM

IRON and STEEL

Leningrad

Moscow

Kharkov

Dnieper R.

Volga R.

Don R.

Volgograd

Omsk

Ob R.

Yenisey R.

Novosibirsk

Alma Ata

Tashkent

Irkutsk

Yakutsk

Lena R.

Vladivostok

Soviet Industrial Resources (1989)

11

Bukhara, the Citadel, Uzbekistan. *Photo Source: William Craft Brumfield*

world because of the ravages of the two world wars, especially the second, and the political purges of the 1930s. (See Chapter 5.)

FACT: The USSR included more than one hundred officially recognized nationalities, twenty-two of which had populations greater than a million in 1989.

FACT: In 1989, 50.8 percent of the Soviet population was ethnically Russian. While a large majority of Russians lived (and continue to live) in the Russian Republic, Russians formed the largest minority in ten of the fourteen other republics. In 1989, Russians made up 35 percent of Latvia's and 38 percent of Kazakhstan's populations, for example.

For the leaders of the Russian Empire and the Soviet Union, the tremendous ethnic diversity of the population was always a potential source of strife, but only in recent years have the full implications of that diversity become readily apparent. Each of the fifteen union republics of the former USSR is home to a particular ethnic group, which has its own language and traditions. In some cases the ethnic group had more in common with a non-Soviet neighbor than with other republics. For example, a large majority of the population of Tadzhikistan shares its religion, Sunni Islam, and other cultural elements with neighboring Afghanistan, and not with Russia. To complicate matters further, most of the republics contain significant minority groups, which do not share language or religion with the majority. (See chart on pp. 16–18.)

A significant trend in recent years has been the population growth among non-Russian (and non-Slavic) peoples. For example, between the censuses of 1979 and 1989, the Tadzhiks of central Asia increased more than eight times the rate of the Russians. The loyalty of some minority nationalities came into question when Soviet troops crossed into Afghanistan in 1979. Many of the invading troops were Muslims from the central Asian republics, and their commanders soon discovered that they were excessively sympathetic to the Muslims of Afghanistan. Entire units of the Red Army in Afghanistan had to be replaced by more reliable, non-Islamic troops. Loyalty became an increasing problem with the advent of *perestroika,* when many ethnic groups in the USSR took advantage of the greater freedom to demand at least greater autonomy, and then outright independence. This issue will be discussed in more detail in Chapter 7.

While the political organization of Eurasia has changed dramatically and continues to change today, the natural environment has not. It is still a land of extremes. It includes flat plains and high mountains, glaciers and deserts, places that are hot and places that are very cold. Over the centuries, its people have had to cope with the extremes. Geographical conditions have made it difficult to earn a living from the land and to feed a constantly growing population. Natural resources other than foodstuffs are abundant but often difficult to extract. Perhaps most important of all, the flatness of the land and the absence of natural boundaries created security problems and a deep-seated fear of invasion. The history of the Russian Empire, the USSR and the peoples of Eurasia has been and continues to be greatly affected by all these geographical factors.

PEOPLES OF THE USSR

The USSR was comprised of many peoples in addition to the ethnic Russians. While there are over one hundred distinct nationality groupings, the chart on page 14 is limited to those nationalities with over a million people; even here, the ethnic variety is obvious. (The prize for the smallest nationality, according to the census of 1979, went to the Negidal—all 504 of them in a northern corner of the USSR.) Note the diversity of languages spoken.

Nationality	Population	% of total	Language Family
Russians	145,071,550	50.78	Slavic
Ukrainians	44,135,989	15.45	Slavic
Uzbeks	16,686,240	5.84	Turkic
Belorussians	10,030,441	3.51	Slavic
Kazakhs	8,137,878	2.85	Turkic
Azerbaijanis	6,791,106	2.38	Turkic
Tatars	6,645,588	2.31	Turkic
Armenians	4,627,227	1.62	Armenian
Tadzhiks	4,216,693	1.48	Iranian
Georgians	3,983,115	1.39	Caucasian
Moldavians	3,355,240	1.17	Romance
Lithuanians	3,068,296	1.07	Baltic
Turkmen	2,718,297	0.95	Turkic
Kirgiz	2,530,998	0.89	Turkic
Germans	2,035,807	0.71	Germanic
Chuvash	1,839,228	0.64	Turkic
Latvians	1,459,156	0.51	Baltic
Bashkirs	1,449,462	0.50	Turkic
Jews	1,449,117	0.50	various
Mordvins	1,153,516	0.40	Finnic
Poles	1,126,137	0.39	Slavic
Estonians	1,027,255	0.36	Finnic

Talbot, Elizabeth, "1989 Soviet Census: Preliminary Results," in *Newsletter of the Russian and East European Center*, University of Illinois at Urbana-Champaign, (April 1990): 1.

The following books were helpful in writing this chapter:

Brown, A., Fennell, J., Kaser, M., and Willetts, H.T., eds. *The Cambridge Encyclopedia of Russia and the Soviet Union*. New York: Cambridge University Press, 1982.
Dewdney, J.C., *USSR in Maps*. New York: Holmes and Meyer, 1982.
East, W.G., *The Soviet Union*, 2nd ed. New York: van Nostrand, 1976.
Symons, L., ed. *The Soviet Union: A Systematic Geography*. New York: Barnes and Noble, 1983.
Whiting, K.R., *The Soviet Union Today*. New York: Praeger, 1962.

For students who are interested, we recommend further reading in the following works:

A Day in the Life of the Soviet Union. New York: Collins, 1987.
    One of a series, this very handsome collection of color photographs attempts to catch the many facets of the USSR at one moment in time.
Blum, D., *Russia: The Land and People of the Soviet Union*. New York: Harry Abrahams, 1980.

This large and lavish volume contains fine color illustrations that vividly convey the Soviet land and its peoples.

Konigsberger, H., *Along the Roads of the New Russia.* New York: Farrar, Straus and Giroux, 1968.

A readable account of everyday life in the Soviet Union by a Dutch-American who traveled through that country in an old Italian army truck.

McDowell, B., *Journey across Russia: The Soviet Union Today.* Washington, D.C.: National Geographic Society, 1977.

The combination of McDowell's text and Conger's photographs makes this a fine, albeit impressionistic, account of many aspects of Soviet life and culture. The authors had access to most parts of the USSR, in return for which the Soviet authorities approved McDowell's text.

Milner-Gulland, R., and Dejevsky, N., *Cultural Atlas of Russia and the Soviet Union.* Oxford: Equinox, 1989.

This oversized book has excellent graphics, lots of maps, and pictures of people and places. It is divided into three parts: geographical background; the historical period (from Rus' to Stalin and after); and regions and republics of the Soviet Union. This last section is particularly valuable for its visuals. This is a good reference work for libraries.

St. George, G., *Siberia and the New Frontier.* New York: David McKay, 1969.

Although its statistics are by now dated, this book remains valuable for its careful description and analysis of the vast territory of Siberia and its inhabitants.

Soloukin, V., *A Walk in Rural Russia.* Translated by S. Miskin. New York: E.P. Dutton, 1967.

This is an unusual account of the adventures of a Russian poet and his wife, who spent the summer of 1956 on a walking tour of the woods, bicycle paths, and tiny villages of the historic region around Vladimir and Suzdal.

Spring, N., *Roaming Russia, Siberia, and Middle Asia.* Seattle: Salisbury Press, 1973.

A photographic essay, in which the reader is treated to remarkable views of countryside, architectural monuments, and historic sites.

Terras, V., ed. *Handbook of Russian Literature.* New Haven: Yale University Press, 1985.

This marvelous book contains a wealth of information and is essential for a history teacher whose course includes works of literature.

The Soviet Union Today. Washington D.C.: National Geographic Society, 1990.

Essentially an updated version of the 1977 *Journey across Russia*, the editors enjoyed much greater freedom this time.

We further recommend the map published by the National Geographic Society in March 1990 in conjunction with this volume. It illustrates the physical and political geography of the USSR with a clarity and precision not possible in most ordinary textbook maps.

ETHNIC AND CULTURAL DIVERSITY IN THE USSR (1989)

Republic* Total population	Population breakdown		Majority Religion	Majority Language Group	Neighbor(s)	Religion	Language Group	Acquired by Russia**	Date of Entry into the USSR as a Union Republic***
Armenia 3.3 million	Armenians Azerbaijanis Russians Kurds	90% 5% 2% 2%	Gregorian Christian	Armenian (Indo-European)	Turkey Iran Azerbaijani SSR Georgian SSR	Sunni Muslim Shi'ite Muslim Shi'ite Muslim Orthodox, Muslim	Turkic Iranian Turkic Caucasian	1828	1936
Azerbaijan 7.0 million	Azerbaijanis Armenians Russians	78% 8% 8%	Shi'ite Muslim	Turkic	Iran Armenian SSR Georgian SSR	Shi'ite Muslim Gregorian Christian Orthodox, Sunni Muslim	Iranian Armenian (Indo-European) Caucasian	1813–1828	1936
Belorussia 10.2 million	Belorussians Russians Poles	79% 12% 4%	Orthodox	Slavic	Russian SFSR Poland Latvian SSR Lithuanian SSR Russian SFSR Ukrainian SSR	Orthodox Catholic Lutheran, Catholic Catholic Orthodox Orthodox, Uniate	Slavic Slavic Baltic Baltic Slavic Slavic	1772–1795	1924
Estonia 1.6 million	Estonians Russians Ukrainians	65% 28% 3%	Lutheran	Finno-Ugric	Finland## Latvian SSR	Lutheran Lutheran, Catholic	Finno-Ugric Baltic	1710–1721	1940
Georgia 5.4 million	Georgians Armenians Russians Azerbaijanis Ossetians Abkhazians	69% 9% 7% 5% 3% 2%	Orthodox, Sunni Muslim	Caucasian	Russian SFSR Turkey Armenian SSR Azerbaijani SSR Russian SFSR	Orthodox Sunni Muslim Gregorian Christian Shi'ite Muslim Orthodox	Slavic Turkic Armenian (Indo-European) Turkic Slavic	1801	1936
Kazakhstan 16.6 million	Kazakhs Russians Ukrainians Tatars	36% 41% 6% 2%	Sunni Muslim	Turkic	China Kirghiz SSR Russian SFSR Turkmen SSR Uzbek SSR	Confucian, Buddhist, Taoist Sunni Muslim Orthodox Sunni Muslim Sunni Muslim	Chinese (Sino-Tibetan) Turkic Slavic Turkic Turkic	1731–1860	1936

Republic / population	Nationality	%	Religion	Language family	Bordering country / republic	Religion	Language family	Date	Year
Kirghizia 4.3 million	Kirghiz	48%	Sunni Muslim	Turkic	China	Confucian, Buddhist, Taoist	Chinese (Sino-Tibetan)	1855–1876	1936
	Russians	26%			Kazakh SSR	Sunni Muslim	Turkic		
	Uzbeks	12%			Tadzhik SSR	Sunni Muslim	Iranian		
	Ukrainians	3%			Uzbek SSR	Sunni Muslim	Turkic		
	Tatars	2%							
Latvia 2.7 million	Latvians	54%	Lutheran	Baltic	Finland##	Lutheran	Finno-Ugric	1710/1721–1772	1940
	Russians	33%	Catholic		Sweden##	Lutheran	Germanic		
	Belorussians	5%			Belorussian SSR	Orthodox, Uniate	Slavic		
	Ukrainians	3%			Estonian SSR	Lutheran	Finno-Ugric		
	Poles	3%			Lithuanian SSR	Catholic	Baltic		
					Russian SFSR	Orthodox	Slavic		
Lithuania 3.7 million	Lithuanians	80%	Catholic	Baltic	Poland	Catholic	Slavic	1795	1940
	Russians	9%			Belorussian SSR	Orthodox, Uniate	Slavic		
	Poles	8%			Latvian SSR	Lutheran, Catholic	Baltic		
	Belorussians	2%			Russian SFSR	Orthodox	Slavic		
Moldavia 4.3 million	Moldavians	64%	Orthodox	Romance	Romania	Orthodox	Romance	1812	1940
	Ukrainians	14%			Ukrainian SSR	Orthodox, Uniate	Slavic		
	Russians	13%							
	Gaugazi	4%							
	Jews	2%							
Russian SFSR 147 million	Russians	83%	Orthodox	Slavic	Poland	Catholic	Slavic	—	1924
	Tatar	4%			Finland	Lutheran	Finno-Ugric		
	Ukrainian	3%			Mongolia	Buddhist	Mongolian		
					Japan++	Buddhist, Shintoist	Japanese		
					China	Confucian, Buddhist, Taoist	Chinese (Sino-Tibetan)		
					North Korea	Buddhist	Korean		
					Azerbaijani SSR	Shi'ite Muslim	Turkic		
					Belorussian SSR	Orthodox, Uniate	Slavic		
					Estonian SSR	Lutheran	Finno-Ugric		
					Kazakh SSR	Sunni Muslim	Turkic		
					Latvian SSR	Lutheran, Catholic	Baltic		
					Lithuanian SSR	Catholic	Baltic		
					Ukrainian SSR	Orthodox, Uniate	Slavic		

ETHNIC AND CULTURAL DIVERSITY IN THE USSR (1989) (CONTINUED)

Republic* Total population	Population breakdown	Majority Religion	Majority Language Group	Neighbor(s)	Religion	Language Group	Acquired by Russia**	Date of Entry into the USSR as a Union Republic***
Tadzhikistan 5.1 million	Tadzhiks 59% Uzbeks 23% Russians 10%	Sunni Muslim	Iranian	Afghanistan China Kirghiz SSR Uzbek SSR	Sunni Muslim Confucian Sunni Muslim Sunni Muslim	Iranian Chinese Turkic Turkic	1865–1876	1929
Turkmenia 3.5 million	Turkmen 68% Russians 13% Uzbeks 9% Kazakhs 3%	Sunni Muslim	Turkic	Afghanistan Iran Kazakh SSR Uzbek SSR	Sunni Muslim Shi'ite Muslim Sunni Muslim Sunni Muslim	Indo-Iranian Iranian Turkic Turkic	1865–1885	1925
Ukraine 51.7 million	Ukrainians 74% Russians 24% Jews 1%	Orthodox, Uniate	Slavic	Poland Romania Czechoslovakia Hungary Belorussian SSR Moldavian SSR Russian SFSR	Catholic Orthodox Catholic Orthodox, Uniate Orthodox Orthodox	Slavic Romance Slavic Finno-Ugric Slavic Romance Slavic	1654–1795	1924
Uzbekistan 19.9 million	Uzbeks 69% Russians 11% Tatars 4% Kazakhs 4% Tadzhiks 4%	Sunni Muslim	Turkic	Afghanistan Kazakh SSR Kirghiz SSR Tadzhik SSR Turkmen SSR	Sunni Muslim Sunni Muslim Sunni Muslim Sunni Muslim	Indo-Iranian Turkic Turkic Iranian Turkic	1865–1876	1925

*Upon gaining independence in 1991, some of the former Soviet republics adopted new English language versions of their names. Belorussia adopted Belarus, Kirghizia became Kyrgyzstan, Moldavia became Moldova, Tadzhikistan became Tajikistan, and Turkmenia became Turkmenistan. The other republics have retained the traditional English language versions of their names.

**Acquisition of these areas by the Russian Empire often occurred over many years, and the criteria for determining incorporation vary; thus, the dates are approximate. Please recognize the limited capacity of a chart to present complicated historical experience.

***In considering the date of entry into the USSR, it is important to remember that the Soviet Union as a federated state was created in 1924. Furthermore, many of the 15 Soviet Socialist Republics were at one time part of other republics or first established as autonomous republics. For example, from 1924 to 1936, Armenia, Georgia, and Azerbaijan formed the Transcaucasian Federation.

‡The Baltic states were independent from 1918 to 1940.

‡‡No land border, but is across the Baltic Sea.

+Moldavia (Bessarabia) was part of Romania from 1918 to 1940.

++No land border, but is across the Sea of Japan.

Source: Adapted from Cole, R.A. and Vaillant, J.G., "Activities for Teaching Russian and Soviet Studies in the High School," Social Science Education Consortium. Boulder, CO 1990, pp 20–22.

Chapter Two

THE ELEMENTS OF OLD RUSSIAN CULTURE

18 pages   3 days
9 stories   2 days

*T*he Soviet Union was a political entity that came into existence as the result of the Russian Revolution of 1917. It was a new state, but it inherited most of its territory and many of its traditions from the Russian Empire and Old Russia. This is the reason that historians begin the history of the Soviet Union by talking about the Russians. In Old Russia, as the period before the reign of Peter the Great (1689–1725) is known, a number of enduring features of Russian culture first made their appearance. In this chapter, we shall examine the origins of Rus' and some elements of Old Russian culture, specifically the adoption of Orthodox Christianity, the impact of the Mongol invasions, the traditions of the Muscovite court, and the culture of the Russian village.

THE FOUNDATIONS OF KIEVAN RUS'

Inquiries into the origins of Russian culture often begin by examining the cultural patterns of tenth and eleventh century Kiev. Kiev, a city on the Dnieper River, was the most important center in an area that was divided at the time into a number of principalities. These principalities did not form a single state and did not have any central administration or common institutions. They were, however, all ruled by princes from the same family. They shared the Orthodox religion, and all developed a written literature in the

21

Church Slavonic language. For these reasons, historians refer to these principalities collectively as Kievan Rus'. Although the Russian state actually emerged after the fall of Kiev, and to its north in the dense forests around Moscow, Muscovite Russia claimed the heritage of the civilization of Kiev and the other cities that formed the realm of Rus'. Today most historians consider that the heritage of Kiev rightly belongs to several nationalities, not only to the Russians, but also to the Belorussians and Ukrainians.

FACT: The first recorded history of Kiev, Novgorod, and the other cities of Rus' begins with the Viking presence in the ninth century.

FACT: Viking expansion in this period was not limited to Rus'. England, France, Sicily, and North America were among the places touched by these adventurous people.

Before the recording of history, Slavic tribes from central Europe had settled along the river trade routes in the western area of what was the Soviet Union. One of the major water roads stretched from the Baltic Sea, along the Dnieper River, to the Black Sea and on to **Constantinople,** the capital of the Byzantine Empire. In the ninth and tenth centuries, the Vikings, whom the Slavs called the Varangians, plied the rivers to exchange the products of the North—slaves, amber, furs, wax, and honey—for the products of the East— spices and fabrics. Varangian trade with Constantinople proved so profitable that the Varangians were determined to control the river routes. To establish their control over the region, they erected a series of fortified sites along the rivers that led from the Baltic Sea to the Black Sea. By the beginning of the tenth century, the Varangians had established rule over the native Slav population and given their name, "Rus'," to the territory centered at Kiev.

FACT: The name Russia comes from "Rus'," the name originally given to the Varangians who entered the area of Novgorod and Kiev in the ninth and tenth centuries.

Varangian and Slav cooperated in commerce, culture, and war. The Varangian ruler's retinue, or **druzhina,** consisted mostly of Varangian warriors, but Slavs were not excluded.

FACT: A *druzhinik* was a member of the prince's household. In eleventh and twelfth century military tales, he is a hero of great valor and skilled horsemanship. The *druzhina* was a small, efficient cavalry. It has been said that the Kievan princes maintained huge stud farms to breed horses, fined heavily anyone who injured a horse, and when a prince died, his favorite horse often was buried with him.

The developments and events of this vigorous period were recorded in chronicles, or annals, which are the only written records for this early history.

Kievan Rus' in the eleventh century. Moscow did not exist in the eleventh century. Because it was not founded until 1147, it is shown in parentheses.

They tell us that late in the ninth century the trading town of Novgorod in the northwest was troubled by disputes and that the people invited a Varangian ruler to settle there to restore order. This man, Rurik, and his successors united several towns into a realm that included Kiev. (See Reading 1.) Kiev eventually became the largest and most important city in Rus'.

FACT: Conclusive evidence that Rurik existed is lacking. He is a great mythic figure. He has been identified with Roric of Jutland, a Dane born in 800 A.D., whose father was an ally of the Holy Roman Emperor Charlemagne.

The Primary Chronicle is the earliest and most literary of the chronicles. Begun about 1040 and continued through 1118, it contains entries about important happenings in Kievan Rus' from the year 852. The chronicle writers, all of whom were monks, stressed certain themes such as the need for the princes to live together harmoniously and the importance of Kievan Rus' in the Christian world. The Primary Chronicle served as a basis for two later historical traditions, that of the North (Russia) and that of the South (Ukraine). The main Russian chronicles of the later period are those of Novgorod and Moscow. The authors of the Moscow Chronicle incorporated the Primary Chronicle as a preface, thereby implying that Moscow was the true successor to Kiev and that Moscow's princes were Kiev's heirs.

THE ADOPTION OF ORTHODOX CHRISTIANITY

The adoption of Christianity in 988 was the greatest single event of the early period. It is recorded in the Primary Chronicle and reverberates throughout it. The chronicler tells us that Prince Vladimir of Kiev (980–1015), a descendant of Rurik, decided that his realm must have a proper religion. He saw several possibilities at the time. He might choose Islam, which had been carried to central Asia by Arab armies and to the upper Volga by Arab traders, or Judaism, which had been embraced by the Khazars, a Turkic people on the lower Volga. Or, he might choose the Christianity of the Germans to the west or that of the Greeks to the south at Constantinople.* He consulted his advisers and decided to send emissaries to visit each area to see for themselves the rituals of each group. When his emissaries returned, they recommended against Judaism, which appeared to have been stigmatized by the Jews' expulsion from the

---

* Although the western and eastern branches of the Christian church had not yet split into two separate churches, already the practices of the Germans to the west and Greeks to the south differed considerably. About seventy years after Kiev adopted Christianity, in 1054, this division in the church was formalized. Thereafter there was a western, Catholic church centered at Rome, and an eastern, Orthodox church centered at Constantinople that was the official religion of the Byzantine Empire.

biblical lands, against Catholicism, which seemed too austere in its observance, and against Islam, which demanded abstention from alcohol. (See Reading 2.)

FACT: Vladimir is reported to have said, "Drinking is the joy of the Rus'. We cannot exist without that pleasure."

The emissaries expressed a profound admiration for the splendor and pageantry of the Byzantine Orthodox church. After attending an Orthodox service, they declared, "We knew not whether we were in heaven or on earth." Vladimir decided to be baptized into the Orthodox Christian faith and ordered that all his people should be baptized or risk his displeasure. Whether this legend is accurate or not, it illustrates two things. First of all, the people of Kievan Rus' in the late tenth century did not feel fully part of any one of the cultural areas marked by the great religions of the time. It also illustrates that the Orthodox church from the beginning was a state church tied to the will of the prince. The notion of a division between church and state, which became so important in western Europe, never developed in the Byzantine Empire nor later in Russia.

In the eleventh and twelfth centuries, the city of Kiev became the center of a rich Christian culture. Imitation of Byzantine Orthodox ritual and tradition was important in the cities where it was cherished by the upper classes, but for most of the rural Slavs, Orthodox practices and beliefs blended with pagan folkways. The early Slavs had worshipped the sun, the wind, fire, and other natural elements and believed their rivers and forests to be populated with spirits. Now, for example, Perun, the Slavic deity of fire and thunder, was merged with the biblical prophet Elijah, whose fiery chariot was prefigured by the famous Firebird of Slavic mythology.

Orthodox churchmen in Kiev borrowed Byzantine literary forms to express their new faith. Epic poems, military tales, and sermons were used to entertain, instruct, and glorify God and his princes. An early Christian writer proclaimed:

> Now hear with the power of your understanding!
> Thus hear, Slavic people!
> Hear the Word which feeds human souls.
> The Word which strengthens the heart and mind.
> This Word ready for the knowledge of God.

But, in fact, Kievan Rus' adopted Orthodox Christianity in its own way. There was great emphasis on ritual, chant, vestments, processions, and blessed icons in beautiful churches, all of which served to elevate and transfix the beholder. Although Kiev soon produced a vibrant Christian culture with numerous holy men and saints, it did not fully take part in the great theological and intellectual life of the Byzantine Empire. The church used the

Slavonic language primarily as a liturgical language in its services rather than to wrestle with religious or political ideas.

FACT: The Greek alphabet and language were not introduced with Orthodoxy. Two great missionaries, Cyril and Methodius, provided the Slavs with an alphabet—the Cyrillic alphabet in the second half of the ninth century, and a written language, Slavonic, based on their vernacular language. Not knowing Greek or Latin, literate Slavs were not able to read philosophy or scientific works written in those languages.

When Vladimir adopted Orthodoxy as the official religion of his realm, he sent for craftsmen from Constantinople to construct and decorate great churches. In this way, the icon, a venerated image of a saint painted on wood, came to Kievan Rus'. Just as the Orthodox church was an earthly reflection of heaven, the icons were a sacred reflection of the saint, the Mother of God, or Christ himself, to whom the faithful prayed. Legends surround miracle-working icons that helped to drive off enemies, and icons of Saint George, the patron saint of the army, were frequently taken into battle. As late as 1914, Tsar Nicholas II used an icon to bless his troops departing for World War I. Icons also were placed in a corner of a peasant's hut, and even today, some Russians continue to have icon corners in their homes.

FACT: Icon painters prayed continuously as they painted the holy images. It was a devotional as well as an artistic act. They sought to portray the super-natural rather than the human qualities of the subject and to copy original icons without allowing their individuality to show in their work. For this reason, the icon remains little changed in style since early times.

By the second half of the eleventh century, Christianity was established, and Kiev flourished under the rule of Yaroslav the Wise (1019–1054). Kiev was an important center of Christian art and learning. A magnificent cathedral dedicated to Saint Sophia (Holy Wisdom) was built, as were several other churches and monasteries. (See Reading 3.)

FACT: The Kievan prince wanted to build an enormous cathedral, Saint Sophia, on the model of the great church of Saint Sophia in Constantinople, then the largest church in the world. The builders did not know how to construct a single large dome, similar to that on the Byzantine church, so they created a new style characterized by many small domes.

Christian education also flourished, and Yaroslav the Wise created a great library in the Cathedral of Saint Sophia. Generous works of charity became the sign of a great prince.

FACT: Anna, daughter of Yaroslav, married King Henry I of France. She seems to have been the only lay person in the French court who could write.

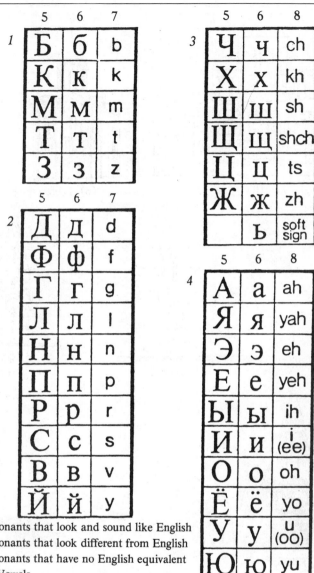

	5	6	7
1	Б	б	b
	К	к	k
	М	м	m
	Т	т	t
	З	з	z

	5	6	7
2	Д	д	d
	Ф	ф	f
	Г	г	g
	Л	л	l
	Н	н	n
	П	п	p
	Р	р	r
	С	с	s
	В	в	v
	Й	й	y

	5	6	8
3	Ч	ч	ch
	Х	х	kh
	Ш	ш	sh
	Щ	щ	shch
	Ц	ц	ts
	Ж	ж	zh
		ь	soft sign

	5	6	8
4	А	а	ah
	Я	я	yah
	Э	э	eh
	Е	е	yeh
	Ы	ы	ih
	И	и	i (ee)
	О	о	oh
	Ё	ё	yo
	У	у	u (oo)
	Ю	ю	yu

1. Russian Consonants that look and sound like English
2. Russian Consonants that look different from English
3. Russian Consonants that have no English equivalent
4. The Russian Vowels
5. Russian Capital Letter
6. Russian Small Letter
7. English Letter
8. Sound

The Cyrillic Alphabet

The Russians still use the Cyrillic alphabet as do the people of Belarus and Ukraine, though in the Ukrainian variant certain letters are different. In the Soviet era, use of the Cyrillic alphabet was imposed on many of the republics. With independence, the non-Slavic republics are considering new written forms of expression, either Latin or Arabic script.

(a) 1037   (b) 1165   (c) 1198

(d) 1475   (e) 1532

(f) 1555   (g) 1693

The Russian Onion Dome

The exact origin of the "onion dome," which typifies most Russian churches, is not known. One theory is that the flat Byzantine dome, seen on the now-destroyed Cathedral of Saint Sophia in Kiev (illus. a), was ill-suited to the heavy snows of the Russian north. Two smaller churches (b and c) illustrate the Russian architects' adaptation to their climate. The Cathedral of the Assumption in the Moscow Kremlin (d) has five domes (three shown here), a style popular in the later Moscow period. The Church of the Ascension in Kolomenskoye (e), built to commemorate the birth of Ivan the Terrible, rises from a low base into a brick spire called a tent. The tent spire and rounded domes combine to create the most famous of all Russian buildings: the Church of the Intercession in Moscow (f), popularly known as Saint Basil's. Finally, the development of the baroque style of architecture from the West is strikingly evident in the Church of the Intercession at Fili (g).

28

She also spoke three languages. Members of the Kievan royal family also married into the ruling houses of the Byzantine Empire, England, Germany, Norway, Poland, and Hungary. Connections with Kievan Rus' were important to western European rulers.

FACT: Some historians think that Kiev was larger than Paris and twice the size of London in the eleventh century. They estimate its population at eighty thousand.

This early period was also characterized by vigorous trading, a growing concern about princely feuding, and a real sense of being God's chosen in the Orthodox faith. Kiev, Novgorod, and smaller towns such as Chernigov*, Galich*, Rostov, and Riazan, linked to Kiev by trade and culture, were centers of a proud tradition. Life in these cities bustled with activity. In Novgorod busy markets resounded with the haggling of merchants and tradesmen over prices and with discussions of politics, especially the merits of their princes. The peal of the **veche** bell in Novgorod was a summons to participation in the vital questions of the day. The *veche* or town council was the place where events of significance were announced and important issues were debated. Novgorod occupied a unique position among early Russian towns. Its chronicle tells how the native inhabitants voted to throw out one high official and replace him with another in the year 1156. The potential for the development of popular self-rule in these towns, especially in Novgorod, appeared to exist. However, subsequent events, namely the Mongol invasions and the rise of Moscow, put an end to the development of self-rule.

A major weakness of the Kievan political system was its practice of princely inheritance. Each son inherited a share of his father's estate. The prince of Kiev assigned his sons and younger brothers to rule different towns on the basis of seniority. The older son usually received a larger town, the younger received a smaller town. This led to jealousies, power struggles, and the political fragmentation that plagued Rus'. (See Reading 3.)

The princely rivalries prevented the development of a strong monarchy or a unified state. No feeling based on a spirit of common interest and cooperation took root in this loosely organized realm. In fact, the princes feuded continually and with such bitterness that they were unable even to unite against outside invaders. The chronic disunity allowed the Polovtsians, horsemen from the east, and later the Mongols, to overrun the southern region and sack the cities of Rus'. In the face of impending disaster, some of the Slavs fled to the forests of the north. The way of life that developed in the northern forest combined with Orthodox traditions to become a new culture. A small town in the forest emerged as its center: Moscow. Kiev did not provide the sole basis for the new Russian culture, but its Orthodox Christianity, Slavonic literary language, and

---

* These towns are today in Ukraine. Russians call them Chernigov and Galich; Ukrainians call them Chernihiv and Halych.

the dynasty of Rurik were important elements in the building of a new Russian state.

THE IMPACT OF THE MONGOLS

The disintegration of Rus' actually began in the second half of the twelfth century. The Polovtsians, nomads of Turkic origin, entered the southern steppe regions and interfered with the flow of Kiev's trade with the Byzantine Empire. The invaders demanded tribute from the Kievan princes, occasionally pillaged Kievan towns, and frequently took captives. Military response to the invaders was feeble. The 1185 epic *Tale of Igor's Campaign* tells of the desperate effort of Prince Igor of Novgorod-Seversk, a town on the northeastern frontier of Rus', to expel the invaders and the failure of his brother princes to aid his effort. The epic leaves the reader with a sense of foreboding and impending disaster.

Fifty years after Igor's defeat, Kiev and other towns of Rus' fell under the Mongol yoke. In 1223, the Mongols, united under Genghis Khan, entered the area, but at his death in 1227 returned to Mongolia. A decade later, the Tatars, as the Mongols were called by the Slavs, returned under Genghis Khan's grandson, Batu. This time, the Tatars stayed and forced submission to the khan's will. The Mongols stripped the people of their portable wealth—jewels, gold, fur, and livestock. Land was the only thing of value that the Mongols could not carry away. (See Reading 4.)

Although the Tatar khan was the supreme ruler from 1237 to 1460—the tsar, as the Slavs called him—he did not try to rule the Slav lands. He did tax them. Local political life was never completely stifled, only controlled and altered by Tatar rule. The Tatars were especially efficient in tax-collecting, census-taking, and military recruitment. They imposed a payment of tribute, custom duties, fees, and tolls at all stages of the transportation of goods, and taxes on the sale of livestock. The collection, recording, and management of this money was well organized.

FACT: The Russian terms *kazna* (treasury) and *kaznachei* (treasurer) are of Tatar origin and indicate that this office and position were created after the Mongol pattern.

Competition to possess the *iarlyk,* the Tatar authorization to collect taxes, was intense among rival princes. Whoever had this right gained the favor of the khan and power over his rival princes. The prince of Moscow managed to become the holder of the *iarlyk.*

The collaboration between Moscow's prince and the Mongol khan resulted in the emergence of new institutions that formed the basis of a large, immensely powerful state. Perhaps the greatest consequence of the period of Mongol domination was the growing centralization of power by the new state, the center of which was Moscow.

The Russians also copied the military organization of the Mongols. Though they first met the Mongols as enemies, the Russians later served in the Mongol armies and campaigned with them. The Russian army of the sixteenth century followed the Mongol setup of divisions with five units: a big center unit, a right arm, a left arm, an advance guard, and a rear guard. They employed the Mongol tactic of enveloping the enemy on both flanks and copied the style of Mongol armor and weapons.

Mongol innovation included the recruitment of troops for regular intervals of service. In Kievan times, the rural population was not subject to conscription. The Mongol invasion changed that. A system of military conscription including the rural population was established. Furthermore, the prince created a new privileged group, the *dvoriane*, made up of military servitors who were granted land and position on condition that they serve him. They gradually displaced the powerful independent companions of the prince as his main source of support. This relationship, whereby the *dvoriane* held land and position only so long as it served the prince, was an important factor in the development of princely power.

THE TRADITIONS OF THE MUSCOVITE COURT

The prince of Moscow gradually united all Russia under his authority and assumed the titles of **autocrat** and tsar. His right to collect taxes on behalf of the Mongols was a key factor in his rise to power. Both Ivan the Great (1462–1505) and his grandson Ivan the Terrible (1533–1584) ruled with absolute authority using techniques of control learned from the Mongols.

FACT: Ivan the Terrible was officially crowned tsar in 1547. He used the title autocrat in the sense of a ruler absolutely supreme in the affairs of his country. The title tsar was borrowed from the Byzantines. Russians called the Byzantine emperor *tsar* or *caesar,* applied the title to the Mongol khan, and later took it for themselves.

Ivan the Great and Ivan the Terrible wore the cap of Vladimir Monomakh, a crown said to have been given to this early Kievan prince by the Byzantine emperor as a symbol of power.

FACT: The cap of Vladimir Monomakh is actually a masterpiece of early fourteenth century central Asian art. It was probably given to Ivan I (1325–1341) by the Mongol khan Uzbeg.

Ivan the Great's marriage to Sophia Paleologus, a niece of the last Byzantine emperor, gave added strength to the Russian tsars' later claim that Moscow was the rightful heir of the Byzantine Empire as the center of

Orthodox Christianity. Moscow princes began to view Orthodoxy as the one, true Christian faith and Moscow as its citadel.

FACT: The Ottoman Turks destroyed the Byzantine Empire. The city of Constantinople fell to the Turks in 1453. The Turks later renamed the city Istanbul.

FACT: Moscow claimed to be the "Third Rome." Rome had fallen into the Catholic heresy and Constantinople, the "Second Rome," had been overrun by the Turks. Early in the sixteenth century, the monk Philotheos wrote: "Hear me, pious Tsar, all Christian kingdoms have converged on thine alone. Two Romes have fallen, a third stands, a fourth there shall not be."

The Muscovite court continued the traditions of the Mongols in the conduct of diplomacy. These were often very different from the customs of western Europe. The Russians, like the Mongols, viewed ambassadors as guests who had to be provided with free transportation, lodging, food, drink, and security. Europeans sent to the Muscovite court were kept under constant surveillance. European ambassadors also were expected to offer appropriate gifts to the tsar, and in audience with the tsar they were expected to surrender their swords. Russian ambassadors to Europe were often indignant that they had to pay for their own maintenance. Moscow's familiarity with Mongol protocol made relations with the East more successful than its relations with the West and created a favorable situation for Russian eastward expansion.

FACT: Some Turkic peoples of central Asia considered Moscow a successor state to the Mongol Golden Horde. They called the Russians the White Horde and the tsar, White Tsar.

In fifteenth and sixteenth century Moscow, a new concept of society and its relation to the ruler was introduced. All classes were required to serve the ruler. If a person served and pleased the tsar, he was rewarded with land and men to work it. If he displeased the tsar, his land was taken away. As a result, even the most privileged of the *dvoriane* were totally dependent on the tsar for their economic position, as well as their political influence. The tsar then used the men dependent on him to crush the power of the formerly independent princes and nobles.

It was important to both tsar and landowner that there be adequate labor for the landed estates. Since land was abundant and labor scarce, this posed a problem. A peasant who did not like his situation could simply move away. To ensure a steady, permanent labor force on the estates, a means had to be found to prevent the free movement of peasants. The state established the legal institution of **serfdom.** Laws were introduced that bound peasants to an owner and to the land. Peasants could not move away without the landlord's permission and had to render him services. In effect, the landlord could do whatever he liked with the peasants, now called serfs.

FACT: The process of enserfment of the peasants was a long one. Serfdom was institutionalized in the Code of Laws of 1649. In contrast, by that date in France and England, the last obligations and restrictions on the peasantry were being removed.

By the end of his reign, Ivan the Terrible had succeeded in establishing an autocracy. The formerly independent princes and nobles had become permanent servitors of the tsar. Peasants were increasingly bound to the land as serfs. Military and administrative service became a requirement for the *dvoriane;* serfdom, taxation, and conscription became the burden of the people. Resistance to the new measures was crushed, often with the use of force.

The tsar not only increased his power over his own subjects but he also expanded his authority over his neighbors. This was a long process, with ups and downs, beginning in the Mongol period and continuing through the sixteenth century. Moscow's princes began to demand that they be called *gosudar* (sovereign) by the other Russian princes. In 1487, Ivan the Great backed up his demand that the Novgorodians recognize him as *gosudar* by sending his troops to Novgorod. So ended the town's long history of independence.

FACT: The removal of Novgorod's famous *veche* bell to Moscow in 1487 was a powerful symbol of Moscow's ascendancy. It also symbolized the end of Novgorod's rule by its town council.

FACT: Ivan the Terrible defeated the Tatars at Kazan in the 1550s. They became the first non-Slavic people to be incorporated into the Russian Empire.

Moscow also benefited from a delineated succession policy. The Muscovite succession remained in one family, with power passing from father to oldest son. This principle replaced the earlier practice of Rus' that viewed the realm as the collective property of the ruling dynasty and all its members. Thus Moscow could consolidate its gains.

With the death of Ivan the Terrible's feeble-minded son and heir, Feodor, in 1598, the Rurikid dynasty came to an end. Russians of that time could not conceive of how the realm could continue without a prince of the blood of Rurik. Feodor's death plunged Russia into the Time of Troubles (1598–1613), a prolonged period of dynastic rivalry, social upheaval, and foreign intervention. A series of individuals fought for Moscow's vacant throne: Boris Godunov, a regent appointed in Feodor's reign; Vasili Shuiski, a member of an aristocratic Moscow family; and pretenders supported by Polish Catholic armies. Chaos reigned. Famine and the flight of people to the frontiers worsened the sorrows and suffering of Russia. It seemed that the state would not survive. The Time of Troubles was a period of trial and partial disintegration (see Reading 5).

Yet, the Time of Troubles also precipitated the building of a great empire.

Russia emerged from this cataclysmic episode under a new dynasty, the Romanovs, who ruled without interruption from 1613 to 1917. The new Russian state continued its attachment to many of the traditions and cultural patterns of the past: Orthodox Christianity, autocracy, serfdom, and the relatively self-contained life of the village. (See Reading 8.)

THE TRADITIONS OF THE RUSSIAN VILLAGE

The northern forests were the home of the Russians throughout the formative period of both their state and their culture. By the fifteenth century, Moscow had become a center of Orthodox Slav civilization. This was a cold and remote frontier cut off from Constantinople and also from western Europe.

FACT: In the course of the fourteenth century, mention of Rus' vanished from French literature. Byzantine writers made the distinction between "distant" or "great" Rus', later Russia, and "near" or "little" Rus', later Ukraine.

The homeland of the Russians was poor and inhospitable. Great forests covered a land that had poor soil, bad drainage, and impassable swamps. Winters were long, dark, and bitterly cold. Summers were short and unpredictable. The Russians learned how to survive in these harsh surroundings. From the forest, the peasant took logs for his hut, wax for his candles, bark for his shoes, fur for his clothing, moss for his floors, and pine boughs for his bed. The forest also provided mushrooms, berries, and honey. As the Russians spread throughout the forest, they developed a remarkably durable and adaptive culture marked by the qualities of caution, determination, and endurance.

For most peasants, the world began and ended at the edge of their village. Given the vast distances and difficulties of transportation, each village was isolated from the next and had to be virtually self-sufficient. Like many agricultural peoples who have had to survive in small settlements scattered throughout a harsh natural terrain, the Russians developed a village organization based on the extended family and the principle of shared resources.

FACT: Individual Russians, even today, include the name of their father in their full name. This is their patronymic. The children of Ivan, for example, are called Feodor *Ivanovich* (Feodor, son of Ivan) and Maria *Ivanovna* (Maria, daughter of Ivan).

FACT: The Russian words for country (*rodina*) and people (*narod*) have the same root as the word for birth (*rod*); the words for native land (*otechestvo*) and land ownership (*otchina*) have the same root as the word for father (*otets*).

FACT: The Russian peasant spoke of "Mother Russia," thinking of it less as a political entity than a common mother (*matushka*) and its ruler less a prince than a common father (*batiushka*). Many peasants thought of the tsar as a father who would help them "if only he knew how they suffered," at the hands of the landlords and tax collectors.

The overpowering objective of the peasant village (**commune**), was physical survival. Until the nineteenth century, land was relatively plentiful and was considered the property of the group, not the individual. Each man received a share of the land for his own use. Periodically the land was redivided so that workers and land were equitably matched. As the commune was held jointly responsible for its obligations to the outside world, including the payment of taxes to landlord and state, and the provision of young men for the tsar's army, the group as a whole had an interest in the work habits and behavior of each of its members. If someone did not do his work, he could not contribute his share to the group's well-being, nor help pay its taxes (see Reading 6).

A village council resolved all local issues. It was made up of household heads and a village elder who discussed issues freely and tried to reach

A meeting of the village elders.

consensus. Unanimity and cooperation were important, for with the margin of survival so slight, failure of the village to work together could be life-threatening. Individual differences and self-assertion had to give way once the council had reached a decision. Thus, the culture of the Russian village was characterized by an effort to avoid risk and to maintain unanimity and order. The central importance of shared living in the extended family and commune shaped the traditions of village Russia. This way of life had taken shape by the middle of the sixteenth century. It changed remarkably little right up to the beginning of the twentieth century. Villages such as these formed the world of nearly eighty percent of the Russian people until World War I and the Revolution of 1917.

FACT: The Russian word for village, *mir,* is also the word for world and for peace.

The Russian peasant lived in a hut called an *izba.* Until the early twentieth century, it was made of wood. Nowadays brick sometimes replaces the logs and families are far better protected from fires. Although there were some differences in *izba* design between northern and southern regions, the construction was essentially uniform. The huts in the south tended to be quite small, approximately fifteen feet by twenty-four feet. In the north, the huge trees made it possible for the hut to be considerably larger. Many of the log huts in the north display intricate carving around window frames, shutters, and along the roof ridge. All the carving was done with a simple axe. Birds and animals were popular designs. Huts in the south tended to be painted.

About one-fourth of the space in the *izba* was devoted to the stove. To live through the winter without freezing to death, the peasants made the stove the center of their lives. It was made from clay or brick and provided many other services. On it clothes were dried, bread was baked, and food was cooked for the family. The stove protected the animals, too, during the long, harsh winter, and the warmest bed in the hut was across its top. Until the end of the nineteenth century, many huts had no chimney, and the smoke went out through the door or through a hole in the roof. When a family moved to a different house, coals from the old stove were brought to start a fire in the new stove, and when a bride left her family's house, she took with her a piece of clay from the stove to protect her in her new home.

Today, even in modern apartments, the kitchen is the gathering place for friends, and the stove symbolically retains its central importance. Hospitality among the Russian people has been and remains especially important. To be invited to sit near the stove is a gesture of acceptance and of friendship. People often shared their food from a common bowl.

Certain objects in the *izba* were particularly important. In the corner diagonally opposite the stove, the family would place its icon, usually on a shelf with a small oil lamp suspended before it. In the north of Russia, an axe would certainly be hung on the wall, for the task of clearing the forest was a never-ending struggle against the encroaching trees that threatened the family's tiny, life-supporting field of crops. The northern Russian became extremely adept at using the axe. The famous wooden churches in the area around Lake Onega were all built using no other tool than an axe. In old peasant families, the father of a newborn baby cut the umbilical cord with his axe. This time-honored tradition was his only participation in the delivery.

In the south, an axe was not needed to fell trees, but the grasses of the steppe had to be cut. A long-handled scythe was used, and at harvest time groups of peasants could be seen against the horizon swaying rhythmically to and fro as they cut through the fields.

Folklore and mythology, military tales and events recorded in the chronicles, the ritual of the church, and seasonal observances formed the fabric of early Russian culture. From earliest pre-Christian times, birth, marriage, and death, spring, summer, fall, and winter created cycles the Russian peasant celebrated with an awareness and reverence of nature. The celebrations were later supplemented and solemnized by the glorious rituals of the church.

Many of the early peasant traditions continue to this day. In earliest times, for example, a midwife was called for the birth of a child, and she served

Church of the Dormition, Nikulino, 1599. *Photo Source: William Craft Brumfield*

a special "christening porridge" to all those present at the feast that celebrated the birth. Nowadays, although most children are born in hospitals (with no midwife in attendance), the father is still obliged to eat some over-salted porridge while friends and family joke and tease him. At the time of a marriage, decorated trees are put in the house of the bride and groom. They symbolize virginity and represent a custom that goes back centuries. In some areas today, obstacles are placed in the road when the bride and groom make their way to register their marriage. Although now done in a joking way, the tradition goes back to ancient times when the bride's party set up poles in the road and the groom's party could pass only if it offered wine or food as gifts.

Storytelling is also an old custom in Russia. The dark forest seemed to be inhabited by spirits and creatures, and gradually such popular figures as the witch Baba Yaga, the beautiful maiden Fair Vasilissa, the Snow Maiden, and the Firebird found their way into folk tales that have inspired Russian authors and composers for centuries. Evenings in the *izba* were spent telling tales around the stove, and in the winter a whole village would sometimes crowd into the largest hut to listen to the local story teller. Folk tales and riddles entertained people from all levels of society. (See Readings 7 and 9.)

> *FACT:*   In his childhood, Count Leo Tolstoy, author of *War and Peace,* listened to a serf his grandfather had bought for his storytelling ability. Later in his life, Tolstoy wrote a collection of fairy tales for the children of the serfs on his estate.

Farmers everywhere are keenly aware of the seasons and of any changes in the weather. Russians are no exception, and many holidays are closely related to the change of season and to the Christian liturgical observances that mark them. Christmas was the first major winter holiday. In pre-Christian times, there had probably been a holiday celebrating the winter solstice, the time of the rebirth of the sun. To celebrate the birth of Christ, the family gathered on Christmas Eve for a joyous and peaceful meal. A cross, the symbol of the Christ, formed from all kinds of grains, was placed on the table under the cloth. The grains symbolized fertility. The peasant dreaded infertility in crops, livestock, or offspring: fertility meant life and life meant continuation. The head of the house prayed for health in the coming year for all family members as well as for the family's livestock.

The second winter festival, *Maslenitsa,* was a carnival time before the seven-week fast of Lent. During Lent, preparation for spring work was completed. Lent ends on Easter Eve, and the Russian people then celebrated the greatest feast of all: the Resurrection of Christ. Trinity Week, in the late spring, mirrored the festival at Yuletide, but instead of a fir tree as the central decoration, a birch tree became the focus symbolizing reanimated nature. Birch boughs decorated the *izba,* and the village planted a strong, young birch for new life and continuity.

Russian village traditions provided a meaningful pattern of order for the peasant to counterbalance grave threats, both natural and political, from the outside world. Faced with famine, disease, invasion, and countless repressions, the Russian peasant nevertheless could rejoice in the birth of a son, the marriage of a daughter, or the coming of spring. These traditions endured and provided some continuity in the midst of often drastic change.

Many formidable changes took place in Rus' and in Russia between the ninth and seventeenth centuries. Some were violent and destructive, others were positive and constructive. Despite these upheavals, the peasant's attachment to the land, to the family, to God, and to the tsar created a system of attitudes and values that continued up to the beginning of the twentieth century. (See Reading 8.)

The following books were helpful in writing this chapter:

Dunn, S. and E., *The Peasants of Central Russia*. New York: Holt, Rinehart and Winston, 1967.
Rice, T.T., *A Concise History of Russian Art*. New York: Praeger, 1963.
Vernadsky, G., *Origins of Russia*, Oxford: Clarendon, 1959.
Vernadsky, G., ed., Fisher, R., Jr.,; Ferguson, A.; Lassky, A.; Pushkarev, S., *A Sourcebook for Russian History from Early Times to 1914*. 3 vols. New Haven: Yale University Press, 1972.

For students who are interested, we recommend further reading in the sources from which we have taken excerpts, as well as the following works:

Billington, J.H., *The Icon and the Axe*. New York: Vintage Books, 1970.
Berry, L. and Crummey, R., *Rude and Barbarous Kingdom: Russia in the Accounts of Sixteenth Century English Voyagers*. Madison, Wisc.: University of Wisconsin Press, 1968.
    This is a collection of colorful accounts of sixteenth century English explorers and merchants who visited Russia.
Brumfield, W.C., *Gold in Azure: One Thousand Years of Russian Architecture*. Boston: David R. Godine, 1983.
    Beautiful photographs by the author, accompanied by a scholarly text for those who want to know more.
Downing, C., *Russian Tales and Legends*. New York: Oxford University Press, 1978.
    An attractive, well-selected, and well-edited collection.
Massie, S., *Land of the Firebird*. New York: Simon and Schuster, 1980.
    A wonderfully readable, romanticized narrative history of Russia's cultural heritage, with colorful attention to its art and music, manners and morals, pastimes and celebrations.
Voyce, A., *Art and Architecture of Medieval Russia*, Norman, Okla.: University of Oklahoma Press, 1977.
    One of the few books that covers its subject in an interesting manner.

READINGS
for
Chapter Two

A note to the reader: You are about to enter a new area where you will encounter many unfamiliar names. Do not be alarmed. The purpose of the readings from the early chronicles is to give you a sense of the atmosphere, the flavor of what is being described. You do not need to remember all the names.

1. The Arrival of Rurik

All people have a story to tell of their origins. What follows is the story of the beginning of Rus'. It is the first written account we have.

6367 (859).* The Varangians from beyond the sea imposed tribute upon the Chuds, the Slavs, the Merians, the Ves, and the Krivichians. But the Khazars imposed it upon the Polyanians, the Severians, and the Vyatichians, and collected a squirrel-skin and a beaver-skin from each hearth.

6368-6370 (860-862). The tributaries of the Varangians drove them back beyond the sea and, refusing them further tribute, set out to govern themselves. There was no law among them, but tribe rose against tribe. Discord thus ensued among them, and they began to war one against another. They said to themselves, "Let us seek a prince who may rule over us, and judge us according to the law." They accordingly went overseas to the Varangian Russes: these particular Varangians were known as Russes, just as some are called Swedes, and others Normans, Angles, and Goths, for they were thus named. On account of these Varangians, the district of Novgorod became known as the land of Rus. The present inhabitants of Novgorod are descended from the Varangian race, but aforetime they were Slavs.

2. The Baptism of Vladimir

6495 (987). Vladimir summoned together his vassals and the city-elders, and said to them, "Behold, the Bulgarians [Bulgars who lived on Volga River] came before me urging me to accept their religion. Then came the Germans and praised their own faith; and after them came the Jews. Finally the Greeks appeared, criticizing all other faiths but commending their own, and they

---

Abridged from "The Primary Chronicle." In *Harvard Studies in Philology and Literature*, Vol. XII. Translated by Samuel Cross. Cambridge, Mass.: Harvard University Press, 1930, pp. 66–8.

* The early Slavs dated their history from the Biblical creation. Thus, the year 859 in our calendar was the year 6367 in theirs.

Abridged from "The Primary Chronicle."

spoke at length, telling the history of the whole world from its beginning. Their words were artful, and it was wondrous to listen and pleasant to hear them . . ."

The vassals and the elders replied, "You know, oh Prince, that no man condemns his own possessions, but praises them instead. If you desire to make certain, you have servants at your disposal. Send them to inquire about the ritual of each and how he worships God."

Their counsel pleased the prince and all the people, so that they chose good and wise men to the number of ten, and directed them to go first among the Bulgarians and inspect their faith. The emissaries went their way, and when they arrived at their destination they beheld the disgraceful actions of the Bulgarians and their worship in the mosque; then they returned to their own country. Vladimir then instructed them to go likewise among the Germans, and examine their faith, and finally to visit the Greeks. They thus went into Germany, and after viewing the German ceremonial, they proceeded to Tsargrad [Constantinople], where they appeared before the Emperor. He inquired on what mission they had come, and they reported to him all that had occurred. When the Emperor heard their words, he rejoiced, and did them great honor on that very day.

On the morrow, the Emperor sent a message to the Patriarch to inform him that a Russian delegation had arrived to examine the Greek faith, and directed him to prepare the church and the clergy, and to array himself in his sacerdotal robes, so that the Russes might behold the glory of the God of the Greeks. When the Patriarch received these commands, he bade the clergy assemble, and they performed the customary rites. They burned incense, and the choirs sang hymns. The Emperor accompanied the Russes to the church, and placed them in a wide space, calling their attention to the beauty of the edifice, the chanting, and the offices of the archpriest and the ministry of the deacons, while he explained to them the worship of his God. The Russes were astonished . . . and in their wonder praised the Greek ceremonial. Then the Emperors Basil and Constantine invited the envoys to their presence, and said, "Go hence to your native country," and thus dismissed them with valuable presents and great honor.

Thus they returned to their own country, and the Prince called together his vassals and the elders. Vladimir then announced the return of the envoys who had been sent out, and suggested that their report be heard. He thus commanded them to speak out before his vassals. The envoys reported, "When we journeyed among the Bulgarians, we beheld how they worship in their temple, called a mosque, while they stand ungirt. The Bulgarian bows, sits down, looks hither and thither like one possessed, and there is no happiness among them, but instead only sorrow and a dreadful stench. Their religion is not good. Then we went among the Germans, and saw them performing many ceremonies in their temples; but we beheld no glory there. Then we went on to Greece, and the Greeks led us to the edifices where they worship their God, and we knew not whether we were in heaven or on earth. For on earth there is no such splendor or such beauty, and we are at a loss how to describe it. We only know that God dwells there among men, and their service is fairer than the ceremonies of other nations. For we cannot forget that beauty."

3. Boris and Gleb

The story of the brothers Boris and Gleb is one of the most enduring of those told in the early chronicles. Following the death of Prince Vladimir of Kiev, a struggle developed among his sons. The eldest son, Sviatopolk, plotted the murder of his brothers, and according to the chronicler, neither Boris nor Gleb put up any resistance when Sviatopolk came after them. In the passive acceptance of their fate they resembled Christ and thereby established a tradition unlike that of either Byzantine or western Christianity at the time: that humbleness and meekness in the face of danger and adversity were marks of sainthood.

Sviatopolk settled in Kiev after his father's death, and after calling together all the inhabitants of Kiev, he began to distribute largess among them. They accepted it, but their hearts were not with him, because their brethren were with Boris. When Boris returned with the army, not having met the Pechenegs,* he received the news that his father was dead. He mourned deeply for him, for he was beloved of his father before all the rest.

When he came to the Alta, he halted. His father's retainers then urged him to take his place in Kiev on his father's throne, since he had at his disposal the latter's retainers and troops. But Boris protested: "Be it not for me to raise my hand against my elder brother. Now that my father has passed away, let him take the place of my father in my heart." When the soldiery heard these words, they departed from him, and Boris remained with his servants.

But Sviatopolk was filled with lawlessness. Adopting the device of Cain, he sent messages to Boris that he desired to live at peace with him, and would increase the patrimony he had received from his father. But he plotted against him how he might kill him. So Sviatopolk came by night to Vyshegorod. After secretly summoning to his presence Putsha and the *boyars* of the town, he inquired of them whether they were whole-heartedly devoted to him. Putsha and the men of Vyshegorod replied: "We are ready to lay down our lives for you." He then commanded them to say nothing to any man, but to go and kill his brother Boris. They straightway promised to execute his order . . .

---

* One of the tribes that invaded Kievan territory from the east.

Abridged from Zenkovsky, Serge A. *Medieval Russia's Epics, Chronicles, and Tales.* New York: E. P. Dutton, 1974, pp. 101–4.

These emissaries came to the Alta, and when they approached, they heard the sainted Boris singing vespers. For it was already known to him that they intended to take his life . . . After finishing vespers, he prayed, gazing upon the icon, the image of the Lord, with these words: "Lord Jesus Christ, who in this image hast appeared on earth for our salvation, and who, having voluntarily suffered thy hands to be nailed to the cross, didst endure thy passion for our sins, so help me now to endure my passion. For I accept it not from those who are my enemies, but from the hand of my own brother. Hold it not against him as a sin, O Lord!"

After offering this prayer, he lay down upon his couch. Then they fell upon him like wild beasts about the tent, and overcame him by piercing him with lances. They also overpowered his servant, who cast himself upon his body . . .

The murderers, after attacking Boris, wrapped him in a canvas, loaded him upon a wagon, and dragged him off, though he was still alive. When the impious Sviatopolk saw that he was still breathing, he sent two Varangians* to finish him. When they came and saw that he was still alive, one of them drew his sword and plunged it into his heart. Thus died the blessed Boris, receiving from the hand of Christ our God the crown among the righteous. He shall be numbered with the prophets and the Apostles, as he joins with the choirs of martyrs, rests in the lap of Abraham, beholds joy ineffable, chants with the angels, and rejoices in company with the choirs of saints. After his body had been carried in secret to Vyshegorod, it was buried in the Church of St. Basil.

The impious Sviatopolk then reflected: "Behold, I have killed Boris; now how can I kill Gleb?" Adopting once more Cain's device, he craftily sent messages to Gleb to the effect that he should come quickly, because his father was very ill and desired his presence. Gleb quickly mounted his horse, and set out with a small company, for he was obedient to his father. When he came to the Volga, his horse stumbled in a ditch on the plain, and broke his leg. He arrived at Smolensk, and setting out thence at dawn, he embarked in a boat on the Smiadyn. At this time, Yaroslav received from Predslava the tidings of their father's death, and he sent word to Gleb that he should not set out, because his father was dead and his brother had been murdered by Sviatopolk. Upon receiving these tidings, Gleb burst into tears, and mourned for his father, but still more deeply for his brother. He wept and prayed with the lament: "Woe is me, O Lord! It were better for me to die with my brother than to live on in this world. O my brother, had I but seen thy angelic countenance, I should have died with thee. Why am I now left alone? Where are thy words

---

* Varangian is the name given to the Vikings who traded with Kiev and established fortified trading posts along the rivers.

that thou didst say to me, my brother? No longer do I hear thy sweet counsel. If thou hast received affliction from God, pray for me that I may endure the same passion. For it were better for me to dwell with thee than in this deceitful world."

While he was thus praying amid his tears, there suddenly arrived those sent by Sviatopolk for Gleb's destruction. These emissaries seized Gleb's boat, and drew their weapons. The servants of Gleb were terrified, and the impious messenger, Goriaser, gave orders that they should slay Gleb with dispatch. Then Gleb's cook, Torchin by name, seized a knife, and stabbed Gleb. He was offered up as a sacrifice to God like an innocent lamb, a glorious offering amid the perfume of incense, and he received the crown of glory. Entering the heavenly mansions, he beheld his long-desired brother, and rejoiced with him in the joy ineffable which they had attained through their brotherly love . . .

After Gleb had been slain, his body was thrown upon the shore between two tree trunks, but afterward they took him and carried him away, to bury him beside his brother Boris in the Church of St. Basil. United thus in body and still more in soul, ye dwell with the Lord and King of all, in eternal joy, ineffable light, bestowing salutary gifts upon the land of Russia. Ye give healing to other strangers who draw near with faith, making the lame to walk, giving sight to the blind, to the sick health, to captives freedom, to prisoners liberty, to the sorrowful consolation, and to the oppressed relief. Ye are the protectors of the land of Russia, shining forever like beacons and praying to the Lord in behalf of your countrymen. Therefore must we worthily magnify these martyrs in Christ, praying fervently to them and saying: "Rejoice, martyrs in Christ from the land of Russia, who gave healing to them who draw near to you in faith and love. Rejoice, dwellers in heaven. In the body ye were angels, servants in the same thought, comrades in the same image, of one heart with the saints. To all that suffer ye give relief. Rejoice, Boris and Gleb, wise in God.

4. The Sack of Riazan

The Mongol or Tatar invasion under the leader Batu Khan visited great devastation upon the Russian people. Riazan, a city on the Kievan frontier between the lower Volga and the Don, was the first town to be razed. The towns of Old Russia were forced to accept Mongol overlordship: over two hundred years of the "Tatar yoke."

Zenkovsky, *Medieval Russia's Epics*, 202–3.

The accursed Batu began the conquest of the land of **Riazan,** and soon approached the city of Riazan itself. They encircled the city and fought without surcease for five days. Batu changed his regiments frequently, replacing them with fresh troops, while the citizens of Riazan fought without relief. And many citizens were killed and others wounded. Still others were exhausted by their great efforts and their wounds. On the dawn of the sixth day the pagan warriors began to storm the city, some with firebrands, some with battering rams, and others with countless scaling ladders for ascending the walls of the city. And they took the city of Riazan on the 21st day of December. And the Tatars came to the Cathedral of the Assumption of the Blessed Virgin, and they cut to pieces the Great Princess Agrippina, her daughters-in-law, and other princesses. They burned to death the bishops and the priests and put the torch to the holy church. And the Tatars cut down many people, including women and children. Still others were drowned in the river. And they killed without exception all monks and priests. And they burned this holy city with all its beauty and wealth, and they captured the relatives of the Riazan princes, the princes of Kiev and Chernigov. And churches of God were destroyed, and much blood was spilled on the holy altars. And not one man remained alive in the city. All were dead. All had drunk the same bitter cup to the dregs. And there was not even anyone to mourn the dead. Neither father nor mother could mourn their dead children, nor the children their fathers or mothers. Nor could a brother mourn the death of his brother, nor relatives their relatives. All were dead. And this happened for our sins.

Seeing this terrible letting of Christian blood, the heart of godless Batu became even more hardened, and he marched against the cities of Suzdal and Vladimir, intending to conquer all Russian lands, to uproot the Christian faith, and to destroy the churches of God. At that time a Riazan lord, Eupaty Kolovrat, who was in Chernigov at the time of the destruction of the city of Riazan, heard of Batu's invasion. He left Chernigov with a small force and hurried to Riazan. When he came to the land of Riazan he saw it devastated and the cities destroyed, the rulers killed, and the people dead. And he rushed to the city of Riazan and found it destroyed, the rulers killed, and the people slaughtered. Some of them were cut down, while others were burned, and still others were drowned. And Eupaty wept with great sorrow and his heart became angry. He gathered a small force of seventeen hundred men who had been preserved by God outside the city. And they hurriedly pursued the godless emperor. And with difficulty they caught up with him in the principality of Suzdal, and suddenly fell upon his camp. And there began a battle without mercy, and confusion reigned. And the Tatars lost their heads from fear as Eupaty fought so fiercely that his sword became dull, and, taking a sword from a fallen Tatar, he would cut them down with their own swords. The Tatars thought that the Russians had risen from the dead, and Eupaty was riding through the ranks of the Tatar regiments so bravely that Batu himself became frightened. [Eupaty Kolovrat's brave but unsuccessful defense of the Russian lands won him the respect of Batu Khan.]

5. The Time of Troubles

In the Time of Troubles, dynastic conflict led to the emergence of rivals for the throne: the Godunovs, the Romanovs, and the Shuiskis were contending families. Other pretenders appeared, claiming in turn to be Dmitri, a son of Ivan the Terrible who had been viciously eliminated early in this troubled period. This reading details events in the episode of the first False Dmitri's appearance. He claimed that he had survived the attack in his boyhood and returned in his manhood to claim his rightful position with the support of Polish armies. This account presents the idea of a threat from the West, an idea that preoccupies Russia to this day.

In the year 7113 (1605) a certain monk, whose name was Gregory and who was a scion of the Otrepiev family, and who had been an addict of occult books and other evils, left Russia and went to the Polish Kingdom. Living there, he began to write subversive proclamations, sending them to all parts of Russia, in which he declared that he was the real Dmitry, son of the tsar. He would go from city to city, hiding himself and causing disturbances among the people of both realms. Then he was joined by fugitives from western Russian and Polish cities, by serfs whose time had arrived according to the will of the evil spirit, and by one village after another, and by one city after another, and finally all were tempted. However, his scheme was evident to many. Yet, what a great amount of evil did they cause! And until this day Russia is unable to be rid of this yoke. He and his followers in evil have done so many base deeds in Russia that no one could describe them all, even if he wrote for many years. In two years this unfrocked monk Gregory succeeded in winning over one-quarter of the entire universe, the entirety of Europe; and even the Pope of Rome wrote on his behalf to the entire West, presenting Gregory as an exile from his fatherland. And the Pope ordered the Polish king, Sigismund III, to start a campaign against Russia in order to take revenge for the impostor. Gregory joined the Catholics, that eternal enemy of Christians, and he gave them a written promise that he would bring entire Russia under the blessing of the **Antichrist,** thus delivering all Russians to eternal death through the abomination of the Catholic Communion. And he would have done this, if the Lord hadn't overthrown his evil design . . .

This enemy, the defrocked monk, plotted with the heretics [the Poles] to massacre the Russian people of all ranks, beginning with the courtiers and ending with common officers. And he intended to have a great celebration with the shooting of artillery in the Pond Field at the Sretensk Gate. And when the people went to this celebration, then he would order the gate to be closed and all would be slain.

Abridged from Zenkovsky, Serge A., ed. and trans. *Medieval Russia's Epics, Chronicles and Tales.* New York: E. P. Dutton, 1963, pp. 380–86.

But this base plot did not come to fruition because two days before the celebration was to have taken place . . . this accursed man died an evil death, having reigned for one year. He used to say of himself that he was thirty-four years of age, but his friends, the demons, didn't give him many more years of life . . .

After his death, the people of Moscow gave themselves to drinking in their joy, instead of rendering thanks to God. And everyone bragged about his deeds in murdering the impostor, Pseudo-Dmitry, and all boasted about their courage. But the people forgot to give thanks through prayer in the Church of the Holy Virgin for this most glorious victory . . .

6. The Russian Peasant Community

The culture of the Russian village changed little from the sixteenth century until the beginning of the twentieth. Although Professor Edward Keenan writes here about the sixteenth century village, he also describes the ageless struggle of the Russian peasant. The chapter on geography in this book pointed out the harsh conditions under which a farmer had to grow his crop. This reading further explains the Russian's resistance to taking risks and the importance of maintaining a collective rather than an individual direction.

In most agricultural communities, like the Russian, isolated from trade and the stabilizing influences of neighboring units—the line between prosperity and disaster, for the group as well as the household unit, is a thin and shifting one. One man's field is flooded, another's is not. One family's cow goes dry, another's does not; one couple has four healthy sons, another is barren, and so on. Different cultures develop different institutionalized means of dealing with the fragility and unpredictability of life. In the Russian village these means of self-preservation can, in narrative fashion, be described as follows:

Let us take two new households, Ivan's and Fedor's, both of which contain four healthy individuals (the two adults and two sons in Ivan's case, a son and daughter in Fedor's), have equal and adequate amounts of land, and one horse each. Now for reasons that will become clear in a moment, it is in the village's interest to keep each of these households, individuals, and horses just as productive as possible, that is to match up labor and land and draft power. Thus as Ivan's sons grow, his household will be allotted or acquire more land, will acquire or be loaned draft power, and so on. Ivan will prosper. As he moves up on the economic scale, however, the village will begin to exert certain downward forces on him. He will be required to take in the widow or orphan of a neighbor or the village cripple. He will be expected to bear the expense of the

Abridged from Keenan, Edward L., "Russian Political Culture." *Russian Review* 45(1986): 115–81.

major local feast, and so on. Thus a real ceiling will be placed on his socio-economic movement—he will be kept, as it were, within the orbit of the particles revolving around the nucleus of that village.

Fedor's case might be different. His son dies, and he and his wife and daughter are unable to cultivate their allotment of land, which is correspondingly reduced. His mare foals, but then his house burns and Fedor is killed. Disaster threatens his wife and daughter. But here again the village steps in, because arable land, and useful labor, and two horses are of vital interest to the whole community. Fedor's widow, if still of child-bearing age, will be married, along with one horse and some of the land, to an able-bodied man who has no wife and no horse and no land, as will the daughter—also with a horse and land. Thus a kind of floor is also imposed, and upward forces are brought to bear which keep these unfortunate individuals alive, within the village, and within the productive nexus of the common survival pattern.

Now these all seem to be reasonable arrangements, but of course the question arises of the wishes and motivations of the individuals and family units concerned, and the sanctions applied in case, for example, Ivan doesn't *want* to take in waifs and widows, and wants instead to become rich, or Fedor's daughter or wife doesn't want to marry the hired hand being provided, but wants to enter a nunnery. In extreme cases, of course, the villagers can beat them to death or, in Ivan's case, let loose the red rooster (i.e., burn his house down), but such extreme measures are usually not necessary because this system of reciprocating mechanisms *is* a system and its virtues and sanctions are known to every member of the culture. Given the chanciness and suddenness of fortune and famine in such conditions, all adult members of such a village will have experienced the benefits of both the "ceiling" and the "floor" in their own lifetime—perhaps in their own family, and will understand the importance of the village organization as the warrant of their own future viability. Under normal circumstances they will not only acquiesce, but will force others to do so in their own interest.

Thus the overpowering objective of the peasant village organization—an objective developed over centuries of unchanging subsistence agriculture, an objective whose imperatives created a tight nucleus bound by immense forces of both cohesion and fission—was survival, economic, biological and social survival. Not justice, as the **Slavophiles** and many city-bred ethnographers thought, not material improvement or the accumulation of wealth, not the "preservation of a way of life," but the preservation of life itself, human life, the life of vital stock, the life of life-giving field cultures. And the smallest political unit of peasant life was not the individual (who was unviable in this environment), and not the nuclear family (which, in its extended form, was marginally viable, but too vulnerable to disease or sudden calamity), but the village, to whose interests all others were subordinated. And the primary mode of decision-making of such a collective was minimization of risk, of the danger of the interruption of life through any of the calamities that could come upon an isolated, technologically primitive, necessarily self-sufficient and by consequence vulnerable community. If innovation offered a short-term improvement of the standard of living at the cost of an increased risk of possible calamity, it was rejected. If the interests of an individual reduced the basic viability of the group, they were denied. When faced with danger, the village would hunker down—or pick up and move on—rather than change.

7. The Maiden Tsar

The roots of Russian folk tales can be traced to pagan mythology. The tales have been popular at all levels of society. The Maiden Tsar *introduces two important characters in many Russian folk tales, the Firebird and the witch, Baba Yaga, who flies through the sky in a mortar and pestle.*

In a certain land, in a certain kingdom, there was a merchant whose wife died, leaving him with an only son, Ivan. He put this son in charge of a tutor, and after some time took another wife; and since Ivan, the merchant's son, was now of age and very handsome, his stepmother fell in love with him. One day Ivan went with his tutor to fish in the sea on a small raft; suddenly they saw thirty ships making toward them. On these ships sailed the Maiden Tsar with thirty other maidens, all her foster sisters. When the ships came close to the raft, all thirty of them dropped anchor. Ivan and his tutor were invited aboard the best ship, where the Maiden Tsar and her thirty foster sisters received them; she told Ivan that she loved him passionately and had come from afar to see him. So they were betrothed.

The Maiden Tsar told the merchant's son to return to the same place the following day, said farewell to him, and sailed away. Ivan returned home and went to sleep. The stepmother led the tutor into her room, made him drunk, and began to question him as to what had happened to him and Ivan at sea. The tutor told her everything. Upon hearing his story, she gave him a pin and said: "Tomorrow, when the ships begin to sail toward you, stick this pin into Ivan's tunic." The tutor promised to carry out her order.

Next morning Ivan arose and went fishing. As soon as his tutor beheld the ships sailing in the distance, he stuck the pin into Ivan's tunic. "Ah, I feel so sleepy," said the merchant's son. "Listen, tutor, I will take a nap now, and when the ships come close, please rouse me." "Very well, of course I will rouse you," said the tutor. The ships sailed close to the raft and cast anchor; the Maiden Tsar sent for Ivan, asking him to hasten to her; but he was sound asleep. The servants began to shake him, pinch him, and nudge him. All in vain—they could not awaken him, so they left him.

From Afanas'ev, Alexander, *Russian Fairy Tales*. Translated by Norbert Guterman, 64–66. New York: Random House, 1975. Reprinted by permission of Pantheon Books, a division of Random House.

The Maiden Tsar told the tutor to bring Ivan to the same place on the following day, then ordered her crews to lift anchor and set sail. As soon as the ships sailed away, the tutor pulled out the pin, and Ivan awoke, jumped up, and began to call to the Maiden Tsar to return. But she was far away then and could not hear him. He went home sad and aggrieved. His stepmother took the tutor into her room, made him drunk, questioned him about everything that had happened, and told him to stick the pin through Ivan's tunic again the next day. The next day Ivan again went fishing, again slept all the time, and did not see the Maiden Tsar; she left word that he should come again.

On the third day he again went fishing with his tutor. They came to the old place, and beheld the ships sailing at a distance, and the tutor straightway stuck in his pin, and Ivan fell sound asleep. The ships sailed close and dropped anchor; the Maiden Tsar sent for her betrothed to come aboard her ship. The servants tried in every possible way to rouse him, but no matter what they did, they could not waken him. The Maiden Tsar learned of the stepmother's ruse and the tutor's treason, and wrote to Ivan telling him to cut off the tutor's head, and, if he loved his betrothed, to come and find her beyond thrice nine lands in the thrice tenth kingdom.

The ships had no sooner set sail and put out to sea than the tutor pulled the pin from Ivan's garment; he awoke and began to bemoan his loss of the Maiden Tsar; but she was far away and could not hear him. The tutor gave him her letter; Ivan read it, drew out his sharp saber, and cut off the wicked tutor's head. Then he sailed hurriedly to the shore, went home, said farewell to his father, and set out to find the thrice tenth kingdom.

He journeyed onward, straight ahead, a long time or a short time—for speedily a tale is spun, but with less speed a deed is done—and finally came to a little hut; it stood in the open field, turning on chicken legs. He entered and found Baba Yaga the Bony-legged. "Fie, fie," she said, "the Russian smell was never heard of nor caught sight of here, but now it has come by itself. Are you here of your own free will or by compulsion, my good youth?" "Largely of my own free will, and twice as much by compulsion! Do you know, Baba Yaga, where lies the thrice tenth kingdom?" "No, I do not," she said, and told him to go to her second sister; she might know.

Ivan thanked her and went on farther; he walked and walked, a long distance or a short distance, a long time or a short time, and finally came to a little hut exactly like the first and there too found a Baba Yaga. "Fie, fie," she said, "the Russian smell was never heard of nor caught sight of here, but now it has come by itself. Are you here of your own free will or by compulsion, my good youth?" "Largely of my own free will, and twice as much by compulsion! Do you know, Baba Yaga, where lies the thrice tenth kingdom?" "No, I do not," she said, and told him to stop at her youngest sister's; she might know. "If she gets angry at you," she added, "and wants to devour you, take three horns from her and ask her permission to blow them; blow the first one softly, the second louder, and the third still louder." Ivan thanked the Baba Yaga and went on farther.

He walked and walked, a long distance or a short distance, a long time or a short time, and finally beheld a little hut standing in the open field and turning upon chicken legs, he entered it and found another Baba Yaga. "Fie, fie, the Russian smell was never heard of nor caught sight of here, and now it has come by itself," she said, and ran to whet her teeth, for she intended to eat her uninvited guest. Ivan begged her to give him three horns: he blew one softly, the second louder, and the third still louder. Suddenly birds of all kinds swarmed about him, among them the firebird. "Sit upon me quickly," said the firebird, "and we shall fly wherever you want; if you don't come with me, the Baba Yaga will devour you." Ivan had no sooner sat himself upon the bird's back than the Baba Yaga rushed in, seized the firebird by the tail, and plucked a large handful of feathers from it.

The firebird flew with Ivan on its back; for a long time it soared in the skies, till finally it came to the broad sea. "Now, Ivan, merchant's son, the thrice tenth land lies beyond this sea. I am not strong enough to carry you to the other shore; get there as best you can." Ivan climbed down from the firebird, thanked it, and walked along the shore.

He walked and walked till he came to a little hut; he entered it, and was met by an old woman who gave him meat and drink and asked him whither he was going and why he was traveling so far. He told her that he was going to the thrice tenth kingdom to find the Maiden Tsar, his betrothed. "Ah," said the old woman, "she no longer loves you; if she gets hold of you, she will tear you to shreds; her love is stored away in a remote place." "Then how can I get it?" "Wait a bit! My daughter lives at the Maiden Tsar's palace and she is coming to visit me today; we may learn something from her." Then the old woman turned Ivan into a pin and stuck the pin into the wall; at night her daughter flew in. Her mother asked her whether she knew where the Maiden Tsar's love was stored away. " I do not know," said the daughter, and promised to find out from the Maiden Tsar herself. The next day she again visited her mother and told her: "On this side of the ocean there stands an oak; in the oak there is a coffer; in the coffer there is a hare; in the hare there is a duck; in the duck there is an egg; and in the egg lies the Maiden Tsar's love."

Ivan took some bread and set out for the place she had described. He found the oak and removed the coffer from it; then he removed the hare from the coffer; the duck from the hare, and the egg from the duck. He returned with the egg to the old woman. A few days later came the old woman's birthday; she invited the Maiden Tsar with the thirty other maidens, her foster sisters, to her house; she baked the egg, dressed Ivan the merchant's son in splendid raiment, and hid him.

At midday, the Maiden Tsar and the thirty other maidens flew into the house, sat down to table, and began to dine; after dinner the old woman served them each an egg, and to the Maiden Tsar she served the egg that Ivan had found. The Maiden Tsar ate of it and at once conceived a passionate love for Ivan the merchant's son. The old woman brought him out of his hiding place.

How much joy there was, how much merriment! The Maiden Tsar left with her betrothed, the merchant's son, for her own kingdom; they married and began to live happily and to prosper.

8. Seventeenth Century Moscow

Peter the Great's succession to the throne ushered in major changes in Russian history. This account is based on English travellers' descriptions of life in Moscow on the eve of Peter's accession. It emphasizes how alien Muscovy seemed to the cultivated Englishman.

The secular and religious life of old Moscow was closely intertwined, Byzantine survivals and influences being distinguishable even up to the end of the seventeeth century. Every ceremony, every national or court celebration was primarily religious in form. Straightforward religious festivals, of St. Simeon "bringer in of the New Year," of St. Peter the Thaumaturge, of the blessing of the water at the feast of the Epiphany and of Christmas and other more familiar anniversaries were, of course, commemorated with elaborate and picturesque ritual and closed with ample banquets. The Tsar himself, surrounded by his chamberlains and court dignitaries, took as important a part as the Patriarch of Moscow and his deans, priests and deacons. But functions outside the calendar of the church were apt to assume an equally religious form. The declaration of a war or the celebration of a victory would be the occasion for a solemn service at which the Tsar would eat the holy bread and partake of the "cup of the Mother of God" before regaling the court, moved sometimes to tears by the fervour of the Tsar's or the Patriarch's address, with red and white mead and vodka.

The **boyars** lived in the closest personal contact with the Tsar. The Tsar's position was very much nearer to that of the "head of a family" than has since been the case with a monarch. Every morning the gentry and nobility had to assemble at the court and were received in order, according to the minute gradations of precedence on which the life of the court was hung. What seem the most trivial requests had to be made to the Tsar in person—such as permission to leave Moscow for a week-end to go to a christening. The Tsar dined in public with his whole court and after the usual siesta the rest of the day was given over to business, each public office having its allotted day for attention.

The principle and prerogatives of seniority were extended beyond the dreams of the English public school. A *boyar* spent a large part of his life

From Marsden, Christopher, *Palmyra of the North: The First Days of St. Petersburg*. London: Faber and Faber, 1942, pp. 50–53.

standing on his dignity. Quarrels as to who should sit above whom at the Tsar's table were carried to extraordinary lengths and a member of one family would resort to any expedient rather than yield precedence to a member of another.

Anything more rigidly conservative than the old *boyar* circles would be impossible to imagine. The family—which counted for everything and the individual for nothing—was run on patriarchal and sternly monastic lines. The head of a family was the bourgeois lord-and-master carried to a fantastic degree of authority. Complete obedience to the father was demanded of all, including the wife and everyone who dwelt under the master's roof. Every hour of the day had its appointed prayers and the simplest domestic business was accompanied by religious obeisances. That extraordinary document, the *Domostroi* [guide to household behavior] of the Archimandrite Silvester, minister of Ivan IV, with its recipes for food and drink, its instructions about clothes, furniture, servants, women and domestic utensils, shows very clearly the narrowness, the detail, and at the same time the licence, as regards drunkenness or wife-beating (don't use a "staff tipped with iron," says the Archimandrite), of the religious regulations according to which life had to be lived.

Intellectual life and discussion were entirely lacking. Illiterate, and fettered hand and foot by the most absurd religious bigotry, the Russian was incapable of grasping the difference between the essential and the unessential or, as we see it, between true right and wrong. His penal legislation, farcically unjust, is a case in point. The pettiest details of ritual or tradition assumed for him prodigious importance; change of any kind he considered *ipso facto* sinful and anything foreign was automatically an abomination. He lived in a thick fog of ignorance, bias and superstition, unenlightened by any effort on the part of church or of government.

Intense puritanism marched hand in hand with uncontrolled vice. Singing, card or chess-playing, games and sports of all kinds—the common, harmless amusements of any people—were forbidden as inventions of the Prince of Devils; the universal drunkenness and wife-beating were accepted as a matter of course. The common people had no recreations. And apart from the cruel organized bullying of jesters—the dwarfs, imbeciles, negroes and freaks who were kept by every *boyar* family—heavy drinking was the only amusement of the nobility, and banquets, which always began with an edifying religious service, invariably ended as orgies. Travellers were disgusted by the drunkenness and general bestiality of the Muscovites. It was nothing to see women and children, let alone priests, reeling about in the streets and suddenly falling dead drunk. Their ordinary manners were those of savages. Their behaviour, especially towards women, on their rare appearances outside Russia, led to diplomatic remonstrances. Filthily dirty, clad in long, cumbersome garments which prevented all free movement, with their unkempt hair down to their shoulders and matted beards, they behaved hoggishly at table, dipping their black and greasy fingers indiscriminately into plates and dishes, always eating too much and drinking noisily and greedily out of unwashed vessels.

Yet they lived in a state of pointless asceticism. Their houses were furnished with only the barest benches and tables; they were always dark, as a room lit by more than ten tallow dips was considered extravagantly lighted, and their only ornaments were a few religious icons. Visitors were impressed by the richness and oriental strangeness of the *boyars'* dress at court, but these vestments were only assumed on very solemn occasions and their ordinary attire was the simple girdled caftan. Their food, though all too abundant, was of the simplest—"gross meats and stinking fish;" mead and raw spirit their only drink.

The position of their women was deplorable. Ignorant and uneducated, they were regarded as domestic, barely human and permanently immature creatures, whose chastity would in some mysterious way be tainted by any appearance in public. Their duties in the household were arduous but went unnoticed—unless a mistake was made, when the master, with certain small limitations (he was enjoined not "to humiliate unduly by flogging before men"), was entitled to inflict upon his wife what form of corporal punishment he thought fit. "Yet three or four years ago," wrote Collins in 1671, "a merchant beat his wife as long as he was able, with a whip two inches about, and then caused her to put on a smock dipt in brandy three or four times distilled, which he set on fire, and so the poor creature perished miserably in the flames. And yet what is more strange, none prosecuted her death: for in this case they have no penal law for killing of a wife or slave, if it happen upon correction. Some of these barbarians will tie up their wives by the hair of the head, and whip them stark naked." Within the *terem* [secluded women's area], which was a cross between a fortress and a nunnery, the women spent their days in seclusion while their lords roistered, only appearing, with great formality and timid obeisance, before some distinguished guest to whom the master of the house wished to show special hospitality by displaying his collection. Any journeys they made, such as to church (where special sections were reserved for them) were undertaken in heavily closed carriages or litters. They themselves wore the *fata* [veil] over their faces. To all intents and purposes the Orthodox Russian woman of the seventeenth century was as completely veiled and segregated as her Moslem sister. Indeed the whole outlook on the female sex was entirely Oriental, for the beauty of a woman was placed in her fatness, a neat waist being thought ugly, so that slender girls would have to, as an outraged Englishman put it, 'on purpose to fatten themselves, lie abed all day long drinking Russian brandy (which will fatten extremely), then sleep, and afterwards drink again, like swine designed to make bacon.' Moreover they stained their teeth black—at a time when Louis XIV was on the throne of France! . . .

The light of the Renaissance had by now illuminated almost every corner of western and northern Europe. The Turk held his oppressive sway in the south-east. But Muscovy, cut off until the middle of the seventeenth century from any contact with Europe, illiterate, without culture other than the religious veneer which the now forgotten Byzantine Empire had long ago superimposed upon its Asiatic inheritance, lay in darkness, wallowing in the sordid slough of superstition. . .

9. Riddles of Old Russia

Anecdotes and riddles were often told on festive occasions in Russia, especially during the Christmas season. Old people told stories to the young, and each tested the wits of the other by asking riddles. Many of the riddles are rich in poetic language and imaginative metaphors. Several are told from the point of view of an object and ask a person to guess what it is. There would be dancing, people dressed up as clowns, buffoons, and folk characters such as Baba Yaga, and the telling of riddles and stories. There are accounts of such festivities from as early as the seventeenth century and as recently as the end of the nineteenth century. These riddles come from a Russian folk riddle collection compiled by D. N. Sadovnikov in the mid-1870s.

Try to guess the answers—what is being described. The answers appear at the end of the reading.

1. What has no body, yet can be seen?
2. There flies a bird:
   Its beak is long,
   Its voice is loud,
   Its wings are sharp;
   Tsars are afraid of it;
   Whoever kills it
   Will shed his own blood.
3. What kind of beast eats in winter, but sleeps in summer;
   its body is warm,
   but it has no blood?
4. If I eat grass,
   I'll dull my teeth.
   If I bite sand,
   I'll sharpen them again.
5. They cut me,
   They bind me,
   They beat me mercilessly,
   They break me on the wheel;
   I'll go through fire and water,

From Sadovnikov, D.N., ed., *Riddles of the Russian People: A Collection of Riddles, Parables and Puzzles.* Translated and with an introduction by Ann C. Bigelow. Ann Arbor, MI: Ardis, 1986.

And my end will be
A knife and teeth.
6. I travel and travel, but there is no trail;
I cut and cut, but there is no blood;
I chop and chop, but there are no chips.
7. Pure and lucid like a diamond
Yet of little worth.
Of a mother it is born
Yet itself to her gives birth.
8. Without hands or tiny hatchet
A little hut is being built.
9. Has wings, but doesn't fly;
Has no legs, but you can't catch up with it.
10. Not a bush, but it has leaves.
Not a shirt, but it is sewn.
Not a man, but it tells a story.
11. A peasant was hauling a wolf, a goat and a cabbage and had to cross the
river in a small boat and take each thing across one by one. If he took the
wolf and the goat across, the wolf would eat up the goat; if he took
the cabbage and the goat across, the goat would eat up the cabbage. How
did he take them across?

Answers
1. shadow
2. mosquito
3. stove
4. scythe; the whetstone to sharpen the scythe is made of sandstone
5. grain, harvested with sickle, bound into sheaves, threshed, baked and
eaten in bread
6. water
7. ice
8. birdnest
9. fish
10. book
11. He took the goat twice, first by itself and left the wolf and cabbage. Then
he went back for the cabbage, left it, and returned with the goat. Leaving it,
he took the wolf and returned a last time to get the goat.

Chapter Three

IMPERIAL RUSSIA

30 pages - 5 days

20 readings - 5 days

*I*n 1721, Tsar Peter I accepted a new title for himself and his successors: Father of the Fatherland, Emperor of All Russia. The new title, conferred upon one of Russia's most able and dynamic rulers, effectively symbolized the beginning of a new era in Russian history, generally known as the Imperial Period. This era lasted for approximately two hundred years, until it ended abruptly and violently in 1917. Imperial Russia retained many of the institutions and traditions of Old Russia, but there were profound changes as well. Through continued expansion, many non-Russians and non-Slavs were incorporated into the Russian state, transforming that state into an empire. A new capital on Russia's western border, St. Petersburg, replaced the historic capital, Moscow. In the latter part of the Imperial Period, Russia not only became considerably more urban and industrialized but also came into much closer contact with the European countries to the west than it ever had before. Increased contact led to greater exposure to European ideas and practices. Because they tended to be very different from those of Russia, they had a dramatic impact. To some Russians, "joining" Europe and borrowing from its more advanced societies seemed a positive way to strengthen Russia. Others opposed such borrowing, because they did not want Russia's basic identity changed. The resulting tension, between the need for reform and the fear of what reform might bring, never resolved itself and ultimately contributed to the downfall of the Russian Empire.

WESTERNIZATION: PETER THE GREAT

By the end of the seventeenth century, Russia had already become a large and potentially powerful state. Compared to the European states to its west, however, it was less developed economically, culturally, and technologically. Had Russia been able to remain isolated, this might not have mattered, but isolation was impossible. In wars with neighboring states, Russian armies usually lost. For Russia to be able to compete effectively with these other states, a major transformation was necessary. Such a transformation was difficult to accomplish, however, because most Russians, suspicious of anything new and different, clung to traditional ways. In the latter half of the seventeenth century, a number of farsighted Russian leaders recognized the need for major changes, and Western cultural influences began to make their way gradually into Russia. Peter the Great, however, was determined to speed up Russia's development. He had the vision, power, and energy to impose changes that transformed Russian society to its very foundations. As a result, his long reign (1689–1725) is still regarded as a watershed in Russian history.

FACT: Peter the Great was one of the largest rulers in history, standing nearly seven feet tall and powerfully built.

Peter was interesting and impressive in other ways. Born in a hut, he developed an early fondness for soldiering, boats, drinking, and women. He loved parties and enjoyed playing practical jokes. And he had tremendous curiosity. Contact with foreigners in Moscow's **German Quarter** sparked his fascination for the West. He decided to take a two-year fact-finding tour, called "the Grand Embassy," through Europe in 1697–98. During this trip, Peter deliberately traveled incognito, avoiding ceremony and concentrating on learning. His particular interest lay in technical subjects, so he concentrated on such areas as shipbuilding, munitions, printing, and medicine, but his curiosity extended to many diverse fields. In short, during the trip, which included Prussia, Holland, England, and the Hapsburg Empire, he attempted to absorb as much of Europe as possible.

On his return, Peter immediately began to institute changes in almost every aspect of Russian life. The changes were not so much part of a grand design as they were measures to meet the needs of the day. Primary among them was the need for military reform. War had been commonplace in Russian history before Peter, and he continued the tradition.

FACT: Russia was at war in every year of Peter's reign but one (1725).

Peter inherited a long and indecisive conflict with the Turks, and he also initiated a campaign against Sweden, in the hope of gaining territory on the Baltic Sea. Charles XII of Sweden proved to be a formidable adversary, soundly defeating Peter's army at Narva, near the Baltic, in 1701. Peter responded to this challenge by rebuilding the Russian army. He introduced conscription (for life), created a professional officer class, and ordered the development of new weapons, from bayonets to heavy artillery.

FACT: On orders from Peter, thousands of bells from Russian churches were melted down and made into cannons and cannonballs.

To Peter, cannons were a more vital need than bells, the military more important than the church. By 1720, Peter's army numbered more than 200,000 regular troops, the largest and one of the most effective fighting forces in Europe. Peter's navy, which he built practically from scratch, included 48 ships of the line, 750 auxiliary vessels, and 28,000 sailors. It was larger than the navies of Sweden and Denmark combined and became an imposing presence on the Baltic Sea.

Peter's military reforms paid off. Leading his troops himself, he defeated Charles and the Swedes in the key battle of Poltava, in the Ukraine, in 1709. During this conflict, Russia obtained territory on the Baltic coast roughly equivalent to modern Latvia and Estonia and decisively ended Swedish domination of the Baltic Sea area. Above all, the Poltava victory marked the emergence of Russia as a military power to be reckoned with in Europe.

Peter realized that to make Russia a powerful military state, he had to develop its economy and create a better, more enlightened administration. To achieve these goals and galvanize Russia's energies, he saw that he must play a very active role. Peter was everywhere, a human dynamo exhorting, bullying, leading by example. He introduced sweeping governmental changes, using western European models. A senate was created to supervise affairs when he was away at war. With advice from the German philosopher, Gottfried Wilhelm Leibnitz, Peter established twelve "colleges," prototypes of later ministries, to handle specialized functions such as finance, foreign affairs, and trade and industry. At his directive, the government took steps to stimulate the economy and produce increased revenue. New industries were created. Foreign trade increased by four hundred percent during Peter's reign. He introduced new taxes, including a head or "soul" tax on the entire lower class. By 1724 the revenue collected was five-and-one-half times what it had been in 1680.

Peter left very few areas untouched.

FACT: Peter decreed that all Russian men were to shave their beards or be fined.

Since Frenchmen and Englishmen of the time did not wear beards, they became for Peter a symbol of backwardness, unacceptable in Russia. To facilitate learning from the West, Peter decided that Russians must learn and speak German or Dutch. Later, these languages gave way to French as the favored court language. He also believed that the Orthodox church promoted tradition and superstition, so he placed it under the control of the Holy Synod, a secular office. Peter changed, or tried to change, everything: dress, social customs, the calendar, the language. Among his most dramatic creations was a new capital city to symbolize the new Russia he was trying to construct. Starting in 1703, the new city, St. Petersburg, was built at the mouth of the Neva River, on the Baltic shore. (See Reading 1.) In this location, the new capital became a window on the West for Russia, providing easy access to Europe via the Baltic Sea. To this day, St. Petersburg (once called Leningrad) looks very much like a European city, a northern Venice with its network of canals.

FACT: St. Petersburg was built by the forced labor of huge numbers of serfs who worked under frightful hardships. Some thirty thousand died in the process, mostly of disease. This led to a saying that it was "a city built on bones."

The use of forced labor was typical of Peter's methods. He believed that the transformation of Russia would not occur by itself. It would result only from command and compulsion. In attempting to westernize and modernize his country, Peter thus reinforced one of the oldest and strongest of Russian traditions, the principle of autocracy.

One element emerging in western society that Peter did not introduce into Russia was the rule of law. It is said that when Peter visited the Inns of Court in London and met with a group of lawyers dressed in their formal robes and white wigs, he remarked, "I have only one such scoundrel in the whole of empire—and him I mean to hang when I return!" As is the case with much cultural borrowing, Peter chose to introduce only those features of western society that suited his purpose.

Even an autocrat such as Peter could not accomplish everything by himself, and so he turned to the gentry for assistance. This group had long been required to serve the state, but the obligation was now increased and formalized by the establishment of a "Table of Ranks." It set out a hierarchy of government positions in which promotion was based chiefly on merit. Portions of the gentry thus became not only beardless speakers of German, but even more dependent on the state than they had been in the seventeenth century, their rank determined by the quality of their service.

Peter's reforms were impressive, but at the same time they were both incomplete and controversial. They were incomplete in that they really affected only those members of the upper classes who lived in or near St. Petersburg. The peasants, who comprised the overwhelming majority of the population, were largely untouched and continued to live much as before. They became known as "the Dark People" to the new, westernized gentry, who viewed them as ignorant, superstitious, and backward. Peter's reforms thus created a schism, or division, in Russian society that grew wider as time went on.

Peter's reforms were controversial as well. Some Russians acknowledged their necessity, but most resented them. The gentry was angry at having to change its lifestyle. Peasants resented the crushing new tax burden, military conscription, and forced labor. Many Orthodox Christians opposed Peter's attempt to secularize their church; they called him the **Antichrist**. (See Reading 2.)

FACT: Among the most violent opponents of Peter's programs were the "Old Believers," a group of conservative Christians. Peter's own son Alexis was condemned to death in part for refusing to submit to his father's will on church reform.

For many Russians, the new capital symbolized all that was bad with Peter's Russia. It was western, secular, and soulless, "a city where all is stone, not only the houses but the trees and the inhabitants." It stood in direct contrast to Moscow, which had been largely built of wood, like the peasant huts of rural Russia. The differing views on Peter's reforms became an open debate in the nineteenth century and lasted for the duration of the Imperial Period.

Historians today still debate whether Peter the Great had a positive effect on Russia's modernization and development, or whether his contempt for law and his autocratic methods left a negative legacy that far outweighed the immediate benefit of his policies. Certainly he widened the gap between ruler and ruled that proved to be the curse of Russia throughout the Imperial Period and beyond. (See Reading 3.)

CULTURE AND EXPANSION: CATHERINE THE GREAT

Following Peter's death in 1725, Russia entered a period of considerable political instability. Of the autocrats on the throne during the next thirty-seven years, one was a boy of eleven, one an infant, one mentally unbalanced, and two were empresses whose abilities were modest and whose interests were not primarily political. This weakness at the top permitted the gentry to flourish. They acquired large amounts of land and new privileges, and threw off unwanted obligations. In 1762, the resurgence of the gentry reached a high point when Tsar Peter III rescinded the requirement that gentry serve the state. Thereafter, state service by the gentry was rendered voluntarily and in the expectation of reward. Whereas Peter the Great had kept the gentry under his tight control, his successors increasingly used a different tactic, buying the gentry off and rewarding their particular favorites handsomely. (See Reading 4.)

In 1762, an unusually able and forceful woman gained the throne, Catherine II, also known as Catherine the Great. Holding power until her death thirty-four years later, she restored much of the stability that had been missing since Peter the Great's death.

FACT: Catherine's real name was Sophia. She was neither Romanov nor
Russian. Born and raised in Germany, she married the future Tsar Peter III
in 1745 and took a Russian name. In 1762, she instigated a coup d'etat
against the current tsar, her husband, following which he was murdered.

In many respects, Catherine was like Peter the Great. She possessed great
intelligence, a strong will, boundless energy, and a natural sense of how to rule.
A passionate and clever woman, she was able to turn her romances to the
advantage of the state.

FACT: Catherine once wrote, "The trouble is, my heart is loath to remain even
one hour without love." She had many lovers, of whom several were
distinguished statesmen.

Like Peter, Catherine admired western Europe. But whereas Peter had a
practical nature and was chiefly interested in importing western technology,
Catherine's interests were more cultural and intellectual. Shipbuilding had
fascinated Peter; ideas fascinated Catherine. The eighteenth century was the
period of the Enlightenment in Europe, a period that stressed the expansion of
knowledge and the application of reason to the solution of social problems.
Catherine fancied herself an enlightened ruler and set about to initiate
enlightened programs. Her aim was, as she said, "to do good . . . to bring
happiness, freedom, and well-being to my subjects." In this spirit, she initiated
a reform of local government, encouraged the development of medicine,
patronized the arts and sciences, and established a legislative commission to
codify the country's laws. With her encouragement, the ideas of the European
Enlightenment gradually made their way into Russia, influencing at least the
upper reaches of society. The publication of books increased dramatically.

FACT: During Peter the Great's reign, 600 books were published in Russia.
Between 1775 and 1800, an even shorter period of time, 7,500 were
published.

The books were not written in the archaic and restrictive church Slavonic
language, but in a new, secular Russian language that emerged gradually
during the eighteenth century. One of the pioneers of the new language
was Michael Lomonosov, who wrote the first Russian grammar in 1755.
Lomonosov, whom the poet Alexander Pushkin later dubbed "the first Russian
university," was both a literary figure and a pioneer in various scientific fields.
He conducted notable research in chemistry, was the first to observe the
atmosphere of Venus, and performed experiments in electricity similar to
those of Benjamin Franklin, with whom he corresponded.

The eighteenth century was the golden age of St. Petersburg, which,
under Catherine and her predecessor, Empress Elizabeth, became a city of
extraordinary beauty and culture and very different in style from Moscow.

A view of Moscow in the eighteenth century, with the Kremlin on the right and the Moscow River on the left.

That city is still dominated by architectural masterpieces of the period, notably the magnificent Winter Palace on the shore of the Neva River. The pastel colors and lavish decorations of these creations, all by western architects, continue to this day to bear witness to the opulence and extravagance of Russian court society at the time. Unfortunately, there was a lack of real substance under the outward display.

FACT: To impress Catherine and two visiting monarchs on a grand tour through southern Russia in 1787, her minister and favorite, Gregory Potemkin, is alleged to have created displays consisting of stage fronts, which appeared at a distance to be actual buildings and communities and which thus gave the impression of real economic progress in the area. These displays gave rise to the expression "Potemkin villages," denoting sham and deceit. Historians now dispute the validity of the story, but it suggests an important reality.

The fact is that Catherine's good intentions were not matched by her achievements in bringing "freedom, happiness, and well-being" to her people, most of whom were still peasants. Most Russian peasants were serfs, living in villages that had not changed since the sixteenth century. Unlike the American slave of the same period, the Russian serf and his family lived in their own house and had access to a small amount of land, which they could work after

A street scene in eighteenth century St. Petersburg showing the western-style architecture, which contrasts markedly with the Russian-style of Moscow of the time.

the obligation to the landlord had been satisfied. Still, the serfs' conditions were often little better than slavery, and royal edicts put them increasingly at the landlords' mercy. The landlords rarely acted in brutal fashion, but they interfered constantly in the daily lives of their serfs. As the ones who worked the land, the serfs felt that they should have title to it, and they resented having to support the landlord who stood in their way, controlled their future, and appeared to contribute little to the betterment of society as a whole. Like people close to the soil anywhere, the Russian peasant was conservative in outlook, wary of outsiders, and skeptical of new-fangled ideas and practices. Since most Russians were peasants until the early twentieth century, the influence of the rural background is still strong among today's Russians.

Generally, the Russian peasant accepted his lot in a fatalistic manner, evading obligations when possible and resorting to drink as an escape. *Volia*, the Russian word for will or wish, expressed the peasant dream of freedom. A Russian writer, Vissarion Belinsky, explained this dream in the 1830s:

To our people liberty . . . simply means license. The liberated Russian nation would not go to a parliament, but run to the taverns to drink, break glass, and hang the gentry because they shave their beards and wear European clothes. . . .[1]

Belinsky is here suggesting that there was an anarchic streak in Russians. For them, freedom was the opportunity to do whatever they wanted. They had no concept of freedom as responsible self-rule.

Periodically, the Russian peasants in the spirit of *volia*, rose up in a massive revolt. Such a revolt occurred in 1773, during Catherine's reign. Led by the Cossack Emelian Pugachev, this great rebellion began in the Urals and spread very quickly, fanned by peasant unrest. Soon it encompassed much of Russia east of Moscow. Pugachev was betrayed by one of his followers, however, and his forces fell to the better-organized army of Catherine. Pugachev was taken to Moscow in a cage and executed. (See Reading 5.)

Catherine was shaken by the Pugachev revolt. The threat to the established order convinced her that the gentry was correct in distrusting the Dark People and that if reform was still an ideal, repression and coercion were more immediate requirements. She dissolved the legislative commission, reasserted her autocratic power, and turned increasingly to the gentry for support in return for favors. In 1785, her Charter of the Nobility confirmed the gentry's freedom from state service and granted freedom from taxation. It also gave the gentry the exclusive right to buy and sell both land and the serfs living on such land. When the author Alexander Radishchev pointed out the evils of serfdom in his *Journey from St. Petersburg to Moscow* in 1790, he incurred the great displeasure of Catherine. She first sentenced him to death but later changed the sentence to a ten-year Siberian exile.

Catherine's policies contributed greatly to the crystallization of the Russian social system, in which the gentry evaded political responsibilities while retaining and increasing their privileges. The masses of peasants continued to work the land hard, pay taxes, support the landlords, and lead a very meager existence.

In domestic affairs, Catherine's record is mixed, but in foreign affairs her successes were considerable. During her reign, Russia gained more new territory than in any reign since Ivan the Terrible in the sixteenth century, and most of this territory contained people who were not ethnic Russians or even Slavs. Peter the Great had ended the threat to Russia from Sweden, and Catherine did the same in the case of two other long-term rivals, the Ottoman Empire and Poland. In two wars against the Ottoman Turks, Catherine forced them to cede much of the northern coast of the Black Sea, including the Crimean peninsula. Russia also received the right to send merchant ships through the Turkish-held straits, the Bosporus and Dardanelles. Russia now had ports that were ice-free and close to the major grain-producing regions of the country.

---

[1]Abridged from Berlin, I., *Russian Thinkers*, 165. New York: Penguin, 1979.

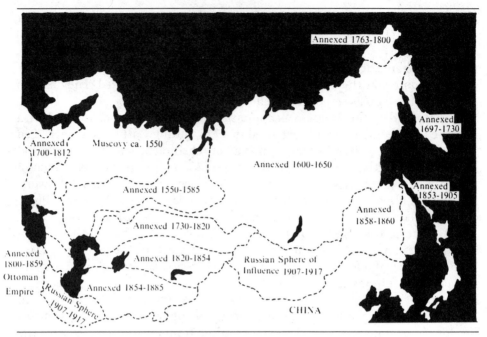

Annexed 1763-1800

Annexed
1697-1730

Annexed
1700-1812   Muscovy ca. 1550

Annexed 1600-1650

Annexed 1550-1585

Annexed
1853-1905

Annexed 1730-1820

Annexed
1858-1860

Annexed
1800-1859

Ottoman

Empire   Annexed 1820-1854   Russian Sphere of
                                         Influence 1907-1917

Russian Sphere
1907-1917   Annexed 1854-1885

CHINA

Territorial Expansion of Russia, 1550–1917

Catherine's second foreign policy success involved Poland. Between 1772 and 1795, a relatively weak Poland was partitioned three times by three stronger neighbors, Austria, Prussia, and Russia. The Russian Empire thereby gained an immense amount of territory in the south and west, including Belorussia and Ukraine. Russian territory now extended into the heart of central Europe for the first time. In the long run, however, these gains produced a mixed blessing. The Poles never accepted the partitions and posed a constant threat of revolt. Also, the partitions brought Russia face to face with another expanding state, and future enemy, Prussia.

REFORM AND REACTION:
ALEXANDER I AND NICHOLAS I

The nineteenth century was a year old when a new tsar, Alexander I, came to the throne, as the result of a coup d'etat against his father, Paul. The early years of this century were ones of great promise for Russia politically, economically, militarily, and diplomatically. By the middle of the century, however, the situation had changed considerably. The promise of political reform gave way to the reality of reaction. Economic progress was limited by the continued existence of serfdom, and military and diplomatic triumph were replaced by embarrassing defeat. In 1801, however, the mood in Russia was optimistic. The new tsar's accession was a cause for rejoicing.

Alexander I (1801–25) has been called "the enigmatic tsar" because of his equivocal and unpredictable nature. Having been raised by an emotionally disturbed father (Paul) and an overpowering and possessive grandmother (Catherine the Great), he learned early to hide his real thoughts and to trust no one. But Catherine had selected French tutors for the young Alexander, and as he came to the throne, he seemed genuinely committed to the principle of reform. In the first decade of his reign, he relaxed travel restrictions and censorship and granted amnesty to thousands who had been unjustly exiled by Paul. He created the Council of State to assist him with legislation, streamlined the ministries, and established a civil service exam to improve the quality of the bureaucracy.

Most important, Alexander dared to question the principle of autocracy, something no tsar had done before.

FACT: Alexander was interested in the idea of constitutional government, and corresponded with Thomas Jefferson about the United States Constitution.

In 1809 Alexander asked a very able minister, Michael Speransky, to draw up a constitution for Russia. Speransky produced a noteworthy document that called for a separation of powers, local self-government, and a national legislative assembly, or **duma.** Had Speransky's plan been implemented, it could have made Russia one of Europe's more progressive states.

This did not occur, however. Progressive as he might have appeared at first, Alexander was, like Catherine, an autocrat at heart. Just as Pugachev's rebellion had influenced Catherine to cease her reform efforts, so events in Europe now convinced Alexander that major reforms were unwise. In France, another absolute monarch, the Bourbon King Louis XVI, had been forcibly overthrown in 1789, and the French revolutionaries were encouraging other peoples of Europe to revolt for "liberty, equality, and fraternity." This became a real threat to Russia when the ambitious French general Napoleon Bonaparte invaded Russia with 600,000 troops in 1812. (See Reading 6.)

FACT: Napoleon's "Grande Armée" was initially successful, getting all the way to Moscow. He found the city abandoned and burned by the Russians. With winter approaching and his supply lines overextended, he was forced to retreat. Harassed by Russian forces and plagued by hunger and frostbite, the French army fell apart. Only one-tenth of its number left Russia alive. It was an epic and popular victory for Russia, later to be justly celebrated in word (Tolstoy's *War and Peace*) and music (Tchaikovsky's *1812 Overture*).

This triumph brought Alexander great prestige, but it also marked the end of his career as reformer. Fearful of future revolutions and Napoleons, he thereafter pursued a reactionary policy. Speransky was sent to Siberia, his constitution consigned to the scrap heap, and Alexander turned for advice to a mystic, the Baroness von Krudener, and an unpleasant, hated minister, Count Alexei Arakcheev.

Realizing that they could not look to the tsar for political reform, other Russians decided to take the initiative. Young army officers, who had come into contact with the radical ideas of the French Revolution after pursuing the French armies back to France in 1814, formed secret societies to press for political change. Similar radical groups were springing up in other European countries, which encouraged the Russian radicals. This early background movement culminated in the Decembrist Revolt of 1825. When Alexander died on December 14, the Decembrist leaders organized a protest against the new tsar, Nicholas, who was reputed to be an extreme reactionary. On the same day, some three thousand rebels gathered on the Senate Square in St. Petersburg.

FACT: The Decembrist Revolt was one of history's least eventful rebellions. The rebels killed the military governor of St. Petersburg when he attempted to negotiate with them but otherwise their only action was to stand in place for five hours, in full battle array and in sub-zero temperatures, until at dusk they were dispersed by loyal troops and their leaders arrested.

Despite its uneventfulness, the Decembrist Revolt was a blatant challenge to Nicholas's authority. He arrested and dealt harshly with the ringleaders. Moreover, the event confirmed Nicholas's belief in order and discipline.

FACT: Since childhood, Nicholas had had a fondness for soldiering and the military. He delighted in the details of army regulations and uniforms. A French visitor, the Marquis de Custine (see Reading 7), said of Nicholas, "The tsar of Russia is a military chief and each of his days is a day of battle."

As a result, his thirty-year reign (1825–55) was marked by a militarism and a preoccupation with the danger of subversion. He imposed strict censorship, created a highly efficient secret police (the Third Section), conducted endless investigations, and made certain that no political opposition could develop. In short, Nicholas, the "Iron Tsar," was a model despot. Whereas Peter the Great had used his autocratic power to change Russia, Nicholas used his to freeze Russia politically and socially for three decades.

Although the Decembrists had failed to provoke change, the martyrs of 1825 inspired others to oppose the regime. New groups drawn from the **intelligentsia** began a revolutionary movement that eventually succeeded in overthrowing tsardom in 1917. The Russian term *intelligentsia* has a very specific meaning in the context of nineteenth century Russian history. It signifies a small group of educated, thinking persons who were alienated from society and particularly from the tsarist regime and who saw it as their duty to oppose that regime. Since open political opposition was not possible, the group had to use other means. Starting in the 1830s, a few began writing philosophical treatises. In these, they agonized over what one of them termed "the accursed questions," by which they meant questions that had no easy or definite answers: questions of right and wrong, truth and justice, freedom and responsibility. At a time when English and French philosophers were becoming increasingly concerned with the material world, Russian thinkers followed the lead of German Romantic philosophers into the world of metaphysics, prophecy, and other forms of abstraction. Like so many Russian thinkers before and after them, they were especially fascinated by the question of Russia's place in history. (See Reading 8.)

Some of the early intelligentsia came to be called Westerners because they believed that Russia's best hope for the future was to follow the lead of Peter the Great and become more like the countries of western Europe. They admired western European constitutions, their increasingly productive economies, and the emphasis they placed on the individual in society. Others, the Slavophiles, disagreed. They believed that Russia had its own greatness and uniqueness. They further suggested that Russia should develop its own culture and in so doing provide inspiration and leadership for the entire world in the future. Whereas the Westerners admired the technological progress and the rational attitude characteristic of the West at the time, the Slavophiles felt that the Occident, as they often called the West, was becoming increasingly soulless and incapable of the kind of spiritual life necessary to keep a society alive and vital. They believed that Russia had not only the material resources necessary for a position of world leadership, but an intangible inner strength, symbolized by the *muzhik* or peasant, whom the Slavophile writers adopted as their hero. Both groups opposed the tsarist regime, however. The tsar was insufficiently western for the Westerners and insufficiently Russian for the Slavophiles. Both groups also found the oppressiveness of the regime and the lack of freedom to express themselves intolerable. Throughout the 1840s and 1850s, they confined their opposition to carefully guarded philosophical speculation. They wrote letters to one another, expounding their views, and joined in discussion groups. Both their numbers and their output remained small and they had no influence whatsoever among the vast majority of Russian people. Still, the intelligentsia are important as the initiators of a tradition of opposition that persisted until the tsarist regime was overthrown in 1917.

There was limited progress in the Russian economy during the reigns of Alexander and Nicholas. By 1860 Russia had three thousand factories, double the number in 1800, but still far fewer than most western European countries. In 1837 the first Russian railroad began operation, between St. Petersburg and nearby **Tsarskoye Selo,** and in 1851 the Moscow-St. Petersburg line was opened.

Boatmen on the Volga River, a familiar scene throughout the Imperial Period. From a painting by Ilya Repin (1844–1930).

FACT: This line, still in use today, is one of the straightest in the world. The legend is that Nicholas settled a dispute over the proper route by taking out a ruler and drawing a straight line on a map. The railroad was built under the supervision of an American engineer, George Washington Whistler.

By 1860, Russian exports had increased in value from 75 to 230 million **rubles,** while imports had risen from 52 to 200 million. Despite these impressive gains, the Russian economy during the first half of the nineteenth century continued to be severely hampered by its inability to increase agricultural productivity.

FACT: In medieval Europe, one seed sown yielded an average of three seeds at harvest time. The result of the low yield was a low standard of living. By 1850 in western Europe, the average yield had increased dramatically, to a one to ten ratio, permitting a larger, nonagricultural population to exist. In Russia, the yield remained at about one to three throughout most of the nineteenth century.

Many Russians believed that serfdom was largely responsible for the low productivity and was also morally wrong. Even Nicholas I recognized this; in a meeting of the State Council in 1842, he said, "There is no doubt that serfdom, as it exists at present in our land, is an evil, palpable and obvious to all." But this did not necessarily mean that serfdom should be abolished. Nicholas continued, "But to touch it now would be a still more disastrous evil . . . the Pugachev rebellion proved how far popular rage can go." Throughout his reign,

Nicholas was worried about the effects of peasant *volia,* and with good reason: During his reign there were over seven hundred officially recorded disturbances caused by serfs. He also worried about another violent reaction, from the landlords, if he were to emancipate the serfs. Hence serfdom continued, agricultural output remained low, and the Russian economy lagged. (See Readings 9 and 10.)

Russian foreign policy during the first half of the nineteenth century followed the same pattern. Its early success and promise gave way to failure. After defeating Napoleon in 1812, Russia gained a prominent position in European affairs. Alexander participated actively in the international settlement that ended the Napoleonic Wars in 1815, and thereafter both he and Nicholas took seriously their role as **gendarme of Europe.** In this role, they were prepared to combat outbreaks of revolution wherever they might occur on the continent. For a time, this policy was successful, but by 1848 too many revolts were occurring throughout Europe for the gendarme to quell completely.

Russia continued to expand, too, during this time. In fact, Russians could be found in a variety of surprising places.

FACT: In 1812 Russian explorers, venturing south to California from their base in Alaska, still a Russian territory, founded Fort Ross, that still stands today. They established a base in Hawaii in 1820. The next year, a Russian expedition seeking a southern route to eastern Siberia discovered Antarctica in the process, naming it "Alexander I Land."

The principal direction of Russian expansion was to the south and east, into the Caucasus, central Asia, and remote Siberia. The expansion began to worry other, more powerful states. England, in particular, viewed Russian expansionism as a threat to her mercantile interests in the Near East and later in the Middle East and Far East as well. With support from France, England sent an expeditionary force to the Crimean peninsula in the Black Sea in 1854. Once again, Russia was on the defensive, invaded by two strong industrialized powers intent on putting the Russian bear back in his lair. The Crimean War, which lasted for two years, was mismanaged on both sides, but the essential fact was that the Russian Empire, with a population of 67 million, could not defeat, on its own soil, an invading force of 70,000.

FACT: During the Crimean War, it took longer for supplies to reach the Russian armies from Moscow than it took for supplies to reach the British and French armies from London and Paris.

After a lengthy siege, the English and French captured the major fortress of Sebastopol, and the Russians sued for peace. In less than two generations,

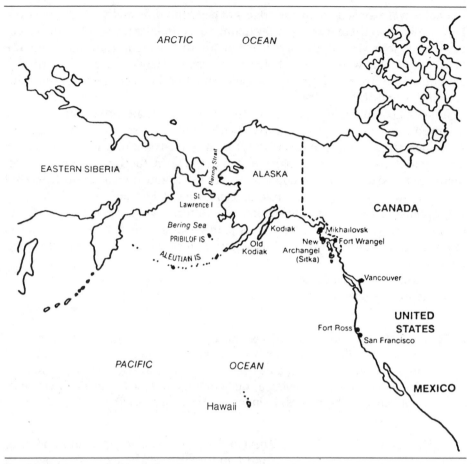

Russian Settlements in North America

the triumph over Napoleon had given way to embarrassing defeat. Once again, Russia had fallen behind other European countries, most obviously England and France, which by this time were well on their way to becoming modern industrial powers. Nicholas I died during the Crimean War, and it was clear that his successor faced a major challenge.

REFORM AND REACTION: ALEXANDER II AND III

The Crimean War demonstrated once again the close relationship between foreign and domestic policy in Russia. An expansionist foreign policy had led to war, and economic backwardness and inefficiency had caused defeat. The Crimean humiliation dramatically showed the need for reform. In the second half of the nineteenth century, Russia repeated the same pattern of reform and reaction that had characterized the reigns of Alexander I and Nicholas I. The need for a complete overhaul was great, but the tsars' desire to preserve the autocracy and the established order was greater. Faced with the more complex challenges of an industrializing world, the tsars of the later nineteenth century hesitated and then abandoned the policy of reform. Russia thus remained relatively backward, and conflicts resulting from continued expansionism turned into defeats. So the cycle was repeated, and as it became more and more apparent that the regime could not or would not break the cycle, the opposition gathered momentum. By 1900 the situation was approaching the crisis stage.

Alexander II (1855–81) was trained for his role from birth and inherited his father Nicholas's belief in autocracy and fondness for militarism. He was also a realist, however, and understood the need for drastic action to strengthen his country and restore its competitive position. He further understood that if he did not take the lead in making the necessary changes, they were likely to occur anyway. "It is better," he said to the Russian nobility in 1856, "to abolish serfdom from above rather than await the time when it will begin to abolish itself from below." Once again, the memory of Pugachev was clear.

Alexander II emancipated the serfs in 1861, despite opposition from most of the landlords, who saw their privileged position severely threatened.

FACT: By this peaceful legal process over 50 million serfs received their freedom. At about the same time, some 4 million black slaves were being freed in the United States, the result of a violent civil war.

Unfortunately, the emancipation process was fatally flawed. The serfs were free as far as they, their families, and their households were concerned. Only about one-third of the land to which they felt entitled was made available to them, however, and it was not free. To buy land, they had to borrow money from the state, to be repaid in installments over forty-nine years. The *mir*, the village community, was collectively responsible for the redemption payments, so individual peasants could not leave the *mir* until all payments had been made. The peasants became disillusioned, a disillusionment that grew as the population increased and their living conditions failed to improve during the remainder of the century.

Alexander was not prepared to establish any sort of legislative assembly on a national scale in Russia, but in 1864 he did institute assemblies, called *zemstvos*, at the local level. These gave propertied Russians a chance to elect representatives who controlled certain local affairs. While limited in scope and authority, the *zemstvos* accomplished much in the fields of education and health, founding schools and hospitals, and seemed to be a training ground for a future representative government at the national level.

Another area badly in need of reform was Russia's judicial system, which was part of the executive and archaic, secretive, and corrupt. In 1864, the judiciary was modernized. It was made a separate branch of government, judicial procedures became public, trial by jury was instituted, and all Russians were declared equal before the law. The Russian judiciary was thus brought more into line with those of the West. It is worth noting, however, that all of Alexander's reforms were accomplished by imperial edict. In Russia, it was still the tsar, and not law, that ruled.

Alexander's reforms, which earned him widespread praise and the unofficial title of Tsar Liberator, did not save him from the increasingly radical opposition. In 1866, a young school dropout named Karakozov attempted to assassinate the tsar.

FACT: Dmitri Karakozov's attempt to assassinate Alexander II in 1866 was the first such attempt on that tsar's life, but it was far from the last: In the following fifteen years, there were no fewer than nine additional attempts, and in 1881 the final attempt was successful.

By this time, a new generation of intelligentsia had appeared. Not satisfied with the philosophizing of the earlier Westerners and Slavophiles, these "new men" or *raznochintsy* (literally, men of diverse rank) were seldom of aristocratic birth, and they tended to be far more impatient than their predecessors. They are often referred to as "men of the sixties," in contrast to the previous generation, the "men of the forties." Not able to rely on inherited income to finance their writing, they scraped by, living on the fringes of society. They raised immediate and practical issues in a direct and blunt manner. They believed that art, literature, and philosophy were useful only if they served a worthy social purpose. There had been enough talk. What was needed now was action. They urged that the old customs and traditions be rejected, the slate wiped clean, and society placed in a position from which it could start afresh.

The attitude of this group is portrayed by the figure of Bazarov in Ivan Turgenev's great novel *Fathers and Sons* (1862). Bazarov, an arrogant, materialistic youth, holds the lifestyle and values of the older generation in contempt. He is a nihilist, one who wishes to destroy the past (a term, based on the Latin word *nihil*, meaning nothing and first used by Turgenev in this work). Though Turgenev intended Bazarov as a caricature, many young radicals of the time took him as their hero. (See Reading 11.)

FACT: Most of the "New Men" (and women) of the 1860s and 1870s were very young. Nicholas Chernyshevsky was a dedicated revolutionary by age 27, but he was old in comparison with his associate, Nicholas Dobrolyubov, who was only 22 when he began writing for the radical journal *The Contemporary*. When Dmitri Pisarev was arrested and jailed in 1862, he was also 22. Pyotr Zaichnevsky was but 19 when he wrote the incendiary pamphlet "Young Russia," Sergei Nechaev 21 when he wrote his "Revolutionary Catechism," and Nicholas Rysakov was barely 18 when he was hanged for his part in the assassination of Alexander II.

Life was not easy for the young revolutionaries. Most were imprisoned, exiled, or otherwise harassed, and many died young, often in obscurity. Their determination was strong, however, and they persevered.

Karakozov's assassination attempt, as well as other outbreaks of violence and the increase of radical thought and writing, prompted Alexander gradually to de-emphasize his program of reform and introduce certain reactionary measures. The 1870s saw greater discipline introduced in schools and universities, new restrictions placed on the press, and the tightening of judicial processes. The new radicals, unsatisfied with Alexander's reforms, were undeterred by his reaction. It only made them more determined to pursue their goal. Most of the radicals had little idea yet of what should replace the hated autocracy, but that did not matter. The immediate task was to overthrow the tsar and to that task they devoted their entire will and energy. After a pause in the early 1870s, a new wave of revolutionary activity broke out in 1878, begun by the shooting of General Feodor Trepov, the military governor of St. Petersburg.

FACT: Trepov was shot by Vera Zasulich, a young revolutionary, who fired one shot, wounding him while he was sitting at his desk. Despite clear and overwhelming evidence of her guilt, she was acquitted by a sympathetic jury at her trial—largely because Trepov was very unpopular.

Vera Zasulich belonged to the People's Will, a revolutionary organization, which in 1879 mounted an all-out campaign of terror against the regime. Not only was it responsible for eight of the assassination attempts on Alexander, including the successful one, but similar and often successful attempts on the lives of prominent tsarist officials. Because of the highly centralized nature of the Russian government, a few assassinations of key officials could wreak havoc. Very rarely in history has such a small group of terrorists caused such disruption. (See Reading 12.)

FACT: The People's Will developed a variety of schemes to make it appear to have a large membership and substantial resources and support. The total membership during its five-year existence was only forty-four.

While this and other revolutionary groups benefited from the lack of sympathy for the tsarist regime among many Russians, the chief reasons for its success were its highly disciplined organization, the thoroughness of its planning, the boldness of its actions, and the complete dedication of its members. That so much could be accomplished by a small group with these attributes was carefully noted by one who was shortly to become a revolutionary, Vladimir Ilyich Lenin.

The assassination of Alexander by a bomb in 1881 was a great triumph for the People's Will, but the crackdown that followed not only broke up that organization, but eliminated revolutionary activity and terror from Russia, with very few exceptions, for twenty years.

After a number of unsuccessful attempts, the revolutionary organization known as the People's Will succeeded in assassinating Tsar Alexander II in 1881. The five key conspirators were arrested and hanged. In this picture, they are receiving the last rites of the church before their execution.

FACT: The five who were directly responsible for the tsar's brutal death were hanged before a crowd of eighty thousand in the last public execution to be held in Russia.

The effect of the assassination was much the same as that of the Decembrist Revolt fifty-six years before. The next tsar, Alexander III (1881–1894), pursued a policy of reaction much like that of Nicholas I.

FACT: Alexander III's nickname was "the Bull." At six feet six, he was the largest tsar since Peter the Great. Stubborn, awkward, and direct, he once responded to a dancing partner's thank-you by saying, "Why can't you be honest? It was just a duty neither of us could have relished. I have ruined your slippers and you have made me nearly sick with the scent you use."

Alexander's reign was generally peaceful, but it was a "peace of the graveyard." He instituted no new political reforms and attempted to undo reforms of the past. Wary of domestic disorder and suspicious of anything foreign, he established a new security policy, the *Okhrana*, to combat subversion. A law of 1881 gave these government officials the authority to declare a state of emergency when they believed public order to be threatened. Armed with this authority, these officials could arrest, imprison, and exile individuals upon suspicion. (See Reading 13.) They could also confiscate property, suppress publications, and close schools. These measures foreshadowed the widespread use of the security police by the Soviet state of the twentieth century. There was a resurgence of pogroms against the Empire's Jewish population. Antisemitism was not uncommon in Europe at this time, but was particularly strong in Russia. While Alexander himself was opposed to **pogroms,** he did institute a campaign to spread the Orthodox religion and to **Russify** the peoples of the Empire. In these policies, Alexander was encouraged by the most reactionary of all nineteenth century Russian statesmen, Constantine Pobedonostsev, procurator of the Holy Synod. Pobedonostsev, a man of brilliant intellect who was tutor to both Alexander and his successor, Nicholas II, once remarked that parliamentary institutions were "the great lie of our age." He is also alleged to have said that the solution to the "Jewish question" was to have one-third convert to Orthodoxy, one-third emigrate, and one-third die. While the Jews were the most blatant target of discrimination, other ethnic groups within the Empire—from the Muslims of central Asia to the Finns in the north—were subject to the official policy of Russification.

Not all of Alexander's advisers were as reactionary, however. Sergei Witte, minister of Finance, was a political conservative who opposed the idea of popular limitations on government. Unlike Pobedonostsev, however, he believed that Russia and the tsarist regime could benefit from industrialization. He argued that this would enable Russia to compete more effectively with the industrialized states of Europe and at the same time would create a prosperous middle class to provide greater economic and political support for the regime. To this end, Witte instituted many ambitious projects: the stabilization of finance based on the import of foreign capital, the construction of the Trans-Siberian Railroad to assist in opening up Siberia, and the development of mining and manufacturing. Indeed, under Witte, the pace of Russian industrialization picked up dramatically. (See Reading 14.)

FACT: During the 1890s, Russian industry grew by an average of eight percent per year. Russian railroads increased in length by forty percent between 1881 and 1894 and doubled again betweeen 1894 and 1905. The growth was greatly facilitated by foreign capital, which by 1900 totalled 900 million rubles.

FACT: One of the most important mining towns in the Donets region, founded in 1870, was named Yuzhovka for its founder, a Welshman named John Hughes.

Territorial expansion continued to be a key element of Russian policy during the second half of the nineteenth century, as it had been since the time of Peter the Great. This was the period of Great Power empires: While Britain, France and others scrambled to divide up Africa, and the United States looked greedily at the Caribbean and the Pacific, Russia continued its pressure on adjacent lands, particularly the Black Sea area and the Balkan peninsula. This was justified by an aggressive **Pan-Slav** ideology, as Russia claimed to be the protector of its fellow Slavs in southeastern Europe. When contained by a gathering of European powers in Berlin in 1878, Russia turned its attention to central Asia and the Far East. Alexander III, and especially his successor Nicholas II, believed that success in these foreign endeavors could restore Russian pride, inspire patriotism, and help the Russian people to forget their domestic grievances. This was not to be, however. After Alexander's death in 1894, these adventures led to conflict with the English in central Asia, and, more seriously, with the Japanese in the Far East. The latter conflict had grave consequences for Alexander's successor, Nicholas II.

RUSSIAN CULTURE TO 1917

Before turning to the reign of the last tsar and the end of the Russian Empire, a brief review of cultural developments in Russia during the nineteenth and early twentieth century is in order. This period witnessed a sustained outburst of creative energy in many fields. In contrast to the previous century, when much of the cultural activity in Russia imitated that of western Europe, nineteenth century art, music, and literature focused on native Russian themes. In all three fields, works of great distinction were produced, with Russian literature in particular gaining a worldwide reputation.

The so-called golden age of Russian literature began with the poet Alexander Pushkin (1799–1837). He and the other authors of the nineteenth century tended to dwell on the most basic and universal of subjects: the nature of man and the problems between the individual and society. The tragic hero of Pushkin's long poem *Eugene Onegin* has difficulty finding a useful place for himself; he feels superfluous. Given a society in which political involvement on the part of individuals was not possible, it is not surprising that the theme of the superfluous man reappears in literature throughout the century. Another common theme is that of conflict between generations, portrayed dramatically in Turgenev's *Fathers and Sons*. Few nineteenth century authors offered solutions for these issues, though Leo Tolstoy (1828–1910) openly condemned the growing materialism he witnessed and advocated a return to the good, simple life close to the soil. Other important writers of the golden age were Mikhail Lermontov, Nikolai Gogol, and Fyodor Dostoevsky.

At the same time, artists and composers were extolling Russian themes in art and music. Painters such as Ilya Repin brought to life individuals and groups from every level and every corner of Russian society. A small group of composers during the latter half of the century created a national school of music, using folk songs and legends to dramatize the Russian past. From this school came many notable works, such as Modeste Mussorgsky's opera *Boris Godunov* and Alexander Borodin's *Prince Igor.*

The twentieth century ushered in a new era in Russia culture, with an emphasis on experimentation and bold new forms. In literature, the period 1900–1917 was called the silver age. In contrast to the more realistic approach of the earlier period, some authors of the silver age emphasized impressions and symbols to convey their messages. The leading prose writers of the early twentieth century were Anton Chekhov, Andrei Bely, and Maxim Gorky, while Alexander Blok was the most prominent poet. Experimentation also characterized the arts of this period. Painters like Wassily Kandinsky, Marc Chagall, and Kazimir Malevich shocked viewers with their revolutionary canvases.

FACT: The world's first totally abstract painting was Russian: Malevich's *Black Square* of 1902.

Composers such as Aleksandr Scriabin and Igor Stravinsky produced similar shock waves in the music world, as did Konstantin Stanislavsky in drama and Sergei Diaghilev in ballet.

FACT: These **avant-garde** Russian authors and artists not only produced startling and puzzling works, but also defied convention in the way they lived and dressed. The poet Vladimir Mayakovsky carried a wooden spoon in his lapel, while his friend and associate David Burliuk had "I am Burliuk" painted on his forehead.

In their fascination with radical forms, these artists helped create a climate for political and social revolution. When such a revolution came in 1917, many of them supported it wholeheartedly. Ironically, the same revolution soon thereafter put an end to artistic experimentation in Russia.

DECLINE AND FALL OF IMPERIAL RUSSIA: NICHOLAS II

When Nicholas II succeeded his father, Alexander III, in 1894, he faced a variety of serious new challenges. The world, including Russia, was fast becoming urbanized and industrialized. Russian agriculture was stagnant. Diplomatic tensions were increasing in Europe. After a lull in the 1880s, opposition groups were once again clamoring for change. The situation required a ruler able and willing to take decisive action, a new Peter the Great. Unfortunately, Nicholas was no Peter. A worthy individual and devout family man, he was a weak and ineffectual emperor. He was conscientious and highly patriotic, but lacked both vision and flexibiltiy.

FACT: Shy and insecure as a youth, Nicholas was tempted to renounce the throne. He always felt ill-prepared to accept the responsibilities and once remarked to a foreign ambassador that he would much rather have been a sailor.

Nicholas relied heavily on reactionary advisers throughout his reign and came increasingly under the influence of his narrow-minded and stubborn wife, Alexandra, to whom he was devoted. Worst of all, Nicholas and Alexandra allowed an ignorant and corrupt peasant named Rasputin into their court. He gradually became a power behind the throne, to the great detriment of the Romanovs, their dynasty, and their country.

FACT: Nicholas and Alexandra had a son, Alexis, who was heir to the throne and who suffered from acute hemophilia, or internal bleeding caused by delayed blood clotting. Rasputin, posing as a holy man and healer, convinced Alexandra that he could stop the bleeding attacks and ease the boy's suffering. She came to trust him completely, first in private matters and eventually in everything, including government policy.

The first few years of Nicholas's reign were quiet and peaceful, but the challenges facing Russia soon changed that. Domestic trouble stemmed from three sources, one of which was the peasantry. Contrary to hopes and expectations, the condition of the Russian peasant grew worse after the emancipation of 1861. Tied to the *mir*, without incentive to improve farming techniques, saddled with redemption payments and taxes, and short of land due to steady population growth, the peasants led a marginal existence and became increasingly bitter. When periodic droughts occurred, as in 1891–92, they brought terrible famine.

FACT: The population of Russia increased from 73 million in 1861 to over 125 million by 1900. Of these, 75 percent were peasants. Calculations show that 28 percent of the peasantry could not support themselves from the land in 1861, and that by 1900 this figure had risen to 52 percent.

A second trouble area was that of the industrial workers, who by 1900 numbered approximately two million. They were concentrated in large, recently constructed factories in St. Petersburg, Moscow, and the Don River basin, so they easily formed sizable and close-knit groups. Workers led an existence even more miserable than that of the peasants. Poorly paid, housed in crowded and filthy slums, their death rate was the highest among industrial workers of all countries. Although they were prohibited from organizing in unions, they went on strike with increasing frequency. (See Reading 16.)

FACT: Serious strikes began in the 1890s and increased dramatically in the early years of the twentieth century. In 1910 there were 226 strikes, involving 46,000 workers. Three years later the totals had escalated to 2,400 strikes staged by 887,000 workers.

A third group that became increasingly restive under the last two tsars was the non-Russian nationalities. Political movements, nationalistic and often revolutionary in attitude, developed in Ukraine, Poland, Finland, the Baltic provinces (Estonia, Latvia, and Lithuania), and the Caucasus region. Murmurs of discontent were also heard as far away as central Asia and eastern Siberia.

A final source of trouble lay in the middle class, which began to emerge in Russia only in the latter part of the nineteenth century. Capitalist businessmen remained largely uninvolved in political concerns, but this was not true of the professional groups. Lawyers, teachers, journalists, and doctors began to take greater and greater interest in politics. Very often their liberal inclinations led them to join the opposition, which began to organize during the 1890s. The more moderate founded the Union of Liberation in 1902 and a political party, the Constitutional Democrats or Cadets, in 1905. The more radical opted for parties that called for revolution. One was the Socialist Revolutionary (SR) party of 1901, which believed that the peasants could be the agents of revolution and advocated terrorism. The SRs became the largest and most popular radical party in Russia prior to 1917.

Other radicals turned to Marxism. Karl Marx, a nineteenth century German philosopher, had explained the causes of social inequity and suffering in *The Communist Manifesto* (1848). He suggested that a proper understanding and application of the laws of history would result in a world where hunger and poverty would be unknown and all men would be equal. In Marx's view, once capitalism had led to the industrialization of society, the working class (proletariat) would rise up against the capitalist factory owners who were exploiting them. In a violent, revolutionary class war, the proletariat would overthrow the capitalists and establish first a dictatorship of the proletariat and later a true communist, or classless, society. History thus proceeded in stages: Capitalist industrialization had to be fully developed before a working class revolution could take place.

Marx's description of the evils of capitalism was vivid and seemed validated by the experience of Russian workers. His accuracy and appeal in this one area suggested that he might well be correct, too, in saying that capitalism was doomed and that revolutionary change for the better was inevitable. No other creed of the time offered such assurance. It is not surprising that many who favored revolution found Marxism attractive.

One of those who embraced Marxism was Vladimir Ilyich Ulyanov, better known by his revolutionary name Lenin. Product of a respectable gentry family, Lenin first studied law, but later turned to radical politics and ultimately to Marxism, in the late 1880s. He soon adopted Marxism completely, involving himself in Marxist discussion groups and the movement to found a Marxist political party in Russia. In 1895, these activities got him arrested and, for the first and last time in his life, he was a political prisoner, confined to a small cell in a St. Petersburg jail for fourteen months. While this was his only incarceration, he did spend much time in exile, first in Siberia (1897–1900), then in western Europe.

FACT: Lenin became a dominant figure in Russian revolutionary activity prior to 1917 despite the fact that, between 1894, when he began his revolutionary career, and 1917, he was in Russia for a total of less than two years.

For Lenin, however, jail and exile simply meant time to refine and promulgate his revolutionary ideology. When he emerged from Siberian exile in 1900, he had a clear notion of what needed to be done, and he spent the next four years trying to convert other Russian Marxists to his way of thinking.

Lenin's views, as they emerged in his writings after 1900, reflected both his strong commitment to Marxism and his impatience for revolution in Russia. He noted, correctly, that in the half-century since Marx had written *The Communist Manifesto*, there had been no revolution of the sort Marx had predicted. He also noted that members of the working class throughout Europe had become generally satisfied with trade unions as a means of improving their lot. His impatience led him to produce a modification of orthodox Marxist theory by introducing the concept of a revolutionary party. Lenin argued that a tightly-organized party of professional revolutionaries, drawn from the intelligentsia, was necessary to lead the workers toward the revolution. Without such leadership, the workers would act "spontaneously" and seek only the material improvements that could be obtained through trade union activity. The party's task was to develop the "consciousness" of the workers, so that they would rise above their search for material benefits, understand the need for revolution, and work actively to bring it about. (See Reading 16.) Lenin's model of a revolutionary party, characterized by small size, centralization of authority, tight discipline, and intolerance of opposition, remained the basic organizing principle of the Communist party until its recent demise.

Lenin brought his ideas to the attention of the Marxist Social Democratic (SD) party at the Second Party Congress, held first in Brussels and then London in 1903. His model of the revolutionary party became the basis of his Bolshevik faction, and later of the Communist party.

FACT: At the Second Congress of the Russian Social Democratic party in 1903, the intransigent Lenin caused a split in the party. Lenin christened his faction Bolsheviks (majority men) and his opponents Mensheviks (minority men), despite the fact that he held a majority only briefly and by a very slim margin. The name stuck, even though in the years to come his Bolsheviks were a small minority within the SD party ranks. The preemption of the term Bolshevik was typical of Lenin's political skill.

From the beginning of his reign, Tsar Nicholas had preferred to live in the calm world of his court. He had little awareness of what was going on outside that world, so he didn't realize that his empire was in deep trouble as the twentieth century began. Strikes, peasant disturbances, and student demonstrations were becoming more frequent. The SRs and SDs called ever more loudly for revolution, and the SRs began an assassination campaign that included over three hundred attempts and eliminated a number of high-level officials between 1902 and 1905. On top of all this, Russia's adventuristic foreign policy in eastern Siberia led to war with Japan in 1904.

In this conflict, fought on land in Manchuria and on Far Eastern waters, the Russian Empire was beaten by a country a fraction of its size. Two Russian fleets were destroyed; their armies fared little better. The consequent embarrassment was greater than in the Crimean War, since now Russia's defeat was at the hands of non-European Japan, which had until recently been undeveloped and was considered by many Russians to be inferior.

FACT: Nicholas, who had nearly been murdered while on a state visit to Japan in 1892 when he was still crown prince, referred to the Japanese as "little short-tailed monkeys" and did little to hide his belief that they were an inferior race.

In 1905 trouble spread from the battlefields of the Far East to the streets of Moscow and St. Petersburg. The opening event in what is generally called the Revolution of 1905 occurred on January 22, 1905, when the people of St. Petersburg made their first major protest against the miserable conditions in which they lived and worked and against the lack of political freedom. Led by Father George Gapon, an Orthodox priest, thousands of St. Petersburg workers and their families marched peacefully to the Winter Palace to present petitions to Nicholas. Unjustifiably alarmed, the palace guard fired on the crowd to disperse it, and by the end of "Bloody Sunday" over a hundred were dead and some eight hundred wounded. This event had two significant results: There were new martyrs for the revolutionary cause, and the common people's long-cherished faith in the tsar as a benevolent father figure was largely destroyed. For years, ordinary Russians had viewed the tsar as their protector against evil landlords and bureaucrats, but increasingly they realized that the tsar himself was largely to blame for their troubles. (See Reading 17.)

Throughout 1905, demonstrations occurred across Russia. Peasants burned their landlords' houses, young radicals assassinated a number of public figures, the sailors of the battleship *Potemkin* mutinied on the Black Sea, national groups initiated protest movements throughout the Empire, and workers went on a series of strikes culminating in a general strike in October.

"Demonstration." A drawing by Boris Kustodiev depicting a typical city scene during the revolutionary year 1905, when the working class first demonstrated in mass protests.

FACT: Discontent among the non-Russian peoples of the Empire was pervasive and included such small groups as the Yakuts of eastern Siberia. Influenced in part by exiled revolutionaries, Yakut school teachers in 1906 organized a congress in Yakutsk which demanded greater autonomy, and a nationalist Yakut newspaper was started.

At the last moment, Nicholas issued the October Manifesto, promising a constitution, an elected state *duma* (parliament), and civil liberties for all. Although the tsar later reneged on many of the promises made in the Manifesto, he temporarily satisfied the moderate politicians. The main reason that the tsar survived the events of 1905, however, was that those who sought to overthrow him had no effective leader. As a result, the multiple outbreaks by workers, peasants, the national minorities, and the military were not synchronized. Twelve years later, this would not be the case.

From 1905 to 1917, Russia appeared at first glance to be a legitimate constitutional monarchy (see Reading 19). Certainly the autocracy had been modified. The Duma turned out to be little more than window dressing, however. It was ineffective as an arena for radical political opposition to voice itself, particularly after the electoral laws were modified in 1907 to increase the voting power of the conservative elements in society. More important, the executive branch was not responsible to it. This period also saw a continuation of the police repression that had existed under Alexander III. The head policeman this time was the extremely able Prime Minister Peter Stolypin, whose policy of "pacification" included summary courts-martial, severe sentences, and countless regulations limiting the civil rights granted in 1905.

FACT: The term "Stolypin's necktie" was created; this was the noose used in the many executions of political radicals.

The repression made life very difficult for the revolutionary parties which, after seeing their hopes first raised and then all but destroyed in 1905, were forced back into exile. There, while the Marxists awaited the expected international revolution, they contemplated the future of their own country with considerable gloom.

FACT: The gloom lasted until 1917. In January of that year Lenin said, "I do not believe that we of the older generation will live to see the revolution . . ."

The pessimism of the revolutionaries stemmed from the fact that, in many respects, the years 1905–14 were good for Russia and its ruler. Stolypin was a perceptive statesman. As Witte had focused on the need to develop Russian industry in the previous decade, Stolypin now attempted to solve the serious problems that continued to haunt agriculture and the rural population. He abolished redemption payments, dissolved the *mirs*, consolidated landholdings, and encouraged the emergence of a new class of strong, independent peasant landowners. He reasoned that a prosperous peasantry would have a stake in the status quo and not lean toward rebellion, as the impoverished peasantry had done in 1905. In one sense, the process was quite successful. Despite some peasant resistance, by 1917 almost half the peasant households in European Russia were independent and on the road to prosperity. On the other hand, the process forced many peasants off the land and into the cities, to be exploited by factory owners.

In other areas, too, there was progress. The *zemstvos* played an increasingly important role in local affairs. Industrialization was given greater priority. A national system of education was established, and literacy became a national goal. Culturally, Russia was a thriving and in many ways a modern society on the eve of the Revolution. Wealthy, liberal Moscow merchants such as Ivan Morosov and Sergei Shchukin not only collected the latest works of such western artists as Matisse and Picasso, but provided a vital source of patronage for Russian artists as well.

FACT: One of the greatest patrons of Russian art in the late Imperial Period was Pavel Tretiakov, a textile manufacturer who in 1892 founded a gallery that still bears his name. It contains the largest collection of Russian art in the world.

There is continued debate among historians about these last years of Imperial Russia. Some argue that Russia's progress between 1905 and 1914 was real and substantial, and that the tsarist regime might well have survived and flourished had it not been for the crisis presented by World War I. Others argue that the regime had a terminal disease and that World War I simply hastened an end that was inevitable. This debate probably will never be settled. Suffice it to say that while things were looking quite good for Russia as late as 1913, the outbreak of war in the following year was far more of a trauma than the regime could bear. Russia was not equipped politically, economically, or militarily to fight a lengthy conflict against Germany, the continent's most heavily industrialized and best-armed power. It was ironic that Russia's aggressive Pan-Slav foreign policy in the Balkan peninsula after 1908 helped to precipitate the outbreak of war in August 1914. In this war, which lasted much longer than anyone expected, the Russians were the first to mobilize and the first to cross into enemy territory on a large scale. (See Reading 19.)

Russia's initial enthusiasm and success didn't last long. By 1915, the tide had turned, and on the German front the tsarist armies began a retreat that never ended. The Romanov dynasty had survived military humiliation in the Crimea in 1855 and again—just barely—in the recent Japanese war. This time it could not. Military defeat was accompanied by growing restiveness among the civilian population, for whom the war crystallized and brought to a head all the long-standing grievances. Symbolic of the disastrous state of affairs in tsardom was the continued presence at court of Rasputin. Hoping that his removal might improve the situation and permit the survival of the status quo a group of Russian aristocrats murdered Rasputin in December 1916. (See Reading 20.) By then, it was much too late. The end of the Russian Empire occurred violently three months later.

Since the reign of Peter the Great, Russia had tried to cope with a modernizing world. Peter had started a process of domestic transformation in order to catch up with the West, but both he and his successors shied away from some of the most necessary changes. When reform did occur, it was fitful,

Nicholas II blesses the troops. Russian soldiers kneel in homage to the tsar at the outbreak of World War I. Nicholas sanctifies the occasion by carrying a holy icon; bearing an icon into battle was a Russian tradition dating back many centuries.

halfhearted, and insufficient. Russia never became capable of competing with the more advanced nations, particularly in the wars that were the inevitable result of its own expansionistic policy. To the very end, Imperial Russia remained a backward autocracy, unsuited to a world of industrialism and political freedom, and unsuited, too, for the leading role it wanted to play in world affairs.

The following books were helpful in writing this chapter:

Crankshaw, E., *The Shadow of the Winter Palace*. New York: The Viking Press, 1976.

Kohn, H., ed. *The Mind of Modern Russia*. New York: Harper and Row, 1962.

Pipes, R., *Russia under the Old Regime*. New York: Scribner's, 1974.

Riasanovsky, N., *A History of Russia*, 3rd ed. New York: Oxford University Press, 1977.

Szamuely, T., *The Russian Tradition*. New York: McGraw Hill, 1974.

Ulam, A., *The Bolsheviks*. New York: Collier, 1965.

For students who are interested, we recommend further reading in the sources from which we have taken excerpts, as well as the following works:

Bergamini, J.D., *The Tragic Dynasty*. New York: Putnam, 1969.
    One of several recent accounts of the Romanovs, with many fascinating anecdotes.

Berlin, I., *Russian Thinkers*. New York: Penguin, 1979.

Lincoln, W.B., *In War's Dark Shadow*. New York: Dial, 1983.
    Subtitled "The Russians before the Great War," this is the first volume in Lincoln's trilogy on the Russian Revolution. It is a fine blend of meticulous scholarship and readability.

Maclean, F., *Holy Russia*. London: Century, 1982.
    Readable narrative history of Russia by well-known British traveler-writer.

Massie, R.K., *Nicholas and Alexandra*. New York: Alfred A. Knopf, 1978.
    Well-researched and colorful account of the reign of the last tsar.

—— *Peter the Great*. New York: Alfred A. Knopf, 1980.
    A similar treatment of Russia's first emperor.

Massie, S., *The Land of the Firebird: The Beauty of Old Russia*. New York: Simon & Schuster, 1980.
    Romanticized but highly readable history.

Obolensky, C., *The Russian Empire: A Portrait in Photographs*. New York: Random House, 1979.
    Photographs taken between 1855 and 1914 convey the sweep and variety of the empire, as well as life among the Russians. Included is a remarkable short introduction by Max Hayward that provides a brilliant overview of imperial Russian history.

Salisbury, H., *Black Night, White Snow*. Garden City, N.Y.: Doubleday, 1978.

A narrative history of the 1905–17 period in Russia by a *New York Times* journalist with much knowledge of Russia. Anecdotal and fast-paced.

Ulam, A., *In the Name of the People.* New York: Viking, 1977.

A fascinating history of the radical revolutionaries of mid-nineteenth century Russia.

Wallace, D.M., *Russia on the Eve of War and Revolution.* Princeton: Princeton University Press, 1964.

Originally published in 1877, updated in 1905 and 1912, and reprinted in 1964 and 1981, this is a classic, authoritative, and highly readable account of Russian life by a correspondent of the London *Times*.

READINGS
for
Chapter Three

1. The Building of St. Petersburg

This reading describes the building of St. Petersburg. It illustrates the degree to which the city took shape as a result of Peter's strong will, with little attention paid to the price in human suffering.

Activity was increased to fever pitch. Encampments, larger than the city itself, swelled to absorb the incoming labour. The work went on winter and summer, day and night, in the face of every obstacle. The privations and setbacks which the workers endured were appalling. Disastrous floods constantly overwhelmed the low-lying islands, and in 1705 the whole city was several feet deep in water. As late as 1721 the Neva was still not controlled; in that year all the streets of St. Petersburg were navigable and Peter was nearly drowned in the **Nevsky Prospekt.** Fire, too—an almost weekly occurrence—played its sinister part. In 1710 all the chief emporiums of the city—the original *Gostinny Dvor* or Bazaar—with hundreds of wood and canvas shops were destroyed in one night. Wolves roamed the streets after dark: even in 1715 a woman was devoured in broad daylight not far from Menshikov's house. There was as yet little at St. Petersburg to attract the people of Moscow. One of Peter's jesters gloomily described the position of the new city in these words: "On one side the sea, on the other sorrow, on the third moss, on the fourth a sigh."

But in 1710 all the members of the Imperial family moved to the new city, together with all government institutions still remaining in Moscow. The same year a *ukase* [proclamation] was issued demanding forty thousand workmen a year, together with their essential tools, to be sent from the provinces. A little later Peter also ordered two thousand thieves and robbers, and all who had been deported or banished, to be sent to the Neva. Then he forbade the erection, owing to the shortage of masons, of any stone buildings in any part of the empire outside St. Petersburg, under penalty of banishment to Siberia and of confiscation of property, while every boat or cart entering the city had to bring a certain quantity of unhewn stones, as stone was sadly lacking in these marshy wastes. It was also forbidden to cut wood on the islands, and, to economize fuel, no one was allowed to heat his bath-house more than once a week. The city was populated by force. All officials, nobles and landowners possessing not less than thirty families of peasant serfs were obliged to settle in St Petersburg and build houses for themselves, of stone, brick, **pise** or wood according to their means: those who owned five hundred peasants had to raise a stone house of two stories, while the poorer ones often found themselves obliged to club together to build one. Such *ukases* continued to be issued. In 1712 came this decree:

Abridged from Marsden, Christopher, *Palmyra of the North: The First Days of St. Petersburg*, 50–3, 55. London: Faber & Faber, 1942.

1. One thousand of the best families of the nobility, etc., are required to build houses of beams, with lath and plaster, in the old English style, along the bank of the Neva from the Imperial palace to the point opposite Nyenskantz.

2. Five hundred of the best known merchant families and five hundred traders less distinguished, must build for themselves wooden houses on the other side of the river, opposite to the dwellings of the nobility, until the government can provide them with stone houses and shops.

3. Two thousand artisans of every kind—painters, tailors, joiners, blacksmiths, etc.—must settle themselves on the same side of the river, right up to Nyenskantz.

The haste with which these dwellings must have been put up is reflected later on in the dilapidated state of the city under Peter's successors; they often did not even stand up to the first winters after the erection and rich banquets in the new houses were spoiled by cracking walls, gaping floors and leaky roofs. They were built with groans and curses both from the wretched labourers and the unwilling occupants, who still saw only evil in every idea and action of the heretical tsar. Nevertheless, in 1712 Peter announced that Sankt Piterburkh [St. Petersburg] was to be the Imperial capital . . .

But already building had been progressing elsewhere than on the two original islands—on the adjacent Isle of Buffaloes, afterwards called Vasilievsky Ostrov, also on the northern bank of the Neva; and on the left bank of the river, opposite Vasilievsky Ostrov, where the Admiralty had been built. There was of course no bridge, not even a pontoon, linking the islands. The twenty boats, manned by ignorant peasants, which were used as ferries were a severe menace to the population. Many people, including such important personages as the Polish Minister, a Major General and one of the tsar's First Physicians, lost their lives in the hazardous transit. On Vasilievsky Ostrov, Peter later wished to have a town on the model of Amsterdam, planted with rows of trees and intersected by navigable canals, and to make this the official centre of his maritime city. Work was begun on the canals, but circumstances eventually made it clear that it would have to be upon the left bank of the river that the life of the city must revolve. As there were no bridges, and as the Neva, at the time of the first ice and again when it breaks, is almost untraversable, the northern islands were virtually cut off from the rest of Russia. Many important buildings, to be sure, were to appear on Vasilievsky Ostrov in Peter's reign and afterwards, as we shall see; but the subsequent history of the city is that of a withdrawal to the mainland—and in the first place to the environs of the Admiralty.

Ten years, then, after the foundation of the city, and with some five hundred houses built, the active influences at work on its architecture are all Germanic: Trezzini and his pupils, Italian and Russian, working in the German-Dutch style of Baltic baroque, and the followers of Schluter—Mattarnovy (who inherited Schluter's plans and models), Schadel, Schwertfeger, Forster and Braunstein—in the equally Dutch-influenced North German manner.

2. Resistance to Peter: Ruthless Razoring

Peter the Great's reforms affected dress and appearance, as well as the organization of his government. Many Russians were particularly disturbed by the order that they must go clean shaven, as they felt to cut their beards was an offense against God. John Perry, the English author of this account, served as an engineer in Peter's service from 1698 to 1712.

It had been the manner of the Russes, like the Patriarchs of old, to wear long beards hanging down upon their bosoms, which they comb'd out with pride, and kept smooth and fine, without one hair to be diminish'd . . . The Czar, therefore, to reform this foolish custom, and to make them look like other Europeans, ordered a tax to be laid, on all gentlemen, merchants, and others of his subjects (excepting the priests and common peasants, or slaves) that they should each of them pay a hundred rubles per annum, for the wearing of their beards, and that even the common people should pay a copeck [100 copecks make up one ruble] at the entrance of the gates of any of the towns or cities of Russia . . . This was look'd upon to be little less than a sin in the Czar, a breach of their religion, and held to be a great grievance for sometime, as more particularly by being brought in by the strangers. But the women liking their husbands and sweethearts the better, they are now for the most part, pretty well reconciled to the practice.

It is most certain, that the Russes had a kind of religious respect and veneration for their beards; and so much the more, because they differed herein from strangers, which was back'd by the humours of the priests . . . and which nothing but the absolute authority of the Czar, and the terror of having them (in his merry humour) pull'd out by the roots, or sometimes taken so rough off, that some of the skin went with them, could ever have prevailed with the Russes to have parted with their beards. On this occasion there were letters drop'd about the streets, sealed and directed to His Czarish Majesty, which charged him with tyranny and heathenism . . .

About this time the Czar came down to Veronize, where I was then on service, and a great many of my men that had worn their beards all their lives, were now obliged to part with them, amongst which, one of the first that I met with just coming from the hands of the barber, was an old Russ carpenter that

---

Abridged from Putnam, Peter, ed., *Seven Britons in Imperial Russia, 1698–1812*, 38–9. Princeton: Princeton University Press, 1952.

had been with me at Camishinka, who was a very good workman with his hatchet, and whom I always had a friendship for. I jested a little with him on this occasion, telling him that he was become a young man, and asked him what he had done with his beard? Upon which he put his hand in his bosom and pull'd it out, and shew'd it to me: farther telling me, that when he came home, he would lay it up to have it put in his coffin and buried along with him, that he might be able to give an account of it to St. Nicholas, when he came to the other world; and that all his brothers (meaning his fellow-workmen, who had been shaved that day) had taken the same care.

3. Alexander Pushkin:
The Bronze Horseman

Alexander Pushkin (1799–1837) is considered one of the greatest Russian poets. Of him, a critic of the 1860s wrote, "In his verse, the living Russian language was made known to us for the first time," and after the Revolution, Lunacharsky, the Soviet Commissar for public enlightenment in the 1920s, wrote, "Pushkin was the Russian Adam." Pushkin was the grandson of an African, an Abyssinian who was adopted and educated by Peter the Great. He met a tragic young death in a duel. This poem, The Bronze Horseman, *is based on a real flood in St. Petersburg and expresses well the ambivalence Pushkin and other patriotic Russians felt toward the titanic figure of Peter the Great. The bronze horseman of its title is the huge statue of Peter that today still looks out over the river Neva. It was raised by an admiring Catherine the Great.*

PROLOGUE

Upon a shore of desolate waves
Stood *he*, with lofty musings grave,
And gazed afar. Before him spreading
Rolled the broad river, empty save
For one lone skiff stream-downward heading.
Strewn on the marshy, moss-grown bank,
Rare huts, the Finn's poor shelter, shrank,
Black smudges from the fog protruding;
Beyond, dark forest ramparts drank
The shrouded sun's rays and stood brooding
And murmuring all about.

Abridged from Pushkin, A., "The Bronze Horseman." In *Alexander Pushkin: Collected Narrative and Lyrical Poetry*. Edited and translated by Walter Arndt, 401–3, 421–3. Ann Arbor: Ardis, 1984.

He thought:
"Here, Swede, beware—soon by our labor
Here a new city shall be wrought,
Defiance to the haughty neighbor.
Here we at Nature's own behest
Shall break a window to the West.
Stand planted on the ocean level;
Here flags of foreign nations all
By waters new to them will call,
And unencumbered we shall revel."

A century passed, and there shone forth
From swamps and gloomy forest prison,
Crown gem and marvel of the North,
The proud young city newly risen.
Where Finnish fisherman before,
Harsh Nature's wretched waif, was plying,
Forlorn upon that shallow shore,
His trade, with brittle net-gear trying
Uncharted tides—now bustling banks
Stand serried in well-ordered ranks
Of palaces and towers; converging
From the four corners of the earth,
Sails press to seek the opulent berth,
To anchorage in squadrons merging;
Neva is cased in granite clean,
Atop its waters bridges hover,
Between its channels, gardens cover
The river isles with darkling green.
Outshone, old Moscow had to render
The younger sister pride of place,
As by a new queen's fresh-blown splendor
In purple fades Her dowager Grace.

I love you, work of Peter's warrant,
I love your stern and comely face,
The broad Neva's majestic current,
Her bankments' granite carapace,
The patterns laced by iron railing,
And of your meditative night
The lucent dusk, the moonless paling;
When in my room I read and write
Lampless, and street on street stand dreaming,
Vast luminous gulfs, and, slimly gleaming,
The Admiralty's needle bright;
And rather than let darkness smother

The lustrous heavens' golden light,
One twilight glow speeds on the other
To grant but half an hour to night.

I love your winter's fierce embraces
That leave the air all chilled and hushed,
The sleighs by broad Neva, girls' faces
More brightly than the roses flushed,
The ballroom's sparkle, noise, and chatter.

. . . .

Thrive, Peter's city, flaunt your beauty,
Stand like unshaken Russian fast,
Till floods and storms from chafing duty
May turn to peace with you at last;
The very tides of Finland's deep
Their long-pent rancor then may bury,
And cease with feckless spite to harry
Tsar Peter's everlasting sleep.

. . . .

[The poet then recounts the sad story of Eugene, whose wife-to-be perished in a flood. Tormented by the discovery of her death, Eugene dreams that he is pursued by the Bronze Horseman. This Peter has no sympathy for the hardships his city has caused the common people like Eugene.]

Eugene's heart shrank. His mind unclouding
In dread, he knew the place again
Where the great flood had sported then,
Where those rapacious waves were crowding
And round about him raged and spun—
That square, the lions, and him—the one
Who, bronzen countenance upslanted
Into the dusk aloft, sat still,
The one by whose portentous will
The city by the sea was planted . . .
How awesome in the gloom he rides!
What thought upon his brow resides!

His charger with what fiery mettle,
His form with what dark strength endowed!
Where will you gallop, charger proud,
Where next your plunging hoofbeats settle?
Oh, Destiny's great potentate!
Was it not thus, a towering idol

Hard by the chasm, with iron bridle
You reared up Russia to her fate?

. . . .

           The dread Tsar's face,
With instantaneous fury burning,
It seemed to him, was slowly turning . . .
Across these empty spaces bound,
Behind his back he heard resound,
Like thunderclouds in rumbling anger,
The deep reverberating clangor
Of pounding hoofs that shook the ground.
And in the moonlight's pallid glamor
Rides high upon his charging brute,
One hand stretched out, 'mid echoing clamor
The Bronze Horseman in pursuit.
And all through that long night, no matter
What road the frantic wretch might take,
There still would pound with ponderous clatter
The Bronze Horseman in his wake.

4. Anna's Ice Palace

The Empress Anna (reigned 1730–40) amused herself with lavish, costly entertainments: fireworks, the creation of ice mountains for sliding on the frozen river Neva, and one of her masterpieces, the ice palace here described.

The winter of 1739–40 was unusually cold, and the scientists of the Academy embarked on a programme of experiments to test the properties of ice that was available in such abundance. Knowing this, a court Chamberlain called Alexander Tatishchev thought of combining it with a new entertainment for the court—building a palace of ice on which artists and artisans as well as scientists could exercise their skills. In the end it turned out to be a setting for another of the Empress's macabre jokes . . .

The Prince [Golitsyn] . . . was in his forties now and long since a widower. But the Empress insisted that he should take another wife. Indeed she chose one for him—Avdotaya Ivanovna, nicknamed "Bujenina" after Anna's favourite dish—roast pork done in a sauce of onions, vinegar and spices. Avdotaya was of Kalmyk origin, extremely ugly and wanted desperately to find a

Abridged from Longworth, P., *The Three Empresses*, 144–5. London: Constable & Co., 1972.

husband. The Empress not only answered her prayers but agreed to pay for the wedding, deciding that it should be made the greatest comic spectacle ever seen in Russia.

A rocket whistled into the air and exploded with a loud report above the city. Within seconds a whole sheaf of rockets was set loose; fountains of coloured fire began to flame, catherine wheels to circle madly. All St. Petersburg was lit up in brilliant flashes of light. The New Year 1740 had arrived.

The Empress attended the usual round of functions, but her own special comedy was due to be staged a few days later. Already the city was alive with excitement and despite the bitter cold, large crowds gathered on the frozen river, hoping to catch a glimpse of what the hundreds of craftsmen were up to concealed behind thick lines of guarding troops.

Then one morning a huge and astonishing procession formed up in the streets. Goats, pigs, cows, camels, dogs and reindeer were seen harnessed to various strange vehicles each of which contained a representative pair from each of the "Barbarous Races" in the Empire. There were Lapps and Kirghiz, Tunguses and Tatars, Bashkirs and Finns—each couple in "national dress." But the centerpiece was an elephant with an iron cage on its back. The cage contained Golitsyn and his unlovely bride.

To the accompaniment of cymbals, bells and the occasional roaring of an angry beast, the procession passed the Palace and eventually arrived at Ernest Biron's covered riding school, where a banquet had been prepared for the captive bridal pair and their guests. By the Empress's express command each couple was served with its own traditional dishes—including such culinary delights as reindeer meat, horse-flesh and fermented mare's milk. There was entertainment too. A poet named Tredyakovski declaimed an ode composed specially for the occasion entitled: "Greetings to the Bridal Pair of Fools," and each pair of guests was made to dance its own "national dance" for the amusement of the onlookers. Then the procession formed up again to accompany the bride and groom to their home for the night—the palace made of ice.

No other material had been used in its construction—walls and steps, baroque balustrades, cornices and columns, even the decorative figurines and window-panes were made of ice. So was the furniture—a huge four-poster bridal bed, chairs, tables, chandeliers, a clock, a commode, a set of playing cards, with the markings coloured in, and a statue of a Cupid. Outside there were other marvels of engineering and the sculptor's art—flowers and trees complete with perching birds, ice cannon which fired real charges, a pair of dolphins which breathed out flames of fire (thanks to a device inside which pumped out naptha), and a life-sized model of an elephant equipped with a machine to squirt out water to a height of two hundred and fifty feet. Everything had been done to excite the eye and astonish the imagination—and all at a cost of only thirty thousand rubles.

The Empress accompanied the bridal pair inside, saw them undressed and laid upon their bed of ice. Then she withdrew. From her bedroom she had an excellent view of the Ice Palace, and next morning she saw Golitsyn and his wife emerge apparently none the worse for their experience. The stove installed inside their chilly bedroom, as the scientists of the Academy took careful note, had proved effective.

5. The Pugachev Rebellion

Emelian Pugachev, instigator of the greatest peasant revolt in Russian history, was a simple Cossack soldier (and deserter). He proclaimed himself Emperor Peter III, claiming that he had survived the plot that had overthrown the real Peter eleven years before. He even set up an imperial court, imitating that in St. Petersburg. Catherine was not amused and issued the following manifesto in December 1773. The great Russian poet Alexander Pushkin (see Reading 3) was fascinated by the Pugachev uprising and wrote a factual history of it, as well as a historical novel, The Captain's Daughter.

By the Grace of God, We, Catherine II, Empress and Autocratix of All the Russias, etc.

Make known to all Our faithful subjects that We have learnt, with the utmost indignation and extreme affliction, that a certain Cossack, a deserter and fugitive from the Don, named Emelian Pugachev, after having traversed Poland, has been collecting, for some time past, in the districts that border on the river Ural, in the government of Orenburg, a troop of vagabonds like himself; that he continues to commit in those parts all kinds of excesses, by inhumanly depriving the inhabitants of their possessions, and even of their lives; and that in order to attract to his party, hitherto composed of robbers, such persons as he meets, and especially the unhappy patriots, on whose credulity he imposes, he has had the insolence to arrogate to himself the name of the late Emperor Peter III. It would be superfluous here to prove the absurdity of such an imposture, which cannot even put on a shadow of probability in the eyes of sensible persons . . .

Since those times, which it is grievous to recollect, all true patriots have enjoyed the fruits of public tranquillity, and shudder with horror at the very remembrance of former troubles. In a word, there is not a man deserving of the Russian name, who does not hold in abomination the odious and insolent lie by which Pugachev fancies himself able to seduce and to deceive persons of a simple and credulous disposition, by promising to free them from the bonds of

Abridged from Dmytryshyn, B., *Imperial Russia: A Source Book, 1700–1917*, 94–6. Hinsdale, Ill.: Dryden, 1974.

submission, and obedience to their sovereign, as if the Creator of the universe had established human societies in such a manner as that they can subsist without an intermediate authority between the sovereign and the people.

Nevertheless, as the insolence of this vile refuse of the human race is attended with consequences pernicious to the provinces adjacent to that district; as the report of the flagrant enormities which he has committed may affright those persons who are accustomed to imagine the misfortunes of others as ready to fall upon them, and as We watch with indefatigable care over the tranquillity of Our faithful subjects, We inform them by the present manifesto that We have taken, without delay, such measures as are the best adapted to stifle the sedition: and in order to annihilate totally the ambitious designs of Pugachev, and to exterminate a band of robbers, who have been audacious enough to attack the small military detachments dispersed about those countries, and to massacre the officers who were taken prisoners. We have dispatched thither, with a competent number of troops, General Alexander Bibikov [1727–1774], general in chief of Our armies, and major of Our regiment of life guards.

Accordingly We have no doubt of the happy success of these measures, and We cherish the hope that the public tranquillity will soon be restored, and that the profligates who are spreading devastation over a part of the government of Orenburg will shortly be dispersed. We are moreover persuaded that Our faithful subjects will justly abhor the imposture of the rebel Pugachev, as destitute of all probability, and will repel the artifices of the ill-disposed, who seek and find their advantage in the seduction of the weak and credulous, and who cannot assuage their avidity but by ravaging their country, and by shedding of innocent blood.

We trust, with equal confidence, that every true son of the country will unremittedly fulfil his duty of the contributing to the maintenance of good order and of public tranquillity, by preserving himself from the snares of seduction, and by duly discharging his obedience to his lawful sovereign. All Our faithful subjects therefore may dispel their alarms and live in perfect security, since We employ Our utmost care, and make it Our peculiar glory, to preserve their property, and to extend the general felicity.

Given at St. Petersburg, December 23, 1773.

6. Napoleon Enters Moscow

This first-hand account is by Baron Claude-François de Meneval, who accompanied Napoleon when the French armies entered Moscow in September 1812.

Abridged from de Meneval, "Napoleon enters Moscow." In *Eyewitness to History*. Edited by J. Carey, 278–80. New York: Avon, 1988.

A curious and impressive sight was this sudden appearance of this great city, Asiatic rather than European, spreading out at the end of a desert and naked plain, topped with its twelve hundred spires and sky-blue cupolas, strewn with golden stars, and linked one to the other with gilded chains. This conquest had been dearly paid for, but Napoleon at that time lulled himself in the hope that he would be able to dictate peace there. The King of Naples, who entered it first, sent word to the Emperor that the city appeared to be deserted and that no civil or military functionary, nor nobleman, nor priest had presented himself. The Russian army had taken away the majority of the inhabitants of Moscow in its train. Some Russian and foreign dealers, who had managed to escape this order, came to see the Emperor and implored him to protect them against the pillaging with which they thought themselves menaced. There had remained in the city only a few thousand people belonging to the lowest classes of society, who had nothing to lose by awaiting the course of events.

Napoleon passed this night of September 14th in the Dorogomilow *faubourg*, and only entered Moscow on the morrow. This entry was not accompanied by that tumult which marks the taking possession of a great city. No noise disturbed the solitude of the city streets, save only the rumbling of the cannon and of the artillery *caissons*. Moscow seemed asleep in deep sleep, like one of those enchanted cities of which we read in Arabian tales. The streets through which we passed were lined with houses of fine appearance for the most part, with closed windows and doors. Palaces with colonnades, churches and beautiful buildings glittering with the luxury of Europe and of Asia raised themselves side by side with very modest habitations. All bespoke the ease and wealth of a great city enriched by trade and inhabited by a wealthy and numerous aristocracy. Some of the principal houses which we were able to enter were well appointed and well furnished, many even magnificently so, and their inhabitants did not appear to have abandoned them for ever.

The Emperor proceeded directly to the Kremlin, a large citadel placed in the centre of the town, on the top of a hill, surrounded with an embattled wall and flanked at intervals with towers armed with cannon. The Kremlin is a second city. It contains the imperial palace, the arsenal, the Senate palace, the archives, the principal public establishments, a large number of churches, temples filled with historical curiosities, objects serving for the coronation of the sovereigns, and lastly trophies and flags taken from the Turks. It is in one of the principal temples that are the tombs of the Tsars . . .

The walls are covered with thick plates of gold and silver on which are figured in relief the principal incidents of the Sacred History. Enormous silver lamps of Byzantine shape hang from the arches of the building, large many-branched chandeliers of the same metal stand on pedestals on the floor. There is also to be seen in this sanctuary a portrait of the Holy Virgin attributed to St. Luke, the frame of this picture is enriched with pearls and precious stones. A great bell-tower, known as the Ivan tower, was surmounted by a gigantic cross in the centre of which was enchased a cross of pure gold containing a fragment of the true cross. This cross and a number of curious objects which could be removed were to be sent to Paris from the Kremlin.

Hardly had the Emperor entered the Kremlin than fire broke out in the Kitaigorod, or Chinese city, an immense bazaar, surrounded by porticoes, in which were heaped up, in large shops or in cellars, the entrances to which were placed in the middle of the streets, precious goods of every kind, such as shawls, furs, Indian and Chinese tissues. Fruitless efforts were made to extinguish the flames, and the burning of the bazaar became the signal for a general conflagration in the city. This conflagration, spreading rapidly, devoured three-quarters of Moscow in three days. Each moment one saw smoke followed by flames breaking out of houses which had remained intact and in the end the fire broke out in every house in the city. The town was one mighty furnace from which sheaves of fire burst heavenwards lighting up the horizon with the glaring flames and spreading a burning heat. These masses of flame, mingling together, were rapidly caught up by a strong wind which spread them in every direction. They were accompanied by a succession of whistling noises and explosions caused by the falling walls and the explosion of inflammable materials which were stored in the shops and houses. To these roaring noises, to these sinister outbreaks added themselves the cries and yells of the wretched people who were caught by the flames in the houses which they had entered to pillage and which many escaped only to perish in the streets which formed a blazing labyrinth from which all escape was impossible. Motionless and in the silence of stupor we looked on at this horrible and magnificent spectacle, with the feeling of our absolute helplessness to render any assistance.

7. A Frenchman's View of Autocracy

The Marquis de Custine was a French aristocrat and opponent of the French Revolution who traveled to Russia in 1839. He expected to find much to admire in the strong government of the tsar. What he actually found was something quite different. Here he describes his reaction to the city of St. Petersburg and the man responsible for its construction. The translator of this selection, Phyllis Penn Kohler, was the wife of the American ambassador to the USSR after World War II. She undertook this translation because she and her friends were struck by the similarity of de Custine's Russia to what they saw in Stalin's day.

I had my pockets full of letters of recommendation which had been given to me in Paris, in part by the Russian ambassador himself, as well as by other equally well-known persons; but as they were sealed I had been afraid to leave

Abridged from Phyllis Penn Kohler, ed. and trans. *Journey For Our Time: The Russian Journals of the Marquis de Custine*, 70–8. Chicago: Henry Regnery, 1951.

them in my portfolio; consequently, I buttoned my coat when I saw the police approaching. They let me pass without searching my person, but when I had to unpack all my trunks before the customs officers, these new enemies undertook the most minute examination of my effects, particularly the books. After being subjected to an interminable examination, all of my books were confiscated—always with the most extreme politeness, but with no regard for my protests. They also took from me two sets of traveler's pistols and an old travel clock. I tried in vain to understand and explain to myself why this latter object should have been subject to confiscation. Everything taken from me was later returned, as they had assured me it would be, but not without a great deal of annoyance and lengthy discussions. Accordingly, I repeat what the Russian gentlemen said: Russia is the country of useless formalities . . .

The highly overrated, famous statue of Peter the Great was the first thing to attract my attention; it seemed to me to have a singularly disagreeable effect; placed on its rock by Catherine, with this inscription—rather conceited in its apparent simplicity—"To Peter I Catherine II." This figure of a man on a horse is neither ancient nor modern; it is a Roman of the time of Louis XV. [See Reading 3.]

I stopped for a moment in front of the scaffolding of a building already famous in Europe, in spite of the fact that it is not finished. This will be the Church of Saint Isaac. Finally, I saw the facade of the new Winter Palace, another prodigious product of the will of a man applied to aligning the strength of men against the laws of nature. The goal was attained, for in one year this palace rose up out of its ashes. I believe it is the largest palace in existence. It is the equivalent of the Louvre and the Tuileries combined.

In order to finish the work in the period specified by the Emperor, unprecedented efforts were required. The interior construction was continued during the bitterest cold of winter. Six thousand laborers were continually at work; a considerable number died each day, but, as the victims were instantly replaced by other champions who filled their places, to perish in their turn in this inglorious gap, the losses were not apparent. And the only purpose of so much sacrifice was to satisfy the caprice of a man! With naturally civilized people, that is to say of an old civilization, men's lives are risked only for common interests whose gravity is recognized by the majority. But how many generations of sovereigns have been corrupted by the example of Peter I!

During freezes of fifteen to twenty degrees below zero, six thousand obscure martyrs, martyrs without merit, martyrs of an involuntary obedience—for this virtue is innate and forced in the Russians—were shut up in rooms heated to eighty-six degrees in order to dry the walls more quickly. Thus these wretches on entering and leaving this abode of death—now become, thanks to their sacrifice, the home of vanity, magnificence and pleasure—underwent a difference in temperature of 100 to 108 degrees.

Work in the mines of the Urals is less injurious to life; however, the laborers employed in Petersburg were not malefactors. I have been told that the unfortunate ones who painted the interior of the hottest rooms were obliged to put a kind of ice cap on their heads in order to keep their senses under the boiling temperature they were condemned to endure while they were working.

If one wished to disgust us with art, gilt, luxury, and with all the pomp of courts, one could not choose a more efficacious means. Nevertheless, the sovereign was called "Father" by men sacrificed in such great numbers under his eyes and for the satisfaction of sheer imperial vanity.

I feel ill at ease in Petersburg since I have seen this palace and heard what it cost in human lives. I guarantee the authenticity of the details; they were given to me by people who are neither spies nor scornful Russians.

The millions spent on Versailles fed as many French workers' families as these twelve months of the Winter Palace killed Slav serfs; but, by means of this sacrifice, the command of the Emperor accomplished miracles and the completed palace, to the general satisfaction, is to be inaugurated by the festivals of a marriage. A prince can be popular without attaching a high price to human life. Nothing colossal is obtained without pain; but when a man is himself both the nation and the government he should impose upon himself the law of employing the great resources of the machine he operates only for the attainment of an end worthy of the effort . . .

An absolute sovereign is wrong to say that he is in a hurry; he should, above all, fear the zeal of his subjects who can use the word of the master, innocent in appearance, like a sword to bring about miracles, but at the cost of an army of slaves! It is great, it is too great; God and mankind will finish by taking vengeance for these inhuman wonders. It is imprudent, to say the least, for a prince to rate satisfaction of vanity at so high a price; but the renown that they gain abroad is more important to the Russian princes than anything else—more important than the reality of power—for in that they are acting in the sense of public opinion; furthermore, nothing can discredit authority with a people for whom obedience has become a condition of life. Some peoples have worshiped light; the Russians worship eclipse. How can their eyes ever be opened?

I do not say that their political system produces nothing good; I say only that it produces at too high a cost.

It is not only now that foreigners are astonished by the love of these people for slavery . . .

[De Custine recalls that in the sixteenth century a German traveler had written about the power of the tsar and the obedience of his subjects. He comments that the same situation still seems true at the time of his visit in the early nineteenth century, and quotes the German traveler:]

He (the Czar) speaks and everything is done: the life, the fortune of the laity and of the clergy, of the nobility and of the citizens, all depend on his supreme will. He has no opposition, and everything in him appears just—as in the Divinity—for the Russians are persuaded that the Great Prince is the executor of celestial decrees. Thus, God and the Prince willed it; God and the Prince know best, such are the ordinary expressions among them; nothing equals their zeal for his service.

I do not know whether it is the character of the Russian nation which has formed such autocrats or whether the autocrats themselves have given this character to the nation . . .

It seems to me, however, that the influence is reciprocal—the Russian government would never have been established anywhere other than in Russia, nor would the Russians have become what they are under a different government.

Today you will hear, in Paris or in Russia, any number of Russians become ecstatic over the miraculous effects of the word of the Emperor; and, while they are priding themselves on the results, not one will be moved to pity by the means employed. The word of the Czar has the power to create, they say. Yes, it brings stones to life, but in doing so it kills men. Despite this small reservation, all Russians are proud of the ability to say to us: "You see, in your country one deliberates three years over the means of rebuilding a theater, whereas our Emperor builds the biggest palace in the world in one year." This childish triumph does not seem to them too dearly paid for by the death of some paltry thousands of workers sacrificed to this regal impatience, to this imperial fantasy, which becomes, to use a fashionable plural, one of the national glories. As for me, however, being French, I see in this only inhuman pedantry. But from one end of this vast Empire to the other, not a single protest is raised against these orgies of absolute sovereignty.

—People and government—here all is harmony. The Russians would not give up the miracles of will of which they are witnesses, accomplices, and victims, if it were a question of bringing back to life all the slaves they have cost. All the same, the thing that surprises me is not that a man, steeped in self-idolatry, a man ascribed as all-powerful by sixty million men, or so-called men, undertakes and brings to conclusions such things; it is that among the voices which recount these accomplishments to the glory of this one man, not one separates itself from the chorus to protest in the name of humanity against the miracles of autocracy. It can be said of the Russians, great and small—they are intoxicated with slavery.

8. Mikhail Lermontov: Prediction

Throughout the nineteenth century, a number of writers made gloomy predictions about what lay ahead for Russia. This is one of the most dire, the work of M. Lermontov, who was an extraordinarily gifted writer and who himself died young. He lived from 1814 to 1841.

> The day will come, for Russia that dark day
> When the Tsar's diadem will fall, and they,
> Rabble who loved him once, will love no more
> And many will subsist on death and gore.
> Downtrodden law no shelter will provide

For child or guiltless woman. Plague will ride
From stinking corpses through the grief-struck
Land where fluttering rags from cottages demand
Help none can give. And famine's gnawing pangs
Will grip the countryside with ruthless fangs.
Dawn on the streams will shed a crimson light.
And then will be revealed the Man of might
Whom thou wilt know, and thou wilt understand
Wherefore a shining blade is in his hand.
Sorrow will by thy lot, grief melt thine eyes
And he will laugh at all thy tears and sighs.

9. Leo Tolstoy: "A Morning of a Landed Proprietor"

Leo Tolstoy (1828–1910) was one of the finest and most enduring of the world's great writers. Best known for his novels War and Peace *and* Anna Karenina, *he also wrote simple stories and fairy tales for children and the peasants on his estate. In this selection, he portrays the world of the landed estate and the attitudes of peasant and landlord toward their world and each other: the suspiciousness and stubborn conservatism of the peasant and the ineffectual good will of a well-meaning young landlord.*

Prince Nekhlyudov was nineteen years old when he came from the Third Course of the university to pass his vacation on his estate, and remained there by himself all summer. In the autumn he wrote in his unformed childish hand to his aunt, Countess Byeloryetski, who, in his opinion, was his best friend and the most brilliant woman in the world. The letter was in French, and ran as follows:

"Dear Aunty: —I have made a resolution on which the fate of my whole life must depend. I will leave the university in order to devote myself to country life, because I feel that I was born for it. For God's sake, dear aunty, do not laugh at me! You will say that I am young; and, indeed, I may still be a child, but this does not prevent me from feeling what my calling is, and from wishing to do good, and loving it.

"As I have written you before, I found affairs in an indescribable disorder. Wishing to straighten them out, and to understand them, I discovered that the

From Berdyaev, Nicolas, *The Origin of Russian Communism*, 80. Ann Arbor: University of Michigan Press, 1960.

Abridged from Tolstoy, Leo, *Childhood, Boyhood, Youth, The Incursion, A Landed Proprietor, The Cossacks, Sevastopol*. Edited and translated by Leo Wiener, Boston: L. C. Page, 1904.

main evil lay in the most pitiable, poverty-stricken condition of the peasants, and that the evil was such that it could be mended by labour and patience alone. If you could only see two of my peasants, Davyd and Ivan, and the lives which they lead with their families, I am sure that the mere sight of these unfortunates would convince you more than all I might say to explain my intention to you.

"Is it not my sacred and direct duty to care for the welfare of these seven hundred men, for whom I shall be held responsible before God? Is it not a sin to abandon them to the arbitrariness of rude elders and managers, for plans of enjoyment and ambition? And why should I look in another sphere for opportunities of being useful and doing good, when such a noble, brilliant, and immediate duty is open to me?

"I feel myself capable of being a good landed proprietor; and, in order to be one, as I understand this word, one needs neither a university diploma, nor ranks [bureaucratic hierarchy], which you are so anxious I should obtain. Dear aunty, make no ambitious plans for me! Accustom yourself to the thought that I have chosen an entirely different path, which is, nevertheless, good, and which, I feel, will bring me happiness. I have thought much, very much, about my future duty, have written out rules for my actions, and, if God will only grant me life and strength, shall succeed in my undertaking.

"Do not show this letter to my brother Vasya. I am afraid of his ridicule; he is in the habit of directing me, and I of submitting to him. Vanya will understand my intention, even though he may not approve of it" . . .

[Nekhlyudov returns to his estate and visits his peasants.]

Nekhlyudov walked into the hut. The uneven, grimy walls were in the kitchen corner covered with all kinds of rags and clothes, while the corner of honour was literally red with cockroaches that swarmed about the images and benches. In the middle of this black, ill-smelling, eighteen-foot hut there was a large crack in the ceiling, and although supports were put in two places, the ceiling was so bent that it threatened to fall down any minute.

"Yes, the hut is in a very bad shape," said the master, gazing at the face of Churis, who, it seemed, did not wish to begin a conversation about this matter.

"It will kill us, and the children, too," the old woman kept saying, in a tearful voice, leaning against the oven under the hanging beds.

"Don't talk!" sternly spoke Churis, and, turning to the master, with a light, barely perceptible smile, which had formed itself under his quivering moustache, he said: "I am at a loss, your Grace, what to do with this hut. I have braced it and mended it, but all in vain."

"How are we to pass a winter in it? Oh, oh, oh!" said the woman.

"Now, if I could put in a few braces and fix a new strut," her husband interrupted her, with a calm, business-like expression, "and change one rafter, we might be able to get through another winter. We might be able to live here, only it will be all cut up by the braces; and if anybody should touch it, not a thing would be left alive; but it might do, as long as it stands and holds together," he concluded, evidently satisfied with his argument.

Nekhlyudov was annoyed and pained because Churis had come to such a state without having asked his aid before, whereas he had not once since his arrival refused the peasants anything, and had requested that everybody should come to him directly if they needed anything. He was even vexed at the peasant, angrily shrugged his shoulders, and frowned; but the sight of wretchedness about him, and Churis's calm and self-satisfied countenance amidst this wretchedness, changed his vexation into a melancholy, hopeless feeling.

"Now, Ivan, why did you not tell me before?" he remarked reproachfully, sitting down on a dirty, crooked bench.

"I did not dare to, your Grace," answered Churis, with the same scarcely perceptible smile, shuffling his black, bare feet on the uneven dirt floor; but he said it so boldly and quietly that it was hard to believe that he had been afraid to approach the master.

"We are peasants: how dare we—" began the woman, sobbing.

"Stop your prattling," Churis again turned to her.

"You cannot live in this hut, that is impossible!" said Nekhlyudov, after a moment's silence. "This is what we will do, my friend—"

"I am listening, sir," Churis interrupted him.

"Have you seen the stone huts, with the hollow walls, that I have had built in the new hamlet?"

"Of course I have, sir," replied Churis, showing his good white teeth in his smile. "We marvelled a great deal as they were building them, —wonderful huts! The boys made sport of them, saying that the hollow walls were storehouses, to keep rats away. Fine huts!" he concluded, with an expression of sarcastic incredulity, shaking his head. "Regular jails!"

"Yes, excellent huts, dry and warm, and not so likely to take fire," retorted the master, with a frown on his youthful face, obviously dissatisfied with the peasant's sarcasm.

"No question about that, your Grace, fine huts."

"Now, one of those huts is all ready. It is a thirty-foot hut, with vestibules and a storeroom, ready for occupancy. I will let you have it at your price; you will pay me when you can," said the master, with a self-satisfied smile, which he could not keep back, at the thought that he was doing a good act. "You will break down your old hut," he continued; "it will do yet for a barn. We will transfer the outhouses in some way. There is excellent water there. I will cut a garden for you out of the cleared ground, and also will lay out a piece of land for you in three parcels. You will be happy there. Well, are you not satisfied?" asked Nekhlyudov, when he noticed that the moment he mentioned changing quarters Churis stood in complete immobility and, without a smile, gazed at the floor.

"It is your Grace's will," he answered, without lifting his eyes.

The old woman moved forward, as if touched to the quick, and was about to say something, but her husband anticipated her.

"It is your Grace's will," he repeated, firmly, and at the same time humbly, looking at his master, and shaking his hair, "but it will not do for us to live in the new hamlet."

"Why?"

"No, your Grace! We are badly off here, but if you transfer us there, we shan't stay peasants long. What kind of peasants can we be there? It is impossible to live there, saving your Grace!"

"Why not?"

"We shall be completely ruined, your Grace!"

"But why it is impossible to live there?"

"What life will it be? You judge for yourself: the place has never been inhabited; the quality of the water is unknown; there is no place to drive the cattle to. Our hemp plots have been manured here since time immemorial, but how is it there? Why, there is nothing but barrenness there. Neither fences, nor kilns, nor sheds, —nothing. We shall be ruined, your Grace, if you insist upon our going there, completely ruined! It is a new place, an unknown place—" he repeated, with a melancholy, but firm, shake of his head.

Nekhlyudov began to prove to the peasant that the transfer would be very profitable to him, that fences and sheds would be put up, that the water was good there, and so forth; but Churis' dull silence embarrassed him, and he felt that he was not saying what he ought to. Churis did not reply; but when the master grew silent, he remarked, with a light smile, that it would be best to settle the old domestic servants and Aleshka the fool in that hamlet, to keep a watch on the grain.

"Now that would be excellent," he remarked, and smiled again. "It is a useless affair, your Grace!"

"What of it if it is an uninhabited place?" Nekhlyudov expatiated, patiently. "Here was once an uninhabited place, and people are living in it now. And so you had better settle there in a lucky hour—Yes, you had better settle there—"

"But, your Grace, there is no comparison!" Churis answered with animation, as if afraid that the master might have taken his final resolution. "Here is a cheery place, a gay place, and we are used to it, and to the road, and the pond, where the women wash the clothes and the cattle go to water; and all our peasant surroundings have been here since time immemorial, —the threshing-floor, the garden, and the willows that my parents have set out. My grandfather and father have given their souls to God here, and I ask nothing else, your Grace, but to be able to end my days here. If it should be your favor to mend the hut, we shall be greatly obliged to your Grace; if not, we shall manage to end our days in the old hut. Let us pray to the Lord all our days," he continued, making low obeisances. "Drive us not from our nest, sir."

While Churis was speaking, ever louder and louder sobs were heard under the beds, in the place where his wife stood, and when her husband pronounced the word "sir," his wife suddenly rushed out and, weeping, threw herself down at the master's feet:

"Do not ruin us, benefactor! You are our father, you are our mother! What business have we to move? We are old and lonely people. Both God and you—" She burst out in tears.

Nekhlyudov jumped up from his seat, and wanted to raise the old woman, but she struck the earth floor with a certain voluptuousness of despair, and pushed away the master's hand.

"What are you doing? Get up, please! If you do not wish, you do not have to," he said waving his hands, and retreating to the door.

When Nekhlyudov seated himself again on the bench, and silence reigned in the hut, interrupted only by the blubbering of the old woman, who had again removed herself to her place under the beds, and was there wiping off her tears with the sleeve of her shirt, the young proprietor comprehended what meaning the dilapidated wretched hut, the broken well with the dirty puddle, the rotting stables and barns, and the split willows that could be seen through the crooked window, had for Churis and his wife, and a heavy, melancholy feeling came over him, and he was embarrassed.

"Why did you not say at the meeting of last week that you needed a hut? I do not know now how to help you. I told you all at the first meeting that I was settled in the estate, and that I meant to devote my life to you; that I was prepared to deprive myself of everything in order to see you contented and happy, —and I vow before God that I will keep my word," said the youthful proprietor, unconscious of the fact that such ebullitions were unable to gain the confidence of any man, least of all a Russian, who loves not words but deeds, and who is averse to the expression of feelings, however beautiful.

The simple-hearted young man was so happy in the sentiment which he was experiencing that he could not help pouring it out.

Churis bent his head sideways and blinking slowly, listened with forced attention to his master as to a man who must be listened to, though he may say things that are not very agreeable and have not the least reference to the listener.

"But I cannot give everybody all they ask of me. If I did not refuse anybody who asks me for timber, I should soon be left with none myself, and would be unable to give to him who is really in need of it. That is why I have put aside a part of the forest to be used for mending the peasant buildings, and have turned it over to the Commune. That forest is no longer mine, but yours, the peasants', and I have no say about it, but the Commune controls it as it sees fit. Come this evening to the meeting; I will tell the Commune of your need: if it resolves to give you a new hut, it is well, but I have no forest. I am anxious to help you with all my heart; but if you do not want to move, the Commune will have to arrange it for you, and not I. Do you understand me?"

"We are very well satisfied with your favour," answered the embarrassed Churis. "If you will deign to let me have a little timber for the outbuildings, I will manage one way or other. The Commune? Well, we know—"

"No, you had better come."

"Your servant, sir. I shall be there. Why should I not go? Only I will not ask the Commune for anything" . . .

Nekhlyudov had long known, not by hearsay, nor trusting the words of others, but by experience, all the extreme wretchedness of his peasants; but all that reality was so incompatible with his education, his turn of mind, and manner of life, that he involuntarily forgot the truth; and every time when he was reminded of it in a vivid and palpable manner, as now, his heart felt intolerably heavy and sad, as though he were tormented by the recollection of some unatoned crime which he had committed.

"Why are you so poor?" he said, involuntarily expressing his thought.

"What else are we to be, your Grace, if not poor? You know yourself what kind of soil we have: clay and clumps, and we must have angered God, for since the cholera we have had very poor crops of grain. The meadows and fields have grown less; some have been taken into the estate, others have been directly attached to the manorial fields. I am all alone and old. I would gladly try to do something, but I have no strength. My old woman is sick, and every year she bears a girl; they have to be fed. I am working hard all by myself, and there are seven souls in the house. It is a sin before God our Lord, but I often think it would be well if he took some of them away as soon as possible. It would be easier for me and for them too, it would be better than to suffer here—"

"Oh, oh!" the woman sighed aloud, as though confirming her husband's words.

"Here is my whole help," continued Churis, pointing to a flaxen-haired, shaggy boy of some seven years, with an immense belly, who, softly creaking the door, had just entered timidly, and morosely fixing his wondering eyes upon the master, with both his hands was holding on to his father's shirt. "Here is my entire help," continued Churis, in a sonorous voice, passing his rough hand through his child's hair. "It will be a while before he will be able to do anything, and in the meantime the work is above my strength" . . .

"I shall wait for the little fellow to grow up. If it is your will, excuse him from school; for a few days ago the village scribe came and said that your Grace wanted him to come to school. Do excuse him: what mind can he have, your Grace? He is too young, and has not much sense yet."

"No; this, my friend, must be," said the master. "Your boy can comprehend, it is time for him to study. I am saying it for your own good. You judge yourself: when he grows up, and becomes a householder, he will know how to read and write, and he will read in church, —everything will go well with you, with God's aid," said Nekhlyudov, trying to express himself as clearly as possible, and, at the same time, blushing and stammering.

"No doubt, your Grace, you do not wish us any harm; but there is nobody at home; my wife and I have to work in the manorial field, and, small though he is, he helps us some, by driving the cattle home, and taking the horses to water. As little as he is, he is a peasant all the same," and Churis, smiling, took hold of his boy's nose between his thick fingers, and cleaned it.

"Still, send him when he is at home, and has time, —do you hear?—without fail."

Churis drew a deep sign, and did not reply. . . .

"Where are these dreams?" now thought the youth, as he approached his house after his visits. "It is now more than a year that I have been seeking happiness upon this road, and what have I found? It is true, at times I feel that I might be satisfied with myself, but it is a kind of dry, mental satisfaction. Yes and no, I am simply dissatisfied with myself! I am dissatisfied because I have found no happiness here, and yet I wish, I passionately wish for happiness. I have not experienced enjoyment, and have already cut off from me everything which gives it. Why? For what? Who has been better off for it? My aunt was right when she said that it is easier to find happiness than to give it to others.

"Have my peasants grown richer? Have they been morally educated and developed? Not in the least. They are not better off, but I feel worse with every day. If I only saw any success in my undertaking, if I saw gratitude—but no, I see the perverted routine, vice, suspicion, helplessness.

"I am wasting in vain the best years of my life," he thought.

10. Alexander Herzen: Thoughts on the Peasant Community

The Russian intelligentsia of the mid-nineteenth century idealized peasant life. For them, the peasant embodied all the virtues of unspoiled rural Russia. Those who favored an egalitarian society even saw in the peasant commune a spontaneous socialism, far in advance of anything western Europe had to offer. Needless to say, few of them knew much about the hard realities of peasant existence nor of the mentality Tolstoy depicts in "A Morning of a Landed Proprietor" (Reading 9). Alexander Herzen was among the intelligentsia, here writing in 1851 from exile in his periodical The Bell, *smuggled into Russia from London.*

The Russian peasant has no real knowledge of any form of life but that of the village commune: he understands about rights and duties only when these are tied to the commune and its members. Outside the commune, there are no obligations for him—there is simply violence . . . The commune has preserved the Russian people from Mongol barbarism, from Imperial civilization, from the Europeanized landowners and from the German bureaucracy: the organic life of the commune has persisted despite all the attempts made on it by authority, badly mauled though it has been at times. By good fortune it has

Abridged from Szamuely, T., *The Russian Tradition*, 203–4. New York: McGraw-Hill, 1974.

survived right into the period that witnesses the rise of socialism in Europe. For Russia this has been a most happy providence . . .

The peasants have remained faithful guardians of the national character, which is based on *communism*, i.e., on the regular division of the fields according to the number of workers and the absence of private landownership . . . The Russian people, crushed by slavery and the Government, cannot follow in the footsteps of European nations and repeat their past revolutions. These were revolutions exclusively of the cities, and anything of that nature would instantly fracture the foundations of our communal system. The opposite is the case: the coming revolution will take place on more native ground . . .

We have none of the Western man's blind prejudices which paralyze and deprive him of half his faculties. Our people's life is based on the village community, with divisions of the fields, with communistic landownership, with elected administration and equal responsibility for each worker . . . The only thing that is conservative on our shifting, unsettled soil is the village community—that is, the only thing deserving preservation . . . I believe, with all my heart and mind, that it is our door on which history is knocking . . .

The word *Socialism* is unknown to our people, but its meaning is close to the hearts of Russians who have lived for ages in the village community.

11. Ivan Turgenev: The Nihilist

The beliefs of the nihilists of the early 1860s are difficult to determine precisely, partly because of their essentially negative outlook and partly because they spoke and wrote as individuals, rather than as spokesmen for a cohesive philosophy. Nevertheless, certain facets of their thinking can be deduced from statements made by and about them. For example, a nihilist named Dmitri Pisarev is said to have once remarked that a good pair of boots was worth more than all the works of Pushkin. The most famous nihilist of all was probably the radical doctor Bazarov in Fathers and Sons, *a novel by Ivan Turgenev. This is ironic because the author clearly intended his portrait of Bazarov to be a caricature. The following reading is a passage from that novel, in which Bazarov is conversing with Pavel Kirsanov, uncle of his friend Arkady. Pavel has just asked Bazarov what he and others like him are up to, and Bazarov replies:*

"I'll tell you what we're doing. Formerly—not very long ago—we used to say that our officials took bribes, that we had no roads, no commerce, no just courts . . ."

Abridged from Turgenev, Ivan, *Fathers and Sons.* Translated by Barbara Makanowitsky, 49–51. New York: Bantam, 1959.

"Well, yes, yes, you are denunciators—it seems that's the term for it. I agree with many of your denunciations, but . . ."

"And then it dawned on us that just to talk on and on about our ulcers wasn't worth the trouble and would only lead to mediocrity and doctrinairism. We observed that our wise men, such as the so-called progressive people and denunciators, are good for nothing, that we spend our time on rot, debating so-called art, meaningless creations, parliamentarianism, jurisprudence, and the devil knows what, when it's a question of our daily bread, when we're being choked by the crudest superstitions, when all our businesses are disintegrating apparently only because of a lack of honest people, when the very freedom the government is fussing about would hardly benefit us because our peasant is glad to rob himself solely in order to drink himself into a stupor in the tavern."

"So," interrupted Pavel, "so: you became convinced of all this and decided not to undertake anything seriously yourselves."

"And decided not to undertake anything," Bazarov repeated gruffly. He had become suddenly annoyed with himself; why had he talked so unrestrainedly in front of that squire?

"Just curse everything?"

"And just curse."

"And that's called nihilism?"

"And that's called nihilism," Bazarov repeated again, this time with marked insolence.

Pavel blinked.

"So that's how it is," he said in a strangely calm voice. "Nihilism is supposed to cure all ills, and you are our libertors and heroes. All right. But why do you abuse the others, including even the denunciators? Aren't you merely talking like everyone else?"

"We've other sins, but not that one," Bazarov muttered through his teeth.

"So, then. You do act, is that it? You're preparing to take action?"

Bazarov didn't answer. Pavel shuddered, but immediately got hold of himself.

"Hmmm! . . . To act, to destroy . . ." he continued. "But how can you destroy without even knowing why?"

"We destroy because we are a force." Arkady remarked . . . [Arkady, a young friend of Bazarov, is also Pavel's nephew].

"Bravo! Bravo! Listen, Arkady—that's how young people today should express themselves! When you think of it, how could they fail to follow you! Young people used to have to study. If they didn't want to be considered ignoramuses, they were forced to exert themselves, like it or not. And now all they have to do is say: Everything in the world is rubbish!—and it's in the bag. Young people are delighted. In reality, while they used to be simply blockheads, now they've suddenly become nihilists."

"And your boasted feeling of personal dignity has failed you," Bazarov remarked phlegmatically, while Arkady boiled with anger, his eyes flashing. "Our argument has gone too far. I believe it would be better to break it off. And

I'll be ready to agree with you,"he added, standing up, "when you give me just one institution in our contemporary existence, in private or public life, which doesn't deserve complete and merciless annihilation."

12. Ivan Turgenev: The Revolutionist's Promise

There are a number of testimonies to the dedication of the young revolutionaries of the 1860s and 1870s. One of the most eloquent is in the form of a prose-poem by Ivan Turgenev, the author of Fathers and Sons, *titled "The Threshold." The heroine of the poem is Sophia Perovskaya, organizer of the plot to assassinate Tsar Alexander II in 1881 and probably Russia's most famous female revolutionary in the nineteenth century. Because of censorship, "The Threshold" did not appear in Turgenev's collected works, but it was published by the underground press of* The People's Will *in 1883.*

I see a huge building. In its front wall is a narrow door, standing ajar; behind the door spreads a gloomy mist. In front of the high threshold is a girl, a Russian girl.

That opaque mist breathes a glacial chill and a slow, hollow voice comes with any icy draught from the depths of the building.

"O thou, who art desirous of crossing this threshold, dost thou know what is awaiting thee?"

"I know," answered the girl.

"Cold, hunger, mockery, scorn, insult, prison, illness, death itself?"

"I know."

"Ostracism, unrelieved loneliness?"

"I know. I am ready. I can endure every suffering, every blow."

"Not only from thy enemies, but from thy families and friends?"

"Yes . . . from them also."

"Good. Thou art prepared to sacrifice thyself?"

"Yes."

"To sacrifice thyself anonymously? Thou wilt perish, and no one, no one will even know whose memory to revere."

"I need neither gratitude nor compassion. I do not need a name."

"Art thou prepared to commit a crime?"

The girl bowed her head: "For that, too, I am ready."

There was a pause before the voice again took up its questioning.

"Dost thou know," it resumed at last, "that thou mayst lose faith in what

From Turgenev, Ivan. "The Threshold." *The Underground Press of the People's Will,* 1883.

thou now believest, that thou mayst come to think that thou hast been mistaken and thrown away thy young life in vain?"

"That, too, I know. And nevertheless I wish to enter."

"Enter!"

The girl crossed the threshold, and a heavy curtain fell behind her.

"Fool!" came the grating voice of someone behind.

"Saint!" was heard from somewhere the reply.

13. Siberian Exiles on the Road

The tsar's secret police arrested many people accused of speaking or working against the autocracy. Both they and regular criminals were sent to work and live in Siberia, sometimes in prisons or labor camps, at other times simply to live there in exile. To get there, they walked in slow-moving caravans, a distance as great as two thousand miles. George Kennan (1845–1924) lived in Russia as a young man and returned there in 1885 to do a report on the Russian prison system. This section of his account gives a glimpse of this special part of the nineteenth century Russian world. It is interesting to compare the communal organization of the prisoners with that of the peasant community. George Kennan was the great-uncle of the twentieth-century diplomat and scholar of the same name.

Marching parties of convicts three or four hundred strong leave Tomsk for Irkutsk weekly throughout the whole year, and make the journey of 1040 miles in about three months. *Etapes,* or exile station-houses, stand along the road at intervals of from twenty-five to forty miles . . .

Each prisoner receives five cents a day in money for his subsistence, and buys food for himself from peasants along the road who make a business of furnishing it. The dress of the exiles in summer consists of a shirt and a pair of trousers of coarse gray linen; square foot-wrappers of the same material in lieu of stockings; low shoes or slippers called *kati;* leather ankle-guards to prevent the leg-fetters from chafing; a visorless Glengarry cap; and a long gray over-coat. The dress of female convicts is the same, except that a petticoat takes the place of the trousers. Women and children who voluntarily accompany relatives to Siberia are permitted to wear their own clothing, and to carry severally as much baggage as can be put into a two-bushel bag. No distinction is made between common convicts and political convicts, except that the latter, if they are nobles or belong to one of the privileged classes, receive seven and a half cents a day for their subsistence instead of five, and are carried in *telegas* [carts] instead of being forced to walk . . .

Abridged from Kennan, George, *Siberia.* Vol. 1, *Siberia and the Exile System.* New York: Devinne Press, Praeger, 1970.

Five or six miles from Tomsk the party passed a *chasovnaya,* or roadside shrine, consisting of an open pavilion, in which hung a ghastly wooden effigy of the crucified Christ. Here, as upon our departure from Tomsk, I noticed that two-thirds of the convicts removed their caps, crossed themselves devoutly, and muttered brief supplications. A Russian peasant may be a highway robber or a murderer, but he continues, nevertheless, to cross himself and say his prayers . . .

Soon after leaving Tomsk, every exile party organizes itself into an **artel,** or "union," elects a chief or head man known as the *starosta,* and lays the foundation of an *artel* fund by levying an assessment upon each of its members, and by selling at auction to the highest bidder the privilege of keeping an exile sutler's store or *maidan,* where the prisoners can openly buy tea, sugar, or white bread, and where they can secretly obtain tobacco, playing-cards, and intoxicating liquor. The organization of the party into an *artel* has for its primary object concerted and combined action against the common enemy—the Government. A single convict, regarded as an individual, has neither rights nor means of self-defense. He is completely at the mercy, not only of the higher authorities in the forwarding prisons and the provincial towns, but of every petty officer in the convoy command that escorts him from *étape* to *étape;* and the only way in which he can acquire even a limited power of self-protection is by associating himself with his fellow-convicts in an *artel,* or union. This *artel,* as an organized body, exercises all of its functions in secret, and strives to attain its ends, first, by enforcing solidarity and joint action on the part of all its members, and, secondly, by deceiving, outwitting, or bribing the officers and soldiers with whom it has to deal. It concerts plans of escape; it contrives means of obtaining forbidden articles, such as playing-cards and tobacco; it hires *telegas,* or sleighs, from the peasants along the road, and sells, or grants, to its members the privilege of riding in them for short distances when exhausted; it bribes executioners to flog lightly; it pays soldiers for smuggling intoxicating liquor into the forwarding prisons and *étapes;* and, finally, it sanctions and enforces all contracts and agreements entered into by its convict members. It is, in short, the body politic of the criminal world; and it fills, in the life of the exile, the same place that the *mir,* or commune, fills in the life of the free peasant. Within the limits of its prison environment the power of the *artel* over its members is absolute. It has its own unwritten laws, its own standards of honor and duty, and its own penal code . . .

The late Colonel Zagarin, inspector of exile transportation for Eastern Siberia, told me that he himself had often made a substantial contribution to the fund of an exile *artel* merely in order to secure from the latter a promise that no attempts to escape should be made within the limits of his jurisdiction. Such promises, he said, were always faithfully observed by the *artel* in its corporate capacity, and were rarely disregarded even by individuals. If, however, an inexperienced "first-timer," tempted by a favorable opportunity, should try to escape, in defiance of the *artel's* prohibition, the veterans of the party, namely, the *brodyags,* would always undertake either to recapture the fugitive, or to bring in some other runaway convict as a substitute, and thus save the honor of the *artel.* He could not remember a single case, he said, in which the *artel* had broken faith. It must not be supposed, however, that the prison commune, in such dealings with the authorities, is actuated by any high or honorable motives. In keeping its promise, in enforcing solidarity, and in punishing disloyalty and disobedience with death, it is merely protecting its own existence and securing what a majority of its members believe to be the greatest good of the greatest number. It has no sentimental regard for truthfulness or faithfulness in the abstract. It simply knows that, at certain times and in certain circumstances, honesty is the best policy, and then it enforces honesty under penalty of death. If however, circumstances so change as to render dishonesty the best policy, then the *artel* sanctions and compels the practice of deception, fraud, untruthfulness, and treachery, under the same tremendous penalty . . .

As the party, wet, tired, and hungry, approaches one of the little log villages that lie along its route, the *starosta,* or chief of the *artel,* asks the convoy officer to allow them to sing the "begging song" as they pass through the settlement. The desired permission is granted; certain prisoners are designated to receive the expected alms; the convicts all remove their gray caps; and entering the village with a slow, dragging step, as if they hardly had strength enough to crawl along, they begin their mournful appeal for pity.

I shall never forget the emotions roused in me by this song when I heard it for the first time . . . Suddenly my attention was attracted by a peculiar, low-pitched, quavering sound which came to us from a distance, and which, although made apparently by human voices, did not resemble anything that I had ever before heard. It was not singing, nor chanting, nor wailing for the dead, but a strange blending of all three. It suggested vaguely the confused and commingled sobs, moans, and entreaties of human beings who were being subjected to torture, but whose sufferings were not acute enough to seek expression in shrieks or high-pitched cries. As the sound came nearer we went out into the street in front of the station-house and saw approaching a chained party of about a hundred bare-headed convicts, who, surrounded by a cordon of soldiers, were marching slowly through the settlement, singing the "exiles' begging song." No attempt was made by the singers to pitch their voices in harmony, or to pronounce the words in unison . . . Rude, artless, and inharmonious as the appeal for pity was, I had never in my life heard anything so mournful and depressing. It seemed to be the half-articulate expression of all the grief, the misery, and the despair that had been felt by generations of human beings in the *étapes,* the forwarding prisons, and the mines.

As the party marched slowly along the muddy street between the lines of gray log houses, children and peasant women appeared at the doors with their hands full of bread, meat, eggs, or other articles of food, which they put into the caps or bags of the three or four shaven-headed convicts who acted as alms-collectors. The jingling of chains and the wailing voices of the exiles grew gradually fainter and fainter as the party passed up the street, and when the sounds finally died away in the distance, and we turned to reenter the post-station, I felt a strange sense of dejection, as if the day had suddenly grown colder, darker, and more dreary, and the cares and sorrows of life more burdensome and oppressive . . .

14. Sergei Witte: A Proposal for Russia's Industrialization

It is important to remember that not all Russian statesmen were reactionaries. This selection from Witte's secret memorandum of 1899 to Tsar Nicholas II indicates that there were farsighted top-level bureaucrats who had ambitious plans for modernizing Russia's economy. All too often, however, their projects were never put into effect or were so badly crippled that they did not come to fruition. This particular discussion of industrialization is a reminder that by the last decade of the nineteenth century and the first decade of the twentieth, tsarist Russia had begun to industrialize and had an economic growth rate that was one of the highest in the world.

The entire economic structure of the empire has been transformed in the course of the second half of the current century, so that now the market and its price structure represent the collective interest of all private enterprises which constitute our national economy . . .

The economic relations of Russia with western Europe are fully comparable to the relations of colonial countries with their metropolises. The latter consider their colonies as advantageous markets in which they can freely sell the products of their labor and of their industry and from which they can draw with a powerful hand the raw materials necessary for them . . . Russia was, and to a considerable extent still is, such a hospitable colony for all industrially developed states, generously providing them with the cheap products of her soil and buying dearly the products of their labor. But there is a radical difference between Russia and a colony: Russia is an independent and strong power. She has the right and the strength not to want to be the eternal handmaiden of states which are more developed economically . . .

We need capital, knowledge, and the spirit of enterprise. Only these three factors can speed up the creation of a fully independent national industry . . .

Industry gives birth to capital, capital gives rise to enterprise and love of learning; and knowledge, enterprise, and capital combined create new industries. Such is the eternal cycle of economic life, and by the succession of such

Abridged from von Laue, Theodore H. "A Secret Memorandum of Sergei Witte on the Industrialization of Imperial Russia." *Journal of Modern History* 26 (March 1954): 64–73.

turns our national economy moves ahead in the process of its natural growth. In Russia this growth is yet too slow, because there is yet too little industry, capital, and spirit of enterprise. But we cannot be content with the continuation of such slow growth . . .

The influx of foreign capital is, in the considered opinion of the minister of finance, the sole means by which our industry can speedily furnish our country with abundant and cheap goods . . . Hence the natural riches of the Russian land and the productive energies of its population will be utilized to a considerably greater extent; our economy will begin to work with greater intensity . . .

If in our present situation we cannot satisfy all our demands from our own resources and have to resort to purchasing abroad, it will be more advantageous for us to buy not finished goods but capital, which is one of the most necessary productive forces, particularly in industry . . . Foreign capital . . . works its way into our industry only because it is satisfied wherever it goes with smaller profits than its Russian predecessors. A new hundred million, flowing into the country from abroad during a given year, lowers by the laws of competition the rate of interest of all capital previously invested in Russian industry, which amounts to billions. If the country pays for these new hundred million rubles ten million in dividends, it gains still a considerably larger sum from the lower interest rates for the capital already invested in its economy. As the billions of national capital become cheaper, the prices of all industrial products will also fall considerably. We have at our disposal cheap labor, tremendous natural riches, and only the high price of capital now stands in the way of getting cheap goods. So why not let foreign capital help us to obtain still more cheaply that productive force of which alone we are destitute? . . .

The import cultural forces thus become an inseparable part of the country itself. Only a disintegrating nation has to fear foreign enslavement . . .

We cannot possibly count on an adequate growth of our industry out of our own national resources, because our store of capital, knowledge, and the spirit of enterprise is altogether insufficient to provide us with cheap industrial goods.

To obtain cheaper goods, of which the population stands in such urgent need, by a substantial tariff reduction would be too expensive. It would forever deprive the country of the positive results of the protective system, for which a whole generation has made sacrifices; it would upset the industries which we have created with so much effort just when they were ready to repay the nation for its sacrifices.

It would be very dangerous to rely on the competition of foreign goods for the lowering of our prices. But we can attain the same results with the help of the competition of foreign capital, which, by coming into Russia, will help Russian enterprise to promote native industry and speed up the accumulation of native capital. . . .

15. The Worker's Life under the Last Tsar

The conditions in which workers lived in Russia at the end of the nineteenth century were terrible by modern standards and sound much like those Charles Dickens described in London more than fifty years before. Such conditions seem to be common in the early stages of industrialization. Henri Troyat describes the conditions as seen by a fictional traveler, Russell, who tells here what he saw when he visited a suburb of Moscow with his Russian guide, Paul Egorovitch Sychkin. Karl Marx had theorized that peasants would never organize or overthrow their landlords because they lived in isolation from one another, whereas workers, crowded together, would see that their shared interest lay in getting rid of the capitalistic factory owners. Troyat puts a similar observation into the mouth of Paul Egorovitch Sychkin.

Whatever his occupation, every worker when engaged received a booklet from his employer, in which the conditions of his employment, the payment of wages, deductions in the form of fines, rents and various liabilities were recorded, and, should the occasion arise, the reason for his dismissal. In brief, it was a sort of professional passport which, together with his official passport, ended by fixing an individual's capabilities and predisposed him to accept his inferior status.

Russell, who thought his own country a century ahead of Russia in social progress, was surprised to learn that the employment of children of less than twelve years and the employment of women at night had been forbidden in Russia . . . and that in Russia there was a medical service at large factories (of more than 100 workers), and that employers' responsibility in the matter of working accidents was constantly recognized . . .

[The Russian, Sychkin, explains to Russell how the Russian workers live.]

In your country the workers live where they like and usually quite a long way from the factory. Even when they are settled in dwellings specially built by their employer, they pay rent in exchange. In short, they forget the factory atmosphere when they go home. In Russia, on the contrary, half the workers live gratuitously, either in the workshops themselves or in huge buildings attached to the factories. This is explained by the fact that in Russia the majority of the population is rural and the peasant who comes to town to seek employment is obviously unable to find a room at a low cost. Moreover, in their *izba* they have acquired the habit of living six, eight or ten together in a smoky room. Why should they be more refined now? If you want to understand

Abridged from Troyat, Henri, *Daily Life in Russia under the Last Tsar*. Translated by Malcolm Barnes, 88–93. London: George Allen & Unwin, 1961.

the life of the Russian worker you must visit a few of these houses exclusively occupied by the workers and their families.

Under the guidance of Paul Egorovitch Sychkin, it did not take Russell long to see that all the large factories were flanked by grey and dejected buildings of several stories, which were simply warehouses of labour. The same architectural style was recognizable in all: they were civilian barracks. Inside, a dark and narrow corridor was flanked by thin plank doors, which opened into dormitories for twenty or thirty workers or into minute rooms *(kamorki)* each sheltering several families. Each family strove to mark off its modest domain in the *kamorka* with hangings made of old pieces of cloth and plaited mats. But these flimsy partitions were not enough to ensure the privacy of couples. The beds (simple plank bunks) touched one another. One chair and one table served ten persons. Men, women and children mingled their voices, odours, illnesses, quarrels and reconciliations. Yet the tenants of a *kamorka* were envied by those who lived in the dormitories. There the bunks stood side by side without the least separation. Often they were placed one above the other, the highest being about two feet below the ceiling. The workers did their washing in the room and dried it on lines strung from wall to wall. A sour odour came from these rags as they dripped upon the muddy floor. The casement windows were clearly too small to permit the ventilation of the premises. In any case, they were carefully nailed up and blocked in.

This kind of dormitory was generally reserved for single men. Nevertheless, Paul Egorovitch Sychkin showed Russell some communal rooms in which, as a result of overpopulation at the factory, women, couples and complete families lived among the bachelors. The beds were separated by wooden partitions fixed to their frames and rising to a height of about three feet six inches. Thus each household had its compartment and the room resembled a stable. According to Sychkin, in certain workers' houses the tenants had on the average only two square yards of space and three or four cubic yards of air per person. And these figures took account only of the number of occupants at a given moment. Now, all the big factories worked continuously, and quite often the same beds were occupied turn and turn about by two workers, one on day shift and the other on night shift. Because of this relief system the dormitory was never empty. In such conditions the quantity of breathable air calculated by Sychkin must be reduced again by half. Appalled by these details, Russell wondered why the Russian worker, himself so badly housed, was not content till he had made his family leave the village to join him.

"It's very simple," said Paul Egorovitch Sychkin. "Having left his own people to work in the town, a man soon sees that he doesn't get money enough to keep both himself and those whom he has left in the country. In forcing his wife and children to join him, he reckons that they will be hired at the factory for a fair wage and that their housing will raise no problem. Doubtless to encourage this kind of family migration, the big manufacturers have built such barracks on their factory land. The Russian peasant has a robust constitution.

Comfort and hygiene do not interest him. He almost distrusts them. What he wants is a corner in which to lie down on bare boards for not too much money. Now the dormitory is always free of charge, and the *kamorki,* at the very most, are let for a deduction of one per cent of the wage, or virtually nothing, so the worker writes home. His wife and children arrive, and the whole lot pile up in some stifling den, already overcrowded with two families, or in the communal room with worn-out bodies strewn upon their litters all around them. With the help of bits of cardboard and cloth hung from nails, the women try to make a refuge in which to protect themselves against indiscreet glances. But no one pays any attention to them. The men are too worn out during the week and on Sundays most of them are drunk. According to statistics which I have consulted, the proportion of women working in the factories in 1855 was 33 per cent, and today it has risen to 44 per cent. In the textile industries they represent as much as 77 per cent of the staff. We are watching a strange phenomenon. So long as the worker's family lives far away from him in the country, he keeps his ties with the soil and with the patriarchal customs of former times. He returns to the village from time to time in order to share in the work in the fields. He knows that there he has his roof, his friends, his graves, his memories. This nostalgic attraction ends abruptly as soon as our man has been able to make his wife and children come and settle in the great barrack. All are employed in the same factory. They have sold their little shanty. They are no longer peasants. And they are proud of it! Gradually a new class is born, homeless, without regrets and without traditions, who have no possessions of their own and live from day to day, lost in an anonymous mass of people just like themselves. As a result of living so close together, they acquire a vague awareness of their strength. Just consider that at the present moment there are no more than two and a half million workers in Russia for a total population of 129 millions. Nevertheless, one can already speak of a "workers' will," while the Russian peasants, many times more numerous, are far from showing the same cohesion in defending their interests.

16. Vladimir Ilyich Lenin: The Organization of the Party

Lenin published a long pamphlet, What is to be Done? *in 1902. It was a vehement attack on his rivals for leadership of the Marxist workers movement. It also gave his blueprint for party organization, a blueprint closely followed both before and after the Revolution of 1917. Lenin emphasizes the need for a small, tightly disciplined, secret,* **vanguard party** *to educate and lead the workers. He also makes a distinction between* **scientific** *and* **democratic**

Abridged from Lenin, V.I., "What Is To Be Done?" Vol. 5, *Collected Works.* 148–68. Moscow: Foreign Language Publishing House, 1964.

socialism, the first and correct type requiring knowledge, and justifying leadership by an elite The second, democratic socialism, according to Lenin, grows muddled, acts "spontaneously" and will never accomplish the revolution. This distinction later justified many authoritarian practices of the Bolsheviks. Until recently, the term scientific socialism was used as a code by which the Soviets indicated approval of a Marxist regime. For definitions of words used by Lenin that have a special meaning, consult the glossary.

Without revolutionary theory there can be no revolutionary movement . . .

The German workers have for the moment been placed in the vanguard of the proletarian struggle. How long events will allow them to occupy this post of honour cannot be foretold. But let us hope that as long as they occupy it, they will fill it fittingly. This demands redoubled efforts in every field of struggle and agitation. In particular, it will be the duty of the leaders to gain an ever clearer insight into all theoretical questions, to free themselves more and more from the influence of traditional phrases inherited from the old world outlook, and constantly to keep in mind that socialism since it has become a science, demands that it be pursued as a science, i.e., that it be studied. The task will be to spread with increased zeal among the masses of the workers the ever more clarified understanding thus acquired, to knit together ever more firmly the organization both of the party and of the trade unions . . .

The strength of the present-day movement lies in the awakening of the masses (principally, the industrial proletariat) and its weakness lies in the lack of consciousness and initiative among the revolutionary leaders . . .

The strikes that followed the famous St. Petersburg industrial war of 1896 assumed a similar general character. Their spread over the whole of Russia clearly showed the depth of the newly awakening popular movement, and if we are to speak of the "spontaneous element" then, of course, it is this strike movement which, first and foremost, must be regarded as spontaneous . . .

The workers were not [in 1890s], and could not be, conscious of the irreconcilable antagonism of their interests to the whole of the modern political and social system, i.e., theirs was not yet Social-Democratic consciousness. In this sense, the strikes of the nineties, despite the enormous progress they represented as compared with the "revolts," remained a purely spontaneous movement.

We have said that there could not have been Social-Democratic consciousness among the workers. It would have to be brought to them from without. The history of all countries shows that the working class, exclusively by its own effort, is able to develop only trade union consciousness, i.e., the conviction that it is necessary to combine in unions, fight the employers, and strive to compel the government to pass necessary labour legislation, etc. The theory of socialism, however, grew out of the philosophic, historical, and economic theories elaborated by educated representatives of the propertied

classes, by intellectuals. By their social status, the founders of modern scientific socialism, Marx and Engels, themselves belonged to the **bourgeois**
intelligentsia . . .

Since there can be no talk of an independent ideology formulated by the
working masses themselves in the process of their movement, the only choice
is—either bourgeois or socialist ideology. There is no middle course (for
mankind has not created a "third" ideology, and moreover, in a society torn by
class antagonisms there can never be a non-class or an above-class ideology).
Hence to belittle the socialist ideology in any way, to turn aside from it in the
slightest degree means to strengthen bourgeois ideology . . .

In order to become a Social-Democrat, the worker must have a clear
picture in his mind of the economic nature and the social and political features
of the landlord and the priest, the high state official and the peasant, the
student and the vagabond; he must know their strong and weak points; he
must grasp the meaning of all the catch-words and sophisms by which each
class and each stratum camouflages its selfish strivings and its real "inner
workings . . ."

Class political consciousness can be brought to the workers only from
without . . .

[Lenin here describes the vanguard party.]

A small, compact core of the most reliable, experienced, and hardened
workers, with responsible representatives in the principal districts and connected by all the rules of strict secrecy with the organization of revolutionaries,
can, with the widest support of the masses and without any formal organization,
perform all the functions of a trade-union organization, in a manner, moreover,
desirable to Social-Democracy. Only in this way can we secure the consolida-
tion and development of a Social-Democratic trade-union movement, despite
all the gendarmes [policemen] . . .

I assert that it is far more difficult to unearth a dozen wise men than a
hundred fools. This position I will defend, no matter how much you instigate
the masses against me for my "anti-democratic" views, etc. As I have stated
repeatedly, by "wise men," in connection with organization, I mean professional revolutionaries, irrespective of whether they have developed from
among students or working men, I assert: (1) that no revolutionary movement
can endure without a stable organization of leaders maintaining continuity; (2)
that the broader the popular mass drawn spontaneously into the struggle,
which forms the basis of the movement and participates in it, the more urgent
the need for such an organization, and the more solid this organization must be
(for it is much easier for all sorts of demagogues to side-track the more
backward sections of the masses); (3) that such an organization must consist
chiefly of people professionally engaged in revolutionary activities; (4) that in
an autocratic state, the more we confine the membership of such an organization to people who are professionally engaged in revolutionary activity and
who have been professionally trained in the art of combating the political

police, the more difficult it will be to unearth the organization; and (5) the greater will be the number of people from the working class and from the other social classes who will be able to join the movement and perform active work in it . . .

The active and widespread participation of the masses will not suffer: on the contrary, it will benefit by the fact that a "dozen" experienced revolutionaries, trained professionally, no less than the police, will centralize all the secret aspects of the work—the drawing up of leaflets, the working out of approximate plans; and the appointing of bodies of leaders for each urban district, for each factory district, and for each educational institution . . .

Try to fit this picture into the frame of our autocracy! Is it conceivable in Russia for all "who accept the principles of the Party programme and render the Party all possible support" to control every action of the revolutionary working in secret? Is it possible for all to elect one of these revolutionaries to any particular office, when, in the very interests of the work, the revolutionary must conceal his identity from nine out of ten of these "all?" Reflect somewhat over the real meaning of the high-sounding phrases . . . and you will realize that "broad democracy" in Party organization, amidst the gloom of the autocracy and the domination of the gendarmerie, is nothing more than a useless and harmful toy. It is a useless toy because, in point of fact, no revolutionary organization has ever practiced, or could practice, broad democracy, however much it may have desired to do so. It is a harmful toy because any attempt to practice "the broad democratic principle" will simply facilitate the work of the police in carrying out large-scale raids, will perpetuate the prevailing primitiveness, and will divert the thoughts of the practical workers from the serious and pressing task of training themselves to become professional revolutionaries to that of drawing up detailed "paper" rules for election systems. Only abroad, where very often people with no opportunity for conducting really active work gather, could this "playing at democracy" develop here and there, especially in small groups . . .

17. Bloody Sunday

There are numerous accounts of the events of January 22, 1905 in St. Petersburg. This one is by the organizer of that day's demonstration, Father George Gapon, in his 1905 The Story of My Life.

"Shall we go straight toward the gate, or by a roundabout route to avoid the soldiers?" I was asked. I shouted huskily, "No; straight through them. Courage! Death or Freedom!" and the crowd shouted in return, "Hurrah!" We

From Gapon, G. "Bloody Sunday: St. Petersburg, 22 January, 1905." In *Eyewitness to History*. Edited by J. Carey, 415–18. New York: Avon, 1988.

then started forward, singing in one mighty, solemn voice the Tsar's hymn, "God Save thy People." But when we came to the line, "Save Nicholas Alexandrovich," some of the men who belonged to the Socialist Party were wicked enough to substitute the words "Save George Appolonovich" [Gapon], while others simply repeated the words, "Death or Freedom!" The procession moved in a compact mass. In front of me were my two bodyguards and a young fellow with dark eyes from whose face his hard labouring life had not yet wiped away the light of youthful gaiety. On the flanks of the crowd ran the children. Some of the women insisted on walking in the first rows, in order, as they said, to protect me with their bodies, and force had to be used to remove them. I may mention also as a significant fact that at the start the police not only did not interfere with the procession, but moved with us with bared heads in recognition of the religious emblems. Two local police officers marched bareheaded in front of us, preventing any hindrance to our advance and forcing a few carriages that we met to turn aside in our favour. In this way we approached the Narva Gate, the crowd becoming denser as we progressed, the singing more impressive, and the whole scene more dramatic.

At last we reached within two hundred paces of where the troops stood. Files of infantry barred the road, and in front of them a company of cavalry was drawn up, with their swords shining in the sun. Would they dare to touch us? For a moment we trembled, and then started forward again.

Suddenly the company of Cossacks galloped rapidly towards us with drawn swords. So, then, it was to be a massacre after all! There was no time for consideration, for making plans, or giving orders. A cry of alarm arose as the Cossacks came down upon us. Our front ranks broke before them, opening to right and left, and down this lane the soldiers drove their horses, striking on both sides. I saw the swords lifted and falling, the men, women and children dropping to the earth like logs of wood, while moans, curses and shouts filled the air. It was impossible to reason in the fever of this crisis. At my order the front rows formed again in the wake of the Cossacks, who penetrated farther and farther, and at last emerged from the end of the procession.

Again we started forward, with solemn resolution and rising rage in our hearts. The Cossacks turned their horses and began to cut their way through the crowd from the rear. They passed through the whole column and galloped back towards the Narva Gate, where—the infantry having opened their ranks and let them through—they again formed line. We were still advancing, though the bayonets raised in threatening rows seemed to point symbolically to our fate. A spasm of pity filled my heart, but I felt no fear. Before we started, my dear friend, the workman K——, had said to me, "We are going to give your life as a sacrifice." So be it!

We were not more than thirty yards from the soldiers, being separated from them only by the bridge over the Tarakanovskii Canal, which here marks the border of the city, when suddenly, without any warning and without a moment's delay, was heard the dry crack of many rifle-shots. I was informed later on that a bugle was blown, but we could not hear it above the singing, and even if we had heard it we should not have known what it meant.

Vasiliev, with whom I was walking hand in hand, suddenly left hold of my arm and sank upon the snow. One of the workmen who carried the banners fell also. Immediately one of the two police officers to whom I had referred shouted out, "What are you doing? How dare you fire upon the portrait of the Tsar?" This, of course, had no effect, and both he and the other officer were shot down—as I learned afterwards, one was killed and the other dangerously wounded.

I turned rapidly to the crowd and shouted to them to lie down, and I also stretched myself out upon the ground. As we lay thus another volley was fired, and another, and yet another, till it seemed as though the shooting was continuous. The crowd first kneeled and then lay flat down, hiding their heads from the rain of bullets, while the rear rows of the procession began to run away. The smoke of the fire lay before us like a thin cloud, and I felt it stiflingly in my throat. An old man named Lavrentiev, who was carrying the Tsar's portrait, had been one of the first victims. Another old man caught the portrait as it fell from his hands and carried it till he too was killed by the next volley. With his last gasp the old man said, "I may die, but I will see the Tsar." One of the banner-carriers had his arm broken by a bullet. A little boy of ten years, who was carrying a church lantern, fell pierced by a bullet, but still held the lantern tightly and tried to rise again, when another shot struck him down. Both the smiths who had guarded me were killed, as well as all those who were carrying the icons and banners; and all these emblems now lay scattered on the snow. The soldiers were actually shooting into the courtyards of the adjoining houses, where the crowd tried to find refuge and, as I learned afterwards, bullets even struck persons inside, through the windows.

At last the firing ceased. I stood up with a few others who remained uninjured and looked down at the bodies that lay prostrate around me. I cried to them, "Stand up!" But they lay still. I could not at first understand. Why did they lie there? I looked again, and saw that their arms were stretched out lifelessly, and I saw the scarlet stain of blood upon the snow. Then I understood. It was horrible. And my Vasiliev lay dead at my feet.

Horror crept into my heart. The thought flashed through my mind, "And this is the work of our Little Father, the Tsar." Perhaps this anger saved me, for now I knew in very truth that a new chapter was opened in the book of the history of our people. I stood up, and a little group of workmen gathered round me again. Looking backward, I saw that our line, though still stretching away into the distance, was broken and that many of the people were fleeing. It was in vain that I called to them, and in a moment I stood there, the centre of a few scores of men, trembling with indignation amid the broken ruins of our movement.

18. The Duma of 1906

This account of the Duma of 1906 conveys the democratic and hopeful spirit of that gathering. The writer of this selection, Bernard Pares, a visiting English historian, was an eyewitness to the events he describes.

He emphasizes here and in other of his writings his view that Russia came very close to developing a constitutional government for itself in the years before the outbreak of World War I. Had the Tsar worked with the Duma, as some of his advisers urged him to do, and not dissolved it, as his strongest adviser, Stolypin, successfully persuaded him to do, the country would have taken an important step toward establishing a representative government with limits on the tsar's autocratic powers.

The Duma met on May 10, 1906. The Emperor, who had not visited his capital since the attempt made upon his life in January, 1905, in a firm and vigorous voice expressed his hope that the labours of the Assembly would be conducive to the welfare of Russia . . .

The Duma now settled down to its work of discussing separate Bills. The family atmosphere, which is so noticeable in Russia, was here peculiarly strong. The Assembly, having complete control of its own house, turned it into something like a vast caravanserai [large inn for caravans]. The beautiful hall soon came to be regarded, even by the peasant members, as a kind of home. The long side lobbies were furnished with great tables covered with green baize, at which peasants and Intelligents sat down indiscriminately to write letters to their families. A constant stream of members was always passing through these rooms; and all congregated from time to time in the great noisy corridor. Here the chief leaders walked up and down arm in arm; and isolated peasants, Russian, **Cossack,** or Polish, sat about on the different benches and were quite ready to converse with any stranger. Members and correspondents gathered without distinction at the buffet and in the restaurant, and little groups of acquaintances wandered through the pleasant gardens outside. The building contained its own postal and telegraph office. If the Duma did nothing else, it brought together for the first time representatives of every class and of every interest in Russia. It was of course far more Imperial than any other European Parliament. It would be difficult to imagine a more picturesque gathering. Each man wore the costume of his class. The country gentry of the Intelligents dressed very simply, but there were Russian priests with long beards and hair, a Roman Catholic bishop in skullcap lined with red, finely accoutred Cossacks from the Caucasus, Bashkirs and Buryats in strange and tinselled Asiatic dress, Polish peasants in the brilliant and martial costumes of

Abridged from Pares, Bernard, *Russia and Reform.* London: Archibald Constable & Co., 1907.

their people, and a whole mass of staid, bearded, and topbooted Russian peasants. Strangers easily obtained admittance; and amongst the most picturesque visitors were the so-called "walking deputies" who were sent by peasant constituents to look after their members, and others who had tramped for hundreds of miles to ask the Duma to settle their private disputes. Groups of members and non-members formed in the corridor to discuss without reticence any question of the moment. Small party conferences, sitting in the committee-rooms, seemed in no way disturbed by passing strangers. Miliukov [leader of Constitutional Democrats—Cadets], in the simple dress of an English country gentleman, walked up and down the corridor receiving the suggestions of various party leaders, which seldom induced him to deviate a yard from the tactics upon which he had determined. One noticed that the Cadets as a body quite failed to get hold of the non-party members. These peasants, who would not sink their individuality in any party formula, expressed the most fresh and interesting opinions of all. Count Heyden [a conservative, far to the right of Miliukov], could often be seen discussing matters with them; he understood them, and they understood him; but Miliukov was hardly ever to be seen talking to a non-party man.

Nearly every newspaper published the fullest reports of the sittings, and these were eagerly devoured in distant villages all over the country . . .

[Pares continues his account] If I may trust the common conclusions of peasant members from almost every part of the Empire, only the least enterprising of the peasants were still in favour of the communal system of land tenure, though all wished to retain the Village Society. The most cherished dream of the intelligent peasant was that of personal property in land . . .

It was now proposed, with the hearty concurrence of the Labour Group, to constitute in the country small committees to investigate the land question in each locality; in other words, the Duma was making a bid to gradually become the Government of the country. The tension between the representatives of the people and the Ministers was too severe to last . . . [The tsar hesitated, undecided as to whether he should name a prime minister from the most numerous party in the Duma. General Trepov urged this course, which would be an important step toward creating a truly parliamentary government.]

At **Peterhof** the counsels of General Trepov were opposed by Mr. Stolypin, the only Minister who had followed the later debates in the Duma. Stolypin's view was clear and consistent; he recognized Russia as having passed into a constitutional regime: that is to say, there would always be a Duma to join in the work of legislation; but he refused to concede the principle that the Ministers should, as a matter of course, be selected from the party prevailing in the Assembly. He was against the formation of a Cadet Ministry, because it would be compelled by its pledges to surrender almost all the power of the administrative system in a single day. The Duma was at war with the Government; if the Government would not make way for a Cadet Ministry, the only step left for it was to dissolve the Duma. The discussion of the two views at Peterhof was long; but by the evening of Saturday, July 21, the view of Mr. Stolypin had prevailed, and the Emperor had signed the decree of dissolution [of the Duma]. The decree expressed in no uncertain terms the Emperor's disappointment at what he regarded as the factious spirit of the Duma. It was read out in churches and posted up in public places all over the Empire; Stolypin himself accepted office as the new Prime Minister.

The dissolution of the Duma was the victory of a single strong-minded man.

Russia had reached a new turning-point in the movement for liberation. There was no question that the people, educated by the events of the last few years into an interest in public affairs, were slowly beginning to find their feet in the new world of politics, and that extremes both of reaction and of revolution were becoming more and more distasteful to them; but as there was now no central and controlling formula, the tension became greater, and violence became more and more possible . . .

19. War Frenzy in St. Petersburg

Less than a decade after the disastrous Russo-Japanese War and the Revolution of 1905, Russia was again at war. Despite the country's many internal troubles, patriotism ran high in August 1914, as evidenced by the following account by Sergei Kurnakov.

There was a crowd in front of a newspaper office. Every few minutes a momentous phrase scribbled in charcoal appeared in the window: "ENGLAND GIVES UP PEACE NEGOTIATIONS. Germany invades Belgium. Mobilization progressing with Great Enthusiam." And at 7.50 p.m.:

"GERMANY DECLARES WAR ON RUSSIA."

Spontaneously the crowd started singing the national anthem. The little pimply clerk who had pasted up the irrevocable announcement was still standing in the window, enjoying his vicarious importance. The people were staring at the sprawling words, as if trying to understand what they actually meant as far as each personal little life was concerned.

Then the edges of the crowd started breaking off and drifting in one direction, up the Nevsky Prospect. I heard the phrase "German Embassy" repeated several times. I walked slowly that way.

The mob pulled an officer from his cab and carried him in triumph.

I went into a telephone box and called up Stana.

"Yes, it's been declared . . . I don't know what I am going to do yet . . . All right, I'll be over about midnight."

From Kurnakov, S.N. "War Frenzy in St. Petersburg." In *Eyewitness to History*. Edited by J. Carey, 448–50. New York: Avon, 1988.

I did not like the way her receiver clicked; there seemed to be contempt in it.

When I got to the St. Isaac Square it was swarming with people. It must have been about nine o'clock, for it was pretty light yet—the enervating, exciting twilight of the northern nights.

The great greystone monstrosity of the German Embassy was facing the red granite of St. Isaac's Cathedral. The crowds were pressing around waiting for something to happen. I was watching a young naval officer being pawed by an over-patriotic group when the steady hammering of axes on metal made me look up at the Embassy roof, which was decorated with colossal figures of overfed German warriors holding bloated carthorses. A flagstaff supported a bronze eagle with spread wings.

Several men were busily hammering at the feet of the Teutons. The very first strokes pitched the mob to a frenzy: the heroic figures were hollow!

"They are empty! . . . A good omen! . . . Another German bluff! . . . We'll show them! . . . Hack them all down! . . . No, leave the horses standing! . . . The national anthem! . . . Lord, Save Thy People!"

The axes were hammering faster and faster. At last one warrior swayed, pitched forward, and crashed to the pavement one hundred feet below. A tremendous howl went up, scaring a flock of crows off the gilded dome of St. Isaac's. The turn of the eagle came; the bird came hurtling down, and the battered remains were immediately drowned in the nearby Moika river.

But obviously the destruction of the symbols was not enough. A quickly organized gang smashed a side door of the Embassy.

I could see flashlights and torches moving inside, flitting to the upper storeys. A big window opened and spat a great portrait of the Kaiser at the crowd below. When it reached the cobblestones, there was just about enough left to start a good bonfire. A rosewood grand piano followed, exploded like a bomb; the moan of the broken strings vibrated in the air for a second and was drowned: too many people were trying to outshout their own terror of the future.

"Deploy! . . . Trot! . . . Ma-a-arch!"

A troop of mounted *gendarmes* was approaching from the other end of the square. The crowd opened up like the Red Sea for the Israelites. A new crowd carrying the portrait of the Emperor and singing a hymn was advancing slowly towards the *gendarmes*. Their officer halted the men and stiffened at the salute; this was the only thing he did towards restoring order. The bonfire was being fed by the furniture, books, pictures, and papers which came hurtling through the windows of the Embassy.

The emblazoned crockery of state came crashing, and the shattering sound whipped the crowd into a new wave of hysteria.

A woman tore her dress at the collar, fell on her knees with a shriek, and pressed her naked breasts against the dusty boots of a young officer in campaign uniform.

"Take me! Right here, before these people! Poor boy . . . you will give your life . . . for God . . . for the Tsar . . . for Russia!"

Another shriek, and she fainted. Men and women were running aimlessly around the bonfire . . . Is it an effect of light and shadow, or do I really see high cheekbones, slanting eyes, and the conic fur caps of Aladin Mirza's horde?

Whew! . . . I let out the breath I had been holding unconsciously during the entire bacchanal.

20. Felix Youssoupoff: The Murder of Rasputin

By 1916, Rasputin's influence in the court of Nicholas II had grown immensely. In the previous year, the tsar had left Petrograd (St. Petersburg) to take direct command of Russian armies at the front. His wife, the Tsaritsa Alexandra, was thus in charge of the court. She relied for advice almost completely on the corrupt peasant Rasputin. Late in 1916, a group of prominent men decided that the situation was intolerable, and that it was their duty to save the Russian state by murdering Rasputin. On the night of December 16, the conspirators gathered in Prince Felix Youssoupoff's palace in Petrograd, and while the others waited upstairs, Youssoupoff invited Rasputin to have drinks with him in the dining room, having previously poisoned some of the wine.

Time passed. I began to get impatient. I poured out two glasses, one for him [Rasputin], the other for myself. I placed his glass in front of him and began to drink out of my own, thinking that he would follow my example.

"Well, let me try it," said Rasputin, stretching out his hand for the wine. It was not poisoned.

Why I first gave him wine in an unpoisoned glass I am at a loss to explain.

He drank it with obvious pleasure. He became animated. "Now give me some Madeira," he said.

I got up to take another glass, but he protested. "Pour it into this one."

I had to give way.

By an apparent accident, however, I soon managed to knock his glass to the floor, where it smashed.

I took advantage of this to pour wine into one of the glasses containing cyanide of potassium.

He drank slowly, taking small sips at a time, just as if he had been a connoisseur.

Abridged from Youssoupoff, Felix, *The End of Rasputin*, 192–6. New York: Dial Press, 1927.

His face did not change; but from time to time he put his hand to his throat as if he found slight difficulty in swallowing. He got up and moved about the room, and when I asked him whether anything was the matter, "Oh, nothing much," he said, "just an irritation in the throat."

There was a nerve-racking pause.

"That's very good Madeira. Give me some more."

The poison still had no effect.

I took no notice of the glass which he held out to me, but seized another poisoned one from the tray. I poured wine into it, and passed it to him.

He drained it: and still the poison had no effect.

There remained the third and last glass.

He looked at me with a cunning smile. I seemed to hear him say: "You see! you can't do me any harm."

But all of a sudden his expression changed into one of fiendish hatred.

I felt that he knew why I had brought him there, and what I intended to do to him. A mute and deadly conflict seemed to be taking place between us. A strange feeling of numbness took possession of me. My head reeled . . . I saw nothing . . . I do not know how long this lasted . . .

I regained my presence of mind and offered him some tea.

While I was pouring out tea, he got up and paced the room. His eye fell on the guitar.

"Play something," he begged, "I love the way you sing."

He sat and listened attentively at first; but as I continued, his head dropped towards the table. He seemed half-asleep.

The moment I stopped he opened his eyes and looked at me with a calm and sad expression: "Sing another," he said.

Time passed . . . The hands of the clocked pointed to half-past two. This nightmare had lasted over two hours.

Upstairs, too, patience had evidently become exhausted. The sounds from that quarter became pronounced, and I was afraid that my friends would come down.

"What's all that noise?" asked Rasputin.

"Probably it's the guests going away; I'll go and see."

As I entered the study [my friends] rushed towards me with revolvers in their hands. Questions showered on me.

"The poison has had no effect," I said.

"Impossible," exclaimed the Grand Duke. "The dose was amply sufficient."

With great difficulty I persuaded them to leave me to finish with Rasputin alone. They had qualms on my behalf.

But finally I took the Grand Duke's revolver and went down to the dining-room.

Rasputin was sitting at the table, just as I had left him. His head was sunken and he was breathing heavily.

"Are you feeling unwell?" I asked.

"Yes, my head is heavy and my stomach is burning. Give me another glass—that will ease me."

I poured him some Madeira; he drank it at a gulp and at once revived and regained his good spirits. All of a sudden he suggested that we should go to the gypsies. I refused on the ground that it was too late.

I had been watching every one of his movements in the expectation of a fatal issue; and now he was suggesting that we should go to the gypsies! But what amazed me most was that in spite of his instinctive knowledge and insight, he should now be so utterly unconscious of his approaching end.

How could his sharp eyes fail to observe that, clenched in my hand behind my back, was a revolver?

As this thought flashed through my mind, I looked round for some reason or other, and my glance fell on a crystal crucifix. I rose and went up to it.

"What are you doing over there so long?" asked Rasputin.

"I love this cross; it's a very beautiful thing."

"Yes, it's a nice thing. How much did you pay for it?"

He came towards me.

"Grigori Efimovich, you had better look at the crucifix, and say a prayer before it."

Rasputin looked at me in amazement, and with a trace of fear.

I saw a new and unfamiliar expression in his eyes, a touch of gentleness and submission. He came right up to me, looking me full in the face, and he seemed to read in my glance something which he was not expecting. I realised that the supreme moment was at hand.

"God give me strength to end it all," I thought, and I slowly brought the revolver from behind my back. Rasputin was still standing motionless before me, his head turned to the right, and his eyes on the crucifix.

"Where shall I shoot?" I thought. "Through the temple or through the heart?"

A streak of lightning seemed to run through my body. I fired.

There was a roar as from a wild beast, and Rasputin fell heavily backwards on the bear-skin rug.

I heard a noise on the staircase: my friends were hurrying to my aid.

We examined the wound. The bullet had passed through the region of the heart. There could be no doubt about it; he was dead.

We all felt elated, so convinced were we that the events of the night would deliver Russia from ruin and dishonour . . .

Chapter Four

RUSSIA IN REVOLUTION, 1917–1928

FACT: The term Russian Revolution is misleading. Actually, there were *two* revolutions in Russia during the year 1917. They are generally known as the February and October Revolutions.

Not only were there two revolutions in Russia in 1917, but they were very different. The first, a popular revolt that succeeded in toppling the Romanov dynasty, took place during the second week of March, according to our calendar, known as the Gregorian. At the time, however, Russia was still using the old Julian calendar, the dates of which were thirteen days behind the Gregorian. (The Soviets changed to the Gregorian in 1918.) Thus the events that we date from March 8, 1917 began, according to the Russian calendar of the time, on February 24. Hence the term February Revolution.

The following autumn there was another revolution, of a very different sort. The Bolshevik party, led by Lenin, overthrew the Provisional Government established by the earlier revolution. Our calendar dates this second, Bolshevik revolution on November 6 and 7, but the Julian dated it on October 24 and 25. It is therefore known as the October Revolution, but was until recently celebrated every November 7. As the USSR's most important political holiday, it paralleled our Independence Day, though it was celebrated in somewhat different fashion, (at least until recently) with strong militaristic overtones. The dates used in this chapter follow the Western calendar.

While the Bolsheviks were able to overthrow the Provisional Government in 1917, it was a full decade before they were able to consolidate their position. This period, 1917–28, was a chaotic one. During it the Bolsheviks had to cope with a devastating civil war, revolts, a bankrupt economy, severe famine, the untimely death of their leader, Lenin, and the question of who would succeed him. Not until 1928, with these issues resolved, could the Bolsheviks, or Communists as they came to be called, finally consider their position secure.

1917: THE FEBRUARY REVOLUTION

The February Revolution began in the capital city of Petrograd.

FACT: Because St. Petersburg sounded German, Russia's capital city was renamed Petrograd in 1914, shortly after the outbreak of World War I. ("Burg" is the German suffix for city, "grad" is the Russian.) The city was called Leningrad until 1991 when residents voted to restore its original name, St. Petersburg.

It erupted quite spontaneously and anonymously at the end of a particularly harsh winter. The participants were not the well-known revolutionary leaders, who were either in jail or exile, but the ordinary people of Petrograd, who were hungry, cold, fed up with the war, and disenchanted with Nicholas II, who seemed unable to remedy the situation.

On March 8, many factory workers went on strike and began to congregate in the city's streets. (See Readings 1 and 2.) In the next three days, more and more joined in, carrying banners calling for "Peace, Land, and Bread." On March 9, the British ambassador cabled London, "Some disorders today, but nothing serious." He could not use those words even one day later, however. By March 10, the disorders had increased, and the city was nearly paralyzed. A general strike was called. Trolleys stopped running. Bread stores closed, as did schools. Nicholas, who was informed of these events while at the front lines with his army, sent a telegram to General Sergei Khabalov, who commanded the troops in the city. It read, "I command you to suppress from tomorrow all disorders on the streets of the capital." The emperor still presumed that a simple order was sufficient to solve such problems.

Unfortunately for him, it wasn't. March 12 proved a turning point when the troops, who were supposed to put an end to the demonstrations, rebelled. The troops were not seasoned soldiers but recently inducted men who were still civilians at heart, and their sympathies lay with the demonstrators. In 1905, the troops had remained loyal to the tsar and fired on the Bloody Sunday demonstrators, saving the regime in the process. In 1917, they did not. By the end of the day on March 12, it really was all over. Without the support of the troops, neither government nor tsar could carry on.

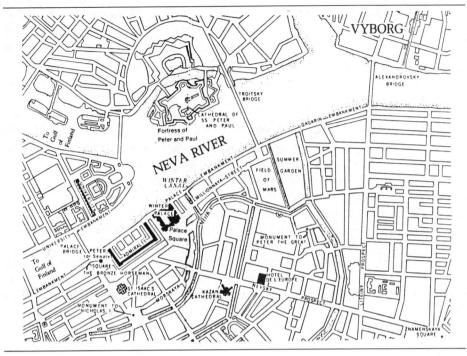

Petrograd in 1917

FACT: The tsar, once Autocrat of All the Russias, ended his reign, and with it the Romanov dynasty, ignominiously. Finally persuaded that he must return to Petrograd to cope with the disturbances, he was prevented from doing so by rebellious railway men, and his royal car was shunted to a siding in the city of Pskov. There on March 15, he was finally persuaded to abdicate, and 304 years of Romanov tsars came to an end.

In Petrograd on March 11, the Duma had appointed a temporary committee to act on its behalf during the crisis. The committee in turn appointed a Provisional Government to carry on the affairs of state until a permanent government could be established. The Provisional Government was an executive group, or cabinet, composed mostly of moderate to conservative members, with Alexander Kerensky, a socialist, the only representative of the left wing. The Provisional Government moved swiftly. It granted amnesty to political prisoners, abolished capital punishment, ended all restrictions based on class, creed, or nationality, guaranteed civil rights, instituted an eight-hour working day, and gave labor the right to organize and strike. Finally, it began immediate preparations for the election of a Constituent Assembly, to produce a constitution and permanent government. Unfortunately, the preparations proceeded very slowly. (See Reading 3.)

At the same time and in the same building that the Provisional Government was formed, another group convened. This was the Petrograd Soviet of Workers' Deputies, a body of workers from factory soviets (councils) throughout the city that had previously appeared briefly in the last months of 1905. This time soldiers were added, and it became the Petrograd Soviet of Workers' *and* Soldiers' Deputies: one deputy for approximately one thousand workers, and one for each company of soldiers. The purpose of the Soviet was to represent the interests of the workers and soldiers during the time of change. While the Soviet initially supported the Provisional Government, it did not hesitate to challenge its policies if it did not agree with them. (See Reading 5.)

The February Revolution thus produced two political organizations that competed for influence and support. An initial crisis between the two groups developed over control of the armed services. The Soviet feared the army as a potential force for counterrevolution. To decrease the threat, the Soviet on March 14 issued Order No. 1 to the soldiers and sailors of Petrograd. The order was designed to reduce the influence of officers in non-combat situations, and to extend the authority of the Soviet to military units through elected political committees of soldiers and sailors within the units. This led to a further breakdown of discipline in an already demoralized army, which in turn reduced its fighting capability.

The February Revolution resulted in the most autocratic country in the world becoming one of the freest countries in the world, all in the space of a week. Tsardom was gone, and there was the promise of a truly democratic government for the first time in Russian history. (See Reading 5.)

FACT: The great change was accomplished at relatively slight cost: By one reckoning, the February Revolution resulted in only 169 killed and 1,264 wounded.

The significance of these events extended beyond the borders of Russia. Now that Russia was a democracy, the American President Woodrow Wilson found it easier to justify American participation in World War I, with his goal of "making the world safe for democracy." The United States entered the war on April 6, 1917.

1917: FROM MARCH TO NOVEMBER

The sense of freedom felt by Russians following the February Revolution was exhilarating. Political groups proliferated, meetings were held, newspapers and journals appeared in large numbers. At all levels of society and in all parts of the country the current situation was discussed and debated with great enthusiasm and excitement. While there were many variations, the central theme of the discussions was how and how soon the fruits of the Revolution might be enjoyed by all. The peasants wanted land; neither emancipation nor the Stolypin reforms had achieved this age-old goal. The workers wanted greater control of their factories to obtain better working conditions. They also sought bread, to relieve hunger. The national minorities, the non-Russian peoples of the empire, wanted greater autonomy, if not independence. And at least by summer everyone, most especially the soldiers, wanted an end to the horrors of war.

It soon became apparent that the Provisional Government was not going to satisfy these aspirations. The Provisional Government felt obligated to Russia's allies to continue fighting. It hoped that the new political leadership would produce a surge of patriotism in the army, which would fight harder and increase the chance of victory. On the domestic front, it was reluctant to institute the most significant and most necessary reforms until a permanent, legal government was established. As a practical matter, even when the Provisional Government wished to take decisive action, it could not do so, as the bureaucracy necessary to carry out its orders had broken down almost completely. In addition, the people of Russia were beginning to ignore orders. Finally, as previously noted, the Soviet was quick to challenge the Provisional Government's authority if it felt the interests of the masses were at stake. For all these reasons, the Provisional Government's accomplishments were greatly limited.

As a result, the initial elation that followed the March events gradually gave way to disappointment and bitterness, cynicism and despair, and fear for the future. Angry, frustrated people began increasingly to take matters into their own hands. An anarchic spirit, which Vissarion Belinsky had called *volia* and which had long been present beneath the surface of Russian life, quickly spread throughout the land. By summer, shortages of basic consumer goods and uncontrolled inflation led to massive worker strikes and demonstrations in Petrograd and other major cities. The national minorities were on the brink of rebellion. Peasants satisfied their desire for land by simply taking it, chasing out landlords, and burning houses in the process. Soldiers, exhausted from combat and anxious to get their share of land, deserted. A genuine social revolution was taking place. (See Reading 6.)

Into this extremely complex and challenging situation there had arrived in mid-April a new and dramatic force: Vladimir Ilyich Lenin. Lenin was in Switzerland when the Revolution broke out. He was determined to return to Russia as soon as possible.

FACT: To solve his problem of how to return to Russia and participate in the Revolution, Lenin contemplated a variety of devices, including traveling by airplane (this before the age of commercial airliners), and posing as a deaf-and-dumb Swede. In the end, he accepted a German offer of safe conduct through Germany in a "sealed train" for himself, his wife, Krupskaya, and a number of associates. (See Reading 7.)

Upon his arrival at Petrograd's Finland Station on April 16, Lenin wasted no time in announcing that he sought to change the course of the Revolution. It was an audacious move. A gambler would have hesitated to wager money on Lenin at that point. Out of the country for a full decade, he had returned under circumstances that suggested collaboration with the German enemy. His Bolshevik party numbered only about twenty-five thousand, far fewer than the other significant parties, and it had very few representatives on the influential Executive Committee of the Petrograd Soviet.

The handicaps did not deter Lenin. Nor did the somewhat mixed reception he received from his fellow Bolshevik leaders upon his arrival. The next day he presented a set of radical propositions concerning the situation. Known as the April Theses, his ideas contrasted sharply not only with the views held by other parties, but with those of his Bolshevik colleagues as well. He proposed an immediate end to the war; no support, not even temporary, for the capitalist Provisional Government; and nationalization of all land. Every point in the radical document was geared to link the Bolshevik party with social revolution and to satisfy popular aspirations. But despite their respect for Lenin, his fellow Bolsheviks found his Theses difficult to accept at first. Most of them were still sufficiently orthodox Marxists to believe that revolution had to proceed in stages, with the ultimate, popular revolution not possible until the capitalists had consolidated their power and industrialized the country. Lenin was not dismayed, however. Never flinching, retreating only when pressure required it, he steadfastly held to his course. The story of 1917 in Russia is the story of how Lenin beat the odds, first winning over his party, then exhorting the people to support it, and finally guiding it to a position from which it could strike for power.

Bolshevik strength began to develop in the late spring. By May, the party claimed a membership of 79,000. This figure increased to 200,000 by August. When the first All-Russian Congress of Soviets convened in June, the Bolsheviks had more than 100 delegates, out of 777, or 12.8 percent of the seats. While still very much a minority, this figure represented an extraordinary gain since March, a gain that increased at an even greater rate during the summer. The results of city council elections in Petrograd and Moscow tell the story.

By the end of September, the Bolsheviks had an absolute majority in the influential Petrograd Soviet and were nearing the point at which a seizure of power could be contemplated realistically.

In the meantime, the Provisional Government was struggling. By early May, banners had appeared in the streets of Petrograd with the legend "Down with the Provisional Government!" Faced with increasing unpopularity and pressure from the Soviet, the Provisional Government in May reorganized itself to include more left wing members. It was at this point that the socialist lawyer Kerensky first emerged as a prominent figure in the government. He was named minister of war. In a second government shakeup in August he became prime minister. But these changes in leadership were not enough. What was needed were new programs, not merely new faces.

Тов. Ленин ОЧИЩАЕТ
землю от нечисти.

The Communists made widespread use of education and propaganda. During and after the Revolution, "Education Trains" took the party's message throughout the land (above left). A political cartoonist in 1920 portrayed Lenin sweeping the world, "clearing it of dirt" in the form of capitalists and kings.

PETROGRAD ELECTIONS AUGUST 20, 1917

Parties	Representatives in old council	Representatives in new council	Total vote
Cadets	47	42	114,485
SRs	54	75	205,666
Mensheviks	40	8	23,552
Bolsheviks	37	67	183,694
Others	22	7	21,982

MOSCOW ELECTIONS 1917

Parties	Reps	June votes	%	Reps	September votes	%
Cadets	17	108,781	17	30	101,106	27
SRs	58	374,885	58	14	54,374	15
Mensheviks	12	76,407	12	4	15,887	4
Bolsheviks	11	85,409	13	47	198,320	54

During the summer of 1917, two serious crises rocked the Provisional Government. The first was a popular uprising in the streets of Petrograd by dissatisfied workers, known as "the July Days." The Provisional Government survived and cracked down on those responsible. While the Bolsheviks had not initiated the disturbances, they had participated, and to avoid arrest Lenin was forced to flee to Finland where he remained until October.

FACT: Lenin's escape to Finland was very tricky, and he was almost caught on several occasions. He shaved his beard and took the identity of Konstantin Petrovich Ivanov, workman. One of his hiding places before leaving Petrograd was the home of a worker named Aliluyev, whose daughter later married Joseph Stalin.

The second crisis was quite different, resulting from an attempted coup d'etat by Army Commander-in-Chief Kornilov in September. To combat the threat from the right wing, Prime Minister Kerensky turned for support to the Bolshevik-dominated Petrograd Soviet and gave its members arms. The Kornilov coup was averted, and the Provisional Government survived, but the incident was a bonanza for the Bolsheviks, who were now not only armed but finding it increasingly easy to pose as champions of the revolutionary cause.

1917: THE OCTOBER REVOLUTION

By October, the political situation in Russia bordered on anarchy. City, countryside, and front line were all out of control, or nearly so, and the Provisional Government was almost completely paralyzed. The Bolsheviks, with their disciplined, authoritarian approach to politics, had a great advantage. People increasingly viewed them as the only group that might be able to get something done. Within the party leadership, however, there was considerable debate over the proper course of action. Some hesitated to take decisive action. Lenin, however, was anxious to move. By the end of September, he was bombarding his colleagues with demands for an armed uprising by the Bolsheviks. At first, the other Bolshevik leaders paid little attention to these demands. Lenin, undaunted, continued his campaign, and as disillusionment with the Provisional Government increased, his position grew stronger. Finally, in a secret, late-night meeting in Petrograd on October 23, Lenin persuaded his party's Central Committee to vote in favor of an armed uprising. In the following two weeks, the Bolsheviks tightened their hold on the leadership of the Petrograd Soviet and set the date for the coup in early November.

While Lenin continued throughout 1917 to be the force behind every move of the Bolsheviks, another figure emerged during the autumn to assist him by taking charge of the detailed operations of the coup. It was Leon Trotsky, a long-time radical but only recently a Bolshevik, a man with immense organizational ability and effectiveness as an orator.

FACT: Just as Lenin had rushed back to Russia from Switzerland, Trotsky had returned from New York City where he had been working for a Russian emigré newspaper.

In November 1917, Trotsky both organized and inspired. In particular, he persuaded the soldiers of the Petrograd garrison to defect from the Provisional Government and become politically neutral. So, when Kerensky later called on government troops to defend the regime, very few responded.

The Bolshevik Revolution began on November 6 and was over within thirty-six hours. Actually, to say that in this short time the Bolsheviks seized power is misleading, since the Provisional Government had effectively disintegrated and there really was no longer any power to be seized. The Bolsheviks filled a power vacuum, and they did so swiftly and easily. (See Readings 8, 9, and 10.)

FACT: The events of November 6–7 did little to interrupt the life of the city. Theaters and movie houses remained open, and their shows went on without interruption. (See Reading 11.)

The coup had been called for by Lenin, engineered principally by Lenin and Trotsky, and carried out by the Bolshevik-dominated Military Revolutionary Committee of the Petrograd Soviet. It was accomplished under the slogan "All Power to the Soviets." That the Bolsheviks did not intend to share power with other socialist parties in the Soviet was clearly hinted on November 8, however, when the Congress of Soviets was informed that the new government would *not* be the Soviet's duly elected Central Executive Committee, as was generally expected. Instead, the Bolsheviks established a new governing body, the Council of People's Commissars (SOVNARKOM), made up entirely of Bolsheviks, with Lenin as chairman. Through the November 6–7 coup, the Soviets became the nominal source of political authority in Russia, but in retrospect, it is clear that the Bolsheviks assumed actual power for themselves alone. Immediately after the coup, the Bolsheviks began the creation of a system in which the legal organs of government coexisted with a single political party, which dictated policy to the government. The parallelism of government and party, with the party calling the shots, became an essential feature of the Stalinist system of government.

The Bolsheviks came to power committed to a set of theories and principles. As Marxists, they believed in the establishment of an ideal communist society in which exploitation would be ended and all people would share equally in society's benefits. More immediately, in decrees issued soon after the coup, Lenin committed his party to securing an immediate end to the war, to distributing land to the peasants, to obtaining greater control of factories by workers, and to permitting greater autonomy for the national minorities. The next few years were to see these goals once again drastically compromised. To some extent, this was due to the very difficult circumstances in which the Bolsheviks found themselves after the October Revolution. (See Reading 12.)

FACT: Lenin himself seemed momentarily awed by his success, which catapulted him into the driver's seat. Said he to Trotsky, "You know, from exile and a life underground, to come suddenly to power . . . it makes one dizzy."

BOLSHEVIK CONSOLIDATION OF POWER

As of the morning of November 8, the Bolsheviks could be pleased with their success of the previous two days, but in reality the success was precarious and would remain so for some time. They held only certain portions of one city, and they faced most of the problems that had caused the downfall of both the tsar and the Provisional Government.

Perhaps the most immediate and serious of these problems was the war against Germany. Lenin realized that if the Revolution were to survive, the war must end, however costly that end might be. Consequently, an armistice was signed in December, and peace negotiations began at the town of Brest-Litovsk. It soon became clear that the Germans would settle only for an extremely harsh treaty, which caused great debate within the Bolshevik leadership. Once again, Lenin's persistence, bolstered by his threat to resign, produced ultimate agreement with his position. On March 3, 1918, the Bolsheviks signed the Treaty of Brest-Litovsk with Germany, ending hostilities between the two countries. The cost to Russia was great.

FACT: With the treaty, Russia was forced to give up 25 percent of its territory, including Ukraine, Finland, Georgia, Poland, and the Baltic states. These lands contained 26 percent of its population, 27 percent of its arable land, 26 percent of its railroads, 33 percent of its manufacturing industries, 73 percent of its iron industries, and 75 percent of its coal and iron mines.

The Germans were not the only problem for the Bolsheviks, however. A domestic problem that faced the Bolsheviks almost immediately was what to do about elections to the Constituent Assembly, already scheduled for late November. The Bolsheviks, not yet daring to interfere with the electoral process and at the same time hoping for a popular mandate, allowed the elections to be held on November 25.

FACT: In this, the freest national election, until 1991, in Russian and Soviet history, the Bolsheviks received 23.5 percent of the vote, whereas the Socialist Revolutionaries received 41 percent.

While hoping for better results, the Bolsheviks were probably not surprised at the outcome. When the Constituent Assembly met in January 1918, the Bolsheviks simply dissolved it by force, branding it counterrevolutionary. (See Reading 14.) Many opposition groups emerged to challenge the Bolsheviks in the six months following the coup. These opponents were originally moderate groups such as the Cadets, who had supported the Provisional Government, and any remaining tsarists. But as the Bolshevik determination to monopolize power became more and more evident, other left wing groups were alienated. While the opposition groups never unified, they posed a very real threat to the new regime.

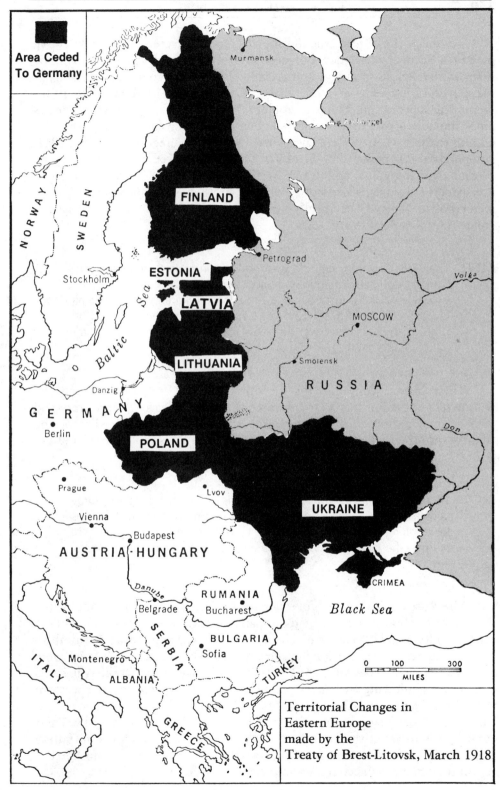

Area Ceded To Germany

FINLAND

ESTONIA

LATVIA

LITHUANIA

POLAND

UKRAINE

RUSSIA

NORWAY

SWEDEN

GERMANY

AUSTRIA-HUNGARY

SERBIA

ITALY

Montenegro

ALBANIA

GREECE

RUMANIA

BULGARIA

TURKEY

Murmansk

Petrograd

Moscow

Smolensk

Stockholm

Danzig

Berlin

Prague

Vienna

Budapest

Belgrade

Bucharest

Sofia

Lvov

CRIMEA

Black Sea

Baltic Sea

Volga

Don

Danube

0   100   300
MILES

To meet the threat, the Bolsheviks issued decrees and took active measures against what they called counterrevolutionary elements. Among them were religious groups, automatically classified as counterrevolutionary. Marx had called religion "the opiate of the people" and attacked it for promoting superstition. The real problem, however, was that religious groups proclaimed allegiance to an authority higher than any on earth. The Bolsheviks, faithful to their atheistic ideology, issued a series of decrees in December 1917, stripping the Orthodox church of its economic power and weakening its control over individual followers. At the same time, a decree shut down newspapers judged to be anti-Bolshevik, and another established the CHEKA, a secret police charged specifically with the task of eliminating opposition groups. (See Readings 15 and 16.)

FACT: The CHEKA, whose full title was the Extraordinary Commission to Combat Counterrevolution and Sabotage, might be considered the successor to the tsarist Okhrana, though the Okhrana was very small and inactive compared to the CHEKA. It has been succeeded in turn by a series of organizations over the years that had a similar mission: the GPU, OGPU, NKVD, MVD, and **KGB.**

Their blatant contempt for the outcome of a free election and the willingness of the Bolsheviks to use force illustrated clearly the arbitrary and authoritarian nature of the new regime and hastened the division of the country into the two factions of the Civil War: the Reds (Bolsheviks) and the Whites (anti-Bolsheviks).

FACT: There was a third group active in the Civil War, partisans sometimes known as the Greens. These were Cossack and peasant units representing local interests, mostly in the south, who liked neither Reds nor Whites, but hurt the latter more because they were located mostly in White territory.

The Russian Civil War broke out in the late spring of 1918 and lasted through 1920, though an associated campaign by the Bolsheviks against Poland continued for an additional year. The Whites enjoyed superiority in numbers and the support of several foreign powers. English and French leaders were angry at the Bolsheviks for having withdrawn Russia from World War I at a critical time, allowing Germany to concentrate all its forces on the western front. Later, Japan and the United States joined England and France, both landing troops at Vladivostok, and the U.S. also at Murmansk, in 1918. Their purpose was to assist the Whites and to prevent allied supplies from falling into German or Bolshevik hands. Beyond this, their presence represented a continuing threat to the Germans on the eastern front.

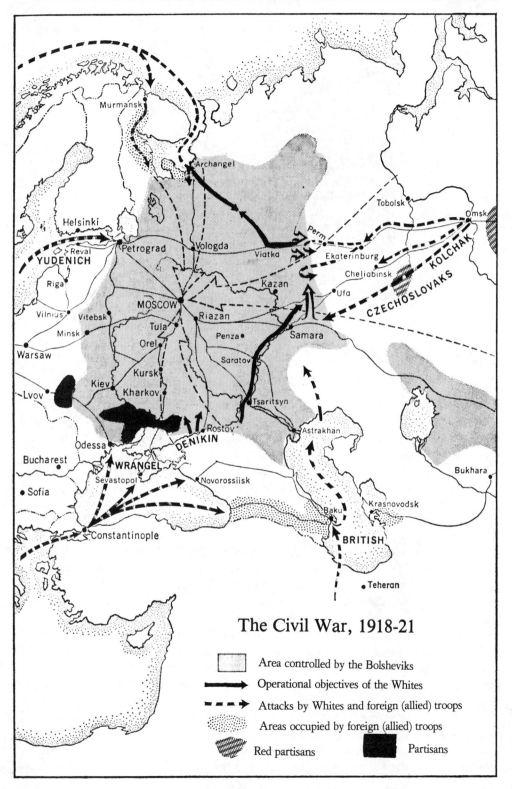

The Civil War, 1918-21

Murmansk

Archangel

Tobolsk

Omsk

Helsinki

Reval

YUDENICH

Petrograd   Vologda   Viatka   Perm

Ekaterinburg

KOLCHAK

Cheliabinsk

Riga

CZECHOSLOVAKS

MOSCOW   Riazan   Kazan   Ufa

Vilnius   Vitebsk

Minsk   Tula   Penza   Samara

Warsaw   Orel   Saratov

Kursk

Lvov   Kiev   Kharkov   Tsaritsyn

Rostov   Astrakhan

Odessa   DENIKIN

Bucharest   WRANGEL

Sofia   Sevastopol   Novorossiisk   Bukhara

Krasnovodsk

Baku

Constantinople   BRITISH

Teheran

	Area controlled by the Bolsheviks
	Operational objectives of the Whites
	Attacks by Whites and foreign (allied) troops
	Areas occupied by foreign (allied) troops
	Red partisans
	Partisans

The United States was among a number of foreign countries that sent troops to Russia during the Civil War. In this photograph, American soldiers are feeding soup to Red soldiers they have captured.

FACT: Fourteen countries intervened in the Russian Civil War. The Japanese force was the largest, at 60,000, and the British second, with 40,000. The United States dispatched about 10,000, mostly to the Far East through Vladivostok. While helpful to the Whites and openly hostile to the Bolsheviks, the foreign detachments normally avoided actual battle. The intervention was mostly over by 1920, having achieved little or nothing except Bolshevik animosity.

The Civil War was a bitter and bloody struggle. (See Readings 17, 18, and 19). Coming as it did on top of the disastrous conflict of 1914–1918, it wreaked further havoc on an already devastated society. The Bolsheviks finally emerged victorious because the Whites were handicapped by lack of leadership, unity of purpose, and geographical fragmentation. The Bolsheviks had interior lines and were under the capable leadership of Leon Trotsky, who headed the Red Army, turning it into a well-organized and effective fighting force. In the end, peasant support for the Reds probably tipped the scale. While they disliked many of the Bolshevik policies, they were even more skeptical of the Whites, who represented the old Russia of the landlords.

The Bolshevik party had been, since its inception in 1903, authoritarian in nature, but the challenge of the Civil War and fear of counterrevolution made it more so. Beset by enemies and fearful for their political lives, the Bolsheviks resorted to increasingly extreme measures to protect their fragile position. Under the CHEKA, the Red Terror was begun during the summer of 1918, with the aim of wiping out enemies of the new regime. Among the victims were former Tsar Nicholas and his family, who were brutally murdered by a local revolutionary group in Ekaterinburg, where they had been sent the previous year. (See Reading 20.) The Bolsheviks themselves calculated that, in twenty provinces of European Russia during 1918 and the first half of 1919, over 8,000 people were shot without trial by the CHEKA and close to 80,000 others arrested without a legal hearing. The actual numbers were doubtless much higher. (See Reading 21.) The crackdown on religion also continued. Priests were deprived of voting rights, church property was confiscated, and many church leaders, including Patriarch Tikhon, were arrested.

The Bolsheviks also cracked down in their economic policy, instituting in 1918 what was called War Communism. Marxism-Leninism taught that, following the overthrow of capitalism, the means of production should be controlled by the state. War Communism sought to achieve this ideological goal by accelerating the transition from a free enterprise economy to a socialist one. There was a pragmatic goal as well, however: to get the stalled economy working again by direct state intervention. To these ends, the Bolsheviks nationalized industries, abolished free trade, requisitioned food from the peasantry by force, and adopted other extreme measures that greatly decreased the freedom of many Russian workers and peasants. In so doing, they incurred increased resistance among these groups. In 1919 alone, 1.7 million peasants deserted the Red Army.

In political affairs the Bolsheviks increased the centralization of authority. The party's Central Committee, which was in charge of everyday matters and directed party policy between party congresses, continued to exist, but its importance decreased. Increasingly, significant decisions were made by a small group within the Central Committee, and in 1919 the small group was formalized as the Political Bureau **(Politburo).** In theory, the Politburo was, and remained until 1991, a subcommittee responsible to the Central Committee. In actuality, however, it soon became the principal source of political authority, to whose decisions the Central Committee would normally give a rubber stamp approval. Originally numbering eight, the Politburo usually contained ten to fifteen members plus half a dozen candidate (non-voting) members.

FACT: In March 1918, Lenin and the Bolshevik party abandoned Petrograd, Peter's window on the West, in favor of Moscow, the ancient capital, and the Kremlin once again became the center of government.

FACT: In that same month, at the seventh Party Congress, Lenin changed the name of his party from the Russian Social Democratic Workers' party (Bolshevik) to the Russian Communist party (Bolshevik). In 1924, it was renamed Communist Party of the Soviet Union (Bolshevik). Finally, in 1949, the parenthetical term Bolshevik was dropped from the title.

THE NEW ECONOMIC POLICY

With the Civil War mostly over by 1920, Lenin and his party controlled the country as a whole for the first time. There were still major challenges to be faced, however, and the Communists devoted the next seven years to facing them and consolidating their control.

Among the challenges the most crucial was that of the economy, which continued to be at a near standstill, causing opposition to the Communist party from its own followers. "I am for the Bolsheviks, but against the Communists," was a saying common among peasants in 1919, symbolic of the fact that much of the support Lenin and his colleagues had enjoyed in 1917 had begun to erode shortly thereafter. To many of the ordinary people of Russia, the Bolsheviks were the party that had accomplished a revolution on their behalf, a revolution from which they could expect greater democracy and a higher standard of living. The Communists, who had imposed unpopular political and economic controls, appeared to be an entirely different group. Workers found that they did not receive control of factories, and a Workers' Opposition movement developed in 1919. Peasants resented War Communism and the forced requisitioning of their produce. They responded by sowing fewer crops and hoarding their surpluses, which in turn produced severe food shortages. Famine occurred in 1921–22, accompanied by epidemics. Deaths from hunger and disease in those two years alone were greater than the total number of Russian battle deaths in World War I and the Civil War.

FACT: The ravages of the famine were so great that the Soviet regime appealed to other countries for help. Despite its anti-communist stance, the United States government responded by organizing the American Relief Administration under future President Herbert Hoover in the summer of 1921. This organization distributed food and medical supplies; in August 1922 alone, it fed more than ten million individuals daily. (See Reading 22.)

Peasant revolts broke out, the most notable of which, in the Tambov region of central Russia in 1920, required fifty thousand Red Army troops to put down. But the most dramatic protest came in 1921, from the sailors of the huge naval base at Kronstadt in the Gulf of Finland.

The sailors of Kronstadt had been among the most ardent supporters of the Bolshevik party. By 1921 they had become disillusioned. They deplored what they called "the arbitrary rule of the commissars," by which they meant the growing centralization of government, the lack of participation by the masses in the decision-making process, and harsh government policies toward both workers and peasants. They drew up a manifesto, hoisted the flag of rebellion, and waited for the Moscow regime to accede to their demands. They misjudged the regime. The Tenth Party Congress, which was meeting at the time, authorized force to put down the revolt, and an army was dispatched under Trotsky's leadership. After a bloody siege, the fortress fell.

FACT: Fifteen thousand Kronstadt defenders who surrendered to Trotsky were executed without even the semblance of a trial.

The manner in which the Communist leadership dealt with the Kronstadt Revolt, by claiming that it was the work of reactionary emigrés, was the clearest indication yet that the new regime was not truly accountable to the wishes of the Russian people.

The protests, opposition movements, and outright revolts of 1919–21 led the Communist party, still very much under Lenin's guiding hand, to institute two new policies, one political and one economic. The political policy was to tighten discipline within the party and eliminate what was defined as factionalism, the right to form political groups within the party and to challenge party decisions. At the Tenth Party Congress in 1921, Lenin introduced a resolution "On Party Unity," which dissolved existing factions and prohibited them in the future. This decision was an important step in the development of the monolithic party that characterized the Stalin period. Thereafter, party discipline was rigidly enforced. One result was the first large purge, or expulsion, of 200,000 party members in 1921.

While tightening political control, Lenin recognized the need to loosen up in the economic area, in order to stabilize the economy, increase production, and decrease popular unrest. War Communism was abandoned and replaced in 1921 by the New Economic Policy (NEP). Forced requisitioning of food was replaced by a tax. In industry, the attempt at total nationalization was also abandoned, and the state retained control only over the "commanding heights" of the economy, large-scale industry and banking. Free trade was reintroduced and private enterprise once again tolerated. While a definite retreat from the communist ideal of public ownership and collectivism, NEP was unquestionably a success economically. By 1928, both the volume of industry and the amount of land under cultivation (but not actual output of grain) exceeded prewar levels, and a degree of prosperity returned to Soviet Russia. The task of reviving the economy and building a new socialist society appealed to many Russians. Taken together with the relaxation of economic controls, it made the NEP period one of enthusiasm and even excitement in the Soviet Union. (See Reading 23.)

The peasants were not the only ones to whom concessions were made during the early 1920s. In fact, it was generally a period of relaxation, with concessions made to various groups in Soviet society. The national minorities were encouraged to develop educational and cultural institutions. The Orthodox church, though restricted in many respects, was formally recognized. Private book printing and publishing reappeared. While some literary figures opposed the new regime, others found it possible to come to terms with it, among them such noteworthy writers as Isaac Babel, Eugene Zamiatin, Yuri Olesha, and

One of the early goals of the Soviet regime was to raise the literacy rate through education. A poster designed to promote this campaign says: "Woman, learn to read and write." The daughter says, "Ah Mama! If you could read and write, you could help me."

Vladimir Mayakovsky, the unofficial poet laureate of the regime. New forms in literature, theater, and art appeared, and under the leadership of Sergei Eisenstein and others, Soviet filmmaking gained prominence. The work of the Russian avant-garde painters caught the attention of artists everywhere.

The regime faced a substantial challenge with regard to the minority nationalities of the former Russian Empire. In 1917, Lenin had called the tsarist empire "the prison house of nationalities" and promised these peoples greater autonomy, but their efforts at self-determination in the years following the Revolution were opposed by the Communist regime. During the Civil War, Red armies brought the Ukrainians, Transcaucasians, and central Asians under party control. In December 1922, a federal state was created, the Union of Soviet Socialist Republics.

FACT: The new USSR initially included Russia, Ukraine, Belorussia, and Transcaucasia. In 1925, it was joined by the Turkmen and Uzbek, and in 1929 by the Tadzhik Republics of central Asia. Later, Transcaucasia was divided into the Armenian, Georgian, and Azerbaijan Republics, and six additional republics were created for the total of fifteen.

In 1924, a constitution for the new state was produced. It guaranteed many freedoms, including the freedom for republics to secede from the union, but as with many of the rights guaranteed by the Soviet constitution, this one was not exercised.

In addition to the various domestic challenges, the Communists faced serious international challenges after 1917. The western powers were still openly hostile to the Communists, for being "godless atheists," for withdrawing Russia from World War I, for repudiating Russia's debts to other countries, and for promoting a worldwide Communist revolution through the **Comintern,** an agency established in 1919 to coordinate and support the activities of Communist parties throughout the world. The western powers particularly resented the intrusion into their domestic political affairs orchestrated by the Comintern. For their part, the Communist leaders felt hostile toward those powers that had intervened in the Russian Civil War and excluded Soviet Russia from the post-World War I settlements and the League of Nations.

By 1921, although Trotsky was still advocating world revolution as a top priority, Lenin and others had begun to realize that such an event, while desirable and inevitable, was not imminent. Here too Lenin recognized the need for compromise, and the emphasis on world revolution was quietly dropped in favor of more traditional diplomatic relations with other countries. Starting with the Treaty of Rapallo with Germany in 1922, Soviet Russia gradually rejoined the world community, a process that climaxed with its admission to the League of Nations in 1934.

FACT: The Treaty of Rapallo contained secret provisions for military cooperation between the two countries. Germany, forbidden to rearm by the Versailles treaty, obtained the right to use Russian bases for training and testing equipment, in return for which Germany agreed to lend expertise and assist in rebuilding Russia's military industry.

THE RISE OF STALIN

Despite the fact that the Bolshevik party had always talked in terms of collective leadership, Lenin was unquestionably the acknowledged leader of the party throughout the revolutionary period. (See Reading 24.) While he avoided titles and discouraged flattery, Lenin nonetheless insisted on having his own way, and a combination of political skill and the great respect in which he was held usually resulted in agreement with his position. Hence, a crisis arose when Lenin became seriously ill in 1921 and intensified when he was incapacitated by a series of strokes beginning in 1922. He died as a result of the strokes in January 1924. (See Reading 25.) While the entire leadership of the party pledged itself at that time to follow Lenin's course and respect the principle of collective leadership, the party clearly needed a single leader. Even before Lenin died, a power struggle developed to determine his successor. The leading candidate was Leon Trotsky, the charismatic figure who had been Lenin's right-hand man during the October Revolution and commander of the Red Army in the Civil War. Trotsky had weaknesses, however: He disliked routine work, preferred to operate by himself, and was vain and self-centered, qualities that did not endear him to his party colleagues.

Another candidate was Joseph Stalin. Stalin was in many respects Trotsky's opposite, lacking in charisma, intellectual distinction, and oratorical ability. He had the apparent disadvantage of being a Georgian, not a Russian. And in 1922, Stalin incurred the ailing Lenin's displeasure by being rude to his wife, Krupskaya. (See Reading 26.) Stalin had strengths, however. A naturally gifted politician, he used a combination of ideological and practical means to advance his position. He championed the theory of "socialism in one country" to oppose Trotsky's idea that the Soviet Union should concentrate on promoting worldwide revolution. Stalin's theory advocated that a buildup of a Communist base in the Soviet Union should precede efforts toward a world revolution.

Stalin maximized his practical advantages as well. Not only was he a member of the influential Politburo, but in 1922 he was named general secretary of the party, a position that enabled him to control party membership, appointments, and promotions. While Trotsky relied on the written and spoken word to gain support, Stalin relied on people who owed him something. He realized that gaining control of the party apparatus would in turn permit control of the government, the military, and the secret police. Quietly, and with great patience, he became familiar with the inner workers of the party and started placing his supporters in key positions. At the same time, he began making alliances with certain party leaders in order to attack others.

Trotsky was the first victim, in 1925. Denounced by a triumvirate Stalin had formed with Gregory **Zinoviev** and Leo **Kamenev,** Trotsky was removed, first as army chief, then from his other positions of leadership. Finally, he was exiled from the USSR in 1927. The other contenders soon followed, like Trotsky victims of Stalin's determination, political shrewdness, and ruthlessness. (See Readings 27 and 28.) By the end of 1927, Stalin was in control of Lenin's party.

By that time, a decade after the successful coup, the Communist regime had made some notable achievements. It had won a civil war and created a new state. It had revived a devastated economy through the NEP and brought both production of goods and standard of living back close to prewar levels. It had reduced class distinctions. It had eliminated political opposition, both inside

When Lenin died in 1924, it was not clear who, if anyone, would be able to assume the powerful position he had established as party leader. By the end of the 1920s, Joseph Stalin had eliminated other candidates and achieved this position. Lenin and his successor are pictured together in 1922. It is now known that this photograph is a fake, a composite of two separate photos commonly displayed to show Stalin at Lenin's side.

and outside the Communist party. It had begun to pull the country out of international isolation. Finally, it had permitted the emergence of a successor to Vladimir Ilyich Lenin. In 1928, however, very few Communists realized the implications of Stalin's emergence. The events of the next decade, under Stalin's leadership, would constitute a revolution that made the events of 1917 to 1928 pale by comparison.

The following books were helpful in writing this chapter:

Chamberlin, W.H., *The Russian Revolution*, 2 vols. New York: Macmillan, 1935.
Daniels, R.V., *Red October*. New York: Scribner's, 1967.
Daniels, R.V., ed., *The Russian Revolution*. Englewood Cliffs, N.J.: Prentice-Hall, 1972.
Dmytryshyn, B., *U.S.S.R. A Concise History*. New York: Scribner's, 1978.
Fitzpatrick, S., *The Russian Revolution*. New York: Oxford University Press, 1982.
Thompson, J.M., *Revolutionary Russia, 1917*. New York: Scribner's, 1981.

For students who are interested, we recommend further reading in the sources from which we have taken excerpts as well as the following works:

Lincoln, W.B., *Passage through Armageddon.* New York: Simon & Schuster, 1986.

Subtitled "The Russians in War and Revolution," this second volume of Lincoln's trilogy covers the period 1914–18. This is narrative history at its best.
————*Red Victory.* New York: Simon & Schuster, 1989.

The final volume of Lincoln's trilogy deals with the Russian Civil War in similarly fine fashion.

McNeal, R.H., *The Bolshevik Tradition.* Englewood Cliffs, N.J.: Prentice-Hall, 1975.

Short, readable, and incisive biographies of four men who rose to the top of the Soviet regime: Lenin, Stalin, Khrushchev, and Brezhnev.

Moorehead, A., *The Russian Revolution.* New York: Harper and Bros., 1958.

Not a scholarly work, but probably the most readable account of the events of 1917 and the background to these events.

Pipes, R., *The Russian Revolution.* New York: Alfred A. Knopf, 1990.

The most recent work on the events of 1917, Pipes's account is lengthy, scholarly, and comprehensive.

Reed, J., *Ten Days that Shook the World.* New York: Penguin, 1966.

An American Communist's eyewitness account of the Bolshevik Revolution of 1917. Authentic and unique.

Sanders, J., *Russia 1917.* New York: Abbeville, 1989.

This handsome volume, combining text with unusual and dramatic photographs from Soviet archives, devotes a chapter to each month of the revolutionary year 1917.

Shukman, H., ed., *The Blackwell Encyclopedia of the Russian Revolution.* Oxford, Basil Blackwell Ltd., 1988.

Everything one might want to know about this momentous event.

READINGS
for
Chapter Four

1. Initial Disturbances:
A Police Account

The February Revolution started with strikes and demonstrations in Petrograd on March 7 (February 23 by the old calendar), as described in the following memorandum sent by the Okhrana (secret police) to its precinct superintendents.

On February 23 at 9:00 A.M., the workers of the plants and factories of the Vyborg district went on strike in protest against the shortage of black bread in bakeries and groceries; the strike spread to some plants located in the Petrograd, Rozhdestvenskii, and Liteinyi districts, and in the course of the day 50 industrial enterprises ceased working, with 87,534 men going on strike.

At about 1:00 P.M., the workmen of the Vyborg district, walking out in crowds into the streets and shouting "Give us bread," started at the same time to become disorderly in various places, taking with them on the way their comrades who were at work, and stopping tramcars; the demonstrators took away from the tram drivers the keys to the electric motors, which forced 15 tramway trains to quit the lines and retire to the Petrograd tramway yard.

The strikers, who were resolutely chased by police and troops summoned (for this purpose), were dispersed in one place but quickly gathered in other places, showing themselves to be exceptionally stubborn; in the Vyborg district order was restored only toward 7:00 P.M.

2. The Mood in the Streets

One of the first eyewitnesses to record his impressions of the early days of the February Revolution was the Socialist Revolutionary Zenzinov. His descriptions capture the mood of those in the streets and suggest the key role the soldiers would play in these events. The dates are those of the old calendar.

These two days—the 23rd and the 24th—I spent most of my time on the streets . . . I roamed the streets without any plan, turning from one into another, observing the crowds, listening in on conversations. There were more than the usual number of people on the streets; common people predominated. (They were) in an excited state, but not irritated—most of all, one could sense the curiosity of the crowd. It was also evident that the people were not so

Abridged from Browder, R.P., and Kerensky, A.F., eds., *The Russian Provisional Government 1917*, 34. Stanford, CA.: Stanford University Press, 1961.
Abridged from Browder and Kerensky, *Russian Provisional Government*, 27.

much residents of these streets as people who had made their way from outlying districts. Chains of soldiers were stationed at many points: undoubtedly their duty was not to let the passers-by go any farther, but they performed this duty poorly. I remember how I was detained for a long time by the Moika [a canal in Petrograd]—the soldiers were given strict orders not to let anyone pass through the chain, but the passers-by kept getting into conversations with them, persuading them to let them go through, explaining the necessity for them to go farther, giving reasons that were obviously fabricated—and the soldiers, looking around them to make sure that their superiors did not notice their indulgence, would let (the people) pass . . . In this way I, too, was allowed to pass. From these fleeting conversations it became clear that all these soldiers were for the most part recently mobilized; i.e., only very recently they had been in the same (position) as the crowds around them.

3. The Provisional Government Proclaims the Revolution

On March 16, the Temporary Committee of the Duma appointed a Provisional Government, in effect a cabinet of ministers (of which there were ten), to rule until a permanent form of government could be decided upon. Four days later the Provisional Government issued its first declaration, outlining its objectives and hopes for the future.

Citizens of the Russian State!

A great event has taken place. By the mighty impulse of the Russian people the old order has been overthrown. A new free Russia has been born. The great upheaval crowns many years of struggle.

By the act of October 17, 1905, under pressure of the awakened popular forces, Russia was promised constitutional liberties. However, those promises were not kept. The spokesman of national hopes, the First State Duma, was dissolved. The Second Duma suffered the same fate. And, powerless to crush the national will, the Government decided, by the Act of June 3, 1907, to retract from the people part of the rights to participate in legislative work which had been granted to them. In the course of nine long years, step by step, the people were deprived of all of the rights which they had gained. Once more the country was plunged into an abyss of arbitrary rule and absolutism. All attempts to make the Government listen to reason proved futile, and the great world struggle into which our motherland was drawn by the enemy found it in a state of moral decay, alienated from the people, indifferent to the future of the motherland, and steeped in the infamy of corruption. Neither the heroic

Browder and Kerensky, *Russian Provisional Government*, 27.

efforts of the army, staggering under the crushing burdens of internal chaos, nor the appeals of the people's representatives who had united in the face of national peril were able to lead the former Emperor and his Government into the path of unity with the people. And when Russia, owing to the illegal and fatal actions of her rulers, was confronted with the gravest disasters, the nation was obliged to take the power into its own hands. The unanimous revolutionary enthusiasm of the people, fully aware of the gravity of the moment, and the determination of the State Duma have created the Provisional Government. And the latter deems it its sacred duty and responsibility to fulfill the people's hopes and lead the country onto the bright path of free civic organization.

The Government believes that the spirit of lofty patriotism, manifested during the struggle of the people against the old regime, will also inspire our valiant soldiers on the field of battle. For its own part, the Government will make every effort to provide our army with everything necessary to bring the war to a victorious conclusion.

The Government will sacredly observe the alliances which bind us to other powers and will unswervingly carry out the agreements entered into with the Allies.

While taking measures to defend the country from the foreign enemy, the Government will, at the same time, deem it to be its primary duty to open a way to the expression of the popular will with regard to the form of government and will convoke the Constituent Assembly within the shortest time possible on the basis of universal, direct, equal, and secret suffrage, also guaranteeing participation in the elections to the gallant defenders of our native land who are now shedding their blood on the fields of battle. The Constituent Assembly will also issue the fundamental laws guaranteeing the country the inalienable rights of justice, equality, and liberty.

Realizing the full gravity of the lack of rights, which oppresses the country and hinders the free creative impulse of the people at a time of grave national upheavals, the Provisional Government deems it necessary to provide the country immediately, even prior to the convocation of the Constituent Assembly, with laws safeguarding civil liberty and equality in order to enable all citizens to apply freely their spiritual forces to creative work for the benefit of the country. The Government will also undertake the enactment of legal provisions to assure all citizens equal participation in the elections of organs of self-government on the basis of universal suffrage.

At this moment of national liberation, the whole country remembers with reverent gratitude those who, in defending their political and religious convictions, fell victims to the vindictive old regime. And the Provisional Government considers it its happy duty to bring back from their exile and imprisonment, with full honors, all those who have suffered for the good of the motherland.

In fulfilling these tasks, the Provisional Government is animated by the belief that it will thus execute the will of the people, and that the whole nation will support it in its honest efforts to ensure the happiness of Russia. This belief inspires it with courage. The Provisional Government sees the only guarantee for the triumph of the new order in the wholehearted support of all of the people.

4. The Petrograd Soviet

The Petrograd Soviet did as the Duma had done and elected an Executive Committee. It immediately began to assume its "watchdog" function, to make sure that the Provisional Government managed the Revolution properly and that the interests of the workers (and later, the soldiers and peasantry) were properly represented. The Socialist Revolutionary N. N. Sukhanov wrote his impressions of these events, which he witnessed.

It was already about 11 o'clock [February 28, old calendar] when the Ex. Com. session opened. I have the impression that during these first days its work went on almost uninterruptedly around the clock. But what work it was! They were not meetings, but a frenzied and exhausting obstacle race.

The agenda had been set up, as pointed out above, in relation to the urgent tasks of the moment. But neither at that session nor in general during the days that followed could there be any questions of fulfilling a programme of work.

Every five or ten minutes business was interrupted by "urgent announcements," or "emergency reports," "matters of exceptional importance" which couldn't "tolerate the slightest delay," and on which the "fate of the revolution depended," etc. These emergency questions were for the most part raised by the Ex. Com. members themselves, who kept getting some sort of information on the side, or prompted by people who were besieging the Ex. Com. But again and again the petitioners, delegates, and messengers from every possible organization and agency, or simply from the nearby crowds, would themselves burst into the meeting.

In the great majority of cases these emergency matters were not worth a barley-corn. I don't remember what the Ex. Com. did during these hours. I remember only unimaginable hubbub, tension, hunger, and the feeling of irritation at these "exceptional reports." There was simply no way of stopping them.

There was no order even in the meeting itself. There was no permanent chairman. Chkheidze, who later performed the chairman's duties almost permanently, didn't do much work in the Ex. Com. during its first days. He was constantly being summoned—either to the Duma Committee or the Soviet sessions or, above all, "to the people," the constantly-changing crowd standing in front of the Tauride Palace. He spoke practically without stopping

Browder and Kerensky, *Russian Provisional Government*, 77–8.

both in the Ekaterinskii Hall and in the street, sometimes to workers and sometimes to soldiers. He would scarcely have time to return to the meeting of the Ex. Com. and take his things off before some delegate would burst in with a categorical demand for Chkheidze, sometimes even reinforced by threats—that the mob would break in. And the tired and sleepy old Georgian would get his fur coat on again with a resigned look, put on his hat, and disappear from the Ex. Com.

There was still no permanent secretary, nor were any minutes taken. If they had been taken and preserved, they would not report any "measures" or "acts of state" during these hours. They would reflect nothing but chaos and "emergency reports" about every possible danger and excess we lacked the means to combat. There were accounts of pillage, fires, and pogroms; pogromist **Black Hundred** leaflets were brought in—handwritten, alas, and thoroughly illiterate. We gave orders not expecting them to be carried out and sent out detachments without any hope that they would really be formed or do their duty.

I don't remember who presided at this meeting, nor whether there was any chairman at all . . . On the writing-desk of the chairman of the former Finance Committee there appeared from somewhere or other tin mugs of tea with crusts of black bread and other eatables. Someone was looking after us. But there was not much food, or else there was simply no time to get it. A feeling of hunger remains in my memory.

5. The Revolution as Seen by a Child

Among the many eyewitness accounts of the events of March 1917 in Petrograd, a particularly interesting one is that of Zinaida Shakhovskoi, who was a child at the time. She was a member of an aristocratic family of some renown and after the Revolution emigrated with them to Paris, where she eventually became a well-known writer and editor of an influential Russian language newspaper. The dates are those of the old calendar.

I was ten years old and since September 1916 a pupil at the Empress Catherine Institute for Young Ladies of Nobility, in Petrograd, when the February revolution occurred.

Sunday, the 26th of February 1917. In the large white-columned reception hall of the Institute, where once a week the pupils could see their parents (under the stares of two solemn looking Empresses, painted in majesty—Catherine the Great and the Dowager Empress Mariya Fedorovna) the usual

Abridged from vonMohrenschildt, D., ed., *The Russian Revolution of 1917*, 100–3. New York: Oxford University Press, 1971.

crowd of visitors was on this particular day considerably thinner, but no rumors of disquietness had penetrated the walls of the Institute.

As my sister and I took leave of my mother, who was accompanied by my brother Dimitry, in his uniform of the pupils of Alexandrovsky Lyceum, and by my two cousins, one of whom was finishing his studies in the Pavlovsky Military Officers School, I joined my classmates in a small neighboring hall where we were allowed to play on Sunday afternoons. There I heard a strange, soon to become familiar, sound: it resembled the dry and regular fall of hail and it was followed by shouting and screams and by the tramping of horseshoes on the pavement. We were even more startled by the hurry with which our mistress in charge, breaking traditional composure, without even bothering to put us in pairs or order us to keep silent, led us to the corridor. At once the grave, somehow monastic atmosphere of the Institute which I found so boring, broke into pandemonium. There were our maids running up and down the stairs, some of them carrying mattresses (as I learned later, to be propped against the windows opening on the quays of Fontanka [a canal in Petrograd]); our janitors, old bemedaled and bearded veterans of the previous war, were hurrying from the entrance hall to the upper floors, where they were never supposed to penetrate. We were shepherded into our classroom overlooking the relative safety of our garden and there our mistresses gave us a summary explanation of what was happening. The unfamiliar word entered my vocabulary: the Revolt, not yet "Revolution."

Of course, the event was beyond our comprehension. The world which I had entered without enthusiasm some months ago, was, in spite of its excellent educational program, remote from reality and nearer the eighteenth century than the twentieth. Over our tight corsets we wore long dresses— green, red or lilac depending on our respective grades—which would have suited the court ladies of Catherine the Great. Our bare arms and ample decolletage were modestly covered by white capes and detachable sleeves. It was a dress which hardly conveyed the idea of the struggle for life.

I must confess, the first day of the February Revolution seemed to us, the seventh-grade pupils, just an exceptionally exciting day which liberated us from the tedious obligation to behave ourselves in a lady-like manner—which meant walking demurely with hands gently crossed over our stomach and making deep reverences when we saw one of our teachers. Discipline was shattered, to our great delight.

While helping other maids to arrange our beds (we were to sleep that night on the floor of our classroom) our young maid Grousha, her arm in a sling, for she was slightly wounded while shutting windows in the great hall, chattered away: "Oh, my dear young ladies, it is terrible what is happening. You see, the crowd thought that they were fired upon from our attic, and they put us under fire. But the police are not here, they are on the roof of Sheremetiev's mansion next door! Oh dear me, what will happen to all of us?! They might well try and burn us during the night." The mysterious "they," who were they exactly? Would "they" roast us during the night? After much speculating on this question, the "young ladies" finally settled down to sleep despite their fears.

The excitement continued during the days that followed as rumors spread that the Pages of the Emperor and the Junkers (student officers) of Pavlovsky Military School would be sent to protect us. The young people of the opposite sex were never, never to be seen outside the great hall! But the awaited defenders didn't come and nobody took the Catherine Institute by assault or fire . . . But there came the day when even we, the youngest of the pupils, became aware that something tragic and final had befallen the Russian Empire and all of us. On March 3, all the pupils and teachers were assembled in the hall as usual for the morning prayers read by one of the highest-ranking pupils. For the first time in about two centuries the prayer for the Tsar and his family was to be omitted, the Emperor having abdicated on the previous day. The girl, who was about 18, stumbled over her words and was unable to pronounce, "Let us pray for the Provisional Government." She started to cry. The teachers and mistresses took to their handkerchiefs and soon the four or five hundred of us were sobbing over something that was lost forever.

The next day the mothers came to take their daughters away; Catherine's Institute was seeing its last days.

Following our mother, my sister Natasha and I stepped out, for good, from the Catherine Institute. I hardly recognized the capital which I had last seen two months ago returning from my winter vacation. All the glamor had left Petrograd; many shops were closed and in front of the others was an unfamiliar sight—long queues were waiting. There were few carriages and no policemen to be seen at the crossings; the streets were full of disorderly soldiers, with a few gloomy civilians hurrying along. Our driver kept saying: "Let's hurry, let's hurry, before the shooting, God forbid, starts again."

6. Anarchy in the Countryside

In the countryside, disorder increased steadily in the months following the February Revolution, as land hungry peasants competed, often violently, for what was left of the landlords' estates. By summer, many parts of rural Russia were in a state of complete anarchy, as suggested by the following report in a Petrograd newspaper.

After arriving home, I was elected to the **volost** committee. In our village there is no order. People live as they did before the Revolution. They make moonshine and sell it for two roubles a bottle. Drunkenness and robbery are on the increase.

Abridged from Pethybridge, R., ed., *Witnesses to the Russian Revolution*, 173–5. New York: Citadel Press, 1967.

The Cossacks who live in the neighbourhood steal from the landholders and peasants and insult the women. They do not even respect the church. In one village the store of the Consumers' Society was looted, and in another the home of a very popular doctor . . .

With the landlords, it is not as it should be. They have planted sugar-beets, and to harvest them they offer labour one and one-half roubles per day, which is not enough to pay for board.

Livestock for the army has been bought in the villages at the rate of eleven roubles the **pud.** It was driven on the land of a certain landowner where many have perished from hunger . . .

Committees are organized in the villages but have no idea where their authority begins or ends. Can the committee dismiss a worthless priest? Can a landowner sell a piece of timber land without the authorization of the committee? . . .

The cost of living and profiteering are on the increase. Speculators buy up bread and sell it later for five roubles the *pud.* There are those who have on hand one thousand or more puds of grain and yet buy more for speculative purposes. Merchants hide manufactured goods and allow only a limited amount on the market, for which they charge high prices. There is an abundance of money in the village and, with it, dissipation and debauchery. For the first time in the history of the village we have a house of ill-fame.

The military unit which was sent here to protect, robs the people of their cattle, fowl and bread, and insults the women . . .

Each year the peasants rented their land from the landowner. This year they went to him as usual and he asked the usual rent. The peasants refused to pay it and, without much bargaining, went home. There they called a meeting and decided to take up the land without paying. They put the ploughs and harrows on their carts and started the field. When they arrived they got into an argument as to the division of the land, because it was not at all the same quality. When they had quarrelled for a time, one of the party proposed that they proceed to the landowner's warehouse, where some good alcohol was kept. They broke into the place, where they found fifty barrels. They drank and drank, but could not drink it all. They became so drunk that they did not know what they were doing and carelessly set the place on fire. Four burned to death; the ninety others escaped. A few days later they returned to the field and once more quarrelled. It ended in a fight in which thirteen were left dead, fifteen were carried off badly injured and, of these, four died.

Soon after that a quarrel started over the rich peasants. In the village there were eighteen farmers who had from twenty-five to thirty **disiatins** of land. They had a reserve of grain of various kinds. About thirty of the villagers seized this reserve. Another village meeting was called. A few of the more intelligent peasants came out strongly against this act of robbery. It ended in another fight in which three were killed and five badly wounded. One of these peasants, whose son was killed, shook his fist and shouted: "I will make you pay for my son."

Three days later one of the village houses caught fire. People came running and asking, "How did it get on fire?" Someone suggested that the man who a few days ago threatened to get even was the incendiary. The mob started for his place and killed him. When that was done, it was learned that the fire was due to the carelessness of the housewife. On that day a strong wind was blowing straight down the street, and 132 houses were burned.

7. Lenin's Arrival

Lenin, the Bolshevik leader who had been in exile in Switzerland for a decade, was caught by surprise by the events of March 1917. Eager to return to Russia to take part in these events, Lenin accepted a German offer of help, in the form of the famous "sealed train," which brought Lenin, his wife Krupskaya, and a small band of associates to Petrograd's Finland Station on April 16. A reception committee was present, composed chiefly of Bolsheviks, but including the Mensheviks Chkheidze and Skobelev, and the journalist N.N. Sukhanov, who wrote this account of the scene at the Finland Station that night.

The throng in front of the Finland Station blocked the whole square, making movement almost impossible and scarcely letting the trams through. The innumerable red flags were dominated by a magnificent banner embroidered in gold: "The Central Committee of the **R.S. Bolsheviks.**" Troops with bands were drawn up under the red flags near the side entrance, in the former imperial waiting-rooms.

There was a throbbing of many motor-cars. In two or three places the awe-inspiring outlines of armoured cars thrust up from the crowd. And from one of the side-streets there moved out on to the square, startling the mob and cutting through it, a strange monster—a mounted searchlight, which abruptly projected upon the bottomless void of the darkness tremendous strips of the living city, the roofs, many-storeyed houses, columns, wires, tramways, and human figures.

Various delegations that had failed to penetrate into the station had found places on the steps of the main entrance and were vainly trying to retain their composure and keep their places in hand-to-hand struggles with the "private" public. Lenin's train was expected around 11.

There was a crush inside the station—more delegations, more flags, and sentries at every step demanding special authority for going any further. The title of member of the Executive Committee [of the Soviet], however, appeased the most conscientious watchdogs, and through the mass of discontentedly grumbling people tightly packed together I made my way right through the

Pethybridge, *Witnesses to the Russian Revolution*, 155–9.

station to a platform, and towards the Tsar's waiting-room, where a dejected Chkheidze sat, weary of the long wait and reacting sluggishly to Skobelev's witticisms. The whole square was clearly visible through the heavily bolted glass doors of the "imperial" waiting-room; the scene was extraordinarily impressive. "Delegates" were enviously clinging to the outside of the windows, and discontented women's voices could be heard: "Party people have to wait in the street, while they let people inside that nobody ever saw before!"

But the indignation was scarcely well-founded: I don't recall seeing any "public," at all well known in politics, science, or literature, that was not Bolshevik. The parties hadn't sent their official representatives; indeed, of the Soviet people or Executive Committee members, besides the **Praesidium,** specially detailed to go, I think there was only myself. In any case there weren't more than three or four people in the "imperial" rooms besides ourselves, since the local Bolshevik commanders had gone to meet Lenin in Finland. While we were waiting for Lenin at the station, he in the train was already familiarizing himself thoroughly with the state of affairs from "immediate sources."

I passed along the platform. There it was even more festive than in the square. Its whole length was lined with people, mostly soldiers ready to "present A-a-a-r-m-s!" Banners hung across the platform at every step; triumphal arches had been set up, adorned with red and gold; one's eyes were dazzled by every possible welcoming inscription and revolutionary slogan, while at the end of the platform, where the carriage was expected to stop, there was a band, and a group of representatives of the central Bolshevik organizations stood holding flowers.

The Bolsheviks, who shone at organization, and always aimed at emphasizing externals and putting on a good show, had dispensed with any superfluous modesty and were plainly preparing a real triumphal entry . . .

We [Sukhanov, Skobelev, and Chkheidze] waited for a long time, the train was very late.

But at long last it arrived. A thunderous **Marseillaise** boomed forth on the platform, and shouts of welcome rang out. We stayed in the imperial waiting-room while the Bolshevik generals exchanged greetings. Then we heard them marching along the platform, under the triumphal arches, to the sound of the band, and between the rows of welcoming troops and workers. The gloomy Chkheidze, and the rest of us after him, got up, went to the middle of the room, and prepared for the meeting. And what a meeting it was, worthy of—more than my wretched pen!

Shliapnikov, acting as master of ceremonies, appeared in the doorway, portentously hurrying, with the air of a faithful old police chief announcing the Governor's arrival. Without any apparent necessity he kept crying out fussily: "Please, Comrades, please! Make way there! Make way there! Comrades make way!"

Behind Shliapnikov, at the head of a small cluster of people behind whom the door slammed again at once, Lenin came, or rather ran, into the room. He wore a round cap, his face looked frozen, and there was a magnificent bouquet in his hands. Running to the middle of the room, he stopped in front of Chkheidze as though colliding with a completely unexpected obstacle. And Chkheidze, still glum, pronounced the following "speech of welcome" with not only the spirit and wording but also the tone of a sermon:

"Comrade Lenin, in the name of the Petersburg Soviet and of the whole Revolution we welcome you to Russia . . . But—we think that the principal task of the revolutionary democracy is now the defense of the Revolution from any encroachments either from within or from without. We consider that what this goal requires is not disunion, but the closing of the democratic ranks. We hope you will pursue these goals together with us."

Chkheidze stopped speaking. I was dumbfounded with surprise: really, what attitude could be taken to this "welcome" and to that delicious "But—"?

But Lenin plainly knew exactly how to behave. He stood there as though nothing taking place had the slightest connection with him—looking about him, examining the persons round him and even the ceiling of the imperial waiting-room, adjusting his bouquet (rather out of tune with his whole appearance), and then, turning away from the Executive Committee delegation altogether, he made this "reply:"

"Dear Comrades, soldiers, sailors, and workers! I am happy to greet in your persons the victorious Russian revolution, and greet you as the vanguard of the world-wide proletarian army . . . The piratical imperialist war is the beginning of civil war throughout Europe . . . The hour is not far distant when . . . the peoples will turn their arms against their own capitalist exploiters . . . The world-wide Socialist revolution has already dawned . . . Germany is seething . . . Any day now the whole of European capitalism may crash. The Russian revolution accomplished by you has prepared the way and opened a new epoch. Long live the world-wide Socialist revolution!"

This was really no reply to Chkheidze's "welcome," and it entirely failed to echo the "context" of the Russian revolution as accepted by everyone, without distinction, of its witnesses and participants.

It was very interesting! Suddenly, before the eyes of all of us, completely swallowed up by the routine drudgery of the Revolution, there was presented a bright, blinding, exotic beacon, obliterating everything we "lived by." Lenin's voice, heard straight from the train, was a "voice from outside." There had broken in upon us in the Revolution a note that was not, to be sure, a contradiction, but that was novel, harsh, and somewhat deafening.

Let us admit that essentially Lenin was right a thousand times over. Personally I was convinced that he was quite right, not only in recognizing the beginning between the World War and the crash of the imperialist system, but in maintaining that we had to steer towards world revolution and evaluate all contemporary historical events in its light. All this was beyond question.

But it was far from enough. It was not enough to acclaim the world-wide Socialist revolution: we had to understand what practical use to make of this idea in our revolutionary policy. If we didn't then the proclamation of the world-wide proletarian revolution would not merely be completely abstract, empty, and futile, but would obscure all the real perspectives and be extremely harmful.

In any case it was all *very* interesting!

The official and public part of the welcome was over. The crowd, burning with impatience, envy, and indignation, was already trying to break through the glass doors from the square. It was noisily and insistently demanding that the newly-arrived leader should come out to it in the street. Shliapnikov again cleared a way for Lenin, shouting: "Comrades, please! Make way there!"

To another Marseillaise, and to the shouts of the throng of thousands, among the red-and-gold banners illuminated by the searchlight, Lenin went out by the main entrance and was about to get into a closed car, but the crowd absolutely refused to allow this. Lenin clambered on to the bonnet of the car and had to make a speech.

". . . any part in shameful imperialist slaughter . . . lies and frauds . . . capitalist pirates . . ." was what I could hear, squeezed in the doorway and vainly trying to get out on to the square to hear the first speech "to the people" of this new star of the first magnitude of our revolutionary horizon.

8. Proclamation of the Military-Revolutionary Committee

Early on the morning of November 6, Kerensky ordered loyal troops to close forcibly the Bolshevik printing press. Believing this to be the first action in a major counterrevolutionary campaign by the Provisional Government, the Military-Revolutionary Committee, which had been set up two days earlier by the Soviets' Central Executive Committee to control the Petrograd garrison, issued an urgent decree, mobilizing forces for the defense of the Revolution.

Soldiers! Workers! Citizens!

The enemies of the people have gone over to the offensive during the night. The Kornilovites at Headquarters are trying to pull cadets and shock battalions in from the outskirts. The Oranienbaum cadets and the shock troops at Tsarskoe Selo have refused to move. A traitorous blow is being devised against the Petrograd Soviet of Workers' and Soldiers' Deputies. The newspapers *"Rabochi Put"* (Worker's Path) and *"Soldat"* (Soldier) have been closed and the printing plant sealed up. The campaign of the counter-revolutionary plotters is directed *against the All-Russian Congress of Soviets* on the eve of its opening, *against the Constituent Assembly, against the*

From Daniels, R.V., ed., *The Russian Revolution*, 121–2. Englewood Cliffs, N.J.: Prentice-Hall, 1972.

people. The Petrograd Soviet of Workers' and Soldiers' Deputies is standing up to defend the revolution. The Military-Revolutionary Committee is leading the resistance to the attack of the plotters. The whole garrison and the whole proletariat of Petrograd are ready to deal a crushing blow to the enemies of the people.

The Military-Revolutionary Committee decrees:

1. All regimental company, and crew committees, together with the commissars of the Soviet, and all revolutionary organizations must meet in constant session, and concentrate in their hands all information about the plans and actions of the plotters.
2. Not a single soldier shall become separated from his unit without the permission of the committee.
3. Two representatives from each unit and five from each district soviet shall immediately be sent to the **Smolny Institute.**
4. Report all actions of the plotters immediately to the Smolny Institute.
5. All members of the Petrograd Soviet and all delegates to the All-Russian Congress of Soviets are summoned immediately to the Smolny Institute for a special session.

The counter-revolution has raised its criminal head.

All the gains and hopes of the soldiers, workers, and peasants are threatened with great danger. But the forces of the revolution immeasurably surpass the forces of its enemies.

The people's cause is in the firm hands. The plotters will be crushed.

No vacillation or doubts. Firmness, steadfastness, perseverance, decisiveness. Long live the revolution!

9. The October Revolution: An Eyewitness Account

Around midnight on November 6 armed groups of Bolsheviks began to occupy key points in the city: government offices, public utilities, transportation facilities, and so on. This turned out to be an extremely easy task since the Provisional Government had by then lost its military support and could no longer maintain its authority or public order. The ease of the operation is described by M.M. Lashevich, a Bolshevik in charge of an important segment of the operation.

Daniels, *Russian Revolution,* 135.

The Military-Revolutionary Committee decided to act. I was ordered to seize the new state bank, the treasury, the telephone exchange, the telegraph office, and the post office during the night.

On approaching the telephone exchange we captured a patrol of cadets. Forcing our way, we burst into the courtyard of the building, after capturing the armored car at the gate. Cadets started to come running into the courtyard. There was a moment when a clash seemed inevitable, and then it would have been woe to the cadets, for in that box (the courtyard of the telephone exchange) anyone who resisted would have been thrashed. By a stratagem we succeeded in avoiding bloodshed.

Hearing the rattle of rifle bolts, I loudly commanded, "Empty your cartridges." Evidently not realizing who was giving the command, the cadets began to unload their rifles, and the Kexholm Regiment men took advantage of this to push the cadets into groups and surround them. The telephone exchange was taken without a shot.

We succeeded in capturing the state bank and the treasury even more easily. The soldiers of the Semenovsky Regiment who were on guard declared that they too were for the Military-Revolutionary Committee, and would not relinquish their posts, considering this an insulting lack of confidence by the representative of the Military-Revolutionary Committee. To avoid delay we had to agree with this, though to assure their loyalty I nevertheless left some of the sailors and Kexholm men there. At the same time the treasury was occupied by a unit sent there, and we got word of the occupation of the post office and the telegraph office. By eight o'clock (on the morning of the 7th) all the orders of the Military-Revolutionary Committee had been executed.

10. The Fall of the Winter Palace

On the night of November 7, the Winter Palace fell to the Bolsheviks, after a short siege. This symbolic event was later dramatized in print and on film, but in actuality it was not particularly difficult or exciting. The following account is by P.N. Maliantovich, minister of justice in the Provisional Government, who was in the palace at the time.

Suddenly a noise arose somewhere and began to grow, spread and roll even nearer. And in its multitude of sounds, fused into a single powerful wave, we immediately sensed something special, unlike the previous noises— something final and decisive. It suddenly became clear that the end was

Pethybridge, *Witness to the Russian Revolution*, 232–4.

coming . . . The noise rose, swelled, and rapidly swept toward us in a broad wave . . . And poured into our hearts unbearable anxiety, like a gust of poisoned air . . . It was clear: this is the onslaught, we are being taken by storm . . . Defense is useless—sacrifices will be in vain . . . The door burst open . . . A military cadet ran in, drew himself up, saluted, his face excited but resolute.

"What are the orders of the Provisional Government? Defense to the last man? We are ready to obey the orders of the Provisional Government."

"No, it is not necessary! It is useless! The picture is clear! We want no bloodshed! We must surrender," they all cried in concert, without discussing the question, merely looking at each other and finding the same feeling and decision in everyone's eyes.

Kishkin came forward. [*Nikolai Kishkin was a personal friend of Kerensky and had been invited to join Kerensky's Coalition Cabinet.*] "If they are here, it means that the Palace is already occupied."

"It is occupied. All entrances are blocked. Everyone has surrendered. This is the only room still under guard. What are the orders of the Provisional Government?"

"Tell them that we want no bloodshed, that we yield to force, that we surrender," said Kishkin.

There was a noise behind the door and it burst open. Like a splinter of wood thrown out by a wave, a little man flew into the room, pushed in by the onrushing crowd which poured in after him and, like water, at once spilled into every corner and filled the room. The little man wore a loose, open coat, a wide felt hat pushed back on his forehead, over his long, reddish hair, and glasses. He had a short, trimmed red moustache and a small beard. His short upper lip rose to his nose when he spoke. The eyes were colourless, the face tired. He flew in and cried in a sharp, small, insistent voice:

"Where are the members of the Provisional Government?"

"The Provisional Government is here," said **Konovalov,** remaining seated. "What do you wish?"

"I inform you, all of you, members of the Provisional Government, that you are under arrest. I am Antonov, chairman of the Military-Revolutionary Committee."

"The members of the Provisional Government yield to force and surrender, in order to avoid bloodshed," said Konovalov.

"To avoid bloodshed! And how much blood have you spilled?" shouted a voice from the mob behind the ring of guards. Many approving exclamations echoed from all sides.

Antonov stopped the outcries.

"Enough, comrades! That's all! we'll straighten that out afterwards . . . Now we must draw up a protocol. I am going to write it now. I shall ask everyone . . . But first I request you to surrender all arms in your possession."

The military surrendered their arms, the rest declared that they carried none.

The room was jammed with soldiers, sailors, Red Guards, some carrying several weapons—a rifle, two revolvers, a sword, two machine-gun ribbons.

When it was learnt that Kerensky had fled, vile oaths were heard from the crowd. Some of the men shouted, inciting the rest to violence:

"These will run off too! . . . Kill them, finish them off, there's no need for protocols! . . .

"Run them through, the sons of bitches! . . . Why waste time with them? They've drunk enough of our blood!" yelled a short sailor, stamping the floor with his rifle—luckily without a bayonet—and looking around. It was almost a call to action. There were sympathetic replies:

"What the devil, comrades! Stick them all on bayonets, make short work of them! . . ."

Antonov raised his head and shouted sharply:

"Comrades, keep calm! All members of the Provisional Government are arrested. They will be imprisoned in the **Fortress of St. Peter and St. Paul.** I'll permit no violence. Conduct yourselves calmly. Maintain order! Power is now in your hands. You must maintain order!"

11. Maxim Gorky: The Gardener

Descriptions of Russia during the year 1917 customarily tend to emphasize the dramatic and violent elements: urban strife, rural anarchy, military failure, attempted coups. It is well to remember, however, that only a tiny portion of Russia's 170 million people were directly involved in the revolutionary events, and that most remained, at least for a little while longer, untouched by them. This point is eloquently made by the great writer Maxim Gorky.

February 1917

Motor-cars, splashing mud against the walls and smothering passers-by, tear rumbling and hooting down the street. They are crowded to overflowing with soldiers and sailors, and bristle with the steel quills of bayonets, like huge hedgehogs running amok. Every now and then there is the crack of a rifle. Revolution! The Russian nation is scurrying about, bewildered with its newly-acquired freedom; it is trying to grasp it, but finds it somewhat elusive.

In the Alexander Park a gardener is engrossed in his solitary work; a thickset man in the fifties. Clumsily and quietly he sweeps away last year's fallen leaves and the litter from paths and flower-beds, and brushes off the freshly fallen snow. He takes not the slightest interest in the bustle that is going on around him, and remains deaf to the screeching of klaxons, the shouts

---

Abridged from Gorky, M., *Fragments from My Diary.* Quoted in Pethybridge, *Witnesses to the Russian Revolution,* 255–6.

and songs and shots. He does not even see the red flags. I watched him to see if he would look up presently and notice the people running about, the motor-lorries glittering with bayonets. But he bent down over his work ad went on with it as stubbornly as a mole. Apparently he is as blind as one also.

March 1917

Along the streets, along the paths in the park, in the direction of the Narodni Dom, hundreds, thousands of soldiers in grey are moving slowly, some of them dragging machine-guns behind them like small iron pigs tied to a string. This is one of the innumerable machine-gun regiments that has just arrived from Oranienbaum. They say that there are more than ten thousand men in it. They do not know what to do with themselves, and ever since they arrived this morning they have been wandering about the town, looking for lodgings. The passers-by step aside when they meet them, for these men are war-weary, hungry and fierce. Some of them, I noticed, had squatted down by a large, round flower-bed and had scattered their rifles and haversacks over it.

Presently, not hurrying himself in the least, the gardener came up with his broom. He surveyed them angrily:

"What sort of a camping ground do you think you've got here? This is a flower-bed—flowers are going to grow here. You know what flowers are, don't you? Are you all blind? This is the children's playground. Come off it, I say. D'you hear me?"

And the fierce, armed men meekly crawled away from the flower-bed.

6 July 1917

Soldiers in steel helmets, just recalled from the front, are surrounding the Peter and Paul Fortress. They are marching leisurely along the pavements and through the park, dragging their machine-guns behind them, their rifles carelessly dangling from their shoulders. Occasionally one of them calls out good-naturedly to a passer-by:

"Hurry up; there's going to be some shooting!"

The inhabitants are all agog to see the battle and are following the soldiers silently, with fox-like movement, dodging from tree to tree and straining their necks, looking eagerly ahead.

In the Alexander Park flowers are growing at the sides of the paths; the gardener is busying himself among them. He has a clean apron on and carries a spade in his hand. As he walks along he scolds both onlookers and soldiers as though they were a flock of sheep.

"Where are you walking, there? Is that grass made for you to trample on? Isn't there enough room for you on the path?"

A bearded, iron-headed peasant in soldier's uniform, his rifle under his arm, says to the gardener:

"You look out yourself, old boy, or we'll shoot you straight away."

"Oh, will you? You just try! Fine shot, you are . . ."

"Don't you know there's a war on? There's going to be some fighting."

"Oh, is there? Well, get on with your fighting, and I'll get on with my job." "I'm with you there. Have you got a fag?" Pulling out his pouch from his pocket the gardener grumbled: "Trampling about where you're not allowed to . . ."

"It's war."

"What's that got to do with me? Fighting's all very well for them that likes it, and you've got plenty of others to help you; but I'm all alone in this job. You'd better clean that rifle of yours a bit; it's all rusty . . ."

There is a whistle and the soldier, unable to light the cigarette in his lips, puts it hastily in his pocket and runs off between the trees.

The gardener spits after him in disgust and shouts angrily:

"What the devil are you running over the grass for? Isn't there any other road you can go by?"

Autumn, 1917

The gardener walks leisurely along the path, a ladder on his shoulders and a pair of shears in his hand. Every now and then he stops to cut off the dead branches by the side of the path. He has grown thinner—seems almost shrivelled; his clothes hang on him like a sail on a mast on a windless day. The shears snip angrily and creakily as he cuts down the barren wood.

Watching him, I could not help thinking that neither an earthquake nor a flood would prevent him from going on with his work. And if the trumpets of the archangels announcing the day of judgment were not shining brilliantly enough, I am quite certain that he would scold the archangels in precisely the same voice as he scolded the soldier.

"You'd better clean those trumpets of yours a bit, they're all dirty."

12. John Reed on Lenin

By the eighth of November, the October Revolution was all over; the Bolsheviks controlled the city, and the Provisional Government had gone the way of the tsars. On that evening, Lenin began the process of constructing a Bolshevik government and planning for the future. The American John Reed, an ardent communist and supporter of Lenin, was present, and described in dramatic fashion the events of the evening.

It was just 8:40 p.m. when a thundering wave of cheers announced the entrance of the presidium, with Lenin—great Lenin—among them. A short, stocky figure, with a big head set down in his shoulders, bald and bulging. Little eyes, a snubbish nose, wide, generous mouth and heavy chin; clean-shaven now, but already beginning to bristle with the well-known beard of his

Abridged from Reed, J., *Ten Days that Shook the World*, 128–44. London: Penguin, 1966.

past and future. Dressed in shabby clothes, his trousers much too long for him. Unimpressive, to be the idol of a mob, loved and revered as perhaps few leaders in history have been. A strange popular leader—a leader purely by virtue of intellect; colourless, humourless, uncompromising and detached, without picturesque idiosyncrasies—but with the power of explaining profound ideas in simple terms, of analysing a concrete situation. And combined with shrewdness, the greatest intellectual audacity . . .

Now Lenin, gripping the edge of the reading stand, letting his little winking eyes travel over the crowd as he stood there waiting, apparently oblivious to the long-rolling ovation, which lasted several minutes. When it finished, he said simply, "We shall now proceed to construct the Socialist order!" Again that overwhelming human roar.

"The first thing is the adoption of practical measures to realize peace . . . We shall offer peace to the peoples of all the belligerent countries upon the basis of the Soviet terms—no annexations, no indemnities, and the right of self-determination of peoples. At the same time, according to our promise, we shall publish and repudiate the secret treaties . . . The question of War and Peace is so clear that I think that I may, without preamble, read the project of a Proclamation to the Peoples of All the Belligerent Countries . . ."

His great mouth, seeming to smile, opened wide as he spoke; his voice was hoarse—not unpleasantly so, but as if it had hardened that way after years and years of speaking—and went on monotonously, with the effect of being able to go on forever . . .

For emphasis he bent forward slightly. No gestures. And before him, a thousand simple faces looking up in intent adoration . . .

[Lenin then read the Proclamation.]

"The Revolution of November 6th and 7th," he ended, "has opened the era of the Social Revolution . . . The labour movement, in the name of peace and Socialism, shall win, and fulfill its destiny . . ."

There was something quiet and powerful in all this, which stirred the souls of men. It was understandable why people believed when Lenin spoke . . .

It was exactly 10:35 when Kamenev asked all in favour of the Proclamation to hold up their cards. One delegate dared to raise his hand against, but the sudden sharp outburst around him brought it swiftly down . . . Unanimous.

Suddenly, by common impulse, we found ourselves on our feet, mumbling together into the smooth lifting unison of the **"Internationale."** A grizzled old soldier was sobbing like a child. **Alexandra Kollontai** rapidly winked the tears back. The immense sound rolled through the hall, burst windows and doors and soared into the quiet sky. "The war is ended! The war is ended!" said a young workman near me, his face shining. And when it was over, as we stood there in a kind of awkward hush, someone in the back of the room shouted, "Comrades! Let us remember those who have died for liberty!" Se we began to sing the Funeral March, that slow, melancholy and yet triumphant chant, so Russian and so moving. The *Internationale* is an alien air, after all, The

Funeral March seemed the very soul of those dark masses whose delegates sat in this hall, building from their obscure visions a new Russia—and perhaps more . . .

For this did they lie there, the martyrs of March, in their cold Brotherhood Grave on Mars Field; for this thousands and tens of thousands had died in the prisons, in exile, in Siberian mines. It had not come as they expected it would come, nor as the *intelligentsia* desired it; but it had come—rough, strong, impatient of formulas, contemptuous or sentimentalism; *real* . . .

Lenin was reading the Decree on Land . . .

At two o'clock the Land Decree was put to vote, with only one against and the peasant delegates wild with joy . . . So plunged the Bolsheviki ahead, irresistible, overriding hesitation and the opposition—the only people in Russia who had a definite programme of action while the others talked for eight long months . . .

It was almost seven when we woke the sleeping conductors and motor-men of the street-cars which the Street Railway Workers' Union always kept waiting at Smolny to take the Soviet delegates to their homes. In the crowded car there was less happy hilarity than the night before, I thought. Many looked anxious; perhaps they were saying to themselves, "Now we are masters, how can we do our will?"

13. Alexander Blok: The Twelve

The symbolist poet Alexander Blok attempted to capture the mood and spirit of the October Revolution in his poem The Twelve, *written in January 1918, from which the following excerpts are taken. Blok's subjects are twelve Red Guards, the paramilitary forces of the Bolsheviks. This revolutionary militia was anarchistic in its outlook and brutal in its actions; to Blok, the Red Guard symbolized the most basic forces unleashed in the events of 1917. The action takes place in a blizzard, which Blok uses to symbolize the Revolution.*

II

The wind plays up: snow flutters down.
Twelve men are marching through the town.

Their rifle-butts on black slings sway.
Lights left, right, left, wink all the way . . .

Abridged from Blok, Alexander, *The Twelve and Other Poems*. Translated by J. Stallworthy and P. France, 145–58. New York: Oxford University Press, 1970.

Cap tilted, fag drooping, every one
looks like a jailbird on the run.

Freedom, freedom,
down with the cross!

Rat-a-tat-tat!

It's cold, boys, and I'm numb!

Rat-a-tat-tat!

Lights left, right, left, lights all the way . . .
Rifles on their shoulders sway . . .

Keep A Revolutionary Step!
The Relentless Enemy Will Not Stop!

Grip your gun like a man, brother!
Let's have a crack at Holy Russia,
Mother
Russia
with her big, fat arse!
Freedom, freedom! Down with the cross!

III

The lads have all gone to the wars
to serve in the Red Guard—
to serve in the Red Guard—
and risk their hot heads for the cause.

Hell and damnation,
life is such fun
with a ragged greatcoat
and a Jerry gun!

To smoke the nobs out of their holes
we'll light a fire through all the world,
a bloody fire through all the world—
Lord, bless our souls!

. . . .

X

Still the storm rages gust upon gust.
What weather! What a storm!

At arm's length you can only just
make out your neighbour's form.

Snow twists into a funnel,
a towering tunnel . . .

"Oh, what a blizzard! . . . Jesus Christ!"
Watch it, Pete, cut out that rot!
You fool, what did Christ and his cross
ever do for the likes of us?
Look at your hands. Aren't they hot
with the blood of the girl you shot?

Keep A Revolutionary Step!
The Enemy Is Near And Won't Let Up!

Forward, and forward again
the working men!

XI

Abusing God's name as they go,
all twelve march onward into snow . . .
prepared for anything,
regretting nothing . . .

Their rifles at the ready
for the unseen enemy
in back streets, side roads
where only snow explodes
its shrapnel, and through quag-
mire drifts where the boots drag . . .
before their eyes
throbs a red flag.

Left, right,
the echo replies.

Keep your eyes skinned
lest the enemy strike!

Into their faces day and night
bellows the wind
without a break . . .

Forward, and forward again
the working men!

14. Dissolution of the Constituent Assembly

The Constituent Assembly was Russia's first democratically elected assembly. As such, it truly represented Russia's voters. Of the 703 delegates, 380 were SRs, and only 168 were Bolsheviks. It met on January 18, 1918, with the Bolshevik leaders having already determined to dissolve it if it did not endorse a pro-Bolshevik program. The leader of the SR party, Victor Chernov, was elected president of the Assembly; the following is his description of the events of that day.

When we, the newly elected members of the Constituent Assembly, entered the Tauride Palace, the seat of the Assembly in Petrograd, on January 18, 1918, we found that the corridors were full of armed guards. They were masters of the building, crude and brazen. At first they did not address us directly, and only exchanged casual observations to the effect that "this guy should get a bayonet between his ribs" or "it wouldn't be bad to put some lead into this one." When we entered the large hall, it was still empty. The Bolshevik deputies had not yet appeared.

The Assembly hall was gradually filled by the deputies. Near the dais were placed armed guards. The public gallery was crowded to overflowing. Here and there glittered rifle muzzles.

At last all the deputies had gathered in a tense atmosphere. The left sector was evidently waiting for something. From our benches rose Deputy Lordkipanidze, who said in a calm, businesslike voice that, according to an old parliamentary custom, the first sitting should be presided over by the senior deputy. The senior was S.P. Shvetsov, an old Socialist Revolutionary (SR).

As soon as Shvetsov's imposing figure appeared on the dais, somebody gave a signal, and a deafening uproar broke out. The stamping of feet, hammering on the desks and howling made an infernal noise. The public in the gallery and the Bolshevik allies, the Left Socialist Revolutionaries, joined in the tumult. The guards clapped their rifle butts on the floor. From various sides guns were trained on Shvetsov. He took the President's bell, but the tinkling was drowned in the noise. He put it back on the table and somebody immediately grabbed it and handed it over, like a trophy, to the representative of the Sovnarkom [Council of People's Commissars], Sverdlov. Taking advantage of a moment of comparative silence, Shvetsov managed to pronounce the sacramental phrase: "The session of the Constituent Assembly is open." These words evoked a new din of protest. Shvetsov slowly left the dais and joined us. He was replaced by Sverdlov, who opened the session for the second

Abridged from vonMohrenschildt, D., ed., *The Russian Revolution of 1917*, 268–72. New York: Oxford University Press, 1971.

time, but now in the name of the Soviets, and presented its "platform." This was an ultimatum: we had just to vote Aye or No.

In the election of the Assembly's President, the Bolsheviks presented no candidate of their own. They voted for Maria Spiridonova, nominated by the Left SRs. Later they threw Spiridonova into jail and tormented her until she was on the verge of insanity. But at this moment they wanted to take full advantage of her popularity and reputation as a martyr in the struggle against Tsarism. My nomination as candidate for the Presidency received even greater support than had been expected. Some leftist peasants evidently could not bring themselves to oppose their own "*muzhik* minister." I obtained 244 votes against 150.

I delivered my inauguration address, making vigorous efforts to keep self-control. Every sentence of my speech was met with outcries, some ironical, others spiteful, often buttressed by the brandishing of guns. Bolshevik deputies surged forward to the dais. Conscious that the stronger nerves would win, I was determined not to yield to provocation. I said that the nation had made its choice, that the composition of the Assembly was a living testimony to the people's yearning for Socialism, and that its convention marked the end of the hazy transition period. Land reform, I went on, was a foregone conclusion: the land would be equally accessible to all who wished to till it. The Assembly, I said, would inaugurate an era of active foreign policy directed toward peace.

I finished my speech amidst a cross-fire of interruptions and cries. It was now the turn of the Bolshevik speakers—Skvortsov and Bukharin. During their delivery, our sector was a model of restraint and self-discipline. We maintained a cold, dignified silence. The Bolshevik speeches, as usual, were shrill, clamorous, provocative and rude, but they could not break the icy silence of our majority. As President, I was bound in duty to call them to order for abusive statements. But I know that this was precisely what they expected. Since the armed guards were under their orders, they wanted clashes, incidents and perhaps a brawl. So I remained silent.

The Social Democratic Tseretelli rose to answer the Bolsheviks. They tried to "scare" him by levelling at him a rifle from the gallery and brandishing a gun in front of his face. I had to restore order—but how? Appeals to maintain the dignity of the Constituent Assembly evoked an even greater noise, at times turning into a raving fury. Dybenko and other demagogues called for more and more assaults. Lenin, in the government box, demonstrated his contempt for the Assembly by lounging in his chair and putting on the air of a man who was bored to death. I threatened to clear the gallery of the yelling public. Though this was an empty threat, since the guards were only waiting for the order to "clear" us out of the hall, it proved temporarily effective. Tseretelli's calm and dignified manner helped to restore peace.

There was a grim significance in the outburst that broke loose when a middle-of-the-road deputy, Severtsov-Odoyesky, started to speak Ukrainian. In the Assembly the Bolsheviks did not want to hear any language except

Russian. I was compelled to state emphatically that in the new Russia, each nationality had the right to use its own language whenever it pleased.

When it appeared that we refused to vote the Soviet "platform" without discussion, the Bolsheviks walked out of the sitting in a body. They returned to read a declaration charging us with counter-revolution and stating that our fate would be decided by organs which were in charge of such things. Soon after that the Left SRs also made up their minds. Just before the discussion of the land reform started, their representative, I. Z. Steinberg, declared that they were in disagreement with the majority, and left the Assembly.

We knew that the Bolsheviks were in conference, discussing what to do next. I felt sure that we would be arrested. But it was of utmost importance for us to have a chance to say the last word. I declared that the next point on the agenda was the land reform. At this moment somebody pulled at my sleeve.

"You have to finish now. There are orders from the People's Commissar."

Behind me stood a stocky sailor, accompanied by his armed comrades.

"What People's Commissar?"

"We have orders. Anyway, you cannot stay here any longer. The lights will be turned out in a minute. And the guards are tired."

"The members of the Assembly are also tired but cannot rest until they have fulfilled the task entrusted to them by the people—to decide on the land reform and the future form of government."

And leaving the guards no time to collect themselves, I proceeded to read the main paragraphs of the Land Bill, which our party had prepared long ago. But time was running short. Reports and debates had to be omitted. Upon my proposal, the Assembly voted six basic points of the bill. It provided that all land was to be turned into common property, with every tiller possessing equal rights to use it. Amidst incessant shouts: "That's enough! Stop it now! Clear the hall!" the other points of the bill were voted.

Fearing that the lights would be extinguished, somebody managed to procure candles. It was essential that the future form of government be voted upon immediately. Otherwise the Bolsheviks would not fail to charge the Assembly with having left the door open for the restoration of the monarchy. The motion for a republican form of government was carried unanimously.

In the dawn of a foggy and murky morning I declared a recess until noon.

At the exit a palefaced man pushed his way to me and beseeched me in a trembling voice not to use my official car. A bunch of murderers, he said, was waiting for me. He admitted that he was a Bolshevik, but his conscience revolted against this plot.

I left the building, surrounded by a few friends. We saw several men in sailor's uniforms loitering near my car. We decided to walk. We had a long distance to go, and when I arrived home I learned that rumors were in circulation that the Constituent Assembly had dispersed, and that Chernov and Tseretelli had been shot.

At noon several members of the Assembly were sent on reconnaissance. They reported that the door of the Tauride Palace was sealed and guarded by a patrol with machine guns and two pieces of field artillery. Later in the day a decree of the Sovnarkom was published by which the Constituent Assembly was "dissolved."

Thus ended Russia's first and last democratic parliament.

15. Terrorism: The Cheka

With the forcible dissolution of the freely elected Constituent Assembly, the Bolsheviks made it clear that their regime was not to be democratic and as a result opposition increased. Defining all opposition as counterrevolutionism, the Bolsheviks in 1918 instituted a policy of terror, implemented by the Cheka. The head of the Cheka, Felix Dzerzhinsky, defined the Cheka's role, in a 1918 interview.

We stand for organized terror—this should be frankly admitted. Terror is an absolute necessity during times of revolution. Our aim is to fight against the enemies of the Soviet Government and of the new order of life. Among such enemies are our political adversaries, as well as bandits, speculators, and other criminals who undermine the foundations of the Soviet Government. To these we show no mercy. We terrorize the enemies of the Soviet Government in order to stop crime at its inception . . .

We judge quickly. In most cases only a day passes between the apprehension of the criminal and his sentence. But this does not mean that our sentences are groundless . . . When confronted with evidence criminals in almost every case confess; and what argument can have greater weight than a criminal's own confession?

16. The Cheka in Action

In February 1918, the following order was issued to implement the goal announced by Dzerzhinsky:

To All Soviets

The All-Russian Extraordinary Commission to Fight Counter-Revolution, Sabotage, and Speculation asks the (local) Soviets to proceed at once to seek out, arrest, and shoot immediately all members . . . connected in one form or another with counter-revolutionary organizations . . . (1) agents of enemy spies, (2) counter-revolutionary agitators, (3) speculators, (4) organizers of

---

Abridged from Bunyan, J., *Intervention, Civil War and Communism in Russia, 1918,* 227. Baltimore: Johns Hopkins Press, 1936.
Bunyan, *Intervention,* 576.

revolts . . . against the Soviet Government, (5) those going to the Don to join the **Kaledin-Kornilov band** and the Polish counter-revolutionary legions, (6) buyers and sellers of arms to be used by the counter-revolutionary bourgeoisie—all these are to be shot on the spot . . . when caught red-handed in the act.

The All-Russian Cheka

17. The Civil War

The attitude of the peasants in the years following the Revolution was described in a piece appearing in the newspaper Our Age *before it was closed down by the Bolsheviks in 1918.*

A DAY IN THE VILLAGE

Colorless, lazy, tedious Riazan has not changed much since the days of Gogol. The raven continues as of old to clamor from the church steeples. All is quiet in the city except for a dance here and there.

In the **uezds** it is frightful. The sleepy Russian village has been aroused by Bolshevism and threatens to destroy everything in sight. In the robbing and killing of landlords Riazan **Gubernia** is notorious . . . conditions are worst in the localities where the deserters and the hidden stills are more numerous . . .

Father Alexander and I took a walk through the village.

"Take note," said the Father, "of the people's blindness . . . and the use that is being made of it . . . At the time of the elections (Constituent Assembly) the women came to me to ask how to vote and while doing so kept looking around to see if anyone was listening. Soldiers went from hut to hut telling the occupants that if they did not vote the Bolshevik ticket their cows, grain, and huts would be taken from them."

While talking we arrived at the schoolhouse . . . A meeting had been called to hear a lecture on how good the Bolsheviks are and what they would give to the people and . . . why other parties were bad. A soldier was reading from a paper. It was not quite clear who sent him here, whether the Riazan Soviet or an emissary of the People's Commissars . . .

During the reading there appeared the commissar himself, in soldier's uniform. He walked with a certain assurance, stepped up to the speaker's desk, took off his cap, knocked on the table, and began to talk:

"Comrades! I should like first of all to call your attention to the importance of the period we are living in. It is a time of the freedom of the people, the triumph of the proletariat, and the solution of important problems . . ."

He spoke rather quickly but not altogether ungrammatically. His speech sounded like an article in *Pravda*, but it was quite evident that he had not

Bunyan, *Intervention*, 547–9.

assimilated what he had read. He likened Kerensky to a dog whose tail had been cut off but (said that) "it should have been the head." When he talked about the bourgeoisie he became so excited that it seemed as if his eyes would pop out . . .

I looked at the auditors. They sat there quietly, drinking in everything, believing everything . . . The village believes him who shouts, beats his breast, and foams at the mouth. The last and loudest speaker has the best chance of carrying his audience with him. But I must return to the speaker of the day.

"Comrades," said the orator, "the time has come when every true peasant and proletarian can say and say loudly: 'Enough! Take the land from the landlords! Go through their bags and pocketbooks!' Do you agree with me, Comrades?"

"We agree!" shouted back the younger men, but the women nudged each other and tried to keep from giggling.

The first speaker was followed by the teacher of the school. He did not know the arts of eloquence, he did not jump up and down, did not fume, and could not get the attention of the audience . . . His arguments, too, were childish. "The Bolsheviks," he said "will soon disappear, for how can it be otherwise?" He failed completely.

Father Alexander came next. He had no more than opened his mouth when someone began to make remarks about him.

I left the room and went outside. Three peasants with long beards stood talking, and I approached them.

"How can listen to such rot, lies, and foolishness?" I remarked.

"Who are you?" asked one.

"One of those city fellows," said another.

"Of course, he does not like to let go of his property," added a third.

The meeting ended and we went home. I spent a miserable night. My room was cold, the baby cried, and the wind howled . . .

When I awoke in the morning and looked out I noticed a streak of light against the grey sky. Later I learned that it was the flames from one of the manor houses which had been set on fire . . .

On my way to the station I passed a number of peasant carts, loaded down with furniture, pictures, and a piano. The piano was without its top and rested on its side. A peasant woman was steadying it with one hand and striking the keys with the other . . .

The train was more than crowded. Every bit of space, including the aisle and the toilet, was occupied. The air was so thick that one almost choked . . . But even under these conditions a young soldier made a speech. He explained the origin of the bourgeoisie:

"Once upon a time there lived Adam and Eve. They had many children. The children settled in villages and cities. In the cities there grew up 'individuals.' These 'individuals' are people of strong will. They united with the priests, that is to say, with all kinds of clergy, and through this combination the bourgeoisie came into existence. What a bourgeoisie! It has been crushing us and it is about time that we got rid of it . . . Tolstoy said the same thing . . ."

I broke in with the question, "What did Tolstoy say?"

He gave me a wicked look of contempt . . . spat on the floor, and turned his back on me. . . .

Russia has lost herself in the darkness. Lord of Heaven, lead Russia out of the darkness!

18. The Peasant's Apology

John Rickman, who provides this anecdote, spent the years 1916–1918 in Russia where he worked as a physician with the Friends' War Victims Relief Unit. He presents this story as typifying an attitude he found among peasants of that time, one that seems to have been formed long before the Revolution of 1917.

Some time before the Bolsheviks were even heard of in our part of Russia, I was driving at dusk through a village on my way back to hospital when a drunken peasant jumped on to the runners of the sledge and demanded that I should stop and treat his headache. He tried to drag me from the sledge by force, so I put my foot on the pit of his stomach and pushed him into a snowdrift. His manner and the strong language he used when he rose were such that a more exact diagnosis and a more medical treatment of his condition did not seem to be indicated. My driver, remarking that the fellow would have a worse head next morning, whipped up the horses and drove on. The trivial incident passed out of my mind.

One day, months later when the snow had gone, an unusual thing happened. A peasant in the waiting-room of the out-patients asked to be seen *last*, in contrast to the usual clamour to be seen first. When all the other comers had been attended to, the *moujik*, [peasant man] standing rather shyly by the door, said "Doctor, don't you recognize me?" I looked at him carefully and said I did not, then turning to the out-patient register, asked when he had been before and what his trouble was. He said he had never been before and had no ailment, but before proceeding he must know that I recognized him . . . [He then began his story.]

"Do you remember months ago in the village of _____ a drunken man set upon you as you were driving through and demanded that you should stop?" The scene came back in a flash. "And do you remember," I said, smiling, "the doctor who put his foot in that man's belly and gave a shove? Damn it all, man, we were quits."

Abridged from Gorer, G., and Rickman, J., *Great Russian Peoples*, 55–61. London: Cresset Press, 1949.

"Now doctor, don't make a joke of it. It's a serious matter." I thought I must have injured him, so apologized and asked him to tell me all about it.

He then began a long story. He had been drunk and felt sick and thick in the head; so seeing me, he suddenly had the bright idea of demanding an instant cure. But his headache made him angry and he tried to do this by force. He had attacked me and that was wrong. Before he asked my forgiveness, it was necessary that I should know exactly who he was and recall the circumstances. He then very shyly produced a document which ran roughly as follows:

This is to certify that I (here there was a space for my name) have received the apology of _____ _____, of the village of _____, on the (space for the date). And this is also to certify that the elders of the said village of _____, after careful examination are convinced that _____ _____'s apologies are from the heart. (Date, signatures of village elders and crosses of attestation.)

The whole thing seemed fantastic; an apology was in the circumstances odd but understandable, but the certificate seemed all out of proportion. I made up my mind to see the village elders and try to clear the matter up.

A few days later my round lay through that village and I called on several of the elders. They said they had been horrified by the attack on me. I had done them no harm, on the contrary had been diligent for their good, and it was necessary to eradicate the evil disposition which had shown itself amongst them that night. I pointed out that my quite adequate physical defence had prevented injury to me being laid on the man's conscience, and also that I had attended patients in the village after the episode just as before, so they need not fear the loss of my assistance; but that was not the point. They felt the attack to be a stain on the honour of the village. They had reproached him the next day and asked him to apologize. He was defiant in refusal . . . Then, since as a group they had not been able to persuade him to apologize, they changed their policy and approached him as individuals. They also got his friends to join in their efforts and for weeks the poor devil was followed wherever he went with reproachful eyes. One day he burst upon them with the news that he would go and apologize. But his manner of saying it did not satisfy them; it was hasty and still somewhat defiant; his heart had not changed. They accepted his consent to apologize as a good sign but not necessarily as an indication of true repentance. Gradually he became more passive and waited patiently to be "released" by the village elders from the yoke of guilt. He then came to me with their certificate . . .

They wished me to know that they felt themselves also to be involved in the insult and hence also in the restoration of the honour of the village.

This was their explanation. There were, of course, other reasons for dealing with me in this way. A physician was an object of value to them. They were helplessly dependent on him and his goodwill, and however familiar he might be as a visitor in their homes and at their councils, they *as a group* could not replace or reproduce him because he belonged to a different civilization, that of the metropolis and of international communications. Towards all members of this civilization they looked with abject submission, envy, and sometimes hatred; from the metropolitan civilization came to them tax gatherers, political police (civil order was maintained, as this story shows, by the villagers themselves in a most unbureaucratic way), landlords (for the most part absentee), priests, a few schoolteachers, and a very few doctors. These, one and all, belonged to the metropolis, not to the village. Over all loomed the distant and terrible, revered and incomprehensible figure of the Czar, who, however widely his characteristics ranged over everything Russian, certainly was not "one of us" . . .

This little episode shows something of the way in which the villagers were bound together by ties of love and how they kept their spirit of their community intact. This spirit gave the members strength when they were in accord with it, and they lived in misery and isolation when they broke, in thought or mood, with the opinion and sentiment of their neighbours. The episode also shows how difficult it was for them to include a member of the alien caste in their way of thought and living.

* * * * *

Some of the social history of the next few years is well known. The Bolsheviks came to power and made all things new. The peasants were collectivized, many were forcibly moved to public works, many more were driven by starvation to seek a living in the towns. The new social unit became the factory, and the old village organization ceased to be typical for the Russian people. But its spirit did not die.

Seventeen years passed, and an Intourist [Soviet travel service for foreign visitors] traveller brought back from one of the large new cities a collection of factory wall-newspapers (the placards on which anyone may freely criticize anyone and anything except the essentials of the new regime). Most of the contents related to the factory statistics, how the shock workers were breaking records, sport, the factory theater, music news, and so forth. Down in a corner (always the same corner of each issue) there was a series of notes which at first glance seemed of the most trivial significance. But their spirit was reminiscent of the village I have mentioned, and heaven knows how many thousand like it. The notes ran somewhat as follows: "We do not like the way Sonia ——— does her work. She doesn't show the right spirit; she slacks." Several times was she thus publicly reproved. Later she was said to show signs of adopting the proper attitude. Finally Sonia was declared an enthusiastic worker who had entered truly into the spirit of the Revolution.

On reading this my mind went back to the peasant whose heart was changed by the silent but not harsh pressure of the group; the steps in this re-entry into the community seemed to be remarkably similar in the two cases; in spite of the greatest imaginable change in the economic and political life the behaviour of the group to a wayward member remained the same. The village spirit, the need to feel that everyone was "one of us," had re-emerged; and I have no doubt that this plays its part in strengthening and consolidating a regime which often seems to us in the West to be based only on force.

19. Isaac Babel: Prishchepa's Vengeance

The horrors of the Civil War also appear in fiction and nowhere more eloquently than in the short stories of Isaac Babel, a Jew from Odessa who accompanied Budenny, the great Bolshevik General, during the Red Army campaigns against the Poles in 1920–21. The following is one story from his collection Red Cavalry. *In these very short stories Babel the intellectual describes with a mixture of outrage and admiration the violent, passionate nature of the Cossacks with whom he served.*

I am on my way to Leszniow, where the Divisional Staff is quartered. My companion, as before, is Prishchepa, a young Cossack from the **Kuban**—a tireless ruffian who has been turned out of the Communist Party, a future rag-and-bone man, a carefree syphilitic, and a happy-go-lucky fraud. He wears a crimson Circassian coat of fine cloth, and a downy Caucasian hood is thrown back over his shoulders. On our journeys he has told me his story.

A year ago, Prishchepa ran away from the Whites. In revenge, these took his parents as hostages and put them to death. Their property was seized by the neighbors. When the Whites were driven out of the Kuban, Prishchepa returned to his native settlement.

It was early morning, daybreak. The peasants' slumber sighed in the acrid stuffiness. Prishchepa hired an official cart and went about the settlement collecting his phonographs, wooden **kvass**-jugs, and the towels his mother had embroidered. He went out into the street in a black felt cloak, a curved dagger at his belt. The cart plodded along behind. Prishchepa went from neighbor to neighbor, leaving behind him a trail of blood-stained footprints. In the huts where he found gear that had belonged to his mother, a pipe that had been his father's, he left old women stabbed through and through, dogs hung above the wells, icons defiled with excrement. The inhabitants of the settlement watched his progress sullenly, smoking their pipes. The young Cossacks were scattered over the steppe, keeping the score. And the score mounted up and up—and still the settlement remained silent.

When he had made an end, Prishchepa went back to his despoiled home and arranged the furniture he had taken back in the places he remembered from childhood. Then he sent for vodka, and shutting himself up in the hut, he drank for two whole days and nights, singing, weeping, and hewing the furniture with his Circassian saber.

Abridged from Babel, I., *The Collected Stories.* Edited and translated by W. Morison, 108–9. New York: New American Library, 1955.

On the third night the settlement saw smoke rise from Prishchepa's hut. Torn, scorched, staggering, the Cossack led the cow out of the shed, put his revolver in its mouth and fired. The earth smoked beneath him. A blue ring of flame flew out of the chimney and melted away, while in the stall the young bull that had been left behind bellowed piteously. The fire shone as bright as Sunday. Then Prishchepa untied his horse, leaped into the saddle, threw a lock of his hair into the flames, and vanished.

20. Murder of the Royal Family

While ex-Tsar Nicholas and his family were in themselves no threat to the Bolsheviks, their presence constituted a symbol and a potential rallying point for the more conservative opposition. The Romanovs were moved from Tobolsk to Ekaterinburg in the Urals in April 1918. The local soviet was hostile to them from the start, and that hostility increased during July, as the anti-Bolshevik Czech Legion drew closer to Ekaterinburg. Acting on orders from Moscow, the locals decided on action. The following is a description by a local workman, who witnessed the events of July 16.

In the evening of July 16th, between 7 and 8 P.M., when the time for my duty had just begun, Commandant Yurovsky [the head of the guard] ordered me to take all the Nagan revolvers from the guards and to bring them to him. I took twelve revolvers from the sentries as well as from some other of the guards, and brought them to the commandant's office. Yurovsky said to me: "We must shoot *them* all tonight, so notify the guards not to be alarmed if they hear shots." I understood, therefore, that Yurovsky had it in his mind to shoot the whole of the Tsar's family, as well as the doctor and the servants who lived with them, but I did not ask him where or by whom the decision had been made. I must tell you that in accordance with Yurovsky's order the boy who assisted the cook was transferred in the morning to the guardroom (in the Popov house). The lower floor of Ipatiev's house was occupied by the Letts from the Letts Commune, who had taken up their quarters there after Yurovsky was made commandant. They were ten in number. At about ten o'clock in the evening, in accordance with Yurovsky's order, I informed the guards not to be alarmed if they should hear firing. About midnight Yurovsky woke up the Tsar's family. I do not know if he told them the reason they had been awakened and where they were to be taken, but I positively affirm that it was Yurovsky who entered the rooms occupied by the Tsar's family. Yurovsky had not ordered me or Dobrynin to awaken the family. In about an hour the whole of the family, the doctor, the maid and the waiters got up, washed and dressed themselves. Just before Yurovsky went to awaken the family, two

---

Pethybridge, *Witnesses to the Russian Revolution*, 290–2.

members of the Extraordinary Commission [of the Ekaterinburg Soviet] arrived at Ipatiev's house. Shortly after one o'clock A.M., the Tsar, the Tsaritsa, their four daughters, the maid, the doctor, the cook and the waiter left their rooms. The Tsar carried the heir in his arms. The Emperor and the heir were dressed in "gimnasterkas" [soldiers' shirts] and wore caps. The Empress and her daughters were dressed but their heads were uncovered. The Emperor, carrying the heir, preceded them. The Empress, her daughters and the others followed him. Yurovsky, his assistant and the two above-mentioned members of the Extraordinary Commission accompanied them. I was also present. During my presence none of the Tsar's family asked any questions. They did not weep or cry. Having descended the stairs to the first floor, we went out into the court, and from there by the second door (counting from the gate) we entered the ground floor of the house. When the room (which adjoins the store-room with a sealed door) was reached, Yurovsky ordered chairs to be brought, and his assistant brought three chairs. One chair was given to the Emperor, one to the Empress, and the third to the heir. The Empress sat by the wall by the window, near the black pillar of the arch. Behind her stood three of the daughters (I knew their faces very well, because I had seen them every day when they walked in the garden, but I didn't know their names). The heir and the Emperor sat side by side almost in the middle of the room. Doctor Botkin stood behind the heir. The maid, a very tall woman, stood at the left of the door leading to the store-room; by her side stood one of the Tsar's daughters (the fourth). Two servants stood against the wall on the left from the entrance of the room.

The maid carried a pillow. The Tsar's daughters also brought small pillows with them. One pillow was put on the Empress's chair; another on the heir's chair. It seemed as if all of them guessed their fate, but not one of them uttered a single sound. At this moment eleven men entered the room: Yurovsky, his assistant, two members of the Extraordinary Commission, and seven Letts. Yurovsky ordered me to leave, saying: "Go on to the streets, see if there is anybody there, and wait to see whether the shots have been heard." I went out to the court, which was enclosed by a fence, but before I got to the street I heard the firing. I returned to the house immediately (only two or three minutes having elapsed), and upon entering the room where the execution had taken place, I saw that all the members of the Tsar's family were lying on the floor with many wounds in their bodies. The blood was running in streams. The doctor, the maid and two waiters had also been shot. When I entered the heir was still alive and moaned a little. Yurovsky went up and fired two or three more times at him. Then the heir was still.

The sight of the murder and the smell of blood made me sick. Before the assassination, when Yurovsky distributed the revolvers, he gave me one but, as I said before, I did not take any part in the murder. After the assassination Yurovsky told me to bring some guards to wash away the blood in the room. On the way to Popov's house I met two of the Senior Guards, Ivan Starkov and Constantin Dobrynin. They were running in the direction of Ipatiev's house. Dobrynin asked me: "Has Nicholas II been shot?" I answered that Nicholas and the whole of his family had been shot. I brought twelve or fifteen guards back with me to the house. These men carried the dead bodies out to the motor lorry that waited near the entrance and the bodies were placed on stretchers made from bedsheets and shafts of sledges taken from the yard. When they were loaded on the truck they were wrapped in soldiers' clothing . . . The members of the Extraordinary Commission sat on the lorry and the truck drove off. I do not know in what direction the lorry went, neither do I know where the bodies were taken.

21. Victims of the Red Terror

While many targets of the terror were from royal or noble backgrounds, its victims were from all walks of life. Typical of its operation is the following account of a single day's (September 17, 1918) work by the Cheka of the Western Region.

The session took place in the presence of seven members of the Extraordinary Commission and two members of the Central Collegium of the Russian Communist Party.

The following were arraigned:

1. Antonevich, S., former (army) officer, an active participant in a counter-revolutionary plot to overthrow Soviet rule. *Decision:* He is to be shot.
2. Gepner, Vladimir, former chief of police of Smolensk. *Decision:* He is to be shot.
3. Korshonboim, former assistant inspector of Smolensk Prison. He flogged political prisoners while holding the position of prison inspector. *Decision:* He is to be turned over to the People's Court and his case is transferred to the Department of Justice.
4. Revknev, I., arrested for serving in the Polish Corps. *Decision:* He is to be released from arrest in view of the fact that he was only a private in the Polish Corps.
5. Sorokin, V., former general and head of the secret police. *Decision:* He is to be shot.
6. Mikhailov, M., a criminal . . . charged with participation in murders and robberies. *Decision:* He is to be shot.
7. Romanov, Zakhar, former police guard . . . notorious for cruelty to peasants. *Decision:* He is to be shot.
8. Kondratiuk, G., charged with drunkenness and murder. *Decision:* He is to be transferred to the People's Court.

Bunyan, *Intervention*, 246–50.

9. Brazhko, charged with drunkenness and murder. *Decision:* Three months in jail.
10. Toptunov, Leiba, charged with giving a bribe. *Decision:* He is to be released from arrest and to receive his money back.
11. Goncharov, E., Piroga, A., Kozlov, and Egorov, members of the militia, charged with violation of official duties. *Decision:* They are to be released.
12. Dorman, M., former general, involved in the organization of a counter-revolutionary plot against the Soviet Government. *Decision:* He is to be shot.
13. Dorman, Vladimir, son of General Dorman . . . *Decision:* Being only fifteen years old, he is to be released.
14. Vitkevich, Maria, proprietress of Smolensk, charged with insulting the Soviet Government. *Decision:* She is to be fined ten thousand rubles and freed from arrest upon payment of the fine.
15. Shustov, Evdokim, a store employee, arrested for having a false permit to carry arms. *Decision:* Because he belongs to the proletarian class Shustov is to be released from arrest.
16. Gladyshev, V., former police official of Smolensk. *Decision:* He is to be shot.
17. Filippov. I., Ventov, F., criminals. *Decision:* They are to be shot.
18. Lukstin, A., arrested for delivering 57,000 rubles to a White Guard organization. *Decision:* He is to be shot.

[An additional 36 names follow, of whom 22 are sentenced to be shot.]

Chairman of the Extraordinary
Commission of the Western
Region

22. The Famine of 1921–22

The famine of 1921–22, caused by drought and the ravages of the Civil War, was so devastating that the Soviet government called for outside help. Among those who responded were Quaker relief organizations from the United States. The following account of the situation in Samara, eight hundred miles southeast of Moscow, is from a report filed by Anna Haines, representative of the American Friends Service Committee in Russia.

I could hear the children crying two blocks away as I approached one of the homes for abandoned children in Samara, the central city of the famine area of Russia. A steady wail that kept up like a moan grew louder as we got nearer. The nurses could do nothing except to go around every morning and

From a report published by The American Friends Service Committee, Philadelphia, 1922.

separate the babies that were going to die that day; and they went around at different times later and felt them to see if they were cold. In the evening those who had died during the day were gathered together and placed in heaps outside the buiding. A garbage-cart stopped each night and the baby bodies were loaded in. The garbage-carts stopped in the same way before all of the children's institutions in Samara and the other cities in the Volga region.

Children's homes, which are emptied of dead babies only to be refilled by the constant flow of abandoned children from the country; men and women and young children falling dead on the street from hunger; farm machinery, which in Russia is more precious than human life at the present time, lying scrapped by the roadside and rusting to pieces, tell the story of the extent and horror of the famine which is destroying the lives of 15,000,000 people in the greatest grain belt of Russia.

Though most of us are more familiar with the larger outlines of the Russian famine story, it is still hard to understand the fact that the great Volga Valley, which has always been the granary of Russia, supplying not only its own population, but most of the rest of European Russia and other areas of the world with wheat and rye, is now bare of any grain. Over an area 800 miles long by 500 miles wide there fell during April, May and June of this year—the critical growing months of the grain crop—less than 2.5 inches, the normal being 14 inches, of rain, and the temperatures averaged 12.6 degrees Fahrenheit hotter than the average for the last seventeen years. While 938,000 tons of grain were needed by this area for its own consumption, but 69,000 were produced. Many of the peasants with whom I talked said that all the grain which their land had produced could have been held in their double hands, and this meant rations for a whole family for a year.

It is impossible at the present time to state accurately the death statistics, but the population of the Volga grain area is approximately 20,000,000, and all of these are vitally affected by the lack of food. We do know, however, that in the children's institutions famine is already making itself felt in dreadful figures. In the institutions for children under three years of age there is a death rate of 90 per cent, and in the homes for older children, those from twelve to fifteen years, there is a death rate of 75 per cent.

A mandate given me by the Commissar of Health, and a working knowledge of the Russian language, enabled me to go to the peasants myself without an interpreter and talk to them personally concerning the conditions under which they were living. I also had the privilege of speaking to the priests, who would be likely to give as opposite statistics from the Soviet figures as truth would allow, because these groups are usually the extreme poles of information in Russia. The members of the co-operative stores also gave valuable information, as they have the best knowledge of the economic situation there today.

We started from Moscow for our trip down into Samara, the largest city affected by the famine. It is situated on the Volga, and is a city of about 300,000 inhabitants, now very much increased in population by the refugees who are constantly pouring in from the country regions. Passing on to Buzuluk, a town formerly containing 20,000 people, now reduced to 12,000 because of the flight of those who could reach Siberia, we traveled out through the country regions.

The steppe ordinarily has no trees; it is a level, slightly rolling plain, with village after village scattered about five or ten miles apart. This fall it looked as though a prairie fire had swept over it. Farms and areas which are usually green or golden with harvest were burned almost black. What grass had grown was only a stunted growth on the surface of the ground. Every few rods as we went along we would scare away the carrion birds which were feasting on the carcasses of the dead horses and dogs that had died along the roadside. There was a continuous stream of refugees going our way, and we passed others going in the opposite direction. They did not much care which way they were going—they were just going to search for food. Some were coming from Uralsk and going to Ufa; some were going from Ufa to Uralsk. One family had passed across the country in June with two horses, small children and a baby, and such household utensils as they could carry. They had been traveling from their home to a place which they had been told contained food. When they reached there they found less food in that town than in their own home, and they were now wandering along the way back, saying that they preferred to die at home rather than in a "foreign land." One horse had died; the one they were using was nothing but a bag of bones. The older children were living upon the rinds of watermelons. Their heads were covered with sores and with flies, and the parents were too listless and tired to care for them.

We entered one of the villages along the wide street which makes up the largest part of a Russian village, with little houses, containing one or two rooms apiece, on either side, and stopped that night at the home of what had been one of the richest peasants in the village. His large wooden house with three rooms was an evidence of his wealth. It was surrounded with barnyards and sheds for stock, all of which were now empty. One of the daughters-in-law said that last year they had twelve horses and six cows. The cows had now all been sold or killed, and all the horses had died but one. The girl showed us the kind of bread the ordinary Russian family is using, and has been using for several months. It was made of grass and leaves and bark which had been ground into flour. There were twelve people in that family, and every day all went out into the countryside for several miles to gather the grass and the leaves and the roots. When this had been ground together the pulp of the hoofs of horses was added to hold it together. That was all this family was living on except soup which was made of horse meat. Later in the evening as the family talked, we learned that they understood that it was not possible for all of them to live until spring.

I talked with the Russian priest and asked if next March would not be the worst month for them. He answered, "No, I think not. This month (September) we will be eating the vegetables and the watermelons and the rinds. In October there will still be the grass, and we can make the grass pancakes. In November, when the snow comes, and we can no longer get anything from the fields, we will still have our little reserve of a few potatoes or a little bit of grass flour. In December people will begin to die, and by the first of the year every bit of the reserve will be gone. In March there will be no one alive in the village."

From all parts of the countryside the abandoned children were being brought daily into the children's homes of the larger towns and cities. These homes, which are hastily prepared as emergency quarters, have no equipment at all. For one of the homes in Samara, a house about six rooms had been taken over in July with the expectation of housing sixty children. At the end of August it contained 400 children. There were thirty-one cups and bowls. There were no sanitary arrangements of any kinds, but the nurses tried to bathe the children and wash as many of the lice from them as possible. But it was of little use, as the same dirty clothing had to be put on them again. There was no attempt at any recreation for the children, nor instruction, because those who had been teachers and caretakers were ill themselves with malaria or dysentery. The children were the most unchildlike babies I have ever seen. They lay perfectly motionless, with lifeless eyes. In the homes for older children the workers would allow them to wander about the streets in the hope of picking up stray bits of garbage as food. But the saddest sights were in the homes for the small babies. These babies were fed the same diet as older children and men and women—the grass bread and the meat soup. They could not digest that food, and it meant simply the question of how many hours the child would live. In one of the homes we visited in Samara the death rate was higher than 90 per cent. It was at these houses that the garbage-cart called daily and, after the bodies were piled in, took them off beyond the city for burial in trenches.

What is the government doing in the face of this appalling disaster? The first thing they concentrated their attention upon was the sending of seed corn into this area. The government realized that even the present famine situation would be as nothing compared to conditions next year if every effort were not given to the planting of seed. It was remarkable to find that the peasants, whose horses were dropping in the field, and whose children were starving, could be seen putting the seed into the ground instead of into their families' mouths. The next most important piece of work it is doing is the attempt to get as many of the people as are not actually needed to plough and plant out of this area into regions where the harvest had been good. It is endeavoring to send all foreigners to the countries of their origin. It is also forming colonies which will settle in Siberia. A group is made up of a bootmaker, a carpenter and other handicraftsmen to form a nucleus about which peasants may be gathered and a new community developed. Several thousands had thus been set out; but while in Siberia they will find wood and possibly grain, there are no materials for building, such as iron, nails or glass; and so the lack of these articles will keep the number who can be sent there relatively small. As many food trains as it is possible to equip from the meager stores at Moscow are being sent into the famine provinces; and food, mostly soup, is fed to the children at railroad junctions. In Samara the government train is feeding 4,000 children a day.

Foreign relief has entered. The American Relief Administration will feed 1,250,000 children. But there are more than twelve million men, women and children who will need food as greatly as those who will be fed by this agency. The number of starving people to whom the Quakers will bring food is limited only by the resources which will be at their command. They are now feeding 50,000 children a day, and their organization is complete enough to enable it to expand this feeding to any limit. The people whom the Quakers will save are those who will not be saved by any other agency, and who will surely die before spring unless aid reaches them.

The morning I left Moscow there was printed in "Pravda," the morning newspaper, a simply worded request which had been sent in by a peasant from the famine area who had heard that the people in Moscow were getting a bread ration. He said:

"I come to you from a far country, where the bread and the buckwheat have failed. Only the noisy vultures are busy in the fields where all day the wind whips up the brown dust. Hunger is here. People moan. Their empty bellies swell. The breasts to which the babies turn are dry. You can hear the groans of the people amid the breaking waves of the Volga. You can hear the shower of their tears. You can hear what they cry out, 'Bring help and bring it soon.' "

23. The 1920s: Reduction of Class Distinctions

Of the results of the 1917 Revolution that became apparent during the 1920s, one of the most apparent was the reduction of class distinctions, a social "leveling," here described by the American historian W.H. Chamberlin, writing in 1930.

Two opposed forces are at work in the soul of the present-day Russian; on the one hand is the influence of centuries of semi-Asiatic passivity and deliberation; on the other is Lenin's injunction that Russia must catch up with and outstrip the technical achievements of the leading capitalist countries. Whether Russia ever will acquire the mechanical efficiency of America and Western Europe is a question for the future. In the meantime the rush and roar of modern industrial life seems to recede and subside as one travels from Berlin or some other European capital to Moscow, where there are only a few score taxicabs.

Abridged from Chamberlin, W.H., *Soviet Russia*, 54–5, 397–9. Boston: Little, Brown, 1931.

A trip through the provinces is calculated to strengthen rather than change the external impressions which one derives in Moscow. The centralized Soviet political and economic system tends to place a stamp of uniformity on the country. Everywhere the same products of the same state trusts and syndicates; everywhere the same articles in newspapers which differ chiefly in their titles; everywhere the same "weeks" to promote cooperation, health, national defense, or some other object.

Of course, historical, racial, and architectural differences cannot be obliterated overnight. The various cities of the Soviet Union have their distinctive traits, although the element of differentiation is probably less than in the older towns of Europe . . .

It is only fair to note that the Russian Revolution, while sweeping away even the poor crumbs of civil liberty which existed under the Tsar (a pale and almost powerless parliament, elected on a narrow franchise, a few newspapers which might very cautiously criticize the official viewpoint, etc.), has brought certain social liberties which to the uneducated or scantily educated masses of the people are probably more valuable than the right to vote for rival parties in elections or to write theoretical critical articles. In judging the effect of the absence of civil liberties on the mood of the Russian people it should never be forgotten that the vast majority of these people have not the slightest conception of what these liberties are; that they are not so far removed from the insurgent soldiers who followed the Dekabristi [Decembrists], shouting, "Constantine and Constitutsia!" ("Constantine and a Constitution!") under the impression that "Constitutsia" was Constantine's wife.

What are the social liberties which are associated with the Revolution? First of all, the disappearance of "superior" social classes, based on wealth and birth. The worker does not have to cringe before the **"red director"** of the Soviet factory as, in pre-war times, he cringed before the private owner of the factory. He can write letters to the press complaining of conditions in the factory and suggesting changes, something which a worker would scarcely do with impunity even in democratic capitalist countries, where factories are private and not public concerns.

A peasant once remarked to me: "After the Revolution there was more freedom; I got land." To him freedom meant, not the opportunity to vote for a parliamentary Peasant Party, but the possession of a slice of the landlord's estate. And this identification of land with liberty is a very traditional attitude of mind with the Russian peasantry. It was no accident that one of the revolutionary societies of the nineteenth century called itself "Land and Liberty." It is true that most peasants have not been singing any very loud hymns to liberty since the Communist Party went over to its more radical agrarian policy in the winter of 1927–1928. To the peasant the pressure exerted to make him sell his grain at low fixed prices seems quite as definite an infringement of liberty as the extortion of high rent by the grasping landlord of pre-revolutionary days. But the big landlords have gone forever; it is rather unlikely that the semi-requisitioning methods which have been used in purchasing the peasants' grain during the last two years will last very long.

In general the common man in Russia today has the sense of release, of social liberty, that comes with the disappearances of classes which are visibly above him in wealth and opportunity, culture and social status. When I called on the Soviet governor of an important industrial province, a man who had held high office in the trade-union movement and accompanied a diplomatic delegation to England, I found him in his office wearing the high boots and colorless blouse that constitute part of the distinctive costume of the Russian worker. Walking on the streets or riding on a train he would have been indistinguishable from the textile workers of the province. He certainly represented a different type of official from the decorated "high excellence" who would most probably have held the corresponding post under the Tsar.

Whether the plebeian leveling which characterizes so many fields of Russian social and cultural life is an unmixed blessing is highly debatable. But that it gives to the masses, at least to those of them who have absorbed some of the revolutionary propaganda, a sense of liberty which they did not possess in former times is, I think, undeniable.

24. Bertrand Russell on Lenin

Until he was incapacitated by illness in 1922, Lenin remained the unchallenged leader of the Communist party and hence of the new Soviet regime. Of the many descriptions of Lenin, one of the most interesting is that of Bertrand Russell, the great British philosopher, who visited Lenin in 1920. Russell was known for his left wing political views, but he found Lenin's authoritarianism distasteful.

Soon after my arrival in Moscow I had an hour's conversation with Lenin in English, which he speaks fairly well. An interpreter was present, but his services were scarcely required. Lenin's room is very bare, it contains a big desk, some maps on the walls, two bookcases, and one comfortable chair for visitors, in addition to two and three hard chairs. It is obvious that he has no love of luxury or even comfort. He is very friendly and apparently simple, entirely without a trace of *hauteur*. If one met him without knowing who he was, one would not guess that he is possessed of great power or even that he is in any way eminent. I have never met a personage so destitute of self-importance. He looks at his visitors very closely, and screws up one eye, which seems to increase alarmingly the penetrating power of the other. He laughs a great deal; at first his laugh seems merely friendly and jolly, but gradually I

Abridged from Russell, B., *The Practice and Theory of Bolshevism*, 32–6. New York: Simon & Schuster, 1964.

came to feel it rather grim. He is dictatorial, calm, incapable of fear, extraordinarily devoid of self-seeking, an embodied theory. The materialist conception of history, one feels, is his lifeblood. He resembles a professor in his desire to have the theory understood and in his fury with those who misunderstand or disagree, as also in his love of expounding. I got the impression that he despises a great many people and is an intellectual aristocrat.

The first question I asked him was as to how far he recognized the peculiarity of English economics and political conditions . . . He does not advocate abstention from Parliamentary contests, but participation with a view to making Parliament obviously contemptible. The reasons which make attempts at violent revolution seem to most of us both improbable and undesirable in this country carry no weight with him, and seem to him mere bourgeois prejudices. When I suggested that whatever is possible in England can be achieved without bloodshed, he waved aside the suggestion as fantastic. I got little impression of knowledge or psychological imagination as regards Great Britain. Indeed the whole tendency of Marxianism is against psychological imagination, since it attributes everything in politics to purely material causes.

I asked him next whether he thought it possible to establish communism firmly and fully in a country containing such a large majority of peasants. He admitted that it was difficult and laughed over the exchange the peasant is compelled to make, of food for paper; the worthlessness of Russian paper (money) struck him as comic. But he said—what is no doubt true—that things will right themselves when there are goods to offer to the peasant. For this he looks partly to electrification in industry, which, he says, is a technical necessity in Russia, but will take ten years to complete . . . Of course he looks to the raising of the blockade as the only radical cure; but he was not very hopeful of this being achieved thoroughly or permanently except through revolutions in other countries. Peace between Bolshevik Russia and capitalist countries, he said, must always be insecure; the Entente might be led by weariness and mutual dissensions to conclude peace, but he felt convinced that the peace would be of brief duration. I found in him, as in almost all leading Communists, much less eagerness than existed in our delegation for peace and the raising of the blockade. He believes that nothing of real value can be achieved except through world revolution and the abolition of capitalism; I felt that he regarded the resumption of trade with capitalist countries as a mere palliative of doubtful value . . .

He said that two years ago neither he nor his colleagues thought they could survive against the hostility of the world. He attributes their survival to the jealousies and divergent interests of the different capitalist nations; also to the power of Bolshevik propaganda. He said that Germans had laughed when the Bolsheviks proposed to combat guns with leaflets, but that the event had proved the leaflets quite as powerful . . .

I think if I had met him without knowing who he was, I should not have guessed that he was a great man; he struck me as too opinionated and narrowly orthodox. His strength comes, I imagine, from his honesty, courage, and unwavering faith—religious faith in the Marxian gospel, which takes the place of the Christian martyr's hopes of paradise, except that it is less egotistical. He has as little love of liberty as the Christians, who suffered under Diocletian and retaliated when they acquired power. Perhaps love of liberty is incompatible with wholehearted belief in a panacea for all human ills. If so, I cannot but rejoice in the skeptical temper of the Western world.

25. Vladimir Mayakovsky: **Komsomolskaya**

Upon his death, Lenin was eulogized in many ways and by many people, beginning what has been called "The Lenin Cult." Among the eulogizers was the poet Vladimir Mayakovsky, writing in 1924.

> "Lenin" and "Death"
> > these words are enemies.
> "Lenin" and "Life"
> > are comrades . . .
> Lenin
> > lived
> Lenin
> > lives
> Lenin
> > will live.

26. Lenin's Testament

With Lenin's illness came the struggle to succeed him as party leader, a struggle that erupted openly in 1923. Although extremely ill and almost totally incapacitated, Lenin in December 1922 dictated notes expressing his concern about a party split and his reservations about some of his leading party colleagues. In this document, called his Testament, *Lenin focused particular attention on Stalin and Trotsky. Early in the next month, he added a postscript, attacking Stalin further, following an incident in which Stalin had been rude to Lenin's wife Krupskaya. Interestingly, this seemingly damning statement by Lenin did not prevent Stalin from succeeding him; Stalin was able to minimize the impact of the* Testament *as the product of a sick man's mind.*

As quoted in Tumarkin, N., *Lenin Lives,* 166. Cambridge: Harvard University Press, 1983.
Abridged from Dmytryshyn, B., *USSR: A Concise History,* 436–7. New York: Scribner's, 1978.

By stability of the Central Committee, of which I spoke above, I mean measures against a split, as far as measures can at all be taken . . .

I have in mind stability as a guarantee against a split in the immediate future, and I intend to deal here with a few ideas concerning personal qualities.

I think that from this standpoint the prime factors in the question of stability are such member of the C.C. as Stalin and Trotsky. I think relations between them make up the greater part of the danger of a split . . .

Comrade Stalin, having become Secretary-General, has unlimited authority concentrated in his hands, and I am not sure whether he will always be capable of using that authority with sufficient caution. Comrade Trotsky, on the other hand . . . is distinguished not only by outstanding ability. He is personally perhaps the most capable man in the present C.C., but he has displayed excessive self-assurance and shown excessive preoccupation with the purely administrative side of the work.

These two qualities of the two outstanding leaders of the present C.C. can inadvertently lead to a split, and if our Party does not take steps to avert this, the split may come unexpectedly . . .

Both of these remarks, of course, are made only for the present, on the assumption that both these outstanding and devoted Party workers fail to find an occasion to enhance their knowledge and amend their one-sidedness.

Lenin

ADDITION TO THE LETTER OF DECEMBER 24, 1922

December 25, 1922

Stalin is too rude and this defect, although quite tolerable in our midst and in dealings among us Communists, becomes intolerable in a Secretary-General. That is why I suggest that the comrades think about a way of removing Stalin from that post and appointing another man in his stead who in all other respects differs from Comrade Stalin in having only one advantage, namely, that of being more tolerant, more loyal, more polite and more considerate to the comrades, less capricious, etc. This circumstance may appear to be a negligible detail. But I think that from the standpoint of safeguards against a split and from the standpoint of what I wrote above about the relationship between Stalin and Trotsky it is not a detail, or it is a detail which can assume decisive importance.

27. Stalin: A Lenin Litany

On the eve of Lenin's funeral in January 1924, Stalin delivered a speech that was like a religious catechism, suggesting the possibility that he was assuming the role of high priest of a rapidly growing Lenin cult.

Abridged from Rigby, T.H., ed., *Stalin*, 40–1. Englewood Cliffs, N.J.: Prentice-Hall, 1966.

Departing from us, Comrade Lenin enjoined us to hold high and guard the purity of the great title of member of the Party. We vow to you, Comrade Lenin, that we shall fulfil your behest with honour! . . .

Departing from us, Comrade Lenin enjoined us to guard the unity of our Party as the apple of our eye. We vow to you, Comrade Lenin, that this behest, too, we shall fulfill with honour! . . .

Departing from us, Comrade Lenin enjoined us to guard and strengthen the dictatorship of the proletariat. We vow to you, Comrade Lenin, that we shall spare no effort to fulfil this behest, too, with honour! . . .

Departing from us, Comrade Lenin enjoined us to strengthen with all our might the alliance of the workers and peasants. We vow to you, Comrade Lenin, that this behest, too, we shall fulfil with honour! . . .

Departing from us, Comrade Lenin enjoined us to strengthen and extend the union of republics. We vow to you, Comrade Lenin, that this behest, too, we shall fulfil with honour! . . .

Departing from us, Comrade Lenin enjoined us to remain faithful to the principles of the Communist International. We vow to you, Comrade Lenin, that we shall not spare our lives to strengthen and extend the union of the working people of the whole world—the Communist International!

28. Stalin: How to Deal with Opposition

Stalin adroitly and ruthlessly maneuvered his way to the top, making use of the Lenin mantle, a shrewd sense, political alliances, the naiveté of his opponents, and above all, his position as party secretary. By picturing himself as the chief proponent of Marxist-Leninist ideology and his opponents as misguided factionalists, as he here does in a speech to the Fifteenth Party Congress in 1927, Stalin convinced many that the future of the party lay with him and with him alone.

From Kamenev's speech it is evident that the opposition does not intend to disarm completely. The opposition's declaration of December 3 indicates the same thing. Evidently, the opposition prefers to be outside the Party. Well, let it be outside the Party. There is nothing terrible, or exceptional, or surprising, in the fact that they prefer to be outside the Party, that they are cutting themselves off from the Party. If you study the history of the Party you will find that always, at certain serious turns taken by our Party, a certain section of the old leaders fell out of the cart of the Bolshevik Party and made room for new people. A turn is dangerous for those who do not sit firmly in the Party cart. Not everybody can keep his balance when a turn is made. You turn the cart—and on looking round you find that somebody has fallen out. (applause)

Rigby, *Stalin*, 41–3.

[There follow examples of Party "turns" in 1903 and 1907–08.]

Our Party is a living organism. Like every organism, it undergoes a process of metabolism: the old and obsolete passes away (applause), the new and growing lives and develops (applause). Some go away, both at the top and at the bottom, and lead the cause forward. That is how our Party grew. That is how it will continue to grow.

The same must be said about the present period of our revolution. We are in the period of a turn from the restoration of industry and agriculture to the reconstruction of the entire national economy, to its reconstruction on a new technical basis, when the building of socialism is no longer merely in prospect, but a living, practical matter, which calls for the surrounding of extremely great difficulties of an internal and external character.

You know that this has proved fatal to the leaders of our opposition, who were scared by the new difficulties and intended to turn the Party in the direction of surrender. And if certain leaders, who do not want to sit firmly in the cart, now fall out, it is nothing to be surprised at. It will merely rid the Party of people who are getting in its way and hindering its progress. Evidently, they seriously want to free themselves from our Party cart. Well, if some of the old leaders who are turning into trash intend to fall out of the cart—a good riddance to them! (Stormy and prolonged applause. The whole congress rises and gives Comrade Stalin an ovation.)

Chapter Five

THE SOVIET PERIOD: 1928–1985

Soviet history from 1928 to 1953 was dominated by a single man, Joseph Stalin. That historians refer to Stalinism, Stalin's Russia, and the Stalinist system, and often discuss Soviet history since Stalin's death in terms of de-Stalinization is eloquent testimony to his domination. It was he who developed the Soviet system of government that Gorbachev inherited in 1985.

FACT: Stalin's real name was Joseph Dzhugashvili. He was born in what is today Soviet Georgia and, like Lenin, took a revolutionary name. Stalin means man of steel. Stalin spoke Russian with a Georgian accent.

By 1927, Stalin had outmaneuvered his political rivals and held firmly the reins of Soviet power. He now put that power to work to bring about a rapid industrialization of Soviet society. The period of industrial transformation is often called the Third Revolution because in many ways it changed the face of the country more than the two revolutions of 1917. Unlike the two earlier revolutions, Stalin's was a revolution from above insofar as it was the government, not the people, that took the initiative.

According to Marx's theory, socialism and communism were possible only in an industrialized country. In 1917, the Bolsheviks had expected the workers of western Europe to join them in an international revolution. Now Stalin began to argue that it would be possible to take the first step toward communism by building socialism in one country. To do that, the Soviet

Union would have to create an industrial base as quickly as possible. Even though the tsarist economy had begun to grow rapidly before the 1917 Revolution, Russia was quite backward economically compared with western Europe. About eighty percent of its population was still isolated in small traditional villages, working the land by primitive and inefficient means. Stalin decided that industrialization, and with it the collectivization of agriculture, was a necessity if the Soviet Union were to survive as a socialist country in a world dominated by capitalist states. As he put it in 1931, "The Soviet Union must march forward so that the world proletariat can look to it as the true fatherland of the working class." And, he added on a more ominous note, "We are fifty or one hundred years behind the advanced countries. We must make good this distance in ten years. Either we do it, or we shall be crushed." The sense of being behind the West that had galvanized the energies of Peter the Great more than two hundred years before also haunted Stalin. As it turned out, precisely ten years later, in June 1941, Hitler launched Operation Barbarossa, his invasion of the Soviet Union. Historians still debate whether Stalin's policies actually helped the Soviets to be ready for Hitler's attack, or whether the collectivization of agriculture and Stalin's purges in fact reduced the Soviet Union's ability to wage war effectively.

COLLECTIVIZATION AND THE EXCITEMENT OF SOCIALIST CONSTRUCTION

The Fifteenth Communist Party Congress in 1927 authorized the First **Five Year Plan.** In it, the Soviet government set very ambitious goals for industrial production. The plan called for an end to private property in industry, which had been allowed in small factories and farms during the period of the New Economic Policy, and set a modest goal for the collectivization of agriculture. Collectivization required peasants to give up their small, individual farms and join together to work large tracts of land collectively. They would share ownership of the land and be paid with a share of their joint production.

FACT: By October 1929, 4.1 percent of peasant households had joined **collective** farms. By March 1930, 58 percent of peasants were collectivized. By 1936, 90 percent of peasants were collectivized.

The government first tried to get the peasants to join collective farms voluntarily. However, few peasants wanted to give up their newly acquired private farms. The government then introduced an all-out campaign to force them to do what they would not do on their own. The poor and landless peasants were set against their richer neighbors (called **kulaks** by the party), with promises of sharing the *kulaks'* land and possessions. Young enthusiasts and party workers from the towns spearheaded what became a second civil war in the countryside. Anyone who resisted was called a *kulak* and either forcibly

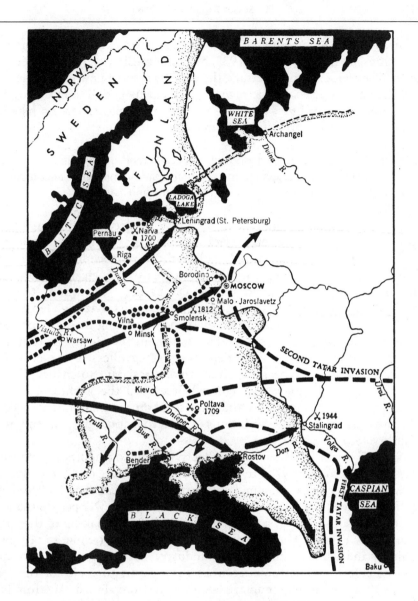

Invasions of Russia / USSR

- – – – TATAR INVASION, 13th CENTURY
- ∿∿∿ EXTENT OF TATAR OCCUPATION
- ▪▪▪▪▪ CHARLES XII, 1701-21
- ●●●●● NAPOLEON, 1812
- ▬▬▬ HITLER INVASION, 1941
- ∿∿∿ EXTENT OF GERMAN OCCUPATION, 1941-42

sent away to settle unpopulated lands in Kazakhstan and Siberia, forced into labor camps, or simply shot. By 1935, over one million exiles had been placed in special settlements to undertake the construction of new enterprises called for in the ambitious economic plan. Recalling this period later during World War II, Stalin confided to Winston Churchill that collectivization had been a terrible struggle, more stressful even than the war.

FACT: It is estimated that fourteen million people died during the collectivization campaign and the man-made famine that accompanied it. Losses were greatest among Ukrainians and Kazakhs.

Nikolai Bukharin, one of Stalin's most talented partners in the early stages of socialist construction, observed, "The worst thing about collectivization, which was a horrible example of brutality to innocent and hardworking peasants, was the deep changes it brought to the psychological outlook of those Communists who participated in the campaign . . . for whom terror was henceforth a normal method of administration." Collectivization led, Bukharin thought, to the dehumanization of the people working in the party. Stalin, unlike Bukharin, was not troubled by such thoughts. He was determined to bring the peasants under government control regardless of the cost. In the nineteenth century, the peasant, stubborn and resistant to change, had lived his life in his own village and ignored or evaded the wishes of the tsar's government. Stalin recognized that the stubborn peasant might become a dangerous obstacle to his ambitions. Collectivization put an end to this possibility. (See Reading 1.)

Why, it might be asked, was collectivization so important? Why was it pushed through so swiftly? In the view of those who supported it, collectivization was a prerequisite for rapid industrialization. Large agricultural units, they believed, could be farmed more productively by fewer people than could the thousands of small peasant farms created by the break-up of the *mir* and the landlords' estates. The large farms would make it possible to use modern machinery and also free manpower for industry. Furthermore, the government would be able to collect produce from these farms to trade for the foreign currency necessary to buy industrial equipment from abroad. And finally, and perhaps most important to Stalin, the government would find it far easier to control the peasants of Russia, once they were gathered into large groups. Collectivization achieved most of these goals, but it was a success bought at the expense of great human suffering. Livestock were slaughtered and eaten by the owners rather than given to the collective. Production was disrupted and there was a terrible famine in which millions of people died of starvation. Not until Stalin's death in 1953 did the production of food regain its precollectivization levels.

Collectivization not only had an enormous cost in human lives, it also left its mark, as Bukharin observed, on the developing style of Soviet administration. The war of 1914, the civil war that followed it, and then the collectivization campaign all helped accustom the new Soviet regime to the use of brutal methods in the service of socialist construction. Lenin himself had taught that the health of the revolution was the highest law. What he meant in effect was that the ends justify the means. Anything that furthered the cause of socialism was permissible. Now Stalin had established himself as the arbiter and last word on what it was that the revolution needed. He had only to say the revolution demanded that he carry out a given policy, regardless of what it cost others, and it was done. His word became law.

The early 1930s were nonetheless a time of rapid industrial growth. As in the 1920s, there was among a large portion of the Soviet population— particularly among Soviet young people—a sense of exhilaration, of new possibilities for themselves personally, and the chance to build a new and better society. The government, which now owned and ran all large factories and other enterprises, set high targets for factory construction and output. Pressure from the central administration to make the targets was intense. Everyone, including women, was expected to work hard to build the socialist future. And work hard they did, under difficult conditions and often with considerable ingenuity. (See Readings 2 and 3.)

FACT: During the First Five Year Plan, which was declared completed after four years, the output of machinery quadrupled and that of oil doubled.

FACT: The number of women in the work force more than doubled between 1928 and 1933, and doubled again by 1940.

Young people worked with enthusiasm to build the foundation of the new industry in such faraway places as Magnitogorsk, the new steel center built in the Urals. Electricity was brought to the countryside (see Reading 4). Education, particularly technical education which bore a direct relation to the regime's economic goals, was widely available. The former peasant, and certainly his son or daughter, could attend night school or the new industrial academies and look forward to being the foreman of a factory, an engineer, or even the manager of a construction project. The contrast between Soviet progress and the Great Depression that was devastating western Europe and the United States added to the sense that the Soviet Union was on the right track. Though the Soviet standard of living was very low at this time, it did seem to be improving.

Stalin's drive for industrialization was accompanied by a tightening of discipline in all areas of Soviet life. Whereas the Revolution of 1917 had been accompanied by ideals of equality and the freedom to experiment with everything from art and literature to education and family relationships, Stalin now introduced tough discipline in school and factory. Factories established sharp wage differentials to encourage workers to get the training necessary to rise in their place of work. Schools were given a dual job: to achieve literacy and improve technical skills, and to inculcate the values of the new Soviet person. As Stalin put it with characteristic bluntness, education is a weapon in

In 1935, workers celebrate the one hundred thousandth tractor built at the Kirov factory, so named in honor of the popular head of the Leningrad party, S.M. Kirov, who was assassinated in 1934.

the hands of the man who holds it. It must teach the virtues of hard work, self-discipline, and loyalty to the Communist party. For Stalin, writers and teachers were to become "engineers of the human soul."

FACT: Literacy as percent of the population

1897	1926	1939	1959	1979
26.3	56.6	89.1	98.5	99.9

The regime also introduced a strict censorship on the media. It required all writers who wanted to be published to follow the canon of **Socialist Realism.** Socialist Realism required writers to portray heroes as models for behavior and to present situations in which good citizens were rewarded and bad ones suffered. Lenin had introduced the idea that literature must be **party-minded,** and serve the state. Now a whole structure of censorship and bureaucracy was developed to make the idea a reality. The regime declared that the job of transforming illiterate, individualistic peasants into cooperative industrial workers was so great that it required the coordinated efforts of everyone, school teachers and artists, radio announcers and writers, as well as political leaders. The result was to put an end to the brilliant creative flowering in the arts that had begun in Russia just before the war and continued in the years immediately after the Revolution. Diaghilev took his Ballet Russe to Paris. The poets Vladimir Mayakovsky and Osip Mandelshtam, and writers such as Andrei Bely, Isaac Babel, Boris Pilnyak, Evgeny Zamiatin, and a host of others were either arrested, left the Soviet Union, or committed suicide. Others remained, but, like the poets **Anna Akhmatova, Marina Tsvetaeva** and **Boris Pasternak,** were forced "to write for the drawer," that is, to give up all hope of getting their work published.

As Stalin moved to tighten the discipline of society by party and state, he also centralized power within the party itself. Lower party organs were strictly controlled by higher ones, so that a decision made at the top would be carried out throughout the land. Stalin also granted increasing power to the security police organization, which he ordered to watch party and government officials to make sure they were loyal to him. People were encouraged to denounce their neighbors.

FACT: Pavlik Morozov was a small boy who denounced his parents for hoarding grain during the collectivization campaign. The parents were arrested. Shortly after that, the outraged villagers killed the boy. Soviet schools and media then made much of little Pavlik as a martyr to the socialist cause. Right up until the 1980s, children were urged to imitate him and give their highest loyalty to the state.

The Communist party congresses that had brought party leaders from all over the country together once a year during Lenin's rule met more and more rarely under Stalin. After the 1927 Party Congress, the next meeting was held in 1930, then 1934, 1939, and not again until 1952. The gap between meetings thus grew from three to four, to five, and finally to thirteen years. The Party Central Committee also met rarely. Power was concentrated in the Politburo and, increasingly, in the person of Stalin.

STALIN'S CULT OF PERSONALITY AND THE PURGES

By 1930, Stalin had begun to develop the cult of his own personality. History was rewritten to illustrate Stalin's genius at every turn. Streets, cities, factories, and mountains were named in his honor. Stalin's picture was put up in every school, store, and factory, while newspapers and radios controlled by the **party-state** continuously trumpeted the accomplishments of the all-wise leader, the genius Stalin.

The cult of personality both reflected and enhanced Stalin's power. It was soon accompanied, however, by a new and terrible development in Soviet history. In December 1934, Kirov, the popular head of the Leningrad party organization, was assassinated. Stalin probably organized this event. In any case, he used it to justify a far-reaching purge of Soviet society and particularly of the party. There had been some arrests and accusations of industrial sabotage in the early 1930s, accompanied by public trials that provided scapegoats for the regime. Those put on trial were blamed for making mistakes and causing all the popular suffering during the time of the first rapid industrialization. More often, of course, that suffering was a side effect of a definite government policy, pushing heavy industry rather than consumer goods or agriculture, for example. There had also been arrests and summary executions in the early years of Bolshevik power when the government felt weak and insecure. What now took place was unprecedented in scale. (See Reading 5.)

FACT: One thousand one hundred eight of the 1,966 delegates to the Seventeenth Communist Party Congress (1934) and 98 of the 139 regular and candidate (non-voting) members elected by that Congress to its Central Committee perished in the purges. Most of them were shot.

If in the 1920s, the party and security police had dealt harshly with any and all who opposed the Bolsheviks, now the security police turned on the party itself. The leadership was hardest hit. All past or potential opponents of Stalin were arrested and accused of outlandish plots, such as conspiring with "Judas Trotsky" to murder Stalin and sabotage the country's economy, or plotting with Germany and Japan to dismember the Soviet Union. In carefully staged, public **show trials** that received wide publicity, many of the early Bolshevik leaders such as Kamenev, Zinoviev, and Bukharin confessed to fictitious crimes after long periods of confinement and torture in prison. Agents of the secret police tracked Trotsky down in Mexico and murdered him there. The purges reached throughout the USSR, into universities and factories, and into towns throughout the Soviet land, striking individuals who had no idea why they were being accused. In some instances, local purges probably served as a means to settle old scores or get rid of a boss who stood in the way of promotion. The purges hit hardest those who had had a measure of responsibility. After purging the party, the police turned on the army. Three of the top five Soviet military leaders were arrested, including Marshal Mikhail Tukhachevsky, who was widely considered the most brilliant Soviet military strategist. Tukachevsky was accused, tried, and executed for plotting with Japan and Germany to dismember the Soviet Union, activities for which there was absolutely no evidence. Some estimate that as a result of the purges the army lost half of its officer corps. (See Reading 6.)

FACT: No one knows exactly how many people were arrested in the purges. Estimates range from 17 to 19 million, about ten percent of the total population. Of these, some 800,000 were executed. Most of the rest were sentenced to labor camps strung out across Siberia. There they joined the vast work force of what the Russian writer Alexander Solzhenitsyn calls the *Gulag Archipelago*—*gulag* was the acronym for Chief Administration of Corrective Labor Camps.

The purges struck down virtually all the original Bolshevik leaders. They also removed the revolutionary generation from positions of leadership throughout the country and made way for the young—the Khrushchevs, Brezhnevs, and Kosygins. These new men had gained education and quick promotion from the Soviet system and now rose rapidly to prominent positions. The purges provided openings for young people who came from peasant and other poor backgrounds. They also created fear and suspicion throughout the Soviet population. It was an atmosphere, Stalin's successor Nikita Khrushchev later said, in which no one felt secure, so no one could work well or with confidence.

Why Stalin ordered the purges remains a matter of debate. The myth that he did not know what was happening has been proved false. Of course, there had in fact been opposition to some of his policies, particularly to his methods of collectivization, but by the late 1930s, those who had opposed him had no power. There is also some evidence that there was, in the early 1930s, some quiet, behind-the-scenes opposition to Stalin's increasingly autocratic ways. It seems unlikely, however, that there was any serious threat to his authority. From the regime's point of view, the arrests and public trials that followed were useful in that they gave it the opportunity to blame many of its problems on wilful wrecking and sabotage by a malevolent few. The arrests and trials also helped develop a siege mentality among the population, providing evidence that devious and determined foreign powers were plotting to overthrow the Soviet socialist state. Such a view of an outside world filled with hostile capitalist states could be used to justify continuous vigilance, sacrifice, and hard work. Nonetheless, it remains hard to understand the reasons for such a large scale attack on the Soviet population. By destroying so many talented people, the purges slowed the growth of the economy, weakened the military, and devastated Soviet science. They drastically reduced the ability of the army to combat the Nazis. Most historians agree that an important reason for the purges was the growing paranoia of Stalin himself and the deterioration of his mental balance. What is really most remarkable about the purges, however, is that the Stalinist system of government was both willing and able to undertake the destruction of so many innocent people.

WORLD WAR II AND ITS AFTERMATH

At the same time, the late 1930s, the international picture was growing darker and more dangerous for the Soviet Union. After Hitler came to power in Germany in 1933, fear of Germany led the USSR to seek improved relations with the democratic capitalist states. In 1933, it established diplomatic relations with the United States which, until then, had refused to recognize what Americans considered to be a dangerous and uncivilized revolutionary government. In 1934, the USSR entered the Leage of Nations and, in 1935, signed bilateral agreements with France and Czechoslovakia. In 1935, the **Comintern** reversed its policy of requiring foreign Communist parties to try to undermine democratic governments and urged them instead to work for a popular front against fascism. By 1935, the Soviets had realized that Fascist Germany, not France or England, posed their greatest threat. In the East, the Comintern supported Chiang Kai-shek and the Chinese Kuomintang against an increasingly militaristic Japan.

While the Soviet Union was continuing to press for alliances and assurances of mutual support from the western powers, especially Britain and France, it also opened secret negotiations with the Nazis. Stalin was determined to avoid war with Germany at any price. He knew that his country was still backward industrially and militarily and further weakened by the purges. Nor did he altogether trust the British and French. He feared they might make a deal with Germany against the Soviet Union. On August 23, 1939, Germany and the Soviet Union signed a nonaggression pact. Each agreed not to go to war against the other and to remain neutral if either side was attacked by a third party. A secret protocol divided up eastern Europe into spheres of influence. Russia's sphere included the eastern regions of Poland, Bessarabia (a province of Rumania), Finland, and the independent nations of Estonia and Latvia. Later the Germans added Lithuania to the Soviet sphere. The Ribbentrop Agreement, as this agreement was called in the West, was what Hitler was waiting for. Free now from the danger of war with the USSR, Germany invaded Poland in September. So began what Americans call World War II and what the Soviets call the Great Patriotic War. The USSR gained peace, at least for a time.

In keeping with their agreement with Hitler, the Soviets annexed Latvia, Estonia, and Lithuania, eastern Poland, and Bessarabia. The three Baltic states became separate republics of the Soviet Union, as did Bessarabia, which was renamed Moldavia. Soviet troops also invaded Finland, in November 1939. The Finns resisted, however, and held the Soviet army to a humiliating standstill in the so-called Winter War of 1939–40. Finland, while ultimately forced to surrender some territory, preserved its independence.

In the summer of 1939, Stalin apparently expected a long war between Germany and the western allies. As it turned out, the Nazis moved far faster than anyone expected. France fell. Britain retreated to its island fortress. On

June 22, 1941, flushed with victory, Hitler turned his panzers eastward against the Soviet Union in Operation Barbarossa.

FACT: Despite warnings from the Allies, the shifting of huge numbers of German troops to the eastern front and frequent flights over Soviet territory by German planes, the Soviet frontiers were barely defended and some troops were without ammunition on the day of the Nazi attack. The Soviet military had made plans to go on the offensive, should war come, but had made no comprehensive plan of defense.

FACT: Stalin did not appear in public for twelve days after the Nazi attack.

Stalin was stunned, so much so that he was unable even to announce to his people what had happened. He left this unpleasant task to one of his subordinates. For a time, the all-wise, all-knowing leader remained invisible to his people. In the Soviet Union, as in western Europe, the Germans moved with surprising speed. By December they were set up on the outskirts of Moscow, Leningrad was under blockade, and most of Soviet Ukraine was under Nazi control.

The situation looked bleak. Not for nineteen long months were the Soviets able to manage their first major victory. Finally, in January 1943, they stopped the Nazi advance at Stalingrad. In that city, they fought hand to hand in the streets, retreating until they had their backs to the broad Volga River. There, when they could retreat no further, they held. The city was almost totally destroyed, but the heroic and costly struggle proved the turning point of the war. Here, as against Napoleon one hundred thirty-one years before, winter and stubborn bravery helped to secure ultimate victory.

FACT: Over one million people died in the nine hundred-day siege and blockade of Leningrad alone, more than ten times the number of people killed by the atomic bomb dropped on Hiroshima. (See Readings 7 and 8.)

FACT: It is estimated that 18 to 24 million Soviet citizens perished during the war, out of a 1939 population of about 190.5 million, or one out of every ten people. United States war losses were about 400,000, out of a population of close to 132 million. (See Reading 9.)

For almost three years, the Soviet Union had to bear the brunt of the Nazi war machine. Although the Americans sent help in the form of vast amounts of equipment and supplies under the Lend-Lease agreement, the Allies were not able to provide what the Soviets most needed, a diversion of German troops to other fronts. Not until three years after the Nazi invasion of the Soviet Union, in June 1944, did the Allies land troops on the Normandy beaches. At last they forced the Nazis to fight what the German generals knew they could not win, a two-front war.

In a series of wartime meetings with Churchill and Roosevelt (and after Roosevelt's death with his successor, Harry Truman), Stalin negotiated with his allies first on military matters and then on the political issues of postwar settlement. During the period that the Soviets were doing most of the fighting and suffering most of the war losses, Stalin held a particularly strong negotiating position. Using this fact and his considerable political skill, Stalin squeezed concessions from the British and Americans. Not only was he treated as an equal partner in all negotiations about the shape of postwar Europe, he also gained the Allies' agreement that there would be friendly states on the Soviet Union's western borders after the war. The historical experience of Polish invasion in the seventeenth century, of Napoleon in the nineteenth century, and the Germans twice in his own century stiffened Stalin's resolve.

Stalin had a very clear idea about what state could be considered a friendly one: It had to be communist and amenable to Soviet direction. It seems unlikely that Churchill, Roosevelt, or Truman fully realized that Stalin understood friendly and communist to be one and the same. They chose to ignore the implications of the Warsaw uprising in the summer of 1944, when Soviet actions foreshadowed events to come. At that time, when the non-communist Polish underground tried to seize the city from the Nazis, the Russian armies halted their advance at the river Vistula on the outskirts of the city. There they remained while the Nazis systematically wiped out the Polish resistance. When the United States government requested access to air bases on Russian-occupied territories so that it could drop supplies to the beleaguered Poles, Stalin refused. Looking back on this strange decision of Stalin's, it is clear that he was not thinking primarily about the military issue of defeating the Germans and saving Polish lives, but that he was already thinking about who would rule Poland after the war. Had the underground liberated Warsaw, its members might have formed a postwar government favorable to the Western allies. Nonetheless, the Allied leaders either did not see what Stalin had in mind, or, if they did see, chose not to protest.

At war's end, Soviet troops occupied the vast territory between their own borders and Berlin. In the next few years, taking advantage of this fact, the Soviets supported Communist parties in their bids for power throughout Eastern Europe. The result was that by 1948, they had what they wanted: friendly communist states on their borders.

FACT: By 1948, Poland, Hungary, Bulgaria, Rumania, Albania, Czechoslovakia, and Yugoslavia all had communist governments, and all but Yugoslavia were dependent on the Soviet government and subservient to its wishes. Finland was not communist but still friendly.

The Soviets called these states "**peoples' democracies.**" The Western powers began to call the same states "Soviet **satellites,**" because their policies depended on Soviet power.

Eastern Europe at the End of World War II

Members of The Warsaw Pact

Communist States — not members of the Warsaw Pact

Areas annexed since World War II

FACT: In 1948, the Yugoslav communist government broke free from Soviet domination. Unlike the Communist party in other East European countries, the Yugoslav party had come to power on its own, and its leader, Tito, enjoyed wide popularity.

After the war, the Soviet Union turned inward to rebuild its devastated economy and to tighten government control of society. During the war, Stalin had relied openly on patriotic appeals, relaxed persecution of the church, and taken many new people into the party. Now such measures to increase popularity were no longer necessary. The cult of personality reemerged stronger even than before the war. (See Reading 10.)

FACT: Of the new Soviet postage stamps issued in 1950, sixty-two had a picture of Stalin, three had a picture of Lenin, and three others pictured the two men together.

Stalin now opened a campaign against what he called cosmopolitanism, by which he meant influences that were not Russian. Jews in particular were singled out for persecution. The regime took stern measures to cut off contact with the West. The cult of the all-wise, all-knowing, awe-inspiring leader reached new heights. There were even signs in 1952 that Stalin was preparing a new purge.

Stalin's repressive domestic policy was matched by a growing distrust of the outside world. Refusal of American help, notably the **Marshall Plan** for postwar reconstruction, which was offered originally to the USSR and Eastern Europe as well as to Western Europe, indicated the lengths to which Stalin would go to avoid Western contact. He did not want Europeans to realize how gravely wounded the Soviet Union had been by war, for he feared they might take advantage of that weakness. Rather than cooperating after the war, the former allies, the Soviet Union and the United States, were led by mutual suspicion into an era of competition and antagonism that was called the Cold War. Speaking in Fulton, Missouri in 1946, Winston Churchill remarked that an iron curtain had descended across the continent of Europe and that those behind it to the east were subject to increasing control from Moscow.

FACT: The iron curtain was not just a figure of speech. The border between most Eastern European countries and Western Europe was fenced, guarded, and mined. Travel from East to West was virtually impossible.

FACT: The United States dropped an atomic bomb on Hiroshima in 1945. Not until 1949 did the USSR detonate its first atomic bomb. The United States held a monopoly on the weapon from 1945 to 1949.

By the end of the 1940s, the allies in war had become enemies in peace. The Western powers saw Soviet domination of Eastern Europe and stubbornness in keeping Germany divided as indications of the Soviet Union's aggressive

Russian and American soldiers meet at the Elbe River, south of Berlin, April 25, 1945.

intentions and feared the growing power of Communist parties in France and Italy. The **Cominform,** a successor organization to the Comintern set up to coordinate the work of Communist parties all over the world, seemed particularly threatening. The Soviets, for their part, felt weak. They still feared Germany. They still feared invasion from the West, across the unbroken central European plain. They seemed surprised that the West could not see this danger or understand why they needed friendly states in Eastern Europe. The American monopoly on the atomic bomb increased the feeling of vulnerability. Yet the Soviets could not see the Marshall Plan as anything other than an American plot to dominate Western Europe and build up West Germany. The

Western powers, however, saw that the Soviet Union controlled large areas of Eastern Europe that had been independent between the two world wars. They feared further Soviet expansion.

When, in 1949, the United States joined with Western European states to create the North Atlantic Treaty Organization (NATO) and establish a joint army, the Soviets began to fear the possibility of Western aggression. Six years later the Soviets joined forces with their Eastern European allies to form a corresponding military alliance, the Warsaw Pact.

Then, on March 5, 1953, Stalin died.

DE-STALINIZATION AND THE KHRUSHCHEV ERA

Stalin's heirs quickly agreed on one thing: There should be no return to the terror of Stalin's rule. As there was no law or established procedure for choosing Stalin's successor, the top party leaders closed ranks and spoke of the need for collective leadership. The dreaded secret police was downgraded in importance and its head, Lavrenty Beria, was shot. Gradually Nikita Khrushchev emerged as the top man. Khrushchev, the son of a simple worker, was one of the men who had risen rapidly into the important positions vacated by victims of the purges, first in Ukraine and then in Moscow. He had profited from the Stalinist system. Nonetheless he moved away from Stalin's methods. Neither he, nor any of his successors, ruled with the arbitrary, absolute power that Stalin had wielded. They depended instead on the support of the members of the highest party council, the Politburo.

At the Twentieth Party Congress in 1956, Khrushchev made the now-famous Secret Speech, so-called because it did not appear in the official transcript of the Congress proceedings. It was, however, read out in meetings throughout the Soviet Union.

FACT: All foreigners were barred from the speech (which was given late at night). The speech was not published in the Soviet Union until 1989.

In his Secret Speech, Khrushchev accused Stalin of numerous crimes and brutality against the Soviet people. Khrushchev ushered in a period of reform, or what is called de-Stalinization. (See Readings 11 and 12.)

FACT: At this time the name of the city of Stalingrad was changed to Volgograd. Before the Revolution, this city had been called Tsaritsyn.

The Soviet leaders now tried to change many of Stalin's policies and methods, while at the same time maintaining the keystones of his system: party control, centralized economic planning, collectivized agriculture, a monopoly on the media, and a willingness to use the police to deal with

The Soviet composer, Dimitri Shostakovich, presents the gold medal for first place in the Tchaikovsky piano competition to Van Cliburn. A picture of Tchaikovsky, the great nineteenth century Russian composer, hangs in the background. In 1958, Van Cliburn became the first American ever to win the competition. This seemed particularly significant in a year when Soviet-American relations were beginning to improve.

troublemakers if necessary. The Khrushchev regime took steps to improve the standard of living, experimented with loosening political controls on literature, and sought ways to increase the participation of rank-and-file party members in responsible positions. Khrushchev also undertook a number of spectacular campaigns, notably his Virgin Lands project to plow and cultivate large tracts of land in Kazakhstan, land previously thought unsuitable for agriculture. He worked for peaceful coexistence with the West, while simultaneously seeking greater influence in the **Third World.** He sought and held a summit meeting with President Eisenhower and appeared before the United Nations. Not all of his projects were successful. De-Stalinization and liberalization at home gave some Eastern European communist governments the idea they could exercise a bit more independence, too, with the result that the loyalty of Poland and the very existence of communist control in Hungary were threatened. The Soviets had to send in tanks to crush the Hungarian Revolution in 1956. China slipped out of the Soviet orbit.

FACT: In 1961, the East Germans built a wall between East and West Berlin to stem the tide of refugees from east to west. An estimated 2.5 million people had fled to the West through Berlin between 1945 and 1961. Just before the wall was built, the flood of refugees reached an average of four thousand per day. The Berlin Wall stood until 1989.

Nikita Khrushchev, President Eisenhower, Mrs. Khrushchev, and Andrei Gromyko meet the press, September 1959.

Seeking to show his skill in foreign affairs, and reduce the military advantage of the United States, Khrushchev took a gamble. In January 1959, Fidel Castro had assumed power in Cuba. Soon thereafter, Castro developed close ties with the Soviet Union. The presence of an ally so close to the United States provided Khrushchev with a temptation he could not resist. He decided to install nuclear missiles in Cuba. The result was the Cuban Missile Crisis of 1962, a frightening confrontation with the United States that was resolved only when Khrushchev agreed to dismantle the missile launch pads in return for an American promise not to try to overthrow the pro-Soviet Cuban government of Fidel Castro.

Problems at home and abroad led to Khrushchev's downfall. In 1964, the Politburo united against him, and Khrushchev was removed from office. For a while Leonid Brezhnev, Aleksei Kosygin, and Nikolai Podgorny formed a collective leadership from which Brezhnev gradually emerged as paramount.

FACT: Unlike Stalin's displaced rivals, who were usually shot, Khrushchev survived to live out his old age and die a peaceful death in 1971.

FACT: In 1967, when the Soviet regime celebrated its fiftieth anniversary, historians could not mention the men who had led the country for forty of those fifty years: Stalin and Khrushchev were both in disgrace.

These facts alone illustrate the difference between Stalin's way of dealing with disagreement and that of his successors. They also illustrate a continuity in the way in which the Soviet regime dealt with unpleasant truths: History was simply rewritten to leave them out.

President John F. Kennedy and Nikita Khrushchev meet in Vienna for a summit meeting in June 1961.

BREZHNEV AND HIS SUCCESSORS

From 1964 until 1985, the Soviet regime was remarkably conservative. There were no dramatic efforts to make revolution from above, such as the collectivization and industrialization campaigns of the 1920s and early 1930s. There were no purges similar to those of the middle and late 1930s. Nor were there experiments and attempts at reform such as those of Khrushchev, who had seemed eager to perfect Soviet socialism and recapture the excitement of its early years. On the contrary, the main goal of the Brezhnev regime and those of his immediate successors, Yuri **Andropov** (1983–84) and Konstantin **Chernenko** (1984–85), was to provide personal and national security. They wanted to perfect the system already in place. The Soviet Union became a conservative state, in the sense that its leaders tried to preserve the institutions established by Stalin and avoid any domestic change.

FACT: Between 1965 and 1972, per capita consumption in the Soviet Union rose five percent per year.

FACT: In 1960, 8 in 100 Soviet families had TV sets; 4 in 100 had a washing machine or a refrigerator. By 1977, 75 in 100 families had TV sets; 65 in 100 had a washing machine or a refrigerator.

From 1964 until the mid-1970s, the Brezhnev regime succeeded quite well in providing both guns and butter, that is, both a strong military and increasing amounts of consumer goods. To do that, it concentrated on developing more efficient management. Education and competence, in addition to political loyalty, became increasingly important as criteria for an important position. Government officials both sought and heeded advice from experts. Professional journalists began to publish differing points of view as to how to solve problems, and so long as those differing opinions did not touch on politics, they were encouraged. Unlike Stalin, Brezhnev and his successors no longer equated minor technical disagreements with disloyalty. Nonetheless, it remained the Communist party that decided what kind of debate would be tolerated and who would prevail.

At the same time that the Brezhnev regime was pressing for efficient management and listening more closely to its experts, it took a very strict line on unwelcome criticism. Experts were encouraged to criticize instances of economic inefficiency, but no one was allowed to point out basic flaws in party management or the government. Khrushchev had experimented with a looser censorship and had allowed publication in 1962 of Alexander **Solzhenitsyn's** frank account of life in a Soviet labor camp, *One Day in the Life of Ivan Denisovich.* Nothing of that sort appeared under Brezhnev. Indeed in 1965 the regime arrested two writers, Andrei **Sinyavsky** and Yuli **Daniel,** because their work had been published abroad. It forced others, among them Solzhenitsyn, to leave the country.

In the 1970s and early 1980s, a few Soviet writers and artists wrote honestly, even though they knew that the official censor would not allow their work to be published. Sometimes they turned to **samizdat,** literally translated "to publish oneself." Writers typed what they had written and circulated it privately among friends.

FACT: In the early 1970s, approximately seventy thousand people were employed in censorship work.

FACT: In the early 1980s, photocopying machines were rare in the Soviet Union and kept in special locked rooms to avoid unauthorized copying of controversial material.

It may seem odd that a state inspired by the writings of Karl Marx, who taught that ideas are a smoke screen to hide economic interests, always considered ideas so powerful and so important. Some governments do not care very much what books are published because they do not think that writers are significant. Not so in the Soviet Union. Great Soviet writers such as Alexander Solzhenitsyn, Marina Tsvetaeva, Anna Akhmatova, and Boris Pasternak came under fire not only when they pointed out shortcomings in the regime, but because they also suggested that there were basic human questions that had not yet been answered even in socialist societies, or portrayed people with religious or humanitarian views in a sympathetic manner. The Soviet regime attributed great power and importance to its writers, and yet it found, like the Russian tsars, that some of its most gifted ones were dangerous. This was one of the many paradoxes of the Soviet system established by Stalin that continued up through the 1980s. (See Reading 13.)

The Brezhnev regime also dealt harshly with those who sought more rights for the non-Russian nationalities, with Christian religious leaders who sought the right to worship in other than officially approved churches, with Jews who sought to emigrate, and with the human rights activists. These persistent and brave men and women were called **dissidents** because they dissented from official views and would not accept the party line.

FACT: **Andrei Sakharov,** well-known in the Soviet Union as one of its most brilliant physicists and father of the Soviet H-bomb, won numerous Stalin and Lenin prizes. When he decided to speak out against human rights abuses and then about the Soviet invasion of Afghanistan, he was put under house arrest in the provincial town of Gorky.

The Soviet **human rights movement** began when a few Soviet citizens decided to monitor their government to see that it obeyed its own constitution. When Soviet citizens were arrested for what they said or wrote, denied the right to an open trial, or stopped from practicing their religion, the human rights activists protested that these were violations of the rights guaranteed by the Soviet Constitution. At first the regime seemed unsure how to deal with this development, but it soon found a solution. The state security policy (KGB) began to harass the activists with late night apartment searches, warnings, and beatings.

FACT: In 1970, Zhores Medvedev, a dissident biochemist, was committed to a mental hospital.

Activists and members of their families lost their jobs, were arrested, and were incarcerated in labor camps and psychiatric hospitals. Some activists were given a choice between going to labor camps or leaving the country. These protests mightily embarrassed the Soviet government, because the Soviet leadership was concerned about world opinion. The leaders were trying to develop a more secure government of laws, but nonetheless continued to ignore their own laws when an important political issue was at stake. (See Reading 14.)

The overriding foreign policy goal of the Brezhnev regime was to maintain a rough military parity with its chief rival, the United States, and to avoid a nuclear war. The devastation of World War II was still a fresh memory, kept alive by frequent references to it in government publications and by huge war monuments that continued to dominate public squares throughout the nation. More than forty-five years later, photo displays about the war were still on the walls in schools. In the Soviet view, however, peace did not require friendship and trust. It only required adequate communication and sufficient agreement to avoid military confrontation. Under the Brezhnev regime, from 1964 to 1982, the Soviet Union engaged in a hugely costly arms race with the United States and realized an age-old dream of the tsars: It was recognized as a military superpower. To that extent, it had caught up with the West at last.

The heritage of Marxist-Leninist ideology, notably the idea that history was leading to socialism, continued to pervade the thinking of Soviet leaders. This assumption influenced their policy in the so-called **Third World**. They believed that in Africa, Asia, and Latin America, people living in poverty were eager to move away from what they called **"capitalist imperialism."** In these areas the Soviet leaders welcomed change and were quite willing to support those opposed to the status quo. They offered military as well as moral support to potential Third World allies. Yet they sought influence in the Third World cautiously, anxious to avoid a direct conflict with the United States. (See Reading 15.)

Even if they believed that historical forces were on their side in the Third World, however, the Soviets were never able to turn reluctant satellites into enthusiastic allies in Eastern Europe. The outpouring of support for **Lech Walesa,** the Polish labor leader who tried in the early 1980s to organize the **Solidarity** labor movement as a force independent of the Polish Communist party, confirmed what the Soviets no doubt already knew: Most Eastern European communist regimes had never achieved real popularity with their people.

FACT: The Soviets twice used troops to put down national political movements in Eastern Europe that had broad popular support: in Hungary in 1956 and in Czechoslovakia in 1968.

During the 1960s and 1970s, even as the Soviet Union and the United States both rushed to develop more advanced and deadly nuclear weapons, trade between the two countries began to grow. Both governments saw advantage in improving relations.

FACT: President Richard Nixon visited the Soviet Union in 1972. He was the first American president to visit the USSR while in office.

The first **SALT treaty** (Strategic Arms Limitation Talks) was signed in 1972, and negotiations for a second SALT agreement got off to a promising start. To be sure, there were at times strains in the Soviet-American relationship, caused by such events as the Soviet military intervention in Czechoslovakia, American military involvement in Vietnam, and Soviet support for Cuban troops in Angola. In spite of those problems, however, during the 1970s the desire to maintain a working dialogue prevailed.

FACT: The first major use of Soviet troops outside of Eastern Europe took place in 1979 when the USSR sent troops to Afghanistan.

Soviet-American relations took a turn for the worse when Soviet troops occupied Afghanistan. The United States reacted with a boycott of the 1980 summer Olympic games held in Moscow and a refusal to ratify the **SALT II** agreement. Thereafter, relations deteriorated rapidly, with each country matching the accusations of the other: President Ronald Reagan called the Soviet Union "an evil empire." (See Reading 16.) The Soviet newspaper *Izvestia* charged that the United States was guilty of **"great power messianism"** and accused it of supporting "fascist terrorist regimes," in such places as Chile and the Philippines. On January 1, 1984, an American elder statesman and former ambassador, **Averell Harriman,** wrote in the *New York Times* that if the pattern continued, the United States might face nuclear war. Each side knew that it was playing a dangerous game, but neither would take the bold step needed to stop its costly and perilous progress.

Despite all the problems, there was a rough social contract between the government and the Soviet peoples that kept the system going during the Brezhnev years. The government no longer used physical violence on a large scale against its own people, as Stalin had done. It kept the country free from foreign invasion, and people felt pride in their superpower status. Jobs were secure, if ill-paid, basic food was cheap, medical care and education were free, and each generation lived a bit better than the one before. Those in the party and other privileged positions gave their loyalty to those at the very top, in return for their share of the best things that the society had to offer. The people knew that under Brezhnev they were safe from the dangers of purge and arrest that had devastated the country in Stalin's time, and members of the elite knew that if they did not criticize or question the system, they could count on a secure and prosperous old age.

FACT: In 1982, the average age of the members of the Politburo, the ruling
          group in the Soviet Union, was sixty-nine.

The system seemed stable. Its leaders were growing old together. Such was the situation in the country where Brezhnev died, and his immediate successors, Chernenko and Andropov, did little to change it.

The following books were helpful in writing this chapter:

Bialer, S., *Stalin's Successors: Leadership, Stability and Change in the Soviet Union.* Cambridge, England & New York: Cambridge University Press, 1980.
Dmytryshyn, B., *USSR: A Concise History.* New York: Scribner's, 1978.
Hough, J.F., and Fainsod, M., *How the Soviet Union Is Governed.* Cambridge, MA & London: Harvard University Press, 1979.
Nove, A., *Stalinism and After.* London: George Allen & Unwin, 1975.
Ulam, A., *Expansion and Coexistence.* New York: Praeger, 1974.

For students who are interested, we recommend further reading in the sources from which we have taken excerpts, as well as the following works:

Catchpole, B., *A Map History of Russia.* London: Heineman Educational Books, 1974, 1976.

Map illustrations and summaries of events written for students.

Chukovskaya, L., *Sofia Petrovna.* Translated by A. Werth, and E.K. Klose. Evanston, Ill.: Northwestern University Press, 1988.

This remarkable short novel conveys the horror of the purges in a way that also provides some understanding of how they were possible. The author is a courageous survivor of those times. A worthy alternative to Solzhenitsyn's *One Day in the Life of Ivan Denisovich.*

Conquest, R., *The Great Terror: Stalin's Purges of the Thirties.* New York: Macmillan, 1968, 1973.

A definitive account of this extraordinary phenomenon.

———. *The Harvest of Sorrow.* New York: Oxford University Press, 1986.

A comprehensive, illuminating account of the collectivization campaign of the early 1930s and the famine and terror that accompanied it.

Gladkov, F., *Cement.* New York: Frederick Ungar, 1948.

A novel of the 1920s in the socialist realism mode.

Heller, M., and Nekrich, A., *Utopia in Power: History of the Soviet Union from 1917 to Our Days.* New York: Summit, 1986.

Two outstanding Soviet emigré historians have combined to give detailed insiders' view. Probably suitable only for the more advanced student.

Koestler, A., *Darkness at Noon.* New York: Bantam, 1970.

Fictionalized account of the experience of an old Bolshevik caught in a purge trial.

Lewis, J., *Stalin: A Time for Judgment.* New York: Pantheon, 1990.

An up-to-date survey of Stalin and his times, companion volume to the TV documentary.

Mandelshtam, N., *Hope against Hope.* New York: Athenaeum, 1970.

Nadezhda Mandelshtam's extraordinarily sensitive and moving account of her poet-husband's last four years. Osip Mandelshtam was first arrested in 1934 and disappeared into the gulag after his second arrest in 1938. This is one of the finest accounts of life at the height of the purges.

Salisbury, H.E., *The 900 Days: The Siege of Leningrad.* New York: DaCapo Press, 1985.

Vivid account of the heroism and suffering of the people of Leningrad during World War II.

Solzhenitsyn, A., *One Day in the Life of Ivan Denisovich.* New York: Praeger, 1963.

A spare and moving account of one day in a Soviet labor camp; his short stories such as "Matryona's House" and "For the Good of the Cause" are also easy to read and highly recommended.

READINGS
for
Chapter Five

1. Katya's Account of Collectivization

What the collectivization campaign meant for much of the Soviet population is suggested by this excerpt from the autobiography of Victor Kravchenko, a Soviet defector. Here he tells the story of a child from a kulak family deported from a village in the course of the collectivization campaign. Kulak (the word means fist in Russian) was a pejorative name given to the prosperous farmers. The Bolsheviks purposefully set the poorer villagers against them, thereby setting up what they called a class war in the countryside. Elsewhere in this account, Kravchenko shows how the campaign destroyed the belief of many idealistic young communists.

My cousin Natasha, a Party member who was directing a factory college, was on the train returning from some business trip. A dirt-crusted, ragged little girl of ten or eleven, one of the new crop of "wild children," came into the car, begging for bread in a tremulous, hardly audible voice. The sight was familiar enough, yet something about the child's pitiful eyes and shriveled features touched Natasha to the quick. She brought the waif to our house.

"I suppose it was the temperature," Natasha had apologized to mother. "I couldn't bear the thought of the barefoot, half-naked bit of humanity out in the cold on a night like this. . ."

After supper, when mother went to wash the dishes, Katya said, "Auntie, may I help you?" Carrying the dishes from the table to the kitchen, she seemed for the first time a normal little girl, a touch of masquerade in her dragging grown-up gown. Our neighbor, Olga Ivanovna, came in. She was an active employee of the Regional Party Committee. She not only approved our taking in the child but offered to share the cost of clothes for her. Suddenly we heard the girl weeping in the kitchen.

"Let her cry it out," mother said.

But the weeping grew louder until it became hysterical sobbing. In the primordial singsong wail of the peasant she kept repeating, in Ukrainian, "Where's my mama? Where's my papa? Oh, where's my big brother Valya?" We went into the kitchen. The girl sat hunched over in a chair, wringing her bony little hands, tears streaming down her sunken cheeks.

"Please quiet down, Katya darling," mother pleaded. "No one will do you any harm. You will live with us, we'll get you shoes and clothes, we'll teach you to read and write. Believe me, I'll be a good mother to you."

The child would not be comforted. She began to tell about herself.

Abridged from Kravchenko, Victor, *I Chose Freedom, The Personal and Political Life of a Soviet Official*, 87–90. New York: Scribner's, 1946. Reprinted by Transaction, New Brunswick, N.J., 1988.

"Don't, little dove, don't. You'll tell us some other time," mother urged.

"I can't," Katya sobbed. "I must tell now. I can't stand not talking. I've been a whole year without my folks. A whole year! We lived in Pokrovnaya. My father didn't want to join the **kolkhoz.** All kinds of people argued with him and took him away and beat him but still he wouldn't go in. They shouted he was a *kulak* agent."

"Was your father a *kulak*?" I asked. "Do you know what a *'kulak* agent' means?"

"No, uncle, I don't know what these words mean. Our teacher didn't teach them to us. We had a horse, a cow, a heifer, five sheep, some pigs and a barn. That was all. Every night the constable would come and take papa to the village Soviet. They asked him for grain and didn't believe that he had no more. But it was the truth, I swear it."—She crossed herself solemnly.—"For a whole week they wouldn't let father sleep and they beat him with sticks and revolvers till he was black and blue and swollen all over."

When the last . . . grain had been squeezed out of him, Katya recounted, her father slaughtered a pig. He left a little meat for his family and sold the rest in the city to buy bread. Then he slaughtered the calf. Again "they" began to drag him out every night. They told that killing livestock without permission was a crime.

"Then one morning about a year ago," Katya went on, "strangers came to the house. One of them was from the G.P.U. [internal police] and the chairman of our Soviet was with him too. Another man wrote in a book everything that was in the house, even the furniture and our clothes and pots and pans. Then wagons arrived and all our things were taken away and the remaining animals were driven to the *kolkhoz.*

"*Mamochka,* my dear little mother, she cried and prayed and fell on her knees and even father and big brother Valya cried and sister Shura. But it did no good. We were told to get dressed and take along some bread and salt pork, onions and potatoes, because we were going on a long journey."

The memory was too much for Katya. She again burst into wild sobbing. But she insisted on going on with the story:

"They put us all in the old church. There were many other parents and children from our village, all with bundles and all weeping. There we spent the whole night, in the dark, praying and crying, praying and crying. In the morning about thirty families were marched down the road surrounded by militiamen. People on the road made the sign of the cross when they saw us and also started crying.

"At the station there were many other people like us, from other villages. It seemed like thousands. We were all crushed into a stone barn but they wouldn't let my dog, Volchok, come in though he'd followed us all the way down the road. I heard him howling when I was inside in the dark.

"After a while we were let out and driven into cattle cars, long rows of them, but I didn't see Volchok anywhere and the guard kicked me when I asked. As soon as our car was filled up so that there was no room for more, even standing up, it was locked from the outside. We all shrieked and prayed to the Holy Virgin. Then the train started. No one knew where we were going. Some said Siberia but others said no, the Far North or even the hot deserts.

"Near Kharkov my sister Shura and I were allowed out to get some water. Mama gave us some money and a bottle and said to try and buy some milk for our baby brother who was very sick. We begged the guard so long that he let us go out which he said was against his rules. Not far away were some peasant huts so we ran there as fast as our feet would carry us.

"When we told these people who we were they began to cry. They gave us something to eat right away, then filled the bottle with milk and wouldn't take the money. Then we ran back to the station. But we were too late and the train had gone away without us."

Katya interrupted herself again to wail for her mother, father, brothers and sister. Now most of us in the kitchen were weeping with the child. The harder mother tried to soothe Katya, the louder she wept herself. My father looked grim and said nothing. I could see the muscles of his face working convulsively . . .

We learned to love Katya and she came to feel at home with us. But from time to time, at night, we could hear her smothered sobs and that ancient dirgelike complaint, "Where are you, little mother? Where are you, *pa-pochka*?"

2. Mayakovsky: *Americans Are Astounded*

The poet V. V. Mayakovsky joined the Bolshevik party when he was fifteen and enthusiastically participated in the Revolution of 1917. He served the new regime with his pen, writing advertising jingles and propaganda verse as well as poetry and plays, and became the unofficial poet laureate of the Revolution. Gradually he grew disillusioned with what he saw as the reemergence of bourgeois values. He found his own individuality incompatible with the requirements of Socialist Realism and the Stalinist way. Unhappy in his personal life as well, Mayakovsky committed suicide in 1930. This poem illustrates Mayakovsky's popular, breezy style, as well as the Soviet preoccupation with, and ambivalence toward the United States.

From Mayakovsky, V.V., "Americans Are Astounded." In *Mayakovsky*, edited and translated by Herbert Marshall, 390–91. London: Dobson Books, 1965.

AMERICANS ARE ASTOUNDED

Through horn-rimmed glasses,
           in their unblinking way,
eyes popping
      from shores afar,
standing on tip-toe
      the U.S.A.
sizes-up
    the U.S.S.R.
What sort of people are they,
         a strange breed of man,
dabbling in construction
      in that far clime?
They've concocted
     some sort of
        five-year plan . . .
And want to
    fullfil it
     in four years' time!
You can't measure such
      by the American standard.
Neither dollars
     nor cents
      can procure their seduction,
with all
   their human energy
      extended,
they work the week round
      in continuous production.
What sort of people are they?
      Of what mettle!
To work like that
    by whom
     were they scourged?
No sort of lash
    has driven them
      like cattle—
such steel discipline
    they themselves
      have forged.
Misters,
   you've practised,
     since ancient history,

work-habits
                with money
                        to buy hard.
So to corpulent misters
                    it's an unsolved mystery,
        the roots
            of the zeal
                    of our Communards.
Bourgeoisie,
            astonish
                    at our Communistic shores—
in aeroplanes,
            on tractors,
                    at whatever work task,
your world-famous,
                streamlined America,
                            for sure,
we
    shall overtake
                and surpass.

3. John Scott: A Day in Magnitogorsk

A number of idealistic and adventurous young Americans set out to work in Soviet Russia after the Revolution, and particularly during the Great Depression of the early 1930s. John Scott was one of them. In this reading he explains why he went and the diverse people he found working together to build a vast industrial complex at Magnitogorsk: Americans on contract, technicians who had been accused of sabotage by the Bolsheviks but now had been pressed into service, party activists, and the workers themselves, most of them peasants fresh from the villages or the military front.

I left the University of Wisconsin in 1931 to find myself in an America sadly dislocated, an America offering few opportunities for young energy and enthusiasm.

I was smitten with the usual wanderlust. The United States did not seem adequate. I decided to go somewhere else. I had already been in Europe three times. Now I projected more far-flung excursions. Plans for a motor-cycle trip to Alaska, thence by home-made sailboat to Siberia and China came to naught.

Abridged from Scott, John, *Behind the Urals*. Indiana: Indiana University Press, 1989.

Where would I get the money to finance the project, and what would I do in China? I looked around New York for a job instead. There were no jobs to be had.

Something seemed to be wrong with America. I began to read extensively about the Soviet Union, and gradually came to the conclusion that the Bolsheviks had found answers to at least some of the questions Americans were asking each other. I decided to go to Russia to work, study, and to lend a hand in the construction of a society which seemed to be at least one step ahead of the American.

Following wise parental counsel I learned a trade before going to Russia. I went to work as a welder's apprentice in the General Electric plant in Schenectady, and several months later received a welder's certificate.

In due course of time Soviet consular wheels ground out my visa and I entrained for Moscow. For ten days I bounced back and forth between several Soviet organizations, trying to make arrangements for a job. The welding trust was glad to give me work. They needed welders in many places. They were not able to sign me up, however, until the visa department had given me permission to remain in the Soviet Union as a worker. The latter organization could grant such permission only to people with jobs. Neither would put anything in writing.

Finally arrangements were completed, and I started out on the four-day train trip to a place called Magnitogorsk on the eastern slopes of the Ural Mountains.

I was very happy. There was no unemployment in the Soviet Union. The Bolsheviks planned their economy and gave opportunities to young men and women. Furthermore, they had got away from the fetishization of material possessions, which, my good parents had taught me, was one of the basic ills of our American civilization. I saw that most Russians ate only black bread, wore one suit until it disintegrated, and used old newspapers for writing letters and office memoranda, rolling cigarettes, making envelopes, and for various personal functions.

I was about to participate in the construction of this society. I was going to be one of many who cared not to own a second pair of shoes, but who built blast furnaces which were their own. It was September, 1932, and I was twenty years old . . .

The big whistle on the power house sounded a long, deep, hollow six o'clock. All over the scattered city-camp of Magnitogorsk, workers rolled out of their beds or bunks and dressed in preparation for their day's work.

I climed out of bed and turned on the light. I could see my breath across the room as I woke my roommate, Kolya. Kolya never heard the whistle. Every morning I had to pound his shoulder for several seconds to arouse him.

We pushed our coarse brown army blankets over the beds and dressed as quickly as we could—I had good American long woolen underwear, fortunately; Kolya wore only cotton shorts and a jersey. We both donned army shirts, padded and quilted cotton pants, similar jackets, heavy scarves, and then ragged sheepskin coats. We thrust our feet into good Russian *"valinkis"*—felt boots coming up to the knee. We did not eat anything. We had nothing on hand except tea and a few potatoes, and there was no time to light a fire in our little homemade iron stove. We locked up and set out for the mill.

It was January, 1933. The temperature was in the neighborhood of thirty-five below. A light powdery snow covered the low spots on the ground. The high spots were bare and hard as iron. A few stars crackled in the sky and some electric lights twinkled on the blast furnaces. Otherwise the world was bleak and cold and almost pitch-dark.

It was two miles to the blast furnaces, over rough ground. There was no wind, so our noses did not freeze. I was always glad when there was no wind in the morning. It was my first winter in Russia and I was not used to the cold.

Down beside the foundation of Blast Furnace No. 4 there was a wooden shanty. It was a simple clapboard structure with a corrugated-iron roof nailed on at random. Its one big room was dominated by an enormous welded iron stove placed equidistant from all the walls, on a plate of half-inch steel. It was not more than half-past six when Kolya and I walked briskly up to the door and pushed it open . . .

Kolya, the welder's foreman, was twenty-two, big-boned, and broad. There was not much meat on him, and his face had a cadaverous look which was rather common in Magnitogorsk in 1933. His unkempt, sawdust-colored hair was very long, and showed under his fur hat. The sheepskin coat which he wore was ragged from crawling through narrow pipes and worming his way into various odd corners. At every tear the wool came through on the outside and looked like a Polish customs officer's mustache. His hands were calloused and dirty; the soles of the *valinkis* on his feet were none too good. His face and his demeanor were extremely energetic.

The riggers were youngish and had not shaved for several days. Their blue peasant eyes were clear and simple, but their foreheads and cheeks were scarred with frostbite, their hands dirty and gnarled.

"I don't know what we're going to do with our cow," said a young fellow with a cutting torch stuck in the piece of ragged rope that served him as a belt. He rubbed his chin sorrowfully with the back of his rough hand. His blue peasant eyes were looking through the shanty walls, through the blast-furnace foundation, through the stack of unerected trusses, across two hundred miles of snow-swept steppe back to the little village he had left six months before. "It took us two weeks to get here," he said earnestly to a bewhiskered welder sitting next to him, "walking over the steppe with our bags on our backs and driving that goddam cow—and now she's not giving any milk."

"What the hell do you feed her?" asked the welder thoughtfully.

"That's just the trouble," said the young cutter's helper, slapping his knee."Here we came all the way to Magnitogorsk because there was bread and work on the new construction, and we find we can't even feed the cow, let alone ourselves. Did you eat in the dining-room this morning?"

"Yeah, I tried to," said a clean-cut looking fellow; "only fifty grams of bread and that devilish soup that tastes like it was made of matchsticks." He shrugged his shoulder and spat on the floor between his knees. "But then—if we are going to build blast furnaces I suppose we have to eat less for a while."

"Sure," said a welder, in broken Russian. "And do you think it's any better anywhere else? Back in Poland we hadn't had a good meal in years. That's why our whole village walked across the Soviet frontier. It's funny, though, we thought there would be more to eat here than there is . . ."

At this point a young, boisterous, athletic-looking burner burst into the room and pushed his way up to the stove. "Boy, is it cold!" he said, addressing everybody in the room. "I don't think we should work up on top today. One of the riveters froze to death up there last night. It seems he was off in a bleeder pipe and they didn't find him till this morning."

"Yeah?" said everybody at once. "Who was it?"

But nobody knew who it was. It was just one of the thousands of peasants and young workers who had come to Magnitogorsk for a bread card, or because things were tough in the newly collectivized villages, or fired with enthusiasm for Socialist construction . . .

At about ten o'clock a group assembled in the wooden shanty, far different from that which had been there three hours before. First Syemichkin, the superintendent, arrived. Then came Mr. Harris, the American specialist consultant, with his interpreter; then Tishenko, the burly, sinister prisoner specialist.* They came into the shanty one by one, unbuttoned their coats, warmed their hands, then set to talking over their blueprints. Mr. Harris produced a package of fat "Kuzbas" cigarettes from the special foreigners' store [*beryozka*].** He passed them around with a smile. No one refused. Kolya, who had just come in, got in on it too.

"Well," said Mr. Harris, through his taciturn interpreter, "when do you expect to get the rest of the riveting done up on top of No. 3? They were telling me about this new time limit. The whole top is to be finished by the twenty-fifth. That's ten days."

Tishenko, the chief engineer, convicted of sabotage in the Ramzin trial*** in 1929, sentenced to be shot, sentence commuted, now serving ten years in Magnitogorsk, shrugged his shoulders. He did not speak immediately. He was not a wordy man. He had been responsible engineer for a Belgian company in the Ukraine before the Revolution. He had had a house of his own,

---

*One of several thousand engineers and scientists accused of anti-Soviet activities and exiled to outlying places where they held responsible positions working for Soviet industry.

**Store in USSR where only hard (Western) currency is accepted, mainly used by foreigners.

***1930 show trial of Professor Leonid Ramzin, accused of sabotaging Soviet industry in collaboration with hostile foreigners.

played tennis with the British consul, sent his son to Paris to study music. Now he was old. His hair was white. He had heard a great deal of talk since 1917, and had decided that most of it was worthless. He did his job, systematically, without enthusiasm. He liked to think that he was helping to build a strong Russia where life would one day be better than it was for his son in Paris or his sister in London. It certainly wasn't yet, though.

Mr. Harris looked at Tishenko. He understood the older man's position and respected his silence. Still, he was a consulting engineer being paid good American dollars, being supplied with caviar in a country where there was little bread and no sugar, to push Magnitostroi through to completion on time. He pressed the point. And Tishenko finally answered slowly: "A riveter froze to death last night. Cold and malnutrition. This morning four of the girls we have heating rivets didn't show up. Two of them are pregnant, I think, and it's cold up there. The compressor is working badly." He stopped, realizing it was all beside the point. If he said that the job would be finished by the twenty-fifth he was a liar and a hypocrite and Mr. Harris would be perfectly aware of it. If he said that it would take longer, he was sabotaging the decision of the Commissar of Heavy Industry. He was already under sentence for sabotage. He looked out of the dusty window. "It'll take at least a month," he said . . .

The door opened and Shevchenko came in. Shevchenko was the great activist among the technical personnel . . .

His technical knowledge was limited, and his written Russian contained many mistakes. His present job was sectional assistant director of construction. He was responsible to the director and to the party for the fulfillment of construction plans . . .

We all realized that Shevchenko was a boor and a careerist. But it seemed to take people like that to push the job forward, to overcome the numerous difficulties, to get the workers to work in spite of cold, bad tools, lack of materials, and undernourishment. It took all types to make Magnitogorsk. That was clear . . .

"Now, Mr. Shevchenko," said the American, "orders are orders, but you can't rivet steel with them and you can't heat rivets with them. We must have these things or the job won't be finished by next Christmas. You're an influential man in the party and with the construction administration. It's up to you to get these materials . . ."

The four men, as heterogeneous a group as one could find—a Cleveland engineer, a prisoner specialist, a Red director, and a young, inexperienced Soviet engineer—sat down around the table to discuss the rest of the points on Mr. Harris's list [of what had to be done] . . .

EPILOGUE—1941

The Magnitogorsk I left in early 1938 was producing upward of five thousand tons of steel daily and large quantities of many other useful products. In spite of the purge, the town was still full of rough and earnest young Russians— working, studying, making mistakes and learning, reproducing to the tune of thirty-odd per thousand every year. They were also writing poetry, going to see remarkably good performances of "Othello," learning to play violins and tennis. All this out in the middle of a steppe where, ten years before, only a few hundred impoverished herders had lived.

Today, after little more than a decade, Magnitogorsk stands as one of the largest metallurgical plants in the world. It produces five thousand tons of pig iron, six to seven thousand tons of steel, more than ten thousand tons of iron ore every day, as well as millions of tons of chemical by-products, structural shapes, steel wire, rods, rails, plates, and strips annually. Furthermore, at the present moment, at least one armament factory previously situated near Leningrad has arrived in Magnitogorsk lock, stock, and barrel, complete with personnel, and is already going into production using Magnitogorsk steel. [Note the year this epilogue was written. The reference is to the Soviet policy of moving whole factories eastward away from the 1941 German advance.]

4. Zoshchenko: Poverty

A top priority of the early Soviet regime was electrification of the countryside. The slogan of the party was "Electrification Plus Soviet Power." Mikhail Zoshchenko, a Soviet satirist born in 1895, depicts here, with consummate skill and humor, the mixed blessing of the advances of industrialization.

Nowadays, brothers, what is the most fashionable word there is, eh?

Nowadays, the most fashionable word that can be is, of course, electrification.

I won't argue that it isn't a matter of immense importance to light up Soviet Russia with electricity. Nevertheless, even this matter has its shady side. I am not saying, comrades, that it costs a lot. It costs nothing more expensive than money. That's not what I'm talking about.

This is what I mean.

I lived, comrades, in a very large house. The whole house was using kerosene. Some had kerosene lamps with, some without a glass, and some had nothing—just a priest's candle flickering away. Real hardship!

And then they started installing electric lights. Soon after the Revolution.

The house delegate [building director] installed them first. Well, he installed and installed. He's a quiet man and doesn't let his tongue give him away. But still he walks a bit strangely, and he's always thoughtfully blowing his nose.

Nevertheless, he doesn't let his tongue give him away.

From Zoshchenko, Mikhail, *Scenes from the Bathhouse*, 29-31. Ann Arbor: University of Michigan Press, 1973.

And then our dear little landlady, Elizaveta Ignat'evna Prokhorov, declares to us that she too wants to put in electric lights in our half-dark apartment.

"Everybody," she says, "is installing them. Even the delegate," she says, "has installed them. Why should we be more backward than other people? All the more so," she says, "since it's economical. Cheaper than kerosene."

You don't say! We too began to install.

We installed them, turned them on—my fathers! Muck and filth all around.

The way it was before, you'd go to work in the morning, come home in the evening, drink a bit of tea, and go to bed. And nothing of this kind was visible as long as you used kerosene. But now when we turned on the lights, we see, here someone's old bedroom slipper lying around, there the wallpaper torn in shreds and hanging down, there a bedbug running away at a trot, trying to save himself from the light, here a rag of who-knows-what, there a gob of spit, here a cigar butt, there a flea hopping.

Holy fathers! You wanted to cry for help. Sad to look on such a spectacle.

Take the couch that stood in our room, for example. I used to think, it's all right, it's a couch. It's a good couch. I often sat on it evenings. And now I was burning electricity—holy fathers! What a couch! Everything's sticking out, hanging down, spilling out from inside. I can't sit down on such a couch—my soul cries out.

So, I think, I don't live very well, do I? Better get out of the house. I begin to develop a negative attitude. My work falls from my hands.

I see the landlady, Elizaveta Ignat'evna, is also going around mournfully, muttering to herself, fussing around in the kitchen.

"What," I ask, "is bothering you, landlady?"

She waves her hand.

"My dear man," she says, "I never thought I was living so badly."

I looked at her fixings—and it really wasn't what you'd call luxurious; in fact, her furniture was painful. And all around, disorder, strewings, litter, rubbish. And all this flooded with bright light and staring you in the eye.

I began coming home kind of depressed.

I come in, I turn on the light, stare at the bulb, and hop into the sack.

After giving it a good deal of thought, I got my pay. I bought some whitewash and started to work. I shook out the bed, killed off the bedbugs, painted over the woodwork, banged the couch back together, decorated, decontaminated—my spirit sings and rejoices.

In general, everything was going well, very well indeed.

But our landlady, Elizaveta Ignat'evna, took another course. She cut the installation wires in her room.

"My dear man," she says, "I don't want to live in the light. I don't want," she says, "my modest circumstances to be lit up for the bedbugs to laugh at."

I begged and argued with her—no good. She held her own.

"I don't want," she says, "to live with that light. I have no money to make repairs."

I tell her: "Why, I'll do the repairs for you myself for next to nothing."
She doesn't want that.

"With those bright lights of yours," she says, "I have to keep busy from morning to night with cleaning and washing. I'll manage," she says, "without the light, as I managed before."

The delegate also tried to convince her. And even quarreled with her. He called her an outmoded *petit bourgeois* [small-minded middle class person]. It didn't work. She refused.

Well, let her have it the way she wants. Personally, I live in the electric light and I am quite satisfied with it.

The way I look at it, the light scratches away all our litter and removes the rubbish.

5. Ginzburg: Into the Whirlwind of the Purges

Stalin's purges led to the arrest and imprisonment of many loyal and devoted Communists. Often those arrested had absolutely no idea why they had been chosen and believed that "if Stalin only knew" what was happening to them, he would reprimand the local official responsible for it. Eugenia Ginzburg was less naive than this. She was nonetheless devoted to the communist cause and has told her story in an unusually well-written and interesting autobiography. This selection begins with a description of the first time she was called in for questioning, shortly after her colleague, an historian named Elvov, had been arrested for misinterpreting the significance of the 1905 Revolution in Russia.

The next two years might be called the prelude to that symphony of madness and terror which began for me in February 1937. A few days after Elvov's arrest, a Party meeting was held at the editorial office of *Red Tartary* at which, for the first time, I was accused of what I had *not* done.

I had *not* denounced Elvov as a purveyor of Trotskyist* contraband. I had *not* written a crushing review of the source book on Tartar history he had edited—I had even contributed to it (not that my article, dealing with the nineteenth century, was in any way criticized). I had *not*, even once, attacked him at a public meeting.

My attempts to appeal to common sense were summarily dismissed.

Abridged from Ginzburg, Eugenia, *Journey into the Whirlwind*, 17–19, 411, 413, 417–18. New York: Harcourt, Brace, 1967.
*After Trotsky's ouster by Stalin, real or fabricated connection with him or possession of his writings was cause for arrest.

"But I wasn't the only one—no one in the regional committee [of the party] attacked him!"

"Never you mind, each will answer for himself. At the moment it's you we are talking about."

"But he was trusted by the regional committee. Communists elected him to the municipal board."

"You should have pointed out that this was wrong. What were you given a university training for, and an academic job?"

"But has it ever been proved that he's Trotskyist?"

This naive question provoked an explosion of righteous anger:

"Don't you know he's been arrested? Can you imagine anyone's being arrested unless there's something definite against him?"

All my life I shall remember every detail of that meeting, so notable for me because, for the first time, I came up against that reversal of logic and common sense which never ceased to amaze me in the more than twenty years that followed right up to the Twentieth Party Congress [when Khrushchev gave his Secret Speech; see Reading 11], or at any rate the plenum of September 1953.

During a recess I went off to the editorial office. I wanted a moment to myself to think of what I should do next and how to behave without losing my dignity as a Communist and a human being. My cheeks were burning, and for several minutes I felt as if I should go mad with the pain of being unjustly accused.

The door creaked, and Alexandra Alexandrovna, the office typist, came in. She had done a lot of work for me and we got on well. An elderly, reserved woman who had suffered some kind of disappointment in life, she was devoted to me.

"You're taking this the wrong way, Eugenia Semyonovna. You should admit you're guilty and say you are sorry."

"But I'm not guilty of anything. Why should I lie at a Party meeting?"

"You'll get a reprimand anyway. A political reprimand is a very bad thing. And by not saying you repent you make it worse."

"I won't be a hypocrite. If they do reprimand me, I'll fight till they withdraw it."

She looked at me with her kindly eyes surrounded by a network of wrinkles, and repeated the very words Elvov had said to me at our last meeting:

"You don't understand what's going on. You're heading for a lot of trouble."

Doubtless, if the same thing happened to me today, I would "recant." I almost certainly would, for I too have changed. I am no longer the proud, incorruptible, inflexible being I was then. But in those days this is what I was: proud, incorruptible, inflexible, and no power on earth could have made me join in the orgy of breast-beating and self-criticism that was just beginning.

Large and crowded lecture halls were turned into public confessionals . . . Beating their breasts, the "guilty" would lament that they had "shown political short-sightedness" and "lack of vigilance," "compromised with dubious elements," "added grist" to this or that mill, and were tainted with "rotten liberalism."

Many such phrases echoed under the vaulted roofs of public buildings. The press, too, was flooded with contrite articles by Party theorists, frightened out of their wits like rabbits and not attempting to conceal their fear. The power and importance of the NKVD* grew with every day. . . .

[Mrs. Ginzburg began to live in continuous fear of arrest.]

My mind told me that there was absolutely nothing for which I could be arrested. It was true, of course, that in the monstrous accusations which the newspapers daily hurled at "enemies of the people" there was something clearly exaggerated, not quite real. All the same, I thought to myself, there must be something in it, however little—they must at least have voted the wrong way on some occasion or other. I, on the other hand, had never belonged to the opposition, nor had I ever had the slightest doubt as to the rightness of the Party line.

"If they arrested people like you they'd have to lock up the whole Party," my husband encouraged me in my line of reasoning.

Yet, in spite of all these rational arguments, I could not shake off a feeling of approaching disaster. I seemed to be at the center of an iron ring which was all the time contracting and would soon crush me.

The nights were terrifying. But what we were waiting for actually happened in the daytime . . .

We were in the dining room, my husband, Alyosha, and I. My stepdaughter Mayka was out skating. Vasya was in the nursery. I was ironing some laundry. I often felt like doing manual work; it distracted me from my thoughts. Alyosha was having breakfast, and my husband was reading a story by Valeria Gerasimova aloud to him. Suddenly the telephone rang. It sounded as shrill as on that day in December 1934 [day Kirov was shot].

For a few moments, none of us picked it up. We hated telephone calls in those days. Then my husband said in that unnaturally calm voice he so often used now:

"It must be Lukovnikov. I asked him to call."

He took the receiver, listened, went as white as a sheet, and said even more quietly:

"It's for you, Genia. Vevers, of the NKVD."

Vevers, the head of the NKVD department for special political affairs, could not have been more amiable and charming. His voice burbled on like a brook in spring.

"Good morning, dear comrade. Tell me, how are you fixed for time today?"

---

*Internal police: Its name has changed many times in the course of Soviet history; most recently its initials have been KGB.

"I'm always free now. Why?"

"Oh, dear, always free, how depressing. Never mind, these things will pass. So anyway, you'd have time to come and see me for a moment . . ."

[As she went out the door, not to return for many years, her husband said,]

"Well, Genia, we'll expect you home for lunch."

How pathetic he looked, all of a sudden, how his lips trembled! I thought of his assured, masterful tone in the old days, the tone of an old Communist, an experienced Party worker.

"Good-by, Paul dear. We've had a good life together."

I didn't even say "Look after the children." I knew he would not be able to take care of them. He was again trying to comfort me with commonplaces—I could no longer catch what he was saying. I walked quickly toward the reception room, and suddenly heard his broken cry:

"Genia!"

He had the haunted look of a baited animal, of a harried and exhausted human being—it was a look I was to see again and again, *there* . . .

EPILOGUE

All that this book describes is over and done with. I, and thousands like me, have lived to see the Twentieth and the Twenty-second Party Congress.

In 1937, when this tale begins, I was a little over thirty. Now I am in my fifties. The intervening eighteen years were spent "there."

During those years I experienced many conflicting feelings, but the dominant one was that of amazement. Was all this imaginable—was it really happening, could it be intended? Perhaps it was this very amazement which helped to keep me alive. I was not only a victim, but an observer also. What, I kept saying to myself, will come of this? Can such things just happen and be done with, unattended by retribution?

Many a time, my thoughts were taken off my own sufferings by the keen interest which I felt in the unusual aspects of life and of human nature which unfolded around me. I strove to remember all these things in the hope of recounting them to honest people and true Communists, such as I was sure would listen to me one day.

When I wrote this record, I thought of it as a letter to my grandson. I supposed that by 1980, when he would be twenty years old, these matters might seem remote enough to be safely divulged. How wonderful that I was mistaken, and that the great Leninist truths have again come into their own in our country and Party! Today the people can already be told of the things that have been and shall be no more.

Here, then, is the story of an ordinary Communist woman during the period of the "personality cult."

[Mrs. Ginzburg's book was published in the West in the mid-1960s. It was submitted for publication in the Soviet Union, but, after much discussion, was not published there.]

6. Stalin's Official History of the Purges

The History of the Communist Party of the Soviet Union was approved by Stalin and published in 1938. It was the official version of Soviet history up to that point. Seventy million copies were printed between 1938 and 1953, and it was used in all schools throughout the Soviet Union. In addition to glorifying Stalin, the History *vilifies most of the early Bolshevik leaders who had, by 1938, been arrested and shot in the purges. Those mentioned in this passage, Bukharin, Trotsky, Pyatakov, Zinoviev, Kamenev, Krestinsky, and others were all Old Bolsheviks. There is absolutely no evidence that they plotted against Lenin, betrayed state secrets, or conspired with foreigners. This reading is included less for the facts it recounts than for the tone and language in which these facts are discussed—the tone and language of the purges.*

In 1937, new facts came to light regarding the fiendish crimes of the Bukharin-Trotsky gang. The trial of Pyatakov, Radek and others, the trial of Tukhachevsky, Yakir and others, and, lastly, the trial of Bukharin, Rykov, Krestinsky, Rosengoltz and others, all showed that the Bukharinites and Trotskyites had long ago joined to form a common band of enemies of the people, operating as the "Bloc of Rights and Trotskyites."

The trials showed that these dregs of humanity, in conjunction with the enemies of the people, Trotsky, Zinoviev and Kamenev, had been in conspiracy against Lenin, the Party and the Soviet state ever since the early days of the October Socialist Revolution. The insidious attempts to thwart the Peace of Brest-Litovsk at the beginning of 1918, the plot against Lenin and the conspiracy with the "Left" Socialist-Revolutionaries for the arrest and murder of Lenin, Stalin and Sverdlov in the spring of 1918, the villainous shot that wounded Lenin in the summer of 1918, the revolt of the "Left" Socialist-Revolutionaries in the summer of 1918, the deliberate aggravation of differences in the Party in 1921 with the object of undermining and overthrowing Lenin's leadership from within, the attempts to overthrow the Party leadership during Lenin's illness and after his death, the betrayal of state secrets and the supply of information of an espionage character to foreign espionage services, the vile assassination of Kirov, the acts of wrecking, diversion and explosions, the dastardly murder of Menzhinsky, Kuibyshev and Gorky—all these and similar villainies over a period of twenty years were committed, it transpired, with the

From Commission of the Central Committee of the C.P.S.U., ed., *History of the Communist Party of the Soviet Union* (Bolshevik), 346–48. New York: International Publishers, 1939.

participation or under the direction of Trotsky, Zinoviev, Kamenev, Bukharin, Rykov and their henchmen, at the behest of espionage services of bourgeois states.

The trials brought to light the fact that the Trotsky-Bukharin fiends, in obedience to the wishes of their masters—the espionage services of foreign states had set out to destroy the Party and the Soviet state, to undermine the defensive power of the country, to assist foreign military intervention, to prepare the way for the defeat of the Red Army, to bring about the dismemberment of the U.S.S.R., to hand over the Soviet Maritime Region to the Japanese, Soviet Byelorussia to the Poles, and the Soviet Ukraine to the Germans, to destroy the gains of the workers and collective farmers, and to restore capitalist slavery in the U.S.S.R.

These Whiteguard pigmies, whose strength was no more than that of a gnat, apparently flattered themselves that they were the masters of the country, and imagined that it was really in their power to sell or give away the Ukraine, Byelorussia and the Maritime Region.

These Whiteguard insects forgot that the real masters of the Soviet country were the Soviet people, and that the Rykovs, Bukharins, Zinovievs and Kamenevs were only temporary employees of the state, which could at any moment sweep them out from its offices as so much useless rubbish.

These contemptible lackeys of the fascists forgot that the Soviet people had only to move a finger, and not a trace of them would be left.

The Soviet court sentenced the Bukharin-Trotsky fiends to be shot.

The People's Commissariat of Internal Affairs carried out the sentence.

The Soviet people approved the annihilation of the Bukharin-Trotsky gang and passed on to next business.

7. The Siege of Leningrad

The city of Leningrad had a population of about 2.5 million people when it was surrounded by the German advance in September of 1941. It remained surrounded for almost nine hundred days. Its only supplies had to be dropped by air or, in winter, brought in over an ice road built over Lake Ladoga. During the siege, it is estimated that well over one million people died, mostly from hunger and cold, but also on the front lines and from the German bombardment. This is a Soviet account, published first in the Soviet Union in 1958.

November–December, 1941

November arrived. Cold, cloudy days and heavy snowfalls replaced the clear, dry days of October. The ground was covered by a thick layer of white

---

Abridged from Pavlov, Dmitri, *Leningrad 1941: The Blockade*, 110–13, 118–19, 122–23, 125, 129–31. Chicago: University of Chicago Press, 1965.

that rose in drifts along the streets and boulevards. An icy wind drove powdered snow through the slits of dugouts and shelters, through the broken windows of apartments, hospitals, and stores. Winter came early, snowy, and cold.

The functioning of the city's transportation system deteriorated with each day. Fuel supplies were almost gone, and industry was dying out. Workers and employees, quartered in distant parts of the city, had now to walk several kilometers to work, struggling from one end of the city to the other through deep snow. Exhausted at the close of the working day, they could barely make their way home. There they could throw off their clothes and lie down for a short while to stretch their work-heavy legs. Sleep would come instantly, in spite of the cold, but would constantly be interrupted by cramps of the legs or hands. Rising was hard in the morning. Night did not restore the strength or drive away weariness. The fatigue of great temporary exertion will pass off in a single night's rest; but this was weariness that came from the daily exhausting of physical strength. Soon, however, it would be time for work again. Arm, leg, neck, and heart muscles would have to take up their burdens. The brain worked tensely.

The demands on people's strength increased as their nourishment deteriorated. The constant shortage of food, the cold weather and nervous tension wore the workers down. Jokes and laughter ceased; faces grew preoccupied and stern. People were weaker. They moved slowly, stopping often. Rosy cheeks were like a miracle. People looked at the person with surprise and some suspicion. Few people in November paid any attention to the whistle and burst of shells that had shocked them into alertness only a few days before. The thunder of gunfire was like a distant, aimless, hoarse barking. People were deeply absorbed in their joyless thoughts.

The blockade was now fifty-three days old. The most severe economies in food consumption and the delivery of a small quantity of grain across the lake had only resulted in the following meager amounts being on hand on the first of November: flour for fifteen days; cereals for sixteen days; sugar for thirty days; fats for twenty-two days. There was only a very small quantity of meat. The supply of meat products depended almost wholly on the deliveries by air. Out of the whole city, however—although everyone knew that food was scarce, since the rations were being reduced—the actual situation was known to only seven men. Two specially chosen workers recorded the deliveries of food over the lake and air routes (and later over the Ice Road), and these figures and those for food on hand were restricted to a small inner circle, which made it possible to keep the secret of the beleaguered fortress.

The eve of the twenty-fourth anniversary of the October Revolution arrived [November 7 by revised calendar]. There usually was such a happy fuss and bustle on that evening! Streets and houses would have been ablaze with lights; store windows would delight the eye with their decorations and lavish displays of goods. Fat turkeys, apples, prunes, pastries, thin slices of ham, and a world of other delicacies would lure shoppers. Everywhere, marketing would be going on in lively fashion, as families prepared to spend the holidays with friends. There would have been the noise of happy children excited by the gaiety in the air and the prospect of presents and shows.

In the memorable year of 1941, Leningraders were deprived of pleasure. They had cold, darkness, and the sensation of hunger constantly with them. The sight of the empty shelves in the stores woke a feeling of melancholy in them that was actually painful. The holiday was observed by issuing each child two hundred grams of sour cream and one hundred grams of potato flour. Adults received five salted tomatoes. Nothing more was to be found . . .

[The Leningraders worked to establish an ice road over Lake Ladoga to bring in supplies and evacuate children and old people. In their desperate need to use the road before the ice was thick enough, they lost many trucks that fell through the ice. Even when the ice road could be used, food and fuel were desperately short.]

Not more than thirty carloads of flour per day were used to feed a population of two and one-half million people. To produce even this much required hard fighting with the enemy and the elements.

The sudden drop by more than one-third in the bread ration had pernicious effects on health. Everyone, dependents especially, began to experience acute hunger. Men and women faded before each others' eyes; they moved slowly; they talked slowly, then an emaciated body would suddenly be lifeless. In those days, death drew itself up to its full stature and loomed menacingly, preparing to reap in masses those who crossed its path, regardless of sex or age.

Cold had settled down to stay in the unheated apartments of the city. Remorselessly it froze the exhausted people. Dystrophy and cold sent 11,085 people to their graves during November, the first to fall under death's scythe being the old men. Their bodies, in contrast to those of women of the same age or young men, offered no resistance at all to acute hunger . . .

More and more adults and children died every day. First a person's arms and legs grew weak, then his body became numb, the numbness gradually approached the heart, gripped it as in a vise, and then the end came.

Death overtook people anywhere. As he walked along the street, a man might fall and not get up. People would go to bed at home and not rise again. Often death would come suddenly as men worked at their machines.

Since public transportation was not operating, burial was a special problem. The dead were usually carried on sleds without coffins. Two or three relatives or close friends would haul the sled along the seemingly endless streets, often losing strength and abandoning the deceased halfway to the cemetery, leaving to the authorities the task of disposing of the body. Employees of the municipal public services and health service cruised the streets and alleys to pick up the bodies, loading them on trucks. Frozen bodies, drifted over with snow, lined the cemeteries and their approaches. There was not strength enough to dig into the deeply frozen earth. Civil defense crews would blast the ground to make mass graves, into which they would lay tens and sometimes hundreds of bodies without even knowing the names of those they buried.

—May the dead forgive the living who could not, under those desperate conditions, perform the last ceremonies due honest, laborious lives . . .

There is in Leningrad an Institute of Plant Genetics whose personnel had at one time assembled a rare collection of grain cultures from 118 countries of the world. The work had been done under the direction of Nikolai Ivanovich Vavilov, the famous scientist.[*] By the beginning of the war, the collection contained more than 100,000 different samples of wheat, rye, corn, rice, and other cereal and bean cultures. A broad study of these flora from all over the world had helped agricultural workers in our country solve a number of important problems.

The war interrupted the creative work of the Institute. Many of its people went to the front, where a number died. The Institute of Plant Genetics (and not only it) dropped from sight in the commotion of the war. The authorities had no time for it, as the workers of the Institute knew; they understood they could do as they pleased with the collection, and no one would hold them responsible if the seed samples disappeared. The members of the Institute, despite the loss of colleagues from their ranks, continued to work, adjusting to circumstances as they arose.

When the enemy was approaching the city, the Institute prepared to evacuate the collection. After having been packed and loaded onto freight cars, the seeds and other scientifically valuable objects finally could not be shipped off because of the blockade. The director of the Institute, I. G. Eichfeld, took steps then to store the samples at the Institute on shelves specially equipped to preserve the seeds. A twenty-four hour watch was kept on them. Every Institute employee took a hand in the watch without exception. They disarmed dozens of incendiary bombs that fell on the roof of the building.

Rats caused a great deal of trouble. The creatures easily got into the empty rooms where the collection was stored, climbed up to the shelves, gnawed through packing, and devoured the seeds.

To protect the collection against the invasion of rats, the seeds were repacked in rat-proof metal boxes and stacked in piles so that they could be under the constant surveillance of the scientists. During the first two months of the blockade, the struggle was chiefly with bombs, rats, and isolated sallies by marauders. More strenuous ordeals were in store for the workers during the famine of November and December, 1941, and the beginning of 1942. This enemy dealt them fearful blows.

In December, Institute employees were often too exhausted to get out of

---

[*]Vavilov (1887–1943?) was Russia's leading plant geneticist and at one time head of the Academy of Agricultural Sciences. He was ousted in 1940 for opposing the theories of T.D. Lysenko and imprisoned. He was "rehabilitated" posthumously.

bed, and their work fell to those who could still move about. On one of the coldest days of that dreadful month, the workers heard sorrowful news; their comrade A. Ya. Molibog, the agrometerologist, had been burned to death in a fire at his home. He had grown so weak from hunger that he could not leave his apartment when it was enveloped in flames. Not long after, the biologist S. A. Egis and D. S. Ivanov, the senior scientist in rice culture, died of exhaustion. Twenty-eight other employees of the Institute followed them to the grave from the same cause.

These people all remained interested in the collection to the end. They would smile and their cloudy eyes would brighten when they were told it was still under care and safe . . .

The proximity to grain and the duty of caring for it in the name of the future while slowly dying of starvation was inhuman torture. But by their solidarity and single-mindedness, the Vavilov collection, which took years to put together, was preserved for science and the future. It cost the lives of many people wholeheartedly devoted to the cause of science but they triumphed over their suffering.

In the Piskarevskoye Memorial Cemetery outside St. Petersburg, over half a million victims of Leningrad's nine-hundred-day siege lie buried in mass graves. At one end of the cemetery stands a memorial plaque with the following inscription, written by the Leningrad poet Olga Bergholz, who survived and wrote about the siege.

Here lie the people of Leningrad
Men. Women. Children.
Beside them lie soldiers of the Red Army
who gave their lives
to defend you, Leningrad.
Cradle of the Revolution.
We cannot give all their noble names here.
There are so many under the timeless guard of granite
but all you who gaze on these stones must know:
No one and nothing has been forgotten.

To the city came an enemy clad in iron and armour.
But workers, schoolchildren, teachers, militiamen
rose with the Army
all, as one, declared:
Death will sooner fear us than we death.
The cold, fierce and dark winter of 1941–1942
is not forgotten.
Nor the grim gunfire.
Nor the horrible bombing in 1943.
Not a single life, comrades, has been forgotten.
Under ceaseless fire from air, land, and sea

The statue of Mother Russia in the Piskarevskoye Memorial Cemetery outside Leningrad.

daily heroism
you set forth simply and with dignity
and you and your Motherland
found victory.
Before your immortal selves
let a grateful people,
the Motherland, and the hero-city Leningrad
always lower their banners
to this sad and hallowed ground.

8. A Russian Woman

Quentin Reynolds was a widely published American correspondent during World War II. The following story of a Russian woman is from one of his dispatches.

At first glance, Uliana looks like almost any middle-aged peasant woman. She sits hunched over a little, the way women do who have spent too many years bending over the soil, coaxing it to yield wheat and corn and potatoes. Until she tells you, you don't know that she bends forward slightly because that eases the pain of a half-healed wound. Until she tells you that she is only thirty-three, you would indeed think of her as just another middle-aged peasant woman . . .

She was born in the village of Putivl, which is in the soft, lush region of the Ukraine. She had two young sisters, Alexandra and Maria. They were trained as nurses. Uliana herself was a brilliant student and fervent patriot. Her father was postmaster of the village, and he took great pride in the intellectual

Abridged from Reynolds, Quentin, *The Curtain Rises*, 119–23. New York: Random House, 1944.

achievements of young Uliana. So did the rest of the village, for when the old mayor (who had held office for twenty years) died, they elected young Uliana in his place.

In Russia they do not call the head of a community mayor; they call him president of the local soviet; but it means the same thing. She was enrolled as a party member when she was twenty-four, a great honor in the Soviet Union, for there are only two million party members in the whole country. That is one percent of the population. There is a waiting list of more than a million.

As mayor, Uliana settled local disputes over land boundaries, she administered justice, and the village of Putivl was indeed a happy and contented community. And then the German juggernaut rolled through the smooth plains of the Ukraine. Many in the village quite sensibly left, but not Uliana. When the Germans roared into Putivl, Uliana was there, calm and serene, prepared to do her best to make life easier for her fellow villagers.

But the Germans gave her no chance. They took Uliana and some of the other leading citizens, led them to a near-by monastery, lined them up against a wall and shot them.

"There were eight of us," Uliana told me in a peculiarly detached voice, as though she were telling of something which had happened to someone else. "Three of us, two teachers and I, were women. They marched us to an old monastery. They told us to face the wall and to take off our clothes. By now, of course, I knew that we were going to be shot. The Germans usually make people they are going to shoot or hang take off all their clothes first. It saves them a lot of trouble afterward.

"I undressed slowly, and then the shots came. I still had my stockings and underwear on. Nobody cried out when the shots came. Then I felt something hit me in the side and I fell forward. Things became confused. I half remember being carried into the monastery and down a staircase, then I lost consciousness.

"When I came to, it was dark and there was a weight on me. When my mind began to work, I realized that there were bodies on top of me. Upstairs, soldiers were arguing about the clothes. I could hear them and then I heard someone groaning near me. It was one of the men, a doctor, and he was not dead, though the others were. He cried out to the Germans to come and finish him off, but they didn't hear him. I crawled over to him and said that we should try to get out. We were in the cellar of the monastery."

"How did you get out of there?" I asked.

"When the soldiers left," she continued, "I crawled up the stairs very slowly because my side hurt and I was losing a lot of blood. The doctor followed me. It was night now. We crawled to a farmhouse near by. I couldn't stand up to knock at the door. I lay there, trying to cry out and fearing that the Germans would hear me, but they didn't. The people in the farmhouse took us in. The doctor had a bad wound. He died that night.

"The following night they put me in a wagon, piled hay on top of me and sent me to a farmhouse a few miles away. Each night I would be transferred farther away from my village, farther away from the Germans. Then I reached an unoccupied town which had a hospital. The bullet had gone through my side and had injured my lung, and they didn't think I would live. I did, though, and then when I was better I decided to join the partisans. People in our villages always knew where they could be found."

"Were you expert with a gun?" I asked.

She smiled faintly, "I had never held a gun in my hands before, but I soon learned. We were usually behind the German lines. We kept in touch with the people of the occupied villages. Sometimes we raided these villages. There was a great shortage of salt in the Ukraine. I imagine the Germans sent it back to their country. Once we heard that they had a stock of salt in a certain village. We raided the village, took the salt and distributed it among the people of the neighboring villages. We were well armed, but food, of course, was a problem."

"How would you get food?" I asked her.

"They put me in charge of that," she said. "My wound was giving me trouble and I couldn't go on quick marches. I'd take a few men and lie in wait beside a road. When a convoy of German food trucks came along, we would ambush them and run the loaded trucks back to our headquarters. We shifted headquarters every few nights. We slept by day usually, and fought by night."

"What was the partisans' main job?"

She shrugged her shoulders. "Our main job was to blow up railroads and bridges. We blew up a lot of them, hindering the German advance. They decided to send a good force after us. We heard about it. They sent twenty tanks into the valley where we were, but we outflanked them and blew up five of them with hand grenades. Then we moved somewhere else. We were always on the move."

Uliana lived and fought with the partisans for nearly two years. She doesn't know yet what happened to her mother or to her two younger sisters. She would rather not think about that, she said. Why was she in Moscow? Uliana was a little ashamed of it. Her old wound had given her a lot of trouble, so she had been sent to specialists in the capital. But she would be back with the partisans soon, she said grimly, and then, rather surprisingly, she lost her placidity and became vibrant, alive, dynamic.

"Do your American women know the kinds of beasts we are fighting?" Her eyes flashed now and she no longer bent forward. She no longer looked like a middle-aged peasant woman. She was filled with a righteous hatred of the men who had invaded her country.

"Do they know that every time Germans occupy a village they hang or shoot a group of women just as a lesson to the others?" she said. "As a lesson to make others fall into line and obey them. Their motto is, 'Women and children first.' Yes, first hang the women and starve the children. Have American women ever seen the bodies of children who have starved to death? I have—in many villages of the Ukraine."

Uliana breathed heavily and put her hand to her side. She got up and bowed, and there was a certain majesty about this stocky Russian who couldn't quite stand up straight. She walked out of the room.

9. Soviet War Losses

Soviet war losses in World War II were about 20 million, out of a population of 191 million in 1939. About one in ten people died during the war. On the following charts, compare the numbers of people who were twenty in 1939 and those who were forty in 1959 and also the numbers of men and women in different age groups in 1959.

The United States lost about 400,000 in World War II. In all its wars, including the Civil War which caused more deaths than any other American conflict, the United States has lost an estimated 1,155,059 people.

In the tables below, note that the first two age brackets include ten years, the others five, until age 70.

POPULATION OF THE SOVIET UNION BY AGE

Age	1939	1959
0–9	43,574,658	46,362,362
10–19	41,395,250	31,808,650
20–24	15,785,942	20,343,028
25–29	18,520,257	18,190,129
30–34	15,598,080	18,998,899
35–39	12,957,576	11,590,509
40–44	9,603,495	10,408,095
45–49	7,775,579	12,263,494
50–54	6,635,588	10,446,734
55–59	5,897,046	8,698,854
60–69	8,535,597	11,736,245
70+	4,461,950	7,971,289
Ages not given	35,872	8,362
Total Population	190,677,890	208,826,650

1959 CENSUS

Age	Total	Men	Women
0–9	46,362,362	23,608,300	22,754,062
10–19	31,808,650	16,066,487	15,742,163
20–24	20,343,028	10,055,978	10,287,050
25–29	18,190,129	8,916,969	9,273,160
30–34	18,998,899	8,611,011	10,387,888
35–39	11,590,509	4,528,340	7,062,169
40–44	10,408,095	3,998,239	6,409,856
45–49	12,263,494	4,705,764	7,557,730
50–54	10,446,734	4,010,114	6,436,620
55–59	8,698,854	2,905,486	5,793,368
60–69	11,736,245	4,098,922	7,637,323
70+	7,971,289	2,540,685	5,430,604
Ages not given	8,362	4,008	4,354
Total	208,826,650	94,050,303	114,776,347

From *Itogi Vsesoyuznoi Naseleniia*. Moscow, Central Statistics Bureau, 1962.

10. Stalin in the 1940s

Milovan Djilas was a leading Yugoslav communist who fought with the communist underground against the Nazis and visited the Soviet Union in 1944, 1945, and again in 1948. In this reading, he describes his impression of Stalin in the spring of 1944, then at the height of his prestige.

What could be more exciting for a Communist, one who was coming from war and revolution? To be received by Stalin—this was the greatest possible recognition for the heroism and suffering of our Partisan warriors and our people. In dungeons and in the holocaust of war, and in the no less violent spiritual crises and clashes with the internal and external foes of Communism, Stalin was something more than a leader in battle. He was the incarnation of an idea, transfigured in Communist minds into pure idea, and thereby into something infallible and sinless. Stalin was the victorious battle of today and the brotherhood of the man of tomorrow. I realized that it was by chance that I personally was the first Yugoslav Communist to be received by him. Still, I felt a proud joy that I would be able to tell my comrades about this encounter and say something about it to the Yugoslav fighting men as well . . .

Suddenly everything that had seemed unpleasant about the USSR disappeared, and all disagreements between ourselves and the Soviet leaders lost their significance and gravity, as if they had never happened. Everything disagreeable vanished before the moving grandeur and beauty of what was happening to me. Of what account was my personal destiny before the greatness of the struggle being waged, and of what importance were our disagreements beside the obvious inevitability of the realization of our idea? . . .

The room was not large, rather long, and devoid of any opulence or decor. But the host was the plainest of all. Stalin was in a marshal's uniform and soft boots, without any medals except a gold star—the Order of Hero of the Soviet Union—on the left side of his breast. In his stance there was nothing artificial or posturing. This was not that majestic Stalin of the photographs or the newsreels—with the stiff, deliberate gait and posture.

He was not quiet for a moment. He toyed with his pipe, which bore the white dot of the English firm Dunhill, or drew circles with a blue pencil around words indicating the main subjects for discussion, which he then crossed out with slanting lines as each part of the discussion was nearing an end, and he kept turning his head this way and that while he fidgeted in his seat.

I was also surprised at something else: he was of very small stature and ungainly build. His torso was short and narrow, while his legs and arms were too long. His left arm and shoulder seemed rather stiff. He had a quite large

Abridged from Djilas, Molivan, *Conversations with Stalin,* 57–82, 190–91. New York: Harcourt, Brace, 1962.

paunch, and his hair was sparse, though his scalp was not completely bald. His face was white, with ruddy cheeks. Later I learned that this coloration, so characteristic of those who sit long in offices, was known as the "Kremlin complexion" in high Soviet circles . . . Still the head was not a bad one; it had something of the folk, the peasantry, the paterfamilias about it—with those yellow eyes and a mixture of sternness and roguishness.

I was also surprised at his accent. One could tell that he was not a Russian. Nevertheless his Russian vocabulary was rich, and his manner of expression was vivid and plastic, and replete with Russian proverbs and sayings. As I later became convinced, Stalin was well acquainted with Russian literature—though only Russian—but the only real knowledge he had outside of Russian limits was his knowledge of political history.

One thing did not surprise me: Stalin had a sense of humor—a rough humor, self-assured, but not entirely without finesse and depth. His reactions were quick and acute—and conclusive, which did not mean that he did not hear the speaker out, but it was evident that he was no friend of long explanations. Also remarkable was his relation to Molotov. He obviously regarded the latter as a very close associate, as I later confirmed. Molotov was the only member of the Politburo whom Stalin addressed with the familiar pronoun *ty*, which is in itself significant when it is kept in mind that with Russians the polite form *vy* is normal even among very close friends.

The conversation began by Stalin asking us about our impressions of the Soviet Union. I replied: "We are enthusiastic!"—to which he rejoined: "And we are not enthusiastic, though we are doing all we can to make things better in Russia." It is engraved in my memory that Stalin used the term Russia, and not Soviet Union, which meant that he was not only inspiring Russian nationalism but was himself inspired by it and identified himself with it . . .

I was enthusiastic about this direct, straightforward manner, which I had not till then encountered in Soviet official circles, and particularly not in Soviet propaganda. I felt that I was at the right spot, and moreover with a man who treated realities in a familiar open way. It is hardly necessary to explain that Stalin was like this only among his own men, that is, among Communists of his line who were devoted to him . . .

[Djilas was later invited to dinner.]

In a spacious and unadorned, though tasteful, dining room the front half of a long table was covered with all kinds of foods on warmed heavy silver platters, as well as beverages and plates and other utensils. Everyone served himself and sat where he wished around the free half of the table. Stalin never sat at the head, but he always sat in the same chair—the first to the left of the head of the table . . .

Such a dinner usually lasted six or more hours—from ten at night till four or five in the morning. One ate and drank slowly, during a rambling conversation which ranged from stories and anecdotes to the most serious political and even philosophical subjects. Unofficially and in actual fact a significant part of Soviet policy was shaped at these dinners. Besides they were the most frequent and most convenient entertainment and only luxury in Stalin's otherwise monotonous and somber life.

Apparently Stalin's co-workers were used to this manner of working and living—and spent their nights dining with Stalin or with one of their own number. They did not arrive in their offices before noon, and usually stayed in them till late evening. This complicated and made difficult the work of the higher administration, but the latter adapted itself, even the diplomatic corps, insofar as they had contacts with members of the Politburo.

There was no established order according to which members of the Politburo or other high officials attended these dinners. Usually those attended who had some connection with the business of the guest or with current issues. Apparently the circle was narrow, however, and it was an especial honor to be invited to such a dinner. Only Molotov was always present, and I maintain that this was not only because he was a Commissar, that is, Minister for Foreign Affairs, but also because he was in fact Stalin's substitute.

At these dinners the Soviet leaders were at their closest, most intimate with one another. Everyone would tell the news from his bailiwick, whom he had met that day, and what plans he was making. The sumptuous table and considerable, though not immoderate, quantities of alcohol enlivened spirits and intensified the atmosphere of cordiality and informality. An uninstructed visitor might hardly have detected any difference between Stalin and the rest. Yet it existed. His opinion was carefully noted. No one opposed him very hard. It all rather resembled a patriarchal family with a crotchety head whose foibles always caused the home folks to be apprehensive . . .

Stalin took quantities of food that would have been enormous even for a much larger man . . . He drank moderately, most frequently mixing red wine and vodka in little glasses. I never noticed any signs of drunkenness in him, whereas I could not say the same for Molotov, and especially not for Beria [head of secret police] who was practically a drunkard . . .

It was at these dinners that the destiny of the vast Russian land, of the newly acquired territories, and, to a considerable degree, of the human race was decided . . .

Thanks to both ideology and methods, personal experience and historical heritage, he [Stalin] regarded as sure only whatever he held in his fist, and everyone beyond the control of his police was a potential enemy . . .

The world in which the Soviet leaders lived—and that was my world too—was slowly taking on a new appearance to me; horrible unceasing struggle on all sides. Everything was being stripped bare and reduced to strife which changed only in form and in which only the stronger and the more adroit survived. Full of admiration for the Soviet leaders even before this, I now succumbed to a heady enthusiasm for the inexhaustible will and awareness which never left them for a moment. That was a world in which there was no choice other than victory or death . . .

If we assume the viewpoint of humanity and freedom, history does not know a despot as brutal and as cynical as Stalin was. He was methodical, all-embracing, and total as a criminal. He was one of those rare terrible dogmatists capable of destroying nine tenths of the human race to "make happy" the one tenth.

However, if we wish to determine what Stalin really meant in the history of Communism, then he must for the present be regarded as being, next to Lenin, the most grandiose figure. He did not substantially develop the ideas of Communism, but he championed them and brought them to realization in a society and a state. He did not construct an ideal society—something of the sort is not even possible in the very nature of humans and human society, but he transformed backward Russia into an industrial power and an empire that is ever more resolutely and implacably aspiring to world mastery . . .

Viewed from the standpoint of success and political adroitness, Stalin is hardly surpassed by any statesman of his time. I am, of course, far from thinking that success in political struggles is the only value . . . All in all, Stalin was a monster who, while adhering to abstract, absolute and fundamentally utopian ideas, in practice recognized, and could recognize, only success— violence, physical and spiritual extermination. However, let us not be unjust toward Stalin! What he wished to accomplish, and even that which he did accomplish, could not be accomplished in any other way. The forces that swept him forward and that he led, with their absolute ideas, could have no other kind of leader but him, given the level of Russian and world relations, nor could they have been served by different methods. The creator of a closed social system, he was at the same time its instrument and, in changed circumstances and all too late, he became its victim. Unsurpassed in violence and crime, Stalin was no less the leader and organizer of a certain social system. Today he rates very low, pilloried for his "errors," through which the leaders of that same system intend to redeem both the system and themselves.

11. Khrushchev's Secret Speech

Nikita Khrushchev first publicly criticized Stalin in 1956 at the Twentieth Communist Party Congress. There he revealed what most of his listeners already knew, namely the crimes committed by Stalin, though perhaps the scale of the crimes surprised even those who had helped make them possible. Thereafter it was hard ever again to justify the ruthless tactics Stalin had used. Nonetheless, Khrushchev never attacked Stalin's role in the brutal collectivization of the peasantry nor his ruthless attack on Trotsky and his other rivals. Khrushchev had no intention of changing the Soviet system of collective and state farms, nor of questioning the basic legitimacy of single party rule.

Abridged from U.S. Congress. *Congressional Record*, 84th Cong., 2d sess., 1957. Vol. 102, pt. 7.

Stalin acted not through persuasion, explanation, and patient cooperation with people, but by imposing his concepts and demanding absolute submission to his opinion. Whoever opposed this concept or tried to prove his viewpoint, and the correctness of his position—was doomed to removal from the leading collective and to subsequent moral and physical annihilation. This was especially true during the period following the XVIIth Party Congress, when many prominent Party leaders and rank-and-file Party workers, honest and dedicated to the cause of Communism, fell victim to Stalin's despotism.

We must affirm that the Party had fought a serious fight against the Trotskyites, rightists and bourgeois nationalists, and that it disarmed ideologically all the enemies of Leninism. This ideological fight was carried on successfully as a result of which the Party became strengthened and tempered. Here Stalin played a positive role . . .

Stalin originated the concept "enemy of the people." This term automatically rendered it unnecessary that the ideological errors of a man or men engaged in a controversy be proven; this term made possible the usage of the most cruel repression, violating all norms of revolutionary legality, against anyone who in any way disagreed with Stalin, against those who were only suspected of hostile intent, against those who had bad reputations. This concept, "enemy of the people," actually eliminated the possibility of any kind of ideological fight or the making of one's views known on this or that issue, even those of a practical character. In the main, and in actuality, the only proof of guilt used, against all norms of current legal science, was the "confession" of the accused himself; and, as subsequent probing proved, "confessions" were acquired through physical pressures against the accused.

This led to glaring violations of revolutionary legality, and to the fact that many entirely innocent persons, who in the past had defended the Party line, became victims.

We must assert that, in regard to those persons who in their time had opposed the Party line, there were often no sufficiently serious reasons for their physical annihilation. The formula, "enemy of the people" was specifically introduced for the purpose of physically annihilating such individuals.

It is a fact that many persons, who were later annihilated as enemies of the Party [were] people [who] had worked with Lenin during his life. Some of these persons had made errors during Lenin's life, but, despite this, Lenin benefited by their work, he corrected them and he did everything possible to retain them in the ranks of the Party; he induced them to follow him . . .

Stalin, on the other hand, used extreme methods and mass repressions at a time when the revolution was already victorious, when the Soviet state was strengthened, when the exploiting classes were already liquidated and Socialist relations were rooted solidly in all phases of national economy, when our Party was politically consolidated . . .

The Commission has presented to the Central Committee Presidium lengthy and documented materials pertaining to mass repressions against the delegates to the XVIIth Party Congress and against members of the Central

Committee elected at that Congress. These materials have been studied by the Presidium of the Central Committee.

It was determined that of the 139 members and candidates of the Party's Central Committee who were elected at the XVIIth Congress, 98 persons, i.e., 70 percent, were arrested and shot (mostly in 1937–1938). [Indignation in the hall.]

What was the composition of the delegates to the XVIIth Congress? It is known that eighty percent of the voting participants of the XVIIth Congress joined the Party during the years of conspiracy before the Revolution and during the Civil War; this means before 1921. By social origin the basic mass of the delegates to the Congress were workers (60 percent of the voting members).

For this reason, it was inconceivable that a Congress so composed would have elected a Central Committee, a majority of whom would prove to be enemies of the Party. The only reason why 70 percent of Central Committee members and candidates elected at the XVIIth Congress were branded as enemies of the Party and of the people was because honest Communists were slandered, accusations against them were fabricated, and revolutionary legality was gravely undermined.

The same fate met not only the Central Committee members but also the majority of the delegates to the XVIIth Party Congress. Of 1,966 delegates with either voting or advisory rights, 1,108 persons were arrested on charges of anti-revolutionary crimes, i.e., decidedly more than a majority. This very fact shows how absurd, wild and contrary to common sense were the charges of counterrevolutionary crimes made out, as we now see, against a majority of participants at the XVIIth Party Congress. [Indignation in the hall.]

We should recall that the XVIIth Party Congress is historically known as the Congress of Victors. Delegates to the Congress were active participants in the building of our Socialist State; many of them suffered and fought for Party interests during the pre-revolutionary years in the conspiracy and at the Civil War fronts; they fought their enemies valiantly and often nervelessly looked into the face of death. How then can we believe that such people could prove to be "two-faced" and had joined the camps of the enemies of Socialism during the era after the political liquidation of Zinovievites, Trotskyites and rightists and after the great accomplishments of Socialist construction?

This was the result of the abuse of power by Stalin, who began to use mass terror against the Party cadres . . .

Comrades:

The cult of the individual acquired such monstrous size chiefly because Stalin himself, using all conceivable methods, supported the glorification of his own person. This is supported by numerous facts. One of the most characteristic examples of Stalin's self-glorification and of his lack of even elementary modesty is the edition of his "Short Biography," which was published in 1948.

This book is an expression of the most dissolute flattery, an example of making a man into a godhead, of transforming him into an infallible sage, "the greatest leader," "sublime strategist of all times and nations." Finally, no other words could be found with which to lift Stalin up to the heavens.

We need not give here examples of the loathsome adulation filling this book. All we need to add is that they all were approved and edited by Stalin personally and some of them were added in his own handwriting to the draft text of the book.

What did Stalin consider essential to write into this book? Did he want to cool the ardor of his flatterers who were composing his "Short Biography"? No! He marked the very places where he thought that the praise of his services was insufficient.

Here are some examples characterizing Stalin's activity, added in Stalin's own hand . . .

"Although he performed his task of leader of the Party and the people with consummate skill and enjoyed the unreserved support of the entire Soviet people, Stalin never allowed his work to be marred by the slightest hint of vanity, conceit, or self-adulation."

Where and when could a leader so praise himself? Is this worthy of a leader of the Marxist-Leninist type? No. Precisely against this did Marx and Engels take such a strong position. This also was always sharply condemned by Vladimir Ilyich Lenin.

In the draft text of his book appeared the following sentence: "Stalin is the Lenin of today." This sentence appeared to Stalin to be too weak, so in his own handwriting he changed it to read: "Stalin is the worthy continuer of Lenin's work, or, as it is said in our Party, Stalin is the Lenin of today." You see how well it is said, not by the Nation but by Stalin himself.

It is possible to give many such self-praising appraisals written into the draft text of that book in Stalin's hand. Especially generously does he endow himself with praises pertaining to his military genius, to his talent for strategy.

I will cite one more insertion made by Stalin concerning the theme of the Stalinist military genius.

"The advanced Soviet science of war received further development," he writes, "at Comrade Stalin's hands. Comrade Stalin elaborated the theory of the permanently operating factors that decide the issue of wars, of active defense and the laws of counter-offensive and offensive, of the co-operation of all services and arms in modern warfare, of the role of big tank masses and air forces in modern war, and of the artillery as the most formidable of the armed services. At the various stages of the war Stalin's genius found the correct solutions that took account of all the circumstances of the situation." [Movement in the hall.]

And further, writes Stalin:

"Stalin's military mastership was displayed both in defense and offense. Comrade Stalin's genius enabled him to divine the enemy's plans and defeat them. The battles in which Comrade Stalin directed the Soviet armies are brilliant examples of operational military skill."

In this manner was Stalin praised as a strategist. Who did this? Stalin himself, not in his role as a strategist but in the role of an author-editor, one of the main creators of his self-adulatory biography.

Such, comrades, are the facts. We should rather say shameful facts.

12. De-Stalinization and the Cult of Lenin

Stalin's reputation in the Soviet Union fell, rose, and fell again in the years after his death in 1953. After Khrushchev's revelation of Stalin's crimes, de-Stalinization gained momentum. In 1961, Stalin's tomb was removed from the mausoleum on Red Square in Moscow that housed Lenin's body and, at the Twenty-Second Party Congress that year, his crimes and failings were spelled out in great detail. Historians were urged to reexamine the Soviet past and provide new history books for schools. The city of Stalingrad, the heroic World War II city, was renamed Volgograd. The campaign to discredit Stalin was accompanied by renewed emphasis on the cult of the founder, Vladimir Ilyich Lenin. This new cult is illustrated in D.A. Lazurkina's speech to the Twenty-Second Congress presented here.

In the late 1970s, Stalin's star began to rise again. History was again rewritten to credit him with considerable achievement, and the scope and effects of the purges were minimized. The Russian poet Yevgeny Yevtushenko wrote that, in 1973, he was with a group of Soviet young people when one raised a toast to Stalin. He asked if they knew how many people had died in the purges. One eighteen-year-old guessed fifteen to twenty, another two hundred. Only one in the rather large group suggested a figure over two thousand. They were astonished when Yevtushenko told them that the figure should be reckoned in millions rather than thousands. Such was the effect of Soviet censorship and the rewriting of history, until the advent of **glasnost,** *when the truth about Stalin finally began to emerge.*

SPEECH BY COMRADE D.A. LAZURKINA, PARTY MEMBER SINCE 1902, LENINGRAD PARTY ORGANIZATION

Comrade delegates! I wholly and fully support the proposals of Comrade Spiridonov and other comrades who have spoken here on removing Stalin's body from the Lenin Mausoleum. *(Stormy applause.)*

In the days of my youth I began my work under the leadership of Vladimir Ilyich Lenin, learned from him and carried out his instructions. *(Applause)* . . .

Not for a minute—either when I sat in prison for two and a half years or when I was sent to a camp, and later exiled (I spent 17 years in exile)—not once did I blame Stalin. I always fought for Stalin, who was assailed by the prisoners,

---

Abridged from "Speech of D.A. Lazurkina," *Current Soviet Policies IV,* 215–16. New York: Columbia University Press, 1962.

the exiles and the camp inmates. I would say: "No, it is not possible that Stalin would have permitted what is happening in the Party. This cannot be!" They would argue with me, some would become angry with me, but I stood firm. I had high esteem for Stalin, I knew that he had done great service before 1934, and I defended him.

Comrades! And then I returned completely rehabilitated. I arrived just at the time when the 20th Party Congress was in session. This was the first time I learned the hard truth about Stalin. And now at the 22nd Congress, as I hear about the disclosed evil deeds and crimes that were committed in the Party with Stalin's knowledge, I wholly and fully endorse the proposal for the removal of Stalin's remains from the Mausoleum.

We fought to the end. We did not believe there could be such arbitrariness in our Leninist party. We wrote, wrote endlessly. If one were to look through the files of my letters, he could count volumes. I wrote endlessly to Stalin. I wrote to others also, and I wrote to the Party control body [organization responsible for discipline and expulsion of Party members]. But unfortunately, even our Party control was not at the proper level at the time; it yielded to the common fear and also refused to consider our cases.

Such was the atmosphere created by the cult of the individual. And we must root out the remnants of it! It is good that the 20th Party Congress raised this question. It is good that the 22nd Party Congress is uprooting these remnants.

I think that our wonderful Vladimir Ilyich, the most human of humans, should not lie beside someone who, although he did service in the past, before 1934, cannot be next to Lenin.

N.S. Khrushchev.—Right! *(Stormy, prolonged applause.)*

D.A. Lazurkina.—Comrades! . . . The only reason I survived is that Ilyich was in my heart, and I sought his advice, as it were. *(Applause.)* Yesterday I asked Ilyich for advice, and it was as if he stood before me alive and said: "I do not like being next to Stalin, who inflicted so much harm on the Party." *(Stormy, prolonged applause.)*

13. Polyakov: Fireman Prokhorchuk

This short story was published in Moscow in 1953, the year of Stalin's death. It pokes fun at the severity of censorship under Stalin. While censors in the Soviet Union later became more sophisticated, they continued to monitor everything that was published in the Soviet Union. This was possible because all publishing houses were owned by the state. The only way to escape the

From Polyakov, Vladimir, "The Story of a Story, or Fireman Prokhorchuk." Translated by A. MacAndrew, in *Partisan Review* 28 No. 2 (Summer 1961): 515–18.

censor was to publish things yourself by typing out a manuscript and circulating it illegally.

THE STORY OF A STORY OR FIREMAN PROKHORCHUK

(The action takes place in the editorial offices of a Soviet magazine. A woman writer—a beginner—shyly enters the editor's office.)

She: Pardon me . . . Please excuse me . . . You're the editor of the magazine, aren't you?

He: That's right.

She: My name is Krapivina. I've written a little short story for your magazine.

He: All right, leave it here.

She: I was wondering whether I couldn't get your opinion of it right away. If you'll permit me, I'll read it to you. It won't take more than three or four minutes. May I?

He: All right, read it.

She: It is entitled "A Noble Deed." *(She begins to read.)*

It was the dead of night—three o'clock. Everybody in the town was asleep. Not a single electric light was burning. It was dark and quiet. But suddenly a gory tongue of flame shot out of the fourth-floor window of a large grey house. "Help!" someone shouted. "We're on fire!" This was the voice of a careless tenant who, when he went to bed, had forgotten to switch off the electric hot-plate, the cause of the fire. Both the fire and the tenant were darting around the room. The siren of a fire engine wailed. Firemen jumped down from the engine and dashed into the house. The room where the tenant was darting around was a sea of flames. Fireman Prokhorchuk, a middle-aged Ukrainian with large black mustachios, stopped in front of the door. The fireman stood and thought. Suddenly he rushed into the room, pulled the smoldering tenant out and aimed his extinguisher at the flames. The fire was put out, thanks to the daring of Prokhorchuk. Fire Chief Gorbushin approached him, "Good boy, Prokhorchuk," he said, "you've acted according to regulations!" Whereupon the fire chief smiled and added: "You haven't noticed it, but your right mustachio is aflame." Prokhorchuk smiled and aimed a jet at his mustachio. It was dawning.

He: The story isn't bad. The title's suitable too: "A Noble Deed." But there are some passages in it that must be revised. You see, it's a shame when a story is good and you come across things that are different from what you'd wish. Let's see, how does it start, your story?

She: It was the dead of night—three o'clock. Everybody in the town was asleep . . .

He: No good at all. It implies that the police are asleep and those on watch are asleep, and . . . No, won't do at all. It indicates a lack of vigilance. That passage must be changed. Better write it like this: It was the dead of night—three o'clock. No one in the town was asleep.

She: But that's impossible, it's night time and people do sleep.

He: Yes, I suppose you're right. Then let's have it this way: Everybody in the town was asleep but at his post.

She: Asleep at their posts?

He: No, that's complete nonsense. Better write: Some people slept while others kept a sharp lookout. What comes next?

She: Not a single electric light was burning.

He: What's this? Sounds as if, in our country, we make bulbs that don't work?

She: But it's night. They were turned off.

He: It could reflect on our bulbs. Delete it! If they aren't lit, what need is there to mention them?

She: *(reading on)* But suddenly a gory tongue of flame shot out of the fourth-floor window of a large grey house. "Help!" someone shouted, "we're on fire!"

He: What's that, panic?

She: Yes.

He: And it is your opinion that panic ought to be publicized in the columns of our periodicals?

She: No, of course not. But this is fiction . . . a creative work. I'm describing a fire.

He: And you portray a man who spreads panic instead of a civic-minded citizen? If I were you I'd replace that cry of "help" by some more rallying cry.

She: For instance?

He: For instance, say . . . "We don't give a damn! We shall put it out!" someone shouted. "Nothing to worry about, there's no fire."

She: What do you mean, "there's no fire" when there is a fire?

He: No, "there's no fire" in the sense of "we shall put it out, nothing to worry about."

She: It's impossible.

He: It's possible. And then, you could do away with the cry.

She: *(reads on)* This was the voice of the careless tenant who, when he went to bed, had forgotten to switch off the electric hot-plate.

He: The what tenant?

She: Careless.

He: Do you think that carelessness should be popularized in the columns of our periodicals? I shouldn't think so. And then why did you write that he forgot to switch off the electric hot-plate? Is that an appropriate example to set for the education of the readers?

She: I didn't intend to use it educationally, but without the hot-plate, there'd have been no fire.

He: And would we be much worse off?

She: No, better, of course.

He: Well then, that's how you should have written it. Away with the hot-plate and then you won't have to mention the fire. Go on, read, how does it go after that? Come straight to the portrayal of the fireman.

She: Fireman Prokhorchuk, a middle-aged Ukrainian . . .

He: That's nicely caught.

She: . . . with large black mustachios, stopped in front of the door. The fireman stood there and thought.

He: Bad. A fireman mustn't think. He must put the fire out without thinking.

She: But it is a fine point in the story.

He: In a story it may be a fine point but not in a fireman. Then also, since we have no fire, there's no need to drag the fireman into the house.

She: But then, what about his dialogue with the fire chief?

He: Let them talk in the fire house. How does the dialogue go?

She: *(reads)* Fire Chief Gorbushin approached him. "Good boy, Prokhorchuk," he said, "you've acted according to regulations!" Whereupon the fire chief smiled and added: "You haven't noticed it, but your right mustachio is aflame." Prokhorchuk smiled and aimed a jet at his mustachio. It was dawning.

He: Why must you have that?

She: What?

He: The burning mustachio.

She: I put it in for the humor of the thing. The man was so absorbed in his work that he didn't notice that his mustache was ablaze.

He: Believe me, you should delete it. Since there's no fire, the house isn't burning and there's no need to burn any mustachios.

She: And what about the element of laughter?

He: There'll be laughter all right. When do people laugh? When things are good for them. And isn't it good that there's no fire? It's very good. And so everybody will laugh. Read what you have now.

She: *(reading)* "A Noble Deed." It was the dead of night—three o'clock. Some people slept while others kept a sharp lookout. From the fourth floor window of a large grey house somebody shouted: "We are not on fire!" "Good boy, Prokhorchuk!" said Fire Chief Gorbushin to fireman Prokhorchuk, a middle-aged Ukrainian with large black mustachios, "you're following the regulations." Prokhorchuk smiled and aimed a jet of water at his mustachio. It was dawning.

He: There we have a good piece of writing! Now it can be published!

14. Bukovsky: Dissenters and the KGB

Vladimir Bukovsky was an ardent **human rights** *activist in the USSR, one of those who insisted that he be treated according to Soviet law and the Soviet Constitution. After a number of years in Soviet prisons and psychiatric*

Abridged from Bukovsky, Vladimir, *To Build a Castle.* Translated by Michael Scammell, 291–94, 355–57, 361–62. New York: Viking, 1977.

hospitals, he emigrated to the United States and published a memoir. In this section of it, he recalls his questioning by a KGB agent, illustrating the dilemma these legal protesters caused for the Soviet regime. He describes the camaraderie that springs up between Soviet citizens even when they are on opposite sides of the fence. He also explains why it was that the regime had to resort to psychiatric diagnoses and hospitalization for Soviet dissidents. Bukovsky speaks first in this conversation with his KGB investigator.

" . . . I am a citizen of the USSR."

"What opinions do you hold?"

"What does that have to do with my case? I hope you're not holding me in jail for my opinions?"

"Do you admit your guilt?"

"How can I answer that when I don't understand the charges? Tell me."

Under the law they were obliged to explain them to me . . .

To begin with, of course, they wouldn't give me any copies of the criminal codes. I received a visit from the Lefortovo Prison governor, Colonel Petrenko with his shaggy gray eyebrows sticking out from under a Caucasian fur cap. "It's not allowed."

All right. I wrote another sheaf of complaints and threatened a hunger strike. No more than two days went by before Colonel Petrenko put himself to the trouble of coming to see me again, saying almost tearfully: "We haven't got any codes, we've turned the whole library upside down. All I've got is my own copy, with a dedication from Semichastny. What do you want me to do—give you that?"

I took not only his presentation copy, autographed by the then chairman of the KGB, but also a copy of the Criminal Procedure Code, complete with commentaries, and a whole pile of assorted legal literature. The only thing they couldn't find was a copy of the Constitution. But I was adamant and on the fourth day, puffing and blowing, the deputy governor, Lieutenant Colonel Stepanov, came running in with one.

"Here you are, I've brought you the Constitution," he said in his comical provincial accent. "But it's for the Russian Republic, I couldn't find one for the USSR. Still, they're both the same. Bought it myself. Cost three kopecks. Never mind, we'll settle up later."

Petrenko and I became the best of friends. He would come to my cell, make an effort to knit his shaggy brows into a stern frown beneath his fur cap, gaze thoughtfully at my empty shelves, and ask: "Why haven't you got any food?"

"I've eaten it all. It's all gone."

"When is your next parcel due?"

"Not for a while yet. In a month."

"Write an application. I'll allow you an extra one." And then he would leave.

He himself was a former investigator and now, reading my endless complaints, he could see clearly that the investigation had run up a blind alley. There was nothing to charge me with.

Meanwhile I was devouring the criminal codes as if they were detective novels, memorizing them like multiplication tables, and was discovering to my amazement how many rights I really had. And I started to make the fullest use of those rights.

Now I openly made fun of my investigators, deluged them with complaints, and forced them to write out my statements ten times in a row.

It was summer, the heat was killing, and my investigators sweated away, dreaming of shady woods. "Vladimir Konstantinovich! Surely that's enough? How many more times can it be copied?"

Around the middle of summer they came up against a total dead end and started a new investigation under Article 70.* But this time they began with caution and stealth, not telling me the new charges. What a hope! The law's the law. Tell me the charges and then ask your questions. Another stream of complaints from me: illegal investigation! Criminals! Put them on trial! . . .

Finally the case ground to a complete halt and there was nothing more to talk about. My investigator started calling me in just for the sake of it, for a chat. With all the squabbling going on, neither of us had noticed how friendly we had become, and now he found it boring if he let a day go by without arguing with me over something or other. He himself lived in the provinces, in Yaroslavl, and like all provincials was ashamed of how badly informed he was. "Well, tell me about one of your books. What about that book by Djilas that you were charged with in 1963?** What sort of a whatsit was it?"

"Do you mean to say they don't let you read them either? Don't they trust you either?"

"Not likely. All you get to read in my job is what you turn up in the searches. And back in Yaroslavl, there's nothing to find. Total darkness."

He listened with rapt attention, like people listening to a lecture in a planetarium: "Is there life on Mars?" I told him everything I could remember from the books I had read in *samizdat*—let him take it all back to his Yaroslavl and tell his friends. They were human beings, after all, and dying to hear something new.

In some ways he quite appealed to me—tall, with a broad forehead and a frank, open face. He didn't care for our case or the role he had been assigned to play in it. Our farewell was even touching . . .

It was a matter of fact that most of the participants in the movement, with their precisely formulated civil-rights position and refusal to accept Soviet reality, were peculiarly vulnerable to psychiatric repression. I could

---

*The Article that forbids "agitation or propaganda carried on for the purpose of subverting or weakening the Soviet regime." Dissidents were often charged with its violation.

**Milovan Djilas, a Yugoslav, wrote *The New Class*, suggesting that there was a new privileged group in the USSR. It was banned in the USSR.

easily imagine Lunts* rubbing his hands and croaking: "Tell me, why won't you acknowledge your guilt?"

And all the legal formulations and references to articles in the Code, constitutional freedoms, and the absence of intent, that is, the entire arsenal of the citizen's rights position, devastating as it was to the investigation, would backfire on you, for it offered an irrefutable syndrome:

You don't acknowledge your guilt? Therefore you don't understand the criminal nature of your actions, therefore you cannot answer for them.

You keep talking about the Constitution and the laws, but what normal man takes Soviet laws seriously? You are living in an unreal world of your own invention, you react inadequately to the world around you.

Do you put the blame for your conflict with society on society? What do you mean, the whole of society is wrong? A typical madman's logic.

You had no intent? That means that you are incapable of understanding the consequences of your actions. You didn't even understand that you were certain to be arrested.

"Very well," croaks Lunts. "If you consider yourself to be in the right, why do you refuse to give evidence during the investigation?"

And again you haven't a leg to stand on—your morbid suspicion and distrustfulness are too plain.

"Why have you been doing all these things? What were you hoping to achieve?" None of us expected any practical results—that wasn't the aim of our actions—but from the point of view of common sense, such behavior was pure madness.

As before, this procedure worked very well with the Marxists—they had an obvious reforming mania, an overvalued idea of saving mankind. With the believers it was even simpler, as it had always been, and with the poets—a clear case of schizophrenia.

The theoretical "scientific" base had long since been prepared. In the conditions of socialism, according to the assertions of the country's leading psychiatrists, there were no social causes of criminality; therefore, any antilegal act was *ipso facto* a mental aberration. Under socialism there is no contradiction between society's goals and man's conscience. Existence determines consciousness, hence there is no such thing as a nonsocialist consciousness.

But the psychiatric method had now been worked out in much greater detail. First of all in the form of that old, tried and true diagnosis: *paranoidal development of the personality.* (The following quotations are from Professors Pechernikov and Kosachev of the Serbsky Institute.)

"Most frequently, ideas about a 'struggle for truth and justice' are formed by personalities with a paranoid structure."

---

*Chief of Department Four, the political department, at Serbsky Institute of Forensic Psychiatry.

"Litigiously paranoid states come into being as a result of psychologically traumatic circumstances affecting the subject's interests and are stamped by feelings that the individuals's legal rights have been infringed."

"A characteristic feature of overvalued ideas is the patient's conviction of his own rectitude, an obsession with asserting his 'trampled' rights, and the significance of these feelings for the patient's personality. They tend to exploit judicial proceedings as a platform for making speeches and appeals."

And, of course, complaints about persecution by the KGB, being searched and followed, telephone tapping, the opening of letters, and dismissal from work were pure persecution manias. The more open and public your position, the more obvious your insanity . . .

There was one more incident that attracted attention to psychiatric repressions, and that was the forcible hospitalization of the well-known scientist Zhores Medvedev.* The Soviet academic world was up in arms—the repressions had reached their very doorstep. The most prominent scientists in the Soviet Union led the campaign for his release.

It was all right for Zhores Medvedev, he was well-enough known in the scientific world. But what could be done for the workman Borisov, the bricklayer Gershuni, the students Novodvorskaya and Iofe, or the stage designer Victor Kuznetsov? For them there was no prospect of academicians raising hell with the Central Committee or the world community of scientists threatening a scientific boycott. According to our information, there were hundreds of little-known individuals being held in psychiatric prisons for political reasons. Who would take up the struggle on their behalf?

15. A Soviet View of U.S. Policy

Academician Georgi Arbatov, the author of this official assessment of United States policy, was the leading Soviet expert on the United States. Pravda (the word means truth in Russian), was the daily newspaper of the Community party. The article was published in March 1983. The tone and substance of this article illustrate the kind of information available to the Soviet public at that time.

The fact that the Reagan Administration has reached the midpoint of its term in office with poor results is, generally speaking, disputed by no one except the President himself and his entourage. . . .

---

*Zhores Medvedev, a prominent Soviet biologist and twin brother of the historian Roy Medvedev, was forcibly committed to a mental hospital in June 1970. As the result of a worldwide campaign of protest he was released after nineteen days. He now lives in England.

Abridged from Arbatov, G., "The United States: Will There Be Changes?" *Pravda* (March 1983). In *Current Digest of the Soviet Press* 35 (April 1983): 1–4.

[After detailing the ways in which President Reagan's domestic policy has failed, Arbatov turns to foreign affairs.]

For, whatever U.S. interests we take—economic, domestic-policy, military, foreign-policy, even Reagan's electoral interests—everywhere common sense requires the normalization of the international situation and an end to the arms race. But, alas, many people have long suspected that common sense is now the least of the factors by which American foreign policy is guided. Apart from certain political shifts in the country—quite a bit has been written about them—this seems, to some extent, to be linked to the present administration's unique style and way of thinking and acting.

For example, a good deal has been written about the provincialism of many of the people on the Reagan "team." This is true—not, of course, in the sense that they lack a capital-city gloss, but the fact is that these people have very often lived, built their careers and worked in isolation from the main problems of the country and of the world as a whole, away from the main roads of history and politics. The nature of Washington policy can't help but be affected by how poorly informed, and sometimes downright thickheaded, many of those who are currently making this policy are. Don't forget how some nominees for high posts couldn't answer the most elementary questions when they were before Congress for confirmation. And remember the embarrassing situations that have occurred at press conferences held by prominent Washington officials and in their conversations with foreign leaders.

Much has also been written about the fact that in and around the U.S. government there are now grouped (as advisers) an unusual number of "specialists" in strategy and military policy who hold such extreme views that many of them have in fact been deemed in need of medical assistance.

If to this one adds the administration's political extremism, many of the sources of the present U.S. leaders' striking isolation from reality, which has distinguished their policy so far, will become understandable. This policy is based on distorted ideas about the world and its problems, about countries and about America itself . . .

In the first place, as politicians many of these people are pure products of propaganda, and very second-rate propaganda at that. Their current prophets, . . . are fanatical anticommunists, loudmouths who aren't capable of understanding the complexity of today's world. And sometimes the American leaders derive their wisdom from even more out-of-the-way "thinkers."

In his first major foreign-policy speech, in May 1981, President Reagan told the cadets at the West Point Military Academy that the nation should put its faith not in parchment and paper (i.e., in treaties and agreements) but in weapons. In this connection, he referred to the books "The Treaty Trap" and "Survival and Peace in the Nuclear Age," by one Laurence Beilenson. Journalists rushed out to hunt up this new political prophet. He turned out to be an 82-year-old retired lawyer, a bosom buddy of Reagan's from the time when (even before the ill-famed Senator J. McCarthy emerged on the political stage) both of them had harassed the "Reds" in Hollywood. When Beilenson was located by journalists, this hale and hearty old man told them that nuclear war is inevitable, that "we must overthrow all Communist governments" and that all those who are prepared to fight the Communists should be "openly" offered money ("I call it 'foreign aid for freedom,' you call it subversion—it's all the same") . . .

Having been molded politically and spiritually by such odious propaganda, many people who are now in the top echelons of power in America perceive the world, emerging problems and events and politics itself in purely propagandistic concepts. I have in mind not only the blind and absolutely implacable hatred of the Soviet Union that a number of American leaders have, and not only the extremely noisy and mendacious propaganda campaigns that they are constantly launching.

I'm also talking about the fact that events displeasing to the U.S. rulers are quite often perceived as the results of someone's malicious propaganda. And the response to these events naturally, comes in the form of another propaganda campaign.

An example of this approach is Washington's appraisal of the antiwar movement in Europe (and then in the U.S., too) as the result of Moscow's propaganda intrigues. An effort was promptly launched to expose these propaganda "intrigues." When it became clear that this wouldn't help, Washington agreed to arms limitation talks. But attempts were made to reduce these talks to propaganda, too. If anyone had any doubts on this score, they were dispelled by Reagan's nominee for the post of Director of the Arms Control and Disarmament Agency, K. Adelman, who candidly said: "The arms limitation talks are just a trick, one we simply had to use in order to calm the American people and our European allies."

Should it come as any surprise that the U.S. proposals at the arms limitation talks are designed to produce an impression on an unsophisticated public (just look at the words they use—"zero option," the acronym START for the strategic arms talks, the name Corpus Christi for a new nuclear submarine, Peacekeeper for a nuclear missile) and, at the same time, be obviously unacceptable to the Soviet Union . . .

Since our striving for detente, lasting peace and disarmament remains unchanging, we will be reliable partners in any honest talks and agreements that have these aims in view. But we know very well that peace accords are not achieved by begging and that one has to wage a stubborn and skillful struggle for them, because aggressive circles will not abandon their plans unless they encounter a resolute—very resolute—rebuff.

The fits of anti-Soviet hysteria that follow one after another also prevent us from believing that the policy of Washington's current rulers may change for the better. Frenzied calls are being made for crusades, statements that smack not only of the cold war but sometimes of outright medievalism. And all this is covered up by hypocritical talk about faith and God, about morality, eternal good and eternal evil.

As time goes on, it's becoming clearer that the U.S. administration not only constantly starts confrontations, but, because of its isolation from the realities of the world, starts them in places that are very inconvenient and very disadvantageous for it. Who can seriously see it as the foremost defender of democracy, civil liberties and trade union rights when both the past and the present of many people now in Washington completely refute this? . . .

A great deal is changing now in the world, and in America. People can't continue living under the growing threat of universal death, and they don't want to. Therefore, they are questioning not individual postulates of the U.S.'s peace-endangering nuclear policy and strategy but its very foundations. They want not words but deeds, concrete deeds capable of removing the threat of a catastrophe that is hanging over the world.

16. Ronald Reagan: The Evil Empire

In a speech to the National Association of Evangelists in Orlando, Florida in March 1983, President Ronald Reagan took on the subject of sin and evil in the world. Toward the end of the speech, he identified the Soviet Union as the source of much of this sin and evil. Because of this, he told his audience, any "freeze" of nuclear weapons would be a serious mistake. In this speech, the president demonstrated that for him the Cold War was still a moral crusade, to be continued without letup. Exactly two years later Mikhail Gorbachev came to power.

There is sin and evil in the world, and we are enjoined by Scripture and the Lord Jesus to oppose it with all our might. . . .

During my first press conference as president, in answer to a direct question, I pointed out that as good Marxist-Leninists the Soviet leaders have openly and publicly declared that the only morality they recognize is that which will further their cause, which is world revolution.

I think I should point out I was only quoting Lenin, their guiding spirit, who said in 1920 that they repudiate all morality that proceeds from supernatural ideas or ideas that are outside class conceptions; morality is entirely subordinate to the interests of class war; and everything is moral that is necessary for the annihilation of the old exploiting social order and for uniting the proletariat.

Abridged from Podell, J. and Anzovin, S., eds. *Speeches of the American Presidents,* 759–60. New York: H. W. Wilson Co., 1988.

I think the refusal of many influential people to accept this elementary fact of Soviet doctrine illustrates an historical reluctance to see totalitarian powers for what they are. We saw this phenomenon in the 1930s; we see it too often today. . . .

I intend to do everything I can to persuade them of our peaceful intent; to remind them that it was the West that refused to use its nuclear monopoly in the '40s and '50s for territoral gain and which now proposes 50 percent cuts in strategic ballistic missiles and the elimination of an entire class of land-based, intermediate range nuclear missiles.

At the same time, however, they must be made to understand we will never compromise our principles and standards. We will never give way our freedom. We will never abandon our belief in God.

And we will never stop searching for a genuine peace. But we can assure none of these things America stands for through the so-called nuclear freeze solutions proposed by some. The truth is that a freeze now would be a very dangerous fraud, for that is merely the illusion of peace. The reality is that we must find peace through strength.

I would agree to a freeze if only we could freeze the Soviets' global desires. A freeze at current levels of weapons would remove any incentive for the Soviets to negotiate seriously in Geneva, and virtually end our chances to achieve the major arms reductions which we have proposed. Instead, they would achieve their objectives through the freeze.

A freeze would reward the Soviet Union for its enormous and unparalleled military buildup. It would prevent the essential and long overdue modernization of United States and allied defenses and would leave our aging forces increasingly vulnerable. And an honest freeze would require extensive prior negotiations on the systems and numbers to be limited and on the measures to insure effective verification and compliance.

And the kind of freeze that has been suggested would be virtually impossible to verify. Such a major effort would divert us completely from our current negotiations on achieving substantial reductions.

Let us pray for the salvation of all those who live in totalitarian darkness, pray they will discover the joy of knowing God.

But until they do, let us be aware that while they preach the supremacy of the state, declare its omnipotence over individual man, and predict its eventual domination of all peoples of the earth—they are the focus of evil in the modern world. . . .

So in your discussions of the nuclear freeze proposals, I urge you to beware the temptation of pride—the temptation blithely to declare yourselves above it all and label both sides equally at fault, to ignore the facts of history and the aggressive impulses of an evil empire, to simply call the arms race a giant misunderstanding and thereby remove yourself from the struggle between right and wrong, good and evil.

Chapter Six

SOVIET SOCIETY ON THE EVE OF THE GORBACHEV REFORMS

THE STALINIST LEGACY

*I*t is impossible to understand the challenges facing the peoples of the former Soviet Union without knowledge of the institutions established by Stalin and the situation Gorbachev and his colleagues inherited from Brezhnev. It was these institutions and that society that Gorbachev set out to change.

The Stalinist system had three main features. First, the Soviet Union was a party-state, in the sense that a single political party, the Communist Party of the Soviet Union (CPSU), dominated the government. Second, the Soviet economy was organized according to the principle of **state socialism.** The state owned all productive enterprises, factories, mines, and farms, set economic priorities, and both planned and managed the use of resources. The third important characteristic of the Stalinist system was that the party-state tried to control and organize as much of each person's life as it could. It took an interest in many aspects of life that in Western countries are considered private responsibility. Marxist-Leninist ideology provided the theoretical and moral justification for the system. These three characteristics made up the chief pillars of the Stalinist command administrative system, a highly centralized and authoritarian government. The government presided over a multinational federal state in which peoples of great variety lived together in a relatively peaceful manner.

THE USSR AS A PARTY-STATE

In 1977, the Soviet government approved a new Constitution, its fourth since 1918. In the Soviet Union, the Constitution is not considered a sacred document that rarely should be changed, but a description of the laws appropriate for a society in its current historical situation. Therefore, as society changes, the Constitution also should change. The Soviet Constitution was not always a good guide to understanding how the Soviet system really worked, however. The Constitution of 1977, for example, described the formal structure of government, but never explained that real power belonged to the Communist party.

The Soviet Constitution provided for elections in which all citizens older than eighteen were expected to vote.

FACT: In 1982, 99.8 percent of those eligible voted in the Soviet elections. In 1990, 36 percent of 186 million eligible voters voted in the U.S. elections.

In keeping with the 1977 Constitution, voters in the Soviet Union elected local councils called soviets. Each of the national republics had an elected national council or republic soviet. At the federal level, there was the **Supreme Soviet** of the Soviet Union that had the constitutional right to make laws. The Supreme Soviet elected the leaders of both the executive and judicial branches, as well as a Presidium that had the power to make decisions when the Supreme Soviet was not in session. The Council of Ministers was the top executive body of the state, responsible for running the economy and state-owned enterprises, as well as overseeing the work of the KGB, the ministries of defense and health, and various industries.

The 1977 Constitution also contained a bill of rights. It listed many of the same civil rights promised by the United States Constitution, as well as rights that the United States Constitution does not have, such as the right to work. In the Soviet Constitution of 1977, however, all rights were granted on condition that they did "not injure the interests of society and the rights of other citizens." If the party decided that the right to free speech or organization was not in the best interests of society, for example, a person could be arrested and charged with unlawful activity. This provision was used to justify harsh treatment of religious dissenters, writers, and other protesters during the 1970s and early 1980s (see Chapter 5). Therefore, one should not assume that because the formal institutions of Soviet government resembled those of the United States, the two systems operated in exactly the same way.

FACT: Until Gorbachev came to power, the Supreme Soviet always confirmed proposed legislation. Its decisions were always carefully orchestrated to be unanimous and accompanied by great applause.

The Supreme Soviet meets in 1982 to celebrate the sixtieth anniversary of the formation of the Soviet Union.

FACT: The Supreme Soviet of the USSR, the top federal legislative body, usually met twice a year for a total of less than ten days. All members had other full-time jobs.

Clearly, the Supreme Soviet could not make the difficult decisions about Soviet laws and policies. In Soviet elections there was only one candidate for each office until the 1980s. There was discussion within the Communist party about potential nominees ahead of time, but not on election day. The Soviet Union called itself democratic and used election campaigns to educate the population about important issues. On election day, however, Soviet citizens voted, but they did not choose.

Soviet constitutions through 1977 made no effort to create a separation of powers. There was no independent judiciary, for example, to decide if the government was properly enforcing the laws. Marxism-Leninism teaches that the interests of citizens and a communist government are one and the same, so there was no need for such a safeguard.

Real power in Soviet society belonged to the Communist Party of the Soviet Union (CPSU), and particularly to those who worked full-time for the party, the **secretariat** and its staff, the **apparat.** The CPSU was the only political party and it was reserved for the elite; only about nine percent of the population were members. The party recruited promising young people. It also sponsored large youth organizations. Young adults aged 16 to 28 belonged to

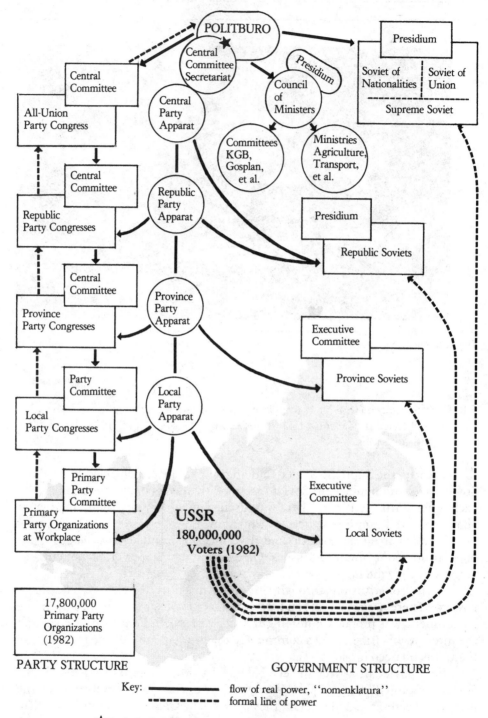

POLITBURO

Central Committee Secretariat ★

Presidium

Council of Ministers

Central Committee

All-Union Party Congress

Central Party Apparat

Committees KGB, Gosplan, et al.

Ministries Agriculture, Transport, et al.

Presidium

Soviet of Nationalities | Soviet of Union

Supreme Soviet

Central Committee

Republic Party Congresses

Republic Party Apparat

Presidium

Republic Soviets

Central Committee

Province Party Congresses

Province Party Apparat

Executive Committee

Province Soviets

Party Committee

Local Party Congresses

Local Party Apparat

Executive Committee

Local Soviets

Primary Party Committee

Primary Party Organizations at Workplace

USSR
180,000,000
Voters (1982)

17,800,000
Primary Party
Organizations
(1982)

PARTY STRUCTURE

GOVERNMENT STRUCTURE

Key: ───────── flow of real power, "nomenklatura"
- - - - - - - - - formal line of power

★ Both the Politburo and the Central Committee
Secretariat are chaired by the General Secretary,
making him the chief executive of the Party.

Institutions of the Party-State; 1982

the **Komsomol.** Students aged 12 to 15 joined the **Young Pioneers,** and small children became **Little Octobrists.** The groups held meetings and organized leisure activities to bring the party message to Soviet youth. Membership in the party was considered a privilege and admission rules were strict. Those who joined were expected to serve as examples to others and to take on extra responsibilities. In return, they received access to scarce consumer goods and the opportunity for the best jobs—all the most important posts in government, top management, the army, and foreign affairs were reserved for party members. Most journalists, editors, and school heads also belonged to the party.

The party was carefully and hierarchically organized. There were numerous local organizations, or party cells, in factories and farms, and in offices and institutes throughout the Soviet Union. The local organizations elected representatives to local congresses, and the local congresses in turn elected delegates to regional congresses. Regional congresses elected delegates to the republic congresses, republic congresses to the federal (All-Union) Party Congress (see diagram). The federal party congress elected the **CPSU Central Committee,** which, in turn, elected an executive Politburo. In theory, the congress at each level elected representatitives to the body above it. This structure made it seem that power flowed upward, from the rank-and-file party members through their representatives to the Politburo. The party seemed to be democratic. In fact, power flowed from the top down. One candidate was selected for each office by party members at the next level up in the hierarchy. For example, in theory the Central Committee elected the Politburo. In fact, the Politburo decided who would be a candidate for election to the Central Committee. As there was only one candidate for each position, the Politburo in effect selected the Central Committee. Furthermore, higher organizations told the lower ones what to do. Decisions of the Politburo, for example, set guidelines for the Central Committee. While there might be, and often was, discussion before decisions were made, once the decision was made by the Politburo, it was supposed to be carried out throughout the land without further discussion.

FACT: The Politburo varied in size and usually had from 10 to 16 full, voting members and about 6 candidate (non-voting) members.

The Politburo made all general policy decisions. Once it had decided on a policy, it was up to the party *secretariat,* and the *apparat,* to see to it that the policy was carried out. The full-time workers of the party *secretariat* and *apparat* made up a powerful, highly centralized administrative organization reaching from Moscow throughout the Soviet Union to monitor the work of government and social and economic agencies, and to select or endorse key personnel. The head of the *secretariat,* the **general secretary,** was the single most powerful position in the USSR. Stalin, Khrushchev, Brezhnev, Andropov, Chernenko, and Gorbachev all held the post of general secretary. The general

In photo on left, Young Pioneers at school in Leningrad. All Soviet children between the ages of ten and fifteen belonged to the Young Pioneers. The red scarf was the Pioneer symbol. Runners enjoy a crisp winter day in the photo on right.

secretary usually served as presidium or government president as well, but his real power depended on his position at the top of the party hierarchy.

The role of the Politburo and *secretariat* of the CPSU in the Stalinist system can be summarized quite simply. They maintained a monopoly on ideology and controlled appointments to all important positions. Because Marxism-Leninism was supposed to provide answers to solve all social problems, and the party and only the party knew how to interpret Marxism-Leninism correctly, the party claimed the right to have the last word on what policy should be and what was right and what was wrong for people in all walks of life. The party's autocratic position was justified by Marxism-Leninism. Lenin had argued that the party understood the science of socialism and therefore had the right and the obligation to guide the state's march toward communism. When different groups in the society disagreed, it was up to the party to find a consensus and set out an authoritative decision. For example, the party declared whether or not wars between capitalist and socialist states were inevitable and whether military or consumer spending should take priority. Such decisions then guided policy. (Review Chapter 3, Reading 17.)

The party *secretariat* also decided who should hold top positions. It developed a system called the **nomenklatura,** a list of all important jobs. Before anyone could hold one of these jobs—newspaper editor, school superintendent, factory manager, or city mayor—he or she had to be approved by the party *secretariat.* By means of the *nomenklatura,* the party made sure that no one who was not loyal to the party could hold an influential position.

While the Communist party made general policy, selected the people to carry it out, informed the Soviet people of its decisions, and took responsibility for educating young people in the spirit of socialism, it was up to the Soviet government to put the policies into effect. The government bureaucracy executed party policy, while the party *secretariat* and its *apparat* watched carefully to make sure that the bureaucrats did what they were supposed to do. It is because of the powerful position of the party that the Soviet Union was called a party-state.

STATE SOCIALISM: THE ECONOMY AND SOCIAL STRATIFICATION

Marx and Lenin taught that as long as there was private property, there would be poverty and exploitation. To get rid of private property was one of the main goals of the Bolshevik Revolution. Therefore, in Stalin's and Brezhnev's Soviet Union, all land, banks, factories, and businesses had to be owned and managed by a collective group or the state, a system known as state socialism. The Soviet economy has been compared to a single giant business corporation that managed a wide variety of industries, but in which all branches had to answer to a single boss, the party-state. There was private property in small things—a house, furniture, or clothing—but according to the Stalinist system of rule, no private person could hire workers, other than to perform a personal service such as baby-sitting.

The Soviet economy also was characterized by central planning. Central planners organized and coordinated all economic activity to serve the collective interest of the Soviet state and people. The system contrasted sharply with a capitalist market economy, such as that of the United States, where independent producers are free to make what they think they can sell without regard to the interests of society as a whole. In theory, in a market economy the government is supposed to regulate economic activity as little as possible. In fact, in the United States today government regulation, subsidies, and tax policy play important parts in determining how the economy actually works.

In keeping with Lenin's teaching about the leading role of the party, it was the Politburo that determined what the collective interest of the Soviet people was and decided on broad economic priorities. The general goals then were translated into specific production targets by the State Planning Commission **(Gosplan)** and presented in the form of a Five Year Plan. *Gosplan* set prices and decided how much would go into investment in new plants and how much into production. The planners collected information from factories, farms, mines, and power plants all over the Soviet Union. With that information in hand, they set production quotas for each factory and productive enterprise.

FACT: In 1860, the per capita production of the Russian Empire was about 40 percent of that of the United States. In 1913, it had fallen to 24 percent; by 1980, Soviet per capita production was estimated to be 60 percent of that of the United States; in 1989, it had fallen to 51 percent or even less of that of the United States.

The Soviet economy grew rapidly after the Revolution under the system of state ownership and central economic planning. Economic growth brought with it a rise in the standard of living. By the 1980s, however, it was clear that economic growth was slowing. Japan surpassed the USSR to become the world's second largest economy. Soviet industry seemed unable to innovate, Soviet farmers were not increasing their productivity, and agriculture in general was not keeping up with popular expectations for a better diet. There is evidence that the quality of the Soviet diet began to decline in the late 1970s. As the economy grew more complex, planners found it increasingly hard to manage all the details. It was especially difficult to plan for the unexpected— the drought that cut grain production or reduced available hydroelectric power, or the fire that destroyed a plant that was supposed to supply tires to a truck manufacturer. When such events occurred, those on the spot could not adapt to the new situation quickly and efficiently because they had to get permission to act from so many different organizations.

The manager of a Soviet factory was judged and rewarded for meeting the quota set by the plan. If he made hats, for example, he had to see to it that the factory produced the number of hats it was supposed to under the plan. It did not matter to him if the hats were ugly or didn't hold their shape. His quota simply required the right number of hats. Selling them was not his problem. The state stores had to take whatever he produced—that was part of their plan. If the factory made stylish hats that sold well, the manager was paid no more than if it made ugly hats that no one wanted. There was no real incentive, then, for good quality work or for innovation. Why risk setting up a new procedure for making hats that might lead to a long-term gain but might also lead to a short-term loss? The manager would not benefit from the gain, and he knew that if the new procedure didn't work, he would pay a penalty. Many of the skills essential for successful management in a competitive market economy, such as innovation, the willingness to take risks, and a concern for quality and marketing, were not rewarded and so they were not developed by Soviet managers.

One of the biggest problems for the Soviet economy was agriculture. Soviet agriculture was organized into farms of two types, state farms (the **sovkhoz**) and collective farms (the *kolkhoz*). The preferred type of farm was the state farm. They were large, and workers, employees of the state, were paid wages just as if they worked in a factory. The collective farms, the *kolkhozes*, were cooperatives in which the farmers shared in the profits of the farm. More often than not, the result was that they were paid very little. Most farm families also had small private plots, about one acre in size. The large collective fields raised much less per acre than private plots, for farmers seem to work better when they know they will profit directly from what they produce.

FACT: In the late 1970s and in the 1980s, the private plots, which made up about 3 percent of the cultivated land, raised at least 12 percent of the food sold in Soviet markets. Some scholars estimated that almost 50 percent of all fruits and vegetables was grown on this 3 percent of cultivated land.

Although such private enterprise went against the Marxist theory that stressed the advantages of collective ownership and collective work, the government accepted it because the food was badly needed by the population.

FACT: Because the state set prices, the price of bread did not rise between the 1950s and 1991.

The Soviet people continued to live poorly by American standards. Most still lived in small houses or crowded apartments and ate less varied food than did most Americans. In the early 1980s, for example, it was estimated that nine million families were living in communal apartments where several families shared a single kitchen and bathroom. Right after World War II, the crowding could be explained because many of the cities in the western part of the country had been badly damaged by the war. Forty or fifty years later it was hard to continue to use that excuse. Poor housing resulted mostly from the fact that consumer comfort was not a high priority for Soviet economic planners. However, such basic necessities as simple food, clothing, medical care, public transportation, and lodging remained very cheap.

Soviet citizens devised ways to make up for the inefficiencies of the planners. Their activities were called the **second economy** and many used to be illegal. Factories bartered for raw materials with one another; there was a brisk secondary rental market in housing in desirable locations; repairmen moonlighted for pay or perhaps bartered their work for food, a new shirt, the services of a dentist, or a tutor for a child. These grey areas of economic activity were outside the planners' control but were tolerated because they were useful in making the system run. There was also considerable illegal activity that flourished despite the regime's effort to stop it. Entrepreneurs bought scarce goods ranging from fashionable clothes that might appear in a store unexpectedly to jeans begged or bought from a foreign tourist, to fruit out of season, or a banned phonograph record. They then resold the goods for large profits. The practice was called speculation and was against the law. From the factories in

The elite of Soviet society included its best artists and athletes, as well as scientists, factory managers, and party leaders. Ballet schools in Moscow and Leningrad continue to train outstanding dancers for the great Russian ballet companies, the Bolshoi and Kirov.

which they worked, people stole wood to fix a house, clothing to sell, or a spare automobile part for a friend. It is almost impossible to estimate accurately the size of the second economy, but it probably represented at least five to ten percent of the total Soviet gross national product in the early 1980s.

A small group of people in the Soviet Union was living well. The top party and government officials and the most successful scientists, writers, athletes, and managers, the so-called *nomenklatura,* did not stand in lines, ride the crowded buses, or spend their weekends in city parks. They enjoyed the special benefits that came with their jobs: chauffeur-driven limousines, vacations in state-owned guest houses, a private house (*dacha*) in an exclusive enclave outside the city, shopping privileges in special stores stocked with fresh food not available elsewhere, and imported clothes and appliances. Such privileges were much more important to Soviet citizens than money. Luxuries could not be bought no matter how much money a person had, but were the reward for holding the right sort of elite job.

Members of the elite also had the opportunity to enjoy the greatest privilege of all, travel abroad. The Soviet government took an unusual attitude toward travel. For many years, those who lived in the countryside, on a state farm or *kolkhoz,* could not travel at all, even within the Soviet Union, without a special permit that was rarely granted. It was especially difficult to get permission to live in Moscow and other big cities such as Kiev. Urban planners did not want their big cities to fill up with the jobless or other people who would aggravate the already difficult housing situation. As for travel abroad, a Soviet citizen could not simply send for a passport and buy an air ticket to travel to Western Europe. Special permission had to come first, and until 1990, it was rarely granted unless the trip was an official one. Even influential people were rarely allowed to take their families with them.

Social mobility based on ability was very high in the early years of Soviet power, provided a person was willing to play along with the party. Pressure on children to study hard, win academic competitions, and get into the right universities was intense. As in many countries, children of farm or factory workers rarely rose to the top in academic, technical, or cultural positions. For them, a job in the party was often a ticket to the top. It was also true that important people in the Soviet Union, as elsewhere, seemed to find ways to get their children into the best schools and into good jobs and so give them a head start on their less-favored peers. Nonetheless it was almost impossible for Soviet citizens to pass on large estates or significant sums of money to their children. Soviet citizens were neither rich nor secure. Everything depended on continuing to please their party superiors. (See Readings 1 to 4.)

EDUCATION AND CULTURE

The preamble to the 1977 Soviet Constitution declared that the state had, among its purposes, "to mold the citizen of the communist society and . . . to raise the cultural level of the working people." This goal had far-reaching implications for education and culture in the Soviet Union. The Soviet government was interested in areas of social activity that in many Western societies are left to the individual. The Soviet government was not satisfied to see to it that its citizens did not bother one another. It expected more than that. It tried to shape citizens' thinking and attitudes, as well as their behavior. The goal of the Soviet government was nothing less than to create "the new Soviet man," a new type of person free from greed and selfishness, laziness, and dishonesty, who would be able to create a truly communist society.

Soviet leaders believed that religion was harmful because it prevented people from developing the proper communist outlook on life. The religious person might obey the laws, but would not accept the party's claim that it had the final knowledge of what was right and wrong. The religious person was considered by the Soviets to be a half-hearted citizen, old-fashioned and superstitious, one who did not live up to the Soviet ideal.

FACT: Although the government outlawed religious education and discouraged religious observance by closing churches, synagogues, and mosques, a survey published in the late 1960s indicated that sixty percent of the babies born in the industrial city of Gorky were baptized.

Two girls at the nursery school at a Moscow factory. To make it possible for Soviet women with young children to work, the Soviet government established numerous schools and all-day programs for small children.

It is important to bear in mind that the Soviets did not believe, as many North Americans do, that the best government is the one that governs least. They did not want to leave individuals free to develop as they chose. On the contrary, they believed that the best government was the one that could organize everyone in an orderly way to work for a common goal, a goal set by the party. The Soviet ideal focused on closing the gap between rich and poor, even though it involved sacrificing political and economic liberties to do so.

FACT: The manual for teaching two- and three-year-olds in nursery schools throughout the Brezhnev era told instructors to teach the children to recognize V. I. Lenin in portraits and illustrations.

The party-state set all school curricula. All school children, as well as medical students, law students, and those in teacher training classes, had to take many courses in Marxist-Leninist ideology designed to teach them to be loyal citizens. As recently as 1990, a person training to be a teacher spent nine hours each week studying Marxism-Leninism. Many values that were stressed in Soviet schools, such as self-discipline, industriousness, punctuality, and honesty, are stressed in schools in most industrial countries. Soviet schools also emphasized the importance of collective work and cooperation. They did not encourage students to develop individual differences or to ask questions. Teachers did not encourage students to compare what they learned in school with their own experiences of the world around them. The new Soviet citizen was not supposed to be a creative individualist but rather a contributor to the collective. (See Reading 4.)

The Soviet regime considered history, literature, and the arts to be powerful means of education. History was written and rewritten to suit the official version of the past. In Stalin's time, the censors made sure that there was no mention of the scope of the purges or the famine that accompanied collectivization.

FACT: For almost twenty years after Khrushchev denounced Stalin, the Soviet national anthem had no words because its original words mentioned Stalin.

In Brezhnev's day, neither Stalin nor Khrushchev was discussed in history textbooks.

Fiction, too, was expected to be educational. Books were supposed to meet the standard of socialist realism. This policy required, for example, that a short story provide examples of good and bad behavior to illustrate that a citizen who cheated would be caught and that the one who worked selflessly for others would be rewarded. All media productions, books, films, television, paintings, and even music were carefully screened and censored to make sure that they provided healthy models for Soviet citizens. It was important that they be easy to understand and inspire desirable behavior. It was not enough that literature not criticize the regime in unwanted ways. It had to take a further step and encourage socially useful activities.

The Soviet regime's goal of shaping thought and behavior led also to suspiciousness of all things foreign, including foreign visitors. Foreign ideas might hurt Soviet society, providing information about political freedoms or the high standard of living in the West, or about rock music that encouraged materialism and sex without love. The result was that visitors usually were watched very carefully. (See Reading 5.)

FACT: The percentage of university-age students in Soviet institutions of higher education was higher than in Great Britain, France, or Germany (but not in the United States).

Despite all the limits on the freedom of expression, however, the Soviet government made education a top priority after the Revolution of 1917. The country had impressive success in achieving literacy and training its citizens

Four men from Azerbaijan gather for sociability, tea, and backgammon. Azerbaijan, Georgia, and Armenia comprised the Transcaucasian Republics of the USSR. Each of the peoples has distinct ethnic traditions that are very different from those of the Slavs.

to be engineers, technicians, and administrators. Once that was accomplished, however, Soviet citizens became more and more impatient with the political constraints on what they could read and say.

THE MULTINATIONAL STATE: THE SOVIET NATIONALITIES

The Soviet Union was home to peoples of many different nationalities. Unlike the United States and Canada, which also contain peoples of many different national origins, most of the peoples of the Soviet Union continued to live in their historic homelands. They did not leave their land voluntarily to go to a new country as did those who emigrated to North America. Rather, the Russian state expanded its control over its diverse neighbors who then became part of the tsar's Empire. Most of the Empire was inherited by the Soviet government, which then created a federal state that was ruled in an authoritarian manner from Moscow.

There was always a built-in tension in Soviet policy toward its nationalities. On the one hand, Soviet constitutions granted important rights to the national republics, much more autonomy than is granted to the American states by the federal Constitution of the United States. Small ethnic groups had their own "autonomous regions" within the republics. Soviet republics had many rights of self-government, as well as the legal right to secede from the Union of Soviet Socialist Republics. In practice, however, their ability to take advantage of those rights was strictly limited by the party until 1990.

The folk arts played a prominent role in the Soviet culture.

The central government, in Stalin's and Brezhnev's time, used all the resources at its command, especially the highly centralized Communist party, to see to it that its non-Russian peoples remained loyal to the Soviet government.

FACT: Russians made up 52 percent of the Soviet population in 1979, but held 67 percent of the seats on the Central Committee of the party. The Slavs (Russians, Ukrainians, and Belorussians) were 72 percent of the population in 1979, but held 86 percent of the Central Committee seats in 1981.

FACT: In non-Russian republics, the first secretary of the party, the top post, was always held by a member of the local nationality. The second secretary, the person who held primary responsibility for job appointments, usually was a Russian and always a Slav.

Soviet policy toward the non-Russian nationalities tried to maintain a delicate balance between making allowances for the reality of cultural differences and exercising central control. The central government recognized the need to use national languages and encouraged the performance of the traditional arts of each people. National languages also were used in schools. In Uzbekistan, for example, a native child would enter a school in which Uzbek was the language of instruction. Soon the child would begin to learn Russian as a second language, because the Soviet government realized that everyone had to be able to communicate with one another if they were to feel a part of a single state. The Russian language seemed to be the logical choice for that purpose. If a native child or the child's parents were eager to have a career of great importance, mastery of Russian was essential. On the other hand, some members of the non-Russian nationalities considered such emphasis on Russian a threat to the survival and development of their national cultures. They objected to the fact that the Russian child growing up in a non-Russian republic rarely learned the local language. Despite those tensions, however, the Soviet party-state managed to keep the peace among its diverse members until the 1990s.

During the long period of the Brezhnev regime, which the people now call the period of stagnation, no one stated publicly what many Soviet leaders knew: The economy was functioning poorly and a well-educated, urbanized population was increasingly restless under party control. There was no incentive to take initiative of any kind or to work well. Everyone repeated what was no longer a joke: "They pretend to pay us and we pretend to work." Creative people in the sciences and the arts were impatient to share ideas with others and to be part of the international community. Party members' interference in running complicated technical or scientific enterprises, hours wasted at party indoctrination meetings, deception about whether the quota really had been fulfilled, preaching by teachers to students about theories and facts both knew to be false, as well as the knowledge that high party bureaucrats were often lazy and dishonest, dragged down the morale of large parts of the population. Corruption and cynicism spread among the young. Juvenile delinquency, alcoholism, and crime increased. Brezhnev himself, vain, aging, and increasingly incompetent, seemed a fitting symbol for a society that had lost its sense of direction.

Such was the situation in 1985 when Mikhail Gorbachev became general secretary of the Communist party. From the outside, the Soviet Union seemed to be a stable society. Its army was powerful and the world accepted the status of the USSR as one of the world's two superpowers. Gorbachev quickly realized, however, that superpower or not, the Soviet Union faced internal problems that could no longer be ignored.

In addition to books used in Chapter 5, the following book was helpful in writing this chapter:

Carrère d'Encausse, H., *Confiscated Power: How Soviet Russia Really Works.* Translated by George Holoch. New York: Harper & Row, 1982.

For students who are interested, we recommend further reading in the sources from which we have taken excerpts, as well as the following works:

American Association for the Advancement of Slavic Studies, *Current Digest of the Soviet Press,* 1314 Kinnear Rd., Columbus, Ohio 43212.
    Useful for students are its periodic compilations of representative articles from the Soviet press.
Bronfenbrenner, Y., *Two Worlds of Childhood: US and USSR.* New York: Russell Sage Foundation, 1970.
    Compares schooling and education in U.S. and USSR. Dated, but good.

Cracraft, J., ed., *The Soviet Union Today*. Chicago: University of Chicago Press, 1988.

> Short essays, most of which appeared in *The Bulletin of the Atomic Scientists*, on various aspects of recent Soviet society, from dissent to the economy, religion, and nationalities.

Cox, A.M., *Russian Roulette: The Superpower Game*. New York: Quadrangle/Times Books, 1982.

> Sensible account of Soviet-American relations in the 70s.

English, R.D., and Halperin, J.J., *The Other Side: How Soviets and Americans Perceive Each Other*. New Brunswick, N.J.: Transaction, 1987.

> Originally published by the Committee for National Security. Worthy treatment of fascinating subject.

Gerhart, G., *The Russian's World: Life and Language*. New York: Harcourt Brace Jovanovich, 1971.

> Intended for language teachers, this book has Russian words interspersed in the text and is not to be read through, but may be consulted for interesting details: how Russian names are formed, plot plans of apartments, sketches of Russian clothing over the centuries.

Hollander, P., *Soviet and American Society: A Comparison*. New York: Oxford, 1970; Chicago: University of Chicago Press, 1978.

> American scholar who grew up in Hungary reflects on two societies.

Rubenstein, J. *Soviet Dissidents, Their Struggle for Human Rights*. Boston: Beacon, 1980.

> A factual summary by Amnesty International activist.

Sivachev, N., and Yakovlev, N., *Russia and the United States: U.S.-Soviet Relations from the Soviet Point of View*. Translated by Olga Adler Titelbaum. Chicago: University of Chicago Press, 1979.

> Survey of Russian-American relations by two Soviet historians.

Shipler, D.K., *Russia: Broken Idols, Solemn Dreams*. New York: Times Books, 1983.

> Account of daily life in the late 70s and early 80s, with perceptive analysis.

Starr, S.F., *Red and Hot: The Fate of Jazz in Soviet Society*. Cambridge, England and New York: Oxford University Press, 1983.

> Readable, pioneering work on popular culture.

READINGS
for
Chapter Six

1. The Public Bath

The public bath in Soviet Russia was a place to enjoy oneself and socialize, just as it was before the Revolution. This description from the mid-1970s would still be valid today.

There is nothing imported about a Russian bath. Russians have been cleaning themselves for centuries with a combination of intense heat, birch leaves and cold water. Every village has a bath, every city has a number of them. The village version is a simple wooden hut with a stove, but in the cities the bath is an elaborate institution. The grandest of all are the 19th-century Sundonovski Baths in Moscow.

Sundonovski built his establishment at the bottom of a hill on a side street a long block from Kuznetski Most, the most fashionable street of shops in pre-revolutionary Moscow. He put up a three-story building a block long, built in the style of 19th-century Moscow—stucco-fronted neo-classical, with rows and rows of large windows. Sundonovski's name is no longer advertised, but everyone still uses it to describe the old building, which has changed very little (and not at all for the better) since 1917.

Sundonovski divided the baths into three classes, a distinction that survives, though the word "class" has been replaced by "department."

The present management (the city of Moscow) demonstrates less concern for the preservation of the old building than the Sundonovski family undoubtedly did, but there is still something grand about the first-class facilities on the second floor.

One senses the grandeur on the circular marble stairway that leads to them. An imposing chandelier and multi-colored, carved ceilings mark the way. The first rooms are paneled in warm, dark wood, and divided into cubicles. Naked men, some wrapped in white sheets, lounge on upholstered seats, some drinking beer, most smoking and talking. (Smoking and drinking are both forbidden by the posted regulations.) They are resting between sessions in the hot room, the shower room or the pool. This last is a Roman monument, Olympic size, surrounded by Corinthian columns and marble walls. The intricate tile floors that Sundonovski selected a century ago are still in place, though whenever a fault appears the repair work is done in a contemporary orange tile that distorts the beautiful old patterns.

According to published descriptions of the baths at the turn of the century, they were then a bastion of luxurious hedonism. A large staff of underpaid boys did the bidding of a wealthy clientele, fetching refreshment, scrubbing and massaging, pressing suits and shining boots. It isn't like that now, though elderly men in white smocks will press a suit or fetch some beer

---

Abridged from Kaiser, Robert, *Russia: The People and the Power*, 74–76, 78–79, New York: Atheneum, 1976.

or a bottle of vodka. And the feeling one gets lounging around the baths of a Friday morning must still approximate the pleasurable sense of self-indulgence that made the establishment so popular before 1917.

The bath attracts all kinds of clients. A group of distinguished professors from the Academy of Sciences* likes to spend most of Saturday there. They come to the first-class section with a good supply of vodka and Armenian brandy, salami, smoked fish and loaves of bread, which they consume— between visits to the hot room and the pool. Their neighbors may be scruffy laborers who come to the bath once a week to dislodge the grime they absorb on the job. Many of the bathers come at the same time on the same day every week, creating societies of friends who have been steaming, drowning and caressing themselves together for years . . .

The atmosphere in the baths is something like that of a locker room, but it isn't a place to dress and undress for some other activity—it *is* the activity. The sheet and pillowcase one gets (for 13 kopeks) to wrap the body and put under the seat make the clients look like Romans in a B movie. The fact that no one has any clothes on seems to reduce the barriers between people. Conversation is easy.

The talk covers every conceivable subject. Jokes are a favorite pastime. The Friday-morning crowd could spend most of the morning chewing dry smoked fish, drinking beer and telling jokes . . .

Most of one's time at the baths is spent on the benches in a series of interludes separating the main business. From the benches in the third-class section the bathers pass through a heavy door into the showering and scrubbing room, a long hall, perhaps 100 feet by 30, lined with marble slabs arranged like beds in a hospital ward. The ceiling of this hall is held up by ancient girders which have been eaten away by rust for decades in the steamy atmosphere, but somehow continue to bear the weight. Men lie asleep on the marble slabs, lounge on them, massage themselves or each other, scrub from head to toe with great mountains of soapsuds. At the end of each marble platform two ancient spigots with smooth wooden handles dispense hot or cold water. Above some of them are shower heads that make it possible to lie under a stream of water for extended periods. Some men fall asleep this way.

The hot room opens off the far end of this hall. It is relatively small, perhaps 25 feet square, on two levels. Just inside the door the heat is strong but not intense. To really feel it one must walk up the tiled steps to the second level, where the old physics lesson about heat rising comes to life. Here the real zealots stand for 20 or 30 minutes, some dressed in little peaked caps and gloves. The head is most sensitive to the heat. The hands start to burn as they collide with the hot air when one whacks himself (or his neighbor) with bunches of leaves. The whacking is meant to open the pores and promote

---

*Soviet Academy of Sciences.** Leading organization of Soviet research in the natural and social sciences to which most successful researchers belonged.

circulation. Serious bathers keep hitting themselves until the leaves come off the dried branches, so the floor is covered with slippery leaves.

The assembled company can never agree on the temperature in the hot room. The fanatics always think it is "weak," and toss small quantities of water onto the big bricks which—made red hot by a gas fire—heat the room. The water creates a fine steam which raises the temperature.

The only unpleasant moments in the bath are the inevitable arguments in the hot room about the temperature. The pretensions to expertise are quite remarkable; at any time there are at least two or three people in the hot room who confidently explain that they know exactly what is best for everyone, what the history of the Russian bath is, why the heat should be higher or lower or unchanged. These experts never agree with each other. Usually, whoever wants it hotter prevails, because he can himself continue tossing water onto the bricks when the others have stopped doing so. Finally it gets too hot for everyone, and there is a stampede of bare bodies down the stairs from the second level.

2. Car Owners' Woes

The Soviet press often carried articles about problems that needed to be remedied: pilfering from factories, alcoholism, absenteeism, and other inefficiencies. This article was quite typical. It is particularly interesting in its suggestion that there might be a place for private initiative in the solution to this problem. To suggest that private initiative might prove a solution was highly unusual in 1981. By 1990, it had become commonplace to think that private enterprise was the answer to all problems. This article indicates how and why the so-called second economy flourished.

Soviet Editors' Note.—Numerous readers have written us in response to the newspaper's Aug. 7 article, "Who Will Fix Automotive Service?" We invited a number of specialists to participate in a round-table discussion of this topic.

Question.—Letters to the editors cite numerous cases of poor performance on the part of automotive service stations. What more needs to be done to improve automotive service in our country?

A. Krutko, Deputy Director of the Moscow Administration for Combating the Embezzlement of Socialist Property and Speculation.—Law violations at automotive service stations have become too widespread. For example, we are presently prosecuting cases of large-scale bribe taking at the Zhiguli Automo-

Abridged from Petrov, V., and Yakovlev, V., "Once Again about Automotive Service," In *Sovetskaya Rossia* (October 1981). *Current Digest of the Soviet Press* 33 (January 1982): 14–15.

tive Service Center on the Warsaw Highway in Moscow. Cheating of car owners is also widespread. We have one such case in which car owners were cheated out of more than 5,000 rubles, altogether. Furthermore, the people who are supposed to be auditing to ensure that billing is correct are sometimes themselves involved in thefts. We have also uncovered cases of large-scale thefts from automotive manufacturers. The situation at the Leninist Young Communist League Automotive Plant is especially disturbing.

S. Petrachenkov, general director of Mosavtotekhobsluzhivaniye [the Moscow Automotive Service Association].—We realize the need for close contacts between automotive service and the agencies charged with combating the embezzlement of socialist property and speculation. One thing that worries us are the auto mechanics who take small bribes or cheat customers out of a ruble or two here and there, but whose offenses are too small to warrant criminal prosecution. There are no legal grounds for firing such people, either. About the only way to punish them would be to deprive them of bonuses, but that wouldn't be any deterrent—they take enough extra money from customers in a week to make up two monthly bonuses. So we are virtually helpless to stop these widespread abuses.

Yu. N. Yagunov, deputy general director of the Moscow Leninist Young Communist League Automotive Plant.—Of course, an effective punishment must be found for such abuses, but it's also necessary to institute effective incentives, so that the amount of money an auto mechanic legally earns is directly proportionate to the quality of work he does.

Q.—What about the fact that it's often the customers themselves who give auto mechanics the opportunity to earn money illegally, "on the side?"

S. N. Vinokurov, Director of Rosavtotekhobsluzhivaniye [the Russian Republic Automotive Service Association].—Considering how much time it normally takes private motorists to get their cars repaired, it's no wonder that they're willing to pay extra money to get the job done more quickly. For example, we recently calculated that a private motorist in Lipetsk Province spends an average of 60 hours just to get one repair performed on his car.

Q.—There's a statistic showing that only four out of every 10 cars that require repairs are repaired at state service stations. If we assume that one private motorist in 10 may do his own car work, that leaves five out of 10 repairs to be done by mechanics working "on the side"—either on state time and at state service stations, or after work but using state materials. Aside from the issue of criminal lawbreaking, don't these enterprising private mechanics constitute an untapped reserve for improving automotive service?

R. Kislyuk, the Volga Automotive Plant's deputy general director for automotive service.—In Hungary, where auto mechanics are allowed to do private work, they buy their own parts and pay income tax to the state. Establishing a similar practice in our country would create healthy competition for state service stations and stimulate them to provide better service.

S. Vinokurov.—Incidentally, this form of service is already being introduced in the Baltic republics.

Q.—What radical steps can be taken to improve state automotive service?

R. Kislyuk.—The reason that illegal practices in automotive service have come to constitute a whole system of their own is that car production is simply outstripping the growth in state automotive service. To provide normal service to all private motorists we would need twice our present service capacity. To keep up with the current production of Zhigulis alone, we should be opening eight new service bays a day, but we are having great difficulty opening even two.

The Volga Automotive Plant's experience demonstrates that the establishment of large specialized service stations with direct ties to auto manufacturers is one way to make service more efficient. Right now the fact that Soyuzav-*totekhobsluzhivaniye* [the All-Union Automotive Service Association] acts as a middleman between service stations and manufacturers greatly slows the process by which the stations obtain spare parts and makes it impossible for us to know which parts and how many each station needs. In addition to specialization, we need to computerize the inventorying and distribution of spare parts. For a long time now there has been talk of setting up an Auto Service Automated Management System, but so far only five of the 50 computers that are needed for this purpose have been installed.

3. Clothes

This reading is from the memoirs of a woman who grew up in Riga, Latvia and then moved to Siberia shortly after World War II. The events she describes took place some twenty years ago, but the search by Soviet citizens for distinctive clothes, preferably imported ones, continues. In the 1970s and 1980s, tourists became a great source for Western goods, and the illegal black market flourished. The Soviet traders made a great deal of money, selling American blue jeans, for example, for one hundred or even two hundred rubles.

Let me tell you about how we got our clothes. I remember the words of a friend of mine who used to say, "If I were to die tomorrow, nobody would know what sort of taste I had in clothes." What she meant was that during our entire lives, we never were able to buy what we liked or what we would choose according to our personal taste, but only what we could find. And what we found was a matter of luck.

What was sold in the stores was very boring and badly made. We wanted to get imported clothes that were stylish and of good quality. There were several ways to find imported clothes. We called one of them the "store way."

Glants, Musya. Interview with Janet Vaillant. Cambridge, Massachusetts, 29 September 1990.

Occasionally imported goods would come into the stores. If, for example, some Austrian boots came in, and you were lucky enough to hear about it, and if you could get away from your job, then you might stand in line four or even six hours to get these boots. When you got to the head of the line, if they hadn't sold all the boots, they might not have them in your size, but you bought them anyway. Then you might trade with a friend, knowing that if they had the good luck to get something that fit you, they would give you something. This took a lot of time and energy. Furthermore, all the imports that came legally to the Soviet Union came in batches. I remember one year Finnish coats came to the city where I lived. They were grey and had a squirrel-fur collar. All those who were lucky enough to get one of the coats looked identical, like students in a school uniform.

The "store way" to get imported clothes really only worked in big cities like Moscow. For a time, I lived in Novokuznets, in Siberia. Then I remember that when people went to Moscow on a business trip, man or woman, everyone would ask them to bring back clothes. We would give them money before they left, so they could buy things. People walked around the stores with big lists of things and the names of the people for whom they were meant to buy them. Nobody at home was afraid that their "buyer" might bring something that wouldn't fit because you could always sell it and gain a friend. Everyone was grateful. And the poor traveller had to find some time from his business trip to walk around in the stores.

There was a better way to get good clothes if you lived in a port city or a place where people had relatives abroad. This way wasn't really legal, but then it wasn't too illegal either. Many of the sailors who traveled with their ships abroad brought things back with them, including imported clothes. We called these things *shmetkii*, a slang word that means all the things you need for a good life. Sailors' wives did the actual selling, and for a very high price. Another source of such *shmetkii* were packages from relatives who lived abroad. I lived in Riga, Latvia. Latvia had been an independent bourgeois republic before World War Two, and because of the war, many people from Latvia moved to other countries during and after the war. Later, in the 1960s, Jews were able to emigrate. These people who lived abroad would send back packages to their relatives. In Riga, there were a lot of goods from these packages that circulated around the city. There were even people who made a business of selling these things. We called them *akooli imperialisma* (sharks of imperialism).

I had my own shark. Of course, she had a name, and she was actually a very nice woman, but we always called her "shark." She used to take a lot of money for things that were not really worth it; however, I never complained. It was because of her that my friends and I were able to look pretty good. She understood us. She would give credit from time to time, so that we could pay for a dress in up to three installments. It was a very serious business. She sold not only what she herself got from packages sent to her, but she took goods sent to other people and sold them on commission. Of course, all this was

secret. To be able to buy from our shark, you had to have special recommenda-
tions and good references as an honest payer and a person who wouldn't gossip.
You had to go quietly and carefully, so the neighbors wouldn't notice you.
Actually our shark gave us much better service than we got in the stores where
often you could not even see what you were buying, much less try it on.

These ways of buying things in the 1960s were a great improvement over
what was possible in the years immediately after the war. Then no imported
things made their way into the country. Then it was difficult to get anything at
all. I remember one expression from my childhood, "to build" a coat or a suit.
It was literally a kind of construction. First of all, you bought the piece of
fabric. Then, after a time, when you had saved up enough money, you bought
the lining. And then, after another lapse of time, the padding that you would
need for warmth. I remember all the pieces for a coat lying in our closet. Last,
there was a very exciting evening when, somewhere, someone found the
crowning piece, the fur collar. Several days later there was a solemn moment
when all these packages were taken to the tailor. Then we waited for weeks,
even months, and had to pay a lot of money before we received the coat. That
coat served, not for a year or two, but for decades. So, step-by-step my family
built such things for everyone in the family.

I remember an American coat that I bought from my shark. It was in
1964, and I didn't say good-bye to that coat until 1979. I wore it for fifteen
years. Even now, I remember how beautiful it was. It was an artificial fur,
American coat. It was an absolutely eternal coat. I got married in that coat. I
wore that coat to the hospital when my daughter was born. I wore it until the
year I emigrated. I changed the collar after a number of years. Then the lining
wore out, and I had to have another one put in.

I don't remember that anyone whom I knew had more than one dress for
work, a blouse and a skirt, and one outfit to go out. Everyone had a summer set
of clothes and a winter set of clothes. Even when I was able to buy more, and I
could afford more, even then I had two or three dresses, not more. It was
natural because these things were very expensive.

I have to explain how much my clothes cost. In 1964, I was working as a
curator in an art museum. My salary was 70 rubles a month.* Later, my salary
increased to 90 rubles. My husband worked then as a technician and received
140 rubles. Several years later, I started to work as an assistant professor at an
institute, and my salary went up to 120 rubles. I have to admit that I spent 300
rubles on my American coat in 1964, more than four months' salary. For many,
many years, I had two jersey dresses, a blue one and a green one. Each one of
them cost 70 rubles. I remember the tragedy I had with my blue dress. I got an
ink stain on it. I was so upset that I cannot express it. Thank God, when I came

---

*About $50 per month at the 1964 official exchange rate. It is very difficult to compare
prices in the U.S. and USSR because some things there were relatively cheap, such as
food, rent, and transportation, others expensive such as clothes and any luxury.

home, my child's baby-sitter, who was a simple village woman, said to me, "Don't worry. I will take it out with milk and a hot iron." And she did. I will always remember her.

When we are talking about clothes, we have to remember how important clothes are in the Soviet Union and how little choice we had about what we could get. Men and women both spent a lot of time and energy trying to get clothes so they could look good.

4. The Soviet People's Court

The People's Courts in the Soviet Union judged petty offenders. Judges often seemed to base their decisions on the character of the defendant as well as on the crime committed. Notice the way the judge suggests the witness should have taken more responsibility for a worker and the lecture about proper behavior and morality.

Soviet trials begin with a short biography of the accused.

A Russian judge would think it silly to deal with Ivan Ivanov, a stranger off the street. Who is this fellow? What is his record at work? In the courts? What about his personal and family background? And so, information about the character and history of the defendant—information which is usually kept secret in English and American courts until guilt or innocence has been decided—is sought and aired at the outset.

[In this case Kondakov has been accused of stealing a pair of galoshes from the place where he works. The judge is questioning a witness.]

"What do you remember about this case? Tell the court everything you know."

"What do I remember? Not very much. I remember it happened on the night shift, sometime in early October—"

"The night of October 11–12?"

"That's right. Kondakov"—she glances in his direction and smiles at him—"arrived about twenty minutes late for work. It was quite clear that he had been drinking. He was pretty drunk. He kept on getting up from his table—I worked next to him—and singing the first stanzas of folk songs. And getting up to congratulate us, I don't know for what. Ordinarily he was a quiet sort.

"Well at about three-thirty he announced loudly that he was going to the bathroom. Of course, I paid no attention. But a few minutes later there was a commotion in the next shop. Everyone ran out—I did too. There he was with the galoshes. He had stuffed them under his coat and the guard noticed it. Well,

---

Abridged from Feifer, George, *Justice in Moscow*. New York: Simon & Schuster, 1964.

that's all I know. The police came and took him away. He seemed confused. Embarrassed. He kept saying, "I never stole a thing in my life."

"Did he swear?"

"Not while I was there. He just muttered to himself, sort of."

"Was he stealing shoes before this incident?"

"I don't know, I have no idea, I don't think so."

"Why do you think he committed this act?"

"I haven't the faintest idea. He was quite drunk."

"But not so drunk that he didn't know he was stealing?"

"I can't say. I don't think so."

"Was he often drunk at work?"

"Not often."

"But he *has* been drunk; did you know he was warned about that?"

"Yes, I knew."

"What can you tell us about his character?"

"He was all right. Decent. I never had any unpleasantness with him."

"But you know that he had 'unpleasantness' with the administration."

"Yes."

"Did you know that he was fired from other jobs and arrested for petty hooliganism [undesirable behavior, juvenile delinquency]?"

"No."

"You didn't know that. Perhaps you ought to have interested yourself in your neighbor. Well, what kind of man was he at work? Did you expect that he might steal? What can you say about his working habits?"

"He wasn't a bad worker. Or unusually good, either. He did his share. I'd call him normal."

"You mean that a normal worker is late and absent and drunk on the job?"

"Uh, he worked well—"

"Worked well! He *stole* well. What about the reprimands he kept getting?"

"During the last couple of months, he worked very hard. I don't think he had any reprimands."

"If you don't count thieving."

"I think he was trying to—"

"Such people have got to be taken under control, they have got to be shown. He drinks, he fails to appear at work, he creates scandals—and now look where he ended. The logical end; he didn't want to heed the warnings. Well, we have a job to do; the people of Moscow need shoes and the Red Hero is trying to supply them. We don't have to put up with people who deliberately stand in the way."

The judge puts back her glasses.

"Now is there anything else you would like to add? Can you tell us anything more about his intentions?"

"I don't know anything more. It was a surprise to me."

The judge turns to the assessors. "Have you any questions?"

They shake their heads, No.

[Kondakov got one year hard labor.]

[In another case, the defendant is a Soviet go-getter, an entrepreneur whose deals are illegal. He is from Azerbaijan, but is being tried in Moscow where he has illegally taken up residence.]

Articles 147 and 198: Swindling and Violation of Passport Regulations. The defendant, a skinny, dark, itinerant Azerbaijanian born in Baku, grins uncontrollably . . .

He has admitted guilt on both charges. The swindling was attempted in a local *rinok* (an open market where collective farmers are permitted to sell produce from their private plots). With a fellow Azerbaijanian he worked a variation of an old confidence game, known in both the East and West as the "pocketbook drop," on a dashing Uzbek soldier on leave in Moscow. Promising to split the contents of a wallet they supposedly found, the two accomplices enticed the victim to part with his own fortune of sixty-three rubles . . .

The second charge is illegal residence in Moscow: the accused has no *propiska* (a residence permit, issued by the police). This permission, which is stamped in the citizen's (internal) passport, is required in the major Soviet cities—Moscow, Leningrad, Kiev—and in the coastal strip along the Black Sea and in other popular areas. A Soviet citizen cannot simply take up residence in these areas as he could, for instance, in Irkutsk. For a newcomer, permission to stay usually depends upon his having a job which would entitle him to a *propiska;* but for most jobs—to complete the vicious cycle—possession of the *propiska* is a prerequisite. The purpose is to deter migration to already overcrowded cities. Thus, the Azerbaijanian, having no steady job, has no legal right to live in Moscow; he has been warned four times during the past two years about his being there.

The judge is a ponderous man who plays with his words and his fingers. "Young man, you have got to get a job, you have got to find yourself an honest place in our socialist society. And you cannot do it in Moscow. Do you understand that you are living at the expense of society? Young man, you are a piece of fungus. You have done nothing with your life but practice the bourgeois creed of getting something for nothing. Why didn't you go back to your homeland and work, like a Soviet man?"

Grinning, the skinny defendant asks for mercy. He knows that he must be punished, of course; he understands that he did wrong—but could the court please make it as light as possible? You see, he has a sick mother in Baku, he has asthma, and he has a burning desire to reform . . .

But the sentence is four years in a labor colony, strict regime. The Azerbaijanian is stunned; the grin becomes a mouth agape, then a grimace of hatred . . .

Four youths stole three rolls of tar paper from their factory: three years each. A drunk sneaked a mirror from a grammar school on Election Day: two years. A sober man took the windshield wipers and mirror from a parked car: one year. An obviously imbecilic old lush insisted on annoying strangers at a metro station: one year. A waitress had been pouring each glass of wine a few drops short and taking home a bottle a fortnight for herself: two years. A man rolled a drunk for his greasy jacket and scruffy shoes: one year. The punishments are astonishingly severe.

5. Soviet Medical Training Under Stalin and Brezhnev

Medical education in the USSR, like education in other fields, included a heavy dose of ideological training. This reduced the time available for the study of medicine itself. In the following excerpts from his autobiography, Russian Doctor, *the emigré Dr. Vladimir Golyakhovsky describes his personal encounter with Marxist-Leninist teachings in the late 1940s, and his son's similar experience in the late 1960s. This practice persisted through the 1980s. To graduate, students had to pass three exams, one in internal medicine, one in surgery, and one in ideology and official history. The ideological exam was abolished in 1990.*

The first lecture on the first day of classes in medical school on Marxism-Leninism-Stalinism was held in an auditorium decorated with big portraits of Lenin and Stalin. The instructor, Professor N. Dubinin, recited quotations and slogans without sense and axioms without proof. Nobody paid any attention to this gobbledygook, of course, and I remember that I gazed at one of my classmates, Lena Kozak, a beautiful blonde, during the whole lecture Nevertheless, these lectures subconsciously taught us that ideological submission was more important than professional accomplishment.

These political lectures took up about a third of my class time during my six years at the medical school. I studied the history of the Communist Party, the basics of Marxism-Leninism, political economy, dialectical materialism, and Marxist-Leninist philosophy. All of this instruction was completely dogmatic. The professors followed a strictly established schedule of instruction based on the textbooks and allowed no deviations or even rational explanations to interfere with the program. The holiest of all Marxist scripture at that time was the fourth chapter of *A Short History of the Bolshevik Party*, because supposedly Stalin Himself had written it.

Abridged from Golyakhovsky, V., *Russian Doctor*, 7–8, 256–57. New York: St. Martin's/ March, 1984.

The official awe toward this chapter went far beyond the awe felt for the Ten Commandments; students were asked to memorize it. Naturally, no one did so, but no one could refuse pretending to do so. As a result all the students murmured the text under their breath, exactly as a hasty parishioner drones a familiar, wearisome prayer. We uttered the words of the text without a thought, and I never discovered what the chapter contained.

If a student failed to do an assignment for any of these classes—for example, if he didn't write a summary of *Lenin's Materialism and Empirocriticism*—the Komsomol (Communist Youth League) called a meeting to threaten the student with expulsion from the school if he missed a second assignment. No such measures were ever taken if a student missed an assignment in any medical courses.

Although my son made it into medical school, after he passed the four oral entrance exams he had to put in two weeks of free work as a laborer's helper on the construction site of a new school building. It was a precondition for any freshman to be allowed to attend classes. This illegal practice had been in force for years, but no one dared object for the writ had been handed down by the Party Committee. Some farsighted freshmen-to-be tried extra hard on the construction site to attract the benevolent attention of the Party bosses. And thereafter, all through the course of study, such students devoted more time and energy to Komsomol duties than to academic endeavors.

Listening to my son's stories and watching him begin his student life, I was struck by how little things had changed over the twenty-two years since I had been a medical student In some respects present-day students had it even harder than I had.

After his first day in school, I asked my son: "What have you learned from your debut?"

"Nothing," he replied.

"What do you mean, nothing?"

"Very simple: our first lecture was in Marxist philosophy. The students talked, getting to know each other, and no one listened to the professor. He muttered inaudibly from his lectern, from time to time making feeble attempts to keep us quiet. The lecture was followed by a meeting at which the secretary of the Party Committee talked at length and very boringly, exhorting us to be worthy of the lofty titles of Soviet students and future physicians. After he was done, another meeting was called for us to elect Komsomol secretaries, and then we were told that each year we would be required to put in a month-long stint on a collective farm, helping harvest the potato crop. Then we were broken down into groups and again had to spend some time electing group leaders and Komsomol secretaries. Some elections, indeed—all the secretaries had been appointed in advance by the Party Committee. And that about sums up the extent of what I learned during my first day."

6. The Intourist Guide

Foreign visitors to the Soviet Union, like visitors to prerevolutionary Russia (see Chapter 3, Reading 5), often commented that they were always accompanied by an official guide, without whom it was very difficult to see or do anything. In the Soviet period, the guides represented Intourist, the government tourist agency. Many visitors suspected that their guides were supposed to watch them and were connected to the KGB. With glasnost, *the suspicions were confirmed. The following account was published in* Moscow News *in 1990.*

It's hard to find another European country where foreign tourists are cared for as much as in the Soviet Union. However, it is even harder to find a country where foreigners are treated with so much suspicion. Paradoxically, this is primarily true of organizations which have been specially designed to cater for the foreigners. This paradox is a special feature of Intourist, which has been employing me as a guide and interpreter for 13 years now.

According to certain "competent bodies" and the Intourist management, the interpreter-guide must at present try to convince foreign tourists that "we have everything but problems in this country." Showing foreigners around the country, we can mention "individual shortcomings" and allude to "temporary difficulties." But, importantly, we must be able to prove to them the superiority of socialism and demonstrate our firm adherence to our beliefs.

But how is this firm belief inculcated in Intourist employees?

I feel ashamed when I look into the eyes of my friends from Sweden when they ask me whether I'm required to report on them to special officers of Intourist. But I'm indeed required to do this, as is specified in the *Rules of the Work of the Interpreter-Guide.* When signing an employment contract, each one of us working at Intourist has to indicate in the application one's agreement to comply with "special conditions" of work.

What is involved in such a report? Everything about everyone. The place of the tourist's birth, employment, knowledge of Russian, attitude towards the USSR, questions asked, acquaintances and contacts with them, participation in excursions and their whereabouts in case they miss some scheduled event. We must specify whether the tourist was conducting spying activities or came to the USSR with "subversive aims."

Some guides diligently think these reports up. Some others compile them in a formal way, still others simply shirk the responsibility. The latter are "educated" through a "dressing down," an oral reprimand, or the refusal of a trip abroad. The person's salary hike can be delayed, or the person can be listed as "not fit to go abroad." One can get on the list for a number of reasons. Until

From "Is It Easy to Be a Guide with Intourist?" *Moscow News* 8, 1990.

1990, Intourist employees were forbidden to give their address or telephone number to foreigners, or to "maintain personal contacts" in general. All personal correspondence had to be carried on exclusively through Intourist.

Now it looks like perestroika has reached our organization as well. We are allowed to give foreigners our address and telephone number. Nevertheless, we got the following explanation from our management at a recent meeting: "You can do that, but we can sack you at a day's notice."

We are still regularly given lectures "on vigilance." The lector continues to reiterate: "At present, when the international situation remains tense, Western secret services are getting ever more active in their work against the USSR. You, interpreter-guides, are on the frontline of the ideological struggle. However, some of you thoughtlessly agree to contacts with foreigners outside your work duties, accept gifts from foreigners, and indulge in unpatriotic conversations with them. We possess full information on such people." Then, we are read the list of those sacked according to Article 254 (p. 1) of the Labour Code of the Russian Federation, which allows no possibility for legally appealing the dismissal. Do you want to know some of the cases? Here you are. An interpreter-guide had a chat with tourist in their room at the Pulkovskaya Hotel at night. A woman guide fell in love with a foreigner, and the latter asked her to marry him. There were instances of dismissal for merely inviting a foreigner home.

The lecture ends with a warning: "We have information on many of you. We know everything and recommend that you comply with the Rules."

Poor guides! Throughout their entire careers some can't find a single "spy" or "anti-Sovieteer." They fail to understand why their humble job as a guide is regarded almost on a par with the job of a special agent out to catch spies.

Lately, guides have been given rights comparable to other Soviet citizens: now they can go abroad on private invitations. I could make a visit abroad (after 12 years of being refused it!). I devoted my life to Scandinavian studies and became a fairly good translator from Swedish. But I saw Sweden only recently for the first time. Can you imagine a peasant divorced from his land, or a philologist for whom books are out of reach? If you can, you will understand my feelings.

However, my triumph was short-lived: the Intourist personnel department keeps a special book to register guides going abroad on private invitation. Our managers believe such visits to be a "misuse of office."

Ilya Nikonov
interpreter-guide

Chapter Seven

THE GORBACHEV REVOLUTION: 1985-1991

Mikhail Gorbachev surprised the world. A few Western observers had noticed that the Soviet Union was losing its dynamism, but most expected the new Soviet government to be much like those that had preceded it. Gorbachev had risen through the ranks of the party. Why should he be different from the gray men who had preceded him?

Once Gorbachev had been chosen general secretary of the party, he systematically replaced many of the aging conservatives who had prospered under Brezhnev with new people who might be expected to be loyal to him. He promised to improve economic production, and moved against corruption. Soon, however, he realized that this was not enough: he began to call for *glasnost* (the Russian word means giving voice to your views), for *perestroika* (restructuring or reconstruction), and for **demokratizatsia** (democratization), as well as for new thinking in foreign affairs. He called for help in removing the log jam that had developed under Brezhnev. When a few of these logs were removed, however, Gorbachev and his advisers discovered that the situation was far more complicated than they had realized. One act led to another, and soon Gorbachev found himself swept along faster and faster by a torrent of demands for change.

---

*This chapter is organized thematically. For a chronology of the key events of the Gorbachev era, see pp. 400–403.

Popular at first, by 1990 Gorbachev was under attack from two sides: by those who wanted him to go faster and by those who thought he had gone too far. The country was in disarray. Economic production had plummeted and the national republics were clamoring for more autonomy and even independence. Then, in August, 1991, a group of highly placed party leaders attempted a coup. When it fell apart, the party itself was discredited and Gorbachev resigned his post as general secretary of the party. The three pillars that had supported the command administrative system—a political monopoly by a single party, the centralized economic planning mechanism, and the penetration of private and social life by the organs of the party-state—had crumbled. Gorbachev had been pushed out and a political and social system that had seemed stable and strong in 1985 had disintegrated in less than a decade. By the end of 1991, the Soviet Union as such had ceased to exist. People had to speak of the former Soviet Union or of individual republics, or of the Commonwealth of Independent States.

GLASNOST AND PERESTROIKA

In the summer of 1986, Gorbachev wrote a book, *Perestroika: New Thinking for Our Country and the World*. In it, he set out his view of the current situation and his plans for the future. He spoke with pride about what Soviet socialism had accomplished: the creation of an economy with a job for everyone, free medical care, free education, and the protection of people from many of the uncertainties of life. Now, he wrote, the country faced challenges that even the great Lenin could not have foreseen. All Soviet leaders before Gorbachev had justified their policies with references to the science of socialism, and to Lenin and Marx. By failing to do so, Gorbachev signaled his readiness to make a radical break with the past. He recognized that new times called for new approaches. (See Reading 1.)

Because the integration of economics, politics, and culture was a basic feature of the Stalinist system, Gorbachev recognized that significant economic reforms were impossible without new policies in cultural and political life. The first of his policies that had dramatic effect was *glasnost*. To identify the sources of the country's problems, and to encourage people to take an active part in the party's economic and anti-corruption campaigns, Gorbachev and his advisers needed to find out what was really happening in their country and to mobilize popular support. Censorship and fear had separated people from one another, but the resulting silence also had prevented the government from getting accurate information. Urged on by Gorbachev, newspapers and journals began to publish articles about corruption and mismanagement. Letters from readers wrote of dishonest party officials and crime.

FACT: In the Brezhnev era, natural catastrophes such as earthquakes and accidents such as airplane crashes were never reported in the Soviet media. Many crimes also went unreported.

One of the first big tests of *glasnost* was the accident at the Chernobyl nuclear reactor in April, 1986. News of this disaster first reached the world in broadcasts from neighboring countries that had identified its nuclear fallout. In the Soviet Union, the reports were delayed and very incomplete at first, but the subsequent degree of openness about the accident, as well as the willingness of the Soviet Union to accept outside help and advice—even from the United States—marked a real change in Soviet behavior. By the end of 1986, most political prisoners had been released, including Andrei Sakharov who returned to Moscow from house arrest in Gorky. Gradually, unevenly, and with occasional setbacks, the Soviet press and television offered hard-hitting investigative reporting, open discussions about the Soviet Union's economic and environmental problems, and revelations about corrupt party officials and the growth of crime. (See Readings 2 and 3.) At first certain subjects remained off limits: the KGB, military spending, delicate matters of foreign policy, and the luxurious lifestyle of high party and government officials. Conservative members of the party *apparat* tried to fight back, well aware that the truth was dangerous to their position. In 1990, reformers finally pushed through a law on freedom of the press.

POLITICAL REFORM

It was clear that if the bureaucracy was to be held accountable for its actions, there would have to be political *perestroika.* In 1988, Gorbachev proposed important changes in the governmental structure that were immediately put into effect. A new, elected 2,250-member body, the Congress of People's Deputies, was created. It was to elect members of a new Supreme Soviet, which would become a standing legislature. The new Supreme Soviet would be a working body with real power, in sharp contrast to the former Supreme Soviet that had met only briefly to rubber stamp party policies. Two years later, Gorbachev created the position of state president and had himself elected to that office by the Congress of People's Deputies. By increasing the power of these government institutions, Gorbachev was consciously creating a force that could counterbalance the power of the party.

Beginning in 1988, elections to all government soviets were contested. For the first time since the Revolution of 1917, there were not only elections, as there had been throughout the Stalin and Brezhnev eras, but real choices among candidates. Government congresses that had been held behind closed doors were now televised in full. Debates became genuine debates about important issues: the economy, laws on property, the cynicism of young people, and the spread of organized crime. Delegates were able to discuss publicly the need for a government of laws rather than of political decrees. By the end of 1989, the reforms had proceeded far enough so that even Gorbachev's policies could be criticized. The result of this increasing openness was the swift political education of the Soviet peoples about the real problems and possibilities that confronted them. (See Reading 4.)

FACT: In 1990, the 28th Party Congress elected a new Central Committee. Only 59 of its 412 members had been in the previous Central Committee, but not all the new delegates were reform-minded.

While the *nomenklatura* system still remained in place, contested elections for party and government positions were weakening its power. The candidate approved by the party did not always win. In local government elections, such as those for the mayors of Moscow and Leningrad, loyal party members were defeated. Boris Yeltsin, for example, a party maverick who had been pushed out of the Politburo and publicly humiliated by Gorbachev, was elected to the Congress of People's Deputies by Moscow voters despite party opposition.

FACT: When Boris Yeltsin was elected president of Russia in 1990, it was the first time in Russian history that the people had directly elected their president.

There seemed to be no stopping the flood of reform. People began to talk about the need for a multiparty system. Gorbachev was criticized for not moving faster toward the total democratization of the country's political system, though other people warned of disorder in the countryside and the need for more disciplined behavior. Many of the administrators responsible for carrying out Gorbachev's reforms tried quietly to sabotage them. Clearly, a fierce struggle was in progress in the Soviet Union, not only over ideals and what was good for the country, but also over bread and butter issues of jobs and privilege. Many members of the *nomenklatura* had a lot to lose.

FACT: A Soviet authority has estimated that in the late 1980s, there were more than one million party and state bureaucrats who benefitted from access to the special stores, cars, and *dachas* that went with their positions. (See Reading 5.)

Many of the full-time, paid party workers and the government bureaucrats who supervised the planned economy or worked in regulatory agencies, could not be expected to support reforms that would almost certainly take away their privileges and possibly put them out of a job. Gorbachev was beginning to undermine the power of the bureaucrats, but he hesitated to move too fast. He was looking for the middle ground between reformers and conservatives.

In 1990 Boris Yeltsin's popularity propelled him to the forefront of the complex Soviet political scene. He is seen here in Cathedral Square of the Kremlin, following the election for the presidency of the Russian Republic, which he won handily.

FACT: For every three young people who had enrolled in the Komsomol (Young Communist League) in 1984, only one enrolled in 1989. Two million people, almost one-tenth of the membership, resigned from the party between 1988 and 1990.

FACT: By March, 1990, ninety-four percent of those Soviet citizens polled thought that the Communist party was responsible for creating a crisis in the Soviet Union.

Boris Yeltsin, president of the Russian Republic, lacked Gorbachev's caution. He resigned from the party in July, 1990 and declared that henceforth there would be no special privileges for party bureaucrats in the Russian Republic. Other reformers such as the mayors of Moscow and Leningrad also resigned from the party. The party had become the enemy in the minds of a large percentage of the Soviet population, and membership a liability for the rising political stars.

THE ECONOMY

Reform of the economy had been Gorbachev's first priority. The main ideas of *perestroika* were to decentralize economic decision-making, to encourage and legalize new types of cooperative and individual property in land and manufacturing, and to introduce features of a market economy. Enterprises were promised more autonomy. Yet few economists or politicians had any real understanding of how a market economy such as that of the United States works. Indeed, the term took on an element of magic, as if the declaration of a market economy would solve all the problems facing the huge country. Tentative steps were taken. Production quotas were reduced, and some factories gained the right to sell surplus products for their own benefit and to negotiate their own prices for goods sold. It became legal to organize cooperatives, small private companies that could hire workers and make the best profit they could. Farmers were granted the right to lease land on a long-term basis and work it for the benefit of themselves and their families. If private plots were so much more productive than collective farms, the thinking went, large family holdings should lead to a significant increase in overall agricultural productivity. Foreign investment and joint business ventures between Soviet and foreign firms also were encouraged.

FACT: In 1990, four Soviet students enrolled in the Harvard Business School.

For much of the Soviet period, those who admired the West were criticized and accused of disloyalty. Now people were urged to learn new skills from the West. The window on the West was opened wide. (See Reading 6.)

The new economic policies had unexpected consequences. For example, Soviet factories had never worried about selling their products. Central planners took care of this for them. Now they had to learn salesmanship and develop marketing skills, something with which they had no experience. They also had to worry about getting supplies and raw materials. Their former suppliers might decide to sell elsewhere. The truck factory, for example, might find that the factory that used to supply it with tires had decided it was more profitable to make bicycle tires. To avert chaos, the planners sometimes had to intervene, demanding from factories a small quota for the planners' purposes. If they did intervene, decentralization and the transition to the market were delayed. If they did not, production went down, and indeed industrial production did fall rapidly.

FACT: In 1990, it cost 2.6 rubles to raise a kilo of meat. The state stores sold that meat for less than two rubles. Meat and many other foods had artificially low prices so that people could afford to buy them.

One of the biggest problems was pricing. The prices set by the central economic planners did not reflect the real cost of the goods being sold. Food

Early in 1990, the first McDonald's restaurant in the Soviet Union opened in Pushkin Square, Moscow, amid considerable fanfare, and immediately drew throngs of customers. This was a joint Canadian-Soviet venture, and was the first of several McDonald's to be built in the USSR.

and housing prices, for example, had been kept artificially low for many years, as a matter of public policy. Cheap food and lodging was one of the achievements of the socialist system. In the late 1980s, food prices in the state stores were permitted to rise slightly. Nonetheless the shelves often remained bare, and when were not, there were long lines. On the other hand, stores run by the new cooperatives were full, but the prices were so high that the average person could not afford to buy anything. People could not help but make a connection between the high prices in the cooperatives and the lack of goods in the state stores, and blame *perestroika* for their problems.

FACT: In 1990, the average Soviet wage was 250 rubles per month. A 25-year-old with a high school education could work in a cooperative and make 600 rubles per month.

FACT: In 1989, a kilo (2.2 lbs.) of potatoes cost 10 to 20 kopecks in Moscow
(100 kopecks equals one ruble). By December 1991, the same potatoes
cost 20 rubles in Moscow.

Many people resent the big profits of the new Soviet entrepreneurs and the high salaries of the people who work in the cooperatives. Even the government, which officially encouraged the cooperatives, was alarmed by the sight of high profits for some and poverty for others. It therefore hesitated to give up all price controls and let the market set the prices. In a situation of shortages, this would create terrible hardship for the great majority of people who had to get by on their fixed, low wages. Nevertheless, by early 1991, food prices were more than doubled in the state stores, and inflation was increasing at dizzying rates. On January 2, 1992, in a desperate move to increase supply, the Russian government freed all prices, except for those of a few food staples. Many salaries were raised as well, helping to fuel an inflation that had begun to spin out of control.

Agriculture has yet to show the improved production expected from *perestroika*. People in the countryside have been reluctant to strike out on their own and take advantage of the new opportunities for family or individual ownership. Where will they get the seed, the fertilizer, or the machines to work their land? These items often belong to the state farm and *kolkhoz* chairmen. The lords of the countryside are not interested in supplying fertilizer to their competitors, nor in leasing them machinery at harvest time when they themselves want it. The tractor driver likes working only eight hours each day for a guaranteed salary. He doesn't want to gamble that he can do better on a family farm. Why risk losing an easy job and low but regular salary? Rural people are conservative in most countries, and few in the Soviet countryside remember a system other than the one they have. They are suspicious of the government. In the past, it brought them little good and much harm. Furthermore, the laws on private ownership remain vague, contradictory and not always enforced. Many fear that the government of tomorrow will change its mind and they will be left isolated and defenseless. (See Reading 7.)

By 1991, the economy found itself caught at a midway point. Soviet leaders tried to encourage innovation and hard work by introducing some aspects of a market system, such as competition and rewards based on results, but they did not dare give up all economic planning and controls. There are numerous technical difficulties, however, in an economy that is half-planned and half-free, where some enterprises operate according to quotas and others are trying to respond to consumer demand. The planners found that they could not guarantee raw materials, spare parts for machinery, or timely deliveries. Some people concluded that all planning should be abolished—which would of course put some powerful people out of their jobs.

As central economic planning has diminished, factory managers had to operate in a new and rapidly changing environment that demands such skills

As *perestroika* failed to bring economic improvement for ordinary Soviet citizens, strikes and demonstrations broke out. In July 1989, coal miners in the Kuzbass region of central Siberia went on strike to call the Soviet leadership's attention to their demands for an improved living standard. Here the striking miners are addressed by one of their leaders.

as financing or marketing—with which they have little or no experience. New businesses need permits and permissions, and many bureaucrats demand bribes for providing them. Organized crime is active in making profits where and when it can, investing in joint-ventures and placing its money in commercial banks. The rules remain unclear. Economic reform was the first concern of Gorbachev's *perestroika* and remained its priority. Yet it has been the economy that has proved the most resistant to successful reform. Economic problems contributed greatly to Gorbachev's downfall and continue to plague the USSR's successor states today.

CULTURE AND SOCIAL LIFE

Glasnost and *perestroika* have had a revolutionary effect on cultural and social life. The lifting of censorship made possible the publication of great writers such as **Bulgakov** and Solzhenitsyn, whose work had been forbidden. Plays with political messages, lectures on politics and philosophy, and exhibitions of abstract art combined to make the cultural life of the large Soviet cities very exciting for the intelligentsia. (See Readings 8 and 9.)

New revelations about the Soviet past have had particularly far-reaching implications.

FACT: Khrushchev's 1956 "Secret Speech" about Stalin's crimes was published for the first time in the Soviet Union in April, 1989.

Glasnost has led to a new understanding and evaluation of the Soviet past. Almost no one in the Soviet Union knew that those killed in the purges numbered many millions, not just a few thousand. Almost no one knew about the secret pact in 1939 between Hitler and Stalin that gave Stalin a free hand in the Baltic republics in return for food and other natural resources from the Soviet Union to support Hitler's war on Poland and western Europe. Few knew that the famine that killed millions of Ukrainians and Kazakhs in the 1930s might have been avoided if the Soviet government had stopped exporting grain, or that millions of those who died in the war were victims of government and military mismanagement. In journals and newspapers, and at open meetings, the blank spots in Soviet history were being filled in. This trend, however, was not without difficulties. (See Reading 10.)

FACT: In June 1988, there were no high school exams in Soviet history. The old "facts" had been discredited, and there was no official version of history upon which to test the students.

For the first time, Soviet citizens could find out the truth about what had happened in their own history. Mass graves were uncovered where lay the bodies of thousands of innocent people who had been shot during the purges. Memorials for the victims of Stalin were erected. Only recently were Soviet citizens able to remember and mourn together losses and family tragedies that had long been painful secrets. Parents often had not even dared to tell their children about their own relatives because they were afraid the children might tell a stranger and the party-state would swoop down to arrest them. Most Soviet citizens became determined to stop the lying. Most, but not all, came to believe that they must know the truth about the past if they were to build a secure future. Much of what they have learned, however, has made them angry.

The revelations about what had been done in the name of the party reinforced a growing sense that the Marxist-Leninist ideology that was to have guided the Soviet Union to a bright communist future had led instead to a dead end, and that the party was guilty of terrible crimes. Most Soviet citizens wondered aloud whether the Revolution itself was a big mistake. Not only Stalin, but Lenin has come under attack. Lenin statues were pulled down by angry crowds. Some continued to defend Lenin and the party, either because their jobs were at stake or because they continued to believe in socialist ideals. (See Reading 11.)

FACT: As recently as 1988, it was illegal for anyone other than a parent to teach children about the Bible.

FACT: In 1990 the city of Gorky changed its name to Nizhny Novgorod, its name before the Revolution. In 1991, Leningrad again became St. Petersburg.

FACT: In 1991, the Russian Republic discarded its Soviet flag with hammer and sickle and replaced it with the traditional tricolor flag of the Russian tsars.

The collapse of the old ideology has created a spiritual and moral vacuum for many people. They have begun to look to the past, to tradition, to religion and to national and ethnic identities. New groups have sprung up to preserve historic buildings, to study local history, and to learn and practice religion. In the summer of 1988, there were huge celebrations in Moscow to celebrate the millennium of the introduction of Christianity to the eastern Slavs. They were attended by high party and government officials, including Gorbachev and his wife, Raisa. Boris Yeltsin appeared at televised Easter services. Three seminaries were reopened and the Russian Orthodox church was allowed to receive 150,000 Russian Bibles from abroad. Bibles became sought after and valued treasures, not only by believers but also by the curious who simply wanted to learn about the teachings of Christianity and its role in the Slavic past. In the Islamic republics, mosques reopened and offered religious education. In Central Asia, too, people took a new interest in their past.

Informal groups of all kinds sprang up like mushrooms after a fall rain. Now there are rock music fan clubs, political clubs, environmental groups, and groups to study the Bible. There are organized groups of yoga enthusiasts, herbal healers, descendants of Cossacks, Hare Krishnas, and admirers of abstract painting. The descendants of the former nobility have formed a group. There are also groups of antisemites and extreme nationalists. Political and social views long kept silenced have had a chance for an open hearing, and not all of them are democratic or tolerant. People have moved quickly to take advantage of their new freedoms. Culture and society have developed a new independent life.

ETHNIC RELATIONS: THE NATIONAL REPUBLICS

The highly centralized party-state effectively maintained Soviet control over the many different ethnic groups that lived within the Soviet Union. When Gorbachev began to decentralize decision-making, however, the republic governments began to gain real authority. *Glasnost* allowed people to develop and express their own points of view and to think about the economic and ecological interests of their own republics. Grievances that had built slowly over many years suddenly burst into the open.

One of the most visible results of the Gorbachev revolution was the reemergence of religion in the USSR. In September, 1990, Orthodox priests carrying icons and shrines leave the Kremlin for a holy procession through Moscow that ended with the consecration of the newly reopened Church of the Resurrection.

Loud claims came first from the Baltic republics. They had been part of the Russian Empire until World War I, independent between the wars, and then incorporated into the Soviet Union in 1940, under the terms of the Stalin-Hitler pact. Estonians and Latvians now expressed their resentment of the Russians who had migrated to their republics, taken jobs, and refused to learn the local languages. Lithuania declared that it would have its independence and, after a show of force proved unsuccessful in preventing it, all three republics declared and gained independence in 1991. Ukraine, Georgia, Armenia, and most of the other republics also declared their wish to be sovereign states. Russian nationalists hastened to point out that they, more than any other group, had suffered from Soviet rule, borne the brunt of the war and the purges, and witnessed the destruction of their culture from a hostile regime seated in their own capital.

FACT: The territory of Nagorno-Karabakh, which is inside Azerbaijan, has a population that is seventy-five percent Armenian.

FACT: In 1989, the population of Kazakhstan was just under forty percent Kazakh. More Russians and Ukrainians live in Kazakhstan than Kazakhs.

Even as the Soviet republics struggled to gain independence from the old central government, however, there were additional disputes within and among the republics. Christian Armenians and Islamic Azerbaijanis fought over the territory of Nagorno-Karabakh. Meskhetian Turks and Uzbeks fought over the fertile Fergana valley, and Uzbeks and Kazakhs fought over disputed territory in Uzbekistan. As independence began to seem like a real possibility, republics took a sharp, hard look at existing borders. The Crimea, part of the Ukrainian Republic, was settled primarily by Russians and Russia had no desire to grant this territory to an independent Ukraine. Additional problems in the Crimea result from the fact that the Crimean Tatars, who were forcibly resettled in the east by Stalin, are returning to claim their historic homeland. Furthermore, many of the republics are themselves multiethnic entities, subject to some of the same pressures and problems that faced the Soviet Union as a whole. In Soviet Georgia, for example, the nationalist government that claimed independence ruthlessly suppressed the Ossetians and Abhazians, minorities within Georgia who wanted more autonomy.

The nationality issues that forced the break-up of the Soviet Union will not be easily resolved. The territory that made up the Soviet Union, and the Russian Empire before it, is an ethnic mosaic where peoples of very different languages and traditions have lived side by side for centuries. Furthermore, the Slavs, particularly Russians and Ukrainians, have relocated throughout the former USSR. Short of massive migration, which would create a whole new set of problems, there is no simple way to create ethnically homogeneous countries on the territory of the former Soviet Union. On the other hand, religion, history, and long memories have combined with modern grievances to create an unstable situation. Now that nationalist emotions and ethnic enmities have been aroused, and are often further inflamed by ambitious politicians, it is difficult to talk soberly and sensibly about the advantages of continued cooperation. (See Reading 12.)

In this unpromising setting, Gorbachev tried and failed to negotiate a union treaty that would establish a new basis for cooperation among the former Soviet republics. Seventy years of membership in a single state with a centrally planned economy had created a web of important production and trade relationships that were threatened with destruction. For example, trucks made in Vladimir, an important Russian industrial center, have long relied on tires made in Armenia. As the planning mechanism has crumbled, the specter of trade barriers among republics threatens to batter further the rapidly worsening economy. Ignoring such dangers, all fifteen republics declared their sovereignty in 1991.

After World War II, the great overseas empires of Great Britain and France broke up. Only the land empire of the Soviet Union survived. Indeed, it was extended to include countries in Eastern Europe that lay on its outskirts. Today, even as Western Europe moves toward greater unity in order to gain the advantages of economic and political cooperation, the former Soviet Union has moved in the opposite direction. Its empire is dissolving in an atmosphere of hostility and resentment. As the new republics seek to divide the spoils and develop new relationships, their leaders and the rest of the world face many challenges. Nuclear weapons positioned throughout the territory of the former Soviet Union and squabbles over their control present a particular danger.

FOREIGN POLICY

Foreign policy, too, was transformed by Gorbachev and his reforms. Gorbachev's new thinking included the idea that systems based on capitalism and socialism could coexist and that their leaders could cooperate to the benefit of both. It also recognized that there could be no victor in a nuclear war, and that true security had to be based on political cooperation, not military might. If one superpower were insecure, Gorbachev maintained, the other would also be insecure because security is a mutual relationship. In December, 1988, during his visit to the United Nations, Gorbachev declared that the Soviet Union supported freedom of choice for all nations, without exception. No longer would Soviet troops be used to maintain control as they had been in Eastern Europe and Afghanistan.

The reflection of Gorbachev's new ideas in concrete policy came soon thereafter. Soviet troops were recalled from Afghanistan. Soviet negotiators offered new proposals and substantial concessions on arms control that led to agreements, new discussions, and further agreements. They worked with the United States to try to settle some of the regional conflicts in the Third World. By the end of the 1980s, the hostile relations that had existed between the United States and the USSR had been transformed with extraordinary speed into cordial relations between the Bush and Gorbachev administrations. Disarmament agreements followed with dizzying speed. The Cold War was over; a new cycle in Soviet-American relations had begun.

Events in Eastern Europe moved even more rapidly. In 1989, one after the other, Communist party governments in Eastern Europe were challenged. People took to the streets in huge mass demonstrations, demanding that Communist leaders be replaced. Governments resigned, coalition governments were formed, and general elections followed. The Soviet government made no effort to intervene, in sharp contrast to its actions in 1956 and 1968 when Soviet troops had put down demonstrations in Hungary and Czechoslovakia, respectively. By the end of the year, each of the satellites had a new government. All but Rumania managed to do so without bloodshed.

In keeping with those developments, East and West Germany moved rapidly towards reunification. The Berlin Wall, symbol of an era of division and hostility in Europe, was torn down stone by stone. Gorbachev joined Western Europeans in accepting that German unity was inevitable and that a sovereign Germany, like other countries, must enjoy freedom of choice about its future.

The result of these events has been the transformation of Europe and the superpower relationship that had existed for forty years. After World War II, Europe was divided into two hostile camps, while the Soviet Union maintained by force, or the threat of force, its hold on unwilling allies. The United States based its foreign policy on the need to meet the Soviet challenge. It joined with West Europeans in the NATO military alliance and supported "freedom fighters" in the Third World. The United States justified interventions in Latin America with dire warnings about the spread of Soviet and communist influence. Suddenly, the relationship upon which all those policies were based, that of two hostile superpowers, had changed. (See Reading 13.)

FACT: In the autumn of 1990, Mikhail Gorbachev won the Nobel Peace Prize for his role in ending the Cold War and in the peaceful transformation of Eastern Europe.

The 1990s began, then, with the end of the Cold War and the system of alliances and policies it had created. With the collapse of the Soviet Union as a federal state, the United States and Western Europe lost both an enemy and a potential partner. Once the euphoria subsided, however, it became clear that there were fresh uncertainties and different dangers. The newly independent republics suddenly began to seek aid from their former enemies: food to feed their populations, financial investment and technical advice to reform their economies and, perhaps most urgent of all, help in dismantling some of their nuclear arsenal and preventing nuclear weapons and technology from falling into the hands of terrorists or other states. The old international system has been destroyed, but a new one is yet to be put in place.

A young girl stands on a pile of rubble in Berlin in February, 1990, shortly after the East Germans began to demolish the wall. Remains of the wall are visible behind the girl.

THE ATTEMPTED COUP AND ITS AFTERMATH

In August 1991, Soviet television announced that Mikhail Gorbachev had taken ill and had asked to be temporarily replaced by his vice-president. In fact he had been placed under house arrest. A small group of well-known conservatives, all of whom had been appointed by Gorbachev, came forward to announce that they would maintain order and stop the country's slide toward disorder and disintegration. The conservative bureaucrats had made their move.

In most of the country, people accepted what had happened without protest, and many local leaders openly supported the coup. In Leningrad and Moscow, however, the people resisted. An important role in the resistance was played by the entrepreneurs, businessmen, and, apparently, elements of organized crime (called the mafia by Russians), as well as some journalists who realized how much they might lose. Yeltsin appeared on the steps of the Russian Republic's government building, rechristened *Belii Dom* (White House) for the occasion, and defied the illegal coup. By some inexplicable error, the coup leaders had failed to arrest Yeltsin at his home or to cut communication links. The elite guard that was then ordered to storm the parliament building refused to do so. Most important of all, it quickly became clear that the army that filled the Moscow streets would not fire on its own people. People did not rally to the coup leaders. Within three days, the coup collapsed. Two of those implicated committed suicide; most of the others claimed to have only followed orders. Those who had greeted the coup with support, and they were many, retracted their statements. (See Reading 14.)

The failure of the coup, which had been led by the party and the KGB, discredited both institutions. It greatly strengthened the hand of the reformers, especially that of Yeltsin, who had cut a defiant figure atop a friendly tank in front of his White House. Yeltsin moved quickly to disband the party, remove the top leadership of the KGB, and to reorganize its functions. He swiftly replaced much of the top leadership of the Russian Republic with new men. Many members of the old administrative elite desperately jumped from positions in the central federal government to similar jobs at the republic level. They continued to cling to the remnants of their long-held privileges. Almost everyone now used words to suggest the support of democracy and the building of a new structure on a new foundation, but most retained the habits of the old structures and the past. When Yeltsin, triumphant after the coup, began to speak of suspending elections and sent personal envoys to provincial cities to ensure that they carried out his policies, many were pleased that a strong man was taking charge. Some were dismayed by this contempt for the new democratic institutions and saw the reemergence of an old autocratic pattern. Others, watching the power and pride of the old Soviet Union dissolve, thought Yeltsin was not firm enough.

One by one, the republics claimed independence, several under the leadership of men who, until recently, had been staunch Communists. Gorbachev tried desperately and in vain to slow the swift break-up of the old union. Finally, on Christmas day, December 25, 1991, he resigned from the presidency of a country that no longer existed. That evening, at 7:32 P.M., the flag of the Soviet Union was lowered from the Kremlin. The USSR was no more.

THE PARADOX OF THE GORBACHEV REVOLUTION

Gorbachev had begun by trying to reform the Soviet system from above, in keeping with a long tradition in Russian history that stretches from Peter the Great and Catherine in the eighteenth century to Lenin and Stalin in the twentieth. As he made clear in his book, *Perestroika*, Gorbachev wanted to reform the system in order to preserve its best features, and to give a better life to the people of his country. He soon realized that true reform could take place only by enlisting the support of large groups of the Soviet population. When he let the people speak, however, they began to make their own demands, to shout, and to demonstrate. Gorbachev found that he had unlocked a Pandora's box with his calls for *glasnost* and *perestroika*. His very success in making the

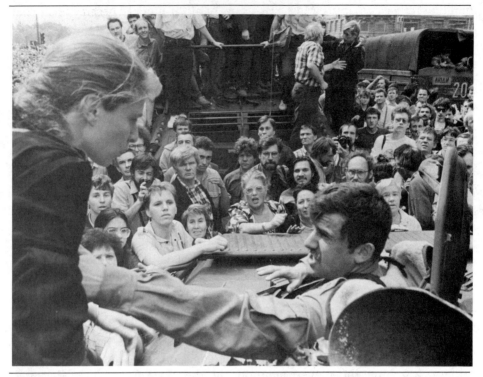

During the attempted coup of August, 1991, Moscow civilians thronged the streets of the city, deliberately confronting the military units deployed by the coup leaders. Here a woman demonstrator, who has climbed onto an armored vehicle on Gorky Street, argues with the vehicle's driver.

people more active led to strikes and blockades, as well as to a free press, democratic elections, and a new group of economic entrepreneurs. Ethnic rivalries reasserted themselves, and national republics demanded their independence.

An active people decided not to accept the Gorbachev agenda. Reform led first to a peaceful revolution and then to increasing disorder and uncertainty, threatening to repeat a pattern equally common in Russian history: a period of reform, leading to disorder that frightens the ruling groups in the society, leading in turn to a period of reaction.

FACT: In 1990, the average Soviet woman spent one and one half hours standing in lines to get food every day. By 1991 that time had more than doubled, and the situation was worsening.

Daily life has grown more difficult for most people since Gorbachev first began his campaign for *perestroika.* Public services have grown worse, not better. The old system of administrative control has broken down and nothing

Shortages of consumer goods in the USSR increased dramatically in 1991. Here people in the coal-mining city of Prokopyevsk in Siberia line up at a bread store.

has appeared to take its place. Consumers have had to put up with shortages of basic items such as soap and sugar, eggs, cheese, tea, and even matches with which to light their stoves. Bread itself is in short supply. Terrible inflation has destroyed many people's life savings overnight, and salaries have not risen to match the rise in food prices.

Almost everyone is glad for the new freedoms, particularly intellectuals who are at last able to pursue their trades honestly as journalists, historians, or teachers. A few entrepreneurs have flourished with their cooperatives. Yet many are angry, angry that the party ruled so long and held so many privileges, angry to learn that many of the sacrifices made by their parents to build socialism were not necessary. They are angry because so many served an evil cause, angry to learn how much better people live in other parts of the world, angry at the liars, the lines, and for lives that seem to have been wasted. They are not only angry, but increasingly afraid for the future. Some talk of sabotage, accusing the conservatives of disrupting the supply of goods on purpose in order to discredit *perestroika*. Others blame the new cooperatives, organized crime, or Gorbachev for having been weak and indecisive; all hope that the new national leaders will get them out of the current crisis. Almost everyone looks at the economy going from bad to worse with a sense of helplessness. (See Readings 15 and 16.)

As the peoples of the former Soviet Union seek to reshape their lives, they face an uncertain future. The old union has broken up; a hastily formed Commonwealth of Independent States grouping most of the former republics seems fragile indeed. In the Russian Republic itself, Yeltsin is struggling with the economic and political problems of the recent past, to which is added the enormous challenge of dividing the assets and liabilities of the former union.

There is an old Chinese curse: "May you live in interesting times." Russians quote a variation: "May you live in times of change." The peoples of the former Soviet Union are living in just such a time, a sharp turning point in their history, a time full of hope and possibility, but also of peril. Gorbachev proved to be a courageous leader who recognized the bankruptcy of the Stalinist system and took steps to destroy it. It proved far easier for him and his advisers to destroy, however, than to create. Out of the complex and revolutionary situation that developed after he took power in 1985, a variety of outcomes are possible. A new system remains to be built, one that must find support in the past as well as adapt itself to the challenges of the present and future.

The following books were helpful in writing this chapter:

Hajda, L., and Beissinger, M., eds., *The Nationalities Factor in Soviet Politics and Society.* Boulder, Colo.: Westview, 1990.
Lane, D., *Soviet Society under Perestroika.* Cambridge, England: Unwin-Hyman, 1990.

For students who are interested, we recommend further reading in the sources from which we have taken excerpts, *the Current Digest of the Soviet Press*, and the following works:

Brumberg, A., ed., *Chronicle of a Revolution.* New York: Pantheon, 1990.
    This book provides a collection of essays, half by Western observers of the Soviet Union and half by Soviet observers of their own country. *Perestroika* in politics, the economy, and history, new voices in literature, and the nationality question are addressed in thoughtful, up-to-date (in 1990) essays.
Goldman, M.F., *Global Studies: The Soviet Union and Eastern Europe.* Guilford, CT: Dushkin, 1988.
    One of a series of area studies, published annually, this book includes essays on contemporary events, useful statistics, and reprints of articles from newspapers and periodicals.
Goldman, M.I., *What Went Wrong with Perestroika.* New York: W.W. Norton, 1991.
    A short, incisive, and highly readable analysis of the difficulties encountered by Gorbachev in his efforts to reform the USSR. A prologue and an epilogue include the events of August, 1991.
Heymann, T.N., *On an Average Day in the Soviet Union.* New York: Fawcett Columbine, 1990.
    Lots of statistics on the USSR presented on a per-day basis, from the number of individuals who become teenagers to the number of hours spent on child care, to the number of theater productions, with comparative figures for the United States in most cases.

Hosking, G., *The Awakening of the Soviet Union.* Cambridge, Mass.: Harvard University Press, 1990.

An extraordinarily good treatment of the exciting changes that have taken place in the USSR since 1985, not so much from Gorbachev's perspective as from the viewpoint of the society he tried to transform. Hosking also places these changes in a historical context.

Loory, Stuart and Imse, Anne, *Seven Days That Shook the World.* Atlanta: Turner Publishing, 1991.

A detailed and dramatic account, in words and photographs, of the attempted coup in August, 1991.

Nove, A., *Glasnost in Action.* Boston: Unwin-Hyman, 1990.

Subtitled "Cultural Renaissance in Russia," this book is an intelligent, readable account of the cultural side of the Gorbachev revolution. It includes a useful guide to select Soviet publications.

Smith, H., *The New Russians.* New York: Random House, 1990.

By the author of *The Russians* (1977), this is the companion volume to Smith's highly acclaimed TV documentary series. Smith is an unusually perceptive observer of the Soviet scene, and he writes extremely well.

Taubman, W., and Taubman, J., *Moscow Spring.* New York: Summit, 1989.

A husband and wife team, both professors at Amherst College, the Taubmans spent five months in Moscow in 1988. This is an account of that time, with emphasis on the Russian intellectuals with whom they associated.

Zalygin, S., comp., *The New Soviet Fiction.* New York: Abbeville, 1989.

A collection of sixteen short stories by prominent contemporary Soviet authors provides a very entertaining way to gain a good understanding of Soviet life in the 1980s.

READINGS
for
Chapter 7

1. Gorbachev on Perestroika

Mikhail Gorbachev wrote his analysis of his country's problems and his thoughts on how to attack the problems in his Perestroika: New Thinking for Our Country and the World, *originally published in 1986. His book was clearly written as much for the outside world, particularly Americans, as for his own citizens. While Gorbachev called for new, innovative thinking, it is interesting to note that he did not see it as at odds with his goal of reviving "the living spirit of Leninism."*

PERESTROIKA—AN URGENT NECESSITY

I think one thing should be borne in mind when studying the origins and essence of perestroika in the USSR. Perestroika is no whim on the part of some ambitious individuals or a group of leaders. If it were, no exhortations, plenary meetings or even a party congress could have rallied the people to the work which we are now doing and which involves more and more Soviet people each day.

Perestroika is an urgent necessity arising from the profound processes of development in our socialist society. This society is ripe for change. It has long been yearning for it. Any delay in beginning perestroika could have led to an exacerbated internal situation in the near future, which, to put it bluntly, would have been fraught with serious social, economic and political crises.

We have drawn these conclusions from a broad and frank analysis of the situation that has developed in our society by the middle of the eighties. This situation and the problems arising from it presently confront the country's leadership, in which new people have gradually appeared in the last few years . . .

At some stage—this became particularly clear in the latter half of the seventies—something happened that was at first sight inexplicable. The country began to lose momentum. Economic failures became more frequent. Difficulties began to accumulate and deteriorate, and unresolved problems to multiply. Elements of what we call stagnation and other phenomena alien to socialism began to appear in the life of society. A kind of "braking mechanism" affecting social and economic development formed. And all this happened at a time when scientific and technological revolution opened up new prospects for economic and social progress.

Something strange was taking place: the huge fly-wheel of a powerful machine was revolving, while either transmission from it to work places was skidding or drive belts were too loose.

Abridged from Gorbachev, M., *Perestroika: New Thinking for Our Country and the World.* New York: HarperCollins, 1987.

Analyzing the situation, we first discovered a slowing economic growth. In the last fifteen years the national income growth rates had declined by more than a half and by the beginning of the eighties had fallen to a level close to economic stagnation. A country that was once quickly closing on the world's advanced nations began to lose one position after another. Moreover, the gap in the efficiency of production, quality of products, scientific and technological development, the production of advanced technology and the use of advanced techniques began to widen, and not to our advantage . . .

Declining rates of growth and economic stagnation were bound to affect other aspects of the life of Soviet society. Negative trends seriously affected the social sphere. This led to the appearance of the so-called "residual principle" in accordance with which social and cultural programs received what remained in the budget after allocations to production. A "deaf ear" sometimes seemed to be turned to social problems. The social sphere began to lag behind other spheres in terms of technological development, personnel, know-how and, most importantly, quality of work.

Here we have more paradoxes. Our society has ensured full employment and provided fundamental social guarantees. At the same time, we failed to use to the full the potential of socialism to meet the growing requirements in housing, in quality and sometimes quantity of foodstuffs, in the proper organization of the work of transport, in health services, in education and in tackling other problems which, naturally, arose in the course of society's development.

An absurd situation was developing. The Soviet Union, the world's biggest producer of steel, raw materials, fuel and energy, has shorfalls in them due to wasteful or inefficient use. One of the biggest producers of grain for food, it nevertheless has to buy millions of tons of grain a year for fodder. We have the largest number of doctors and hospital beds per thousand of the population and, at the same time, there are glaring shortcomings in our health services. Our rockets can find Halley's comet and fly to Venus with amazing accuracy, but side by side with these scientific and techno-logical triumphs is an obvious lack of efficiency in using scientific achievements for economic needs, and many Soviet household appliances are of poor quality.

This, unfortunately, is not all. A gradual erosion of the ideological and moral values of our people began . . .

The presentation of a "problem-free" reality backfired: a breach had formed between word and deed, which bred public passivity and disbelief in the slogans being proclaimed. It was only natural that this situation resulted in a credibility gap: everything that was proclaimed from the rostrums and printed in newspapers and textbooks was put in question. Decay began in public morals; the great feeling of solidarity with each other that was forged during the heroic times of the Revolution, the first five-year plans, the Great Patriotic War and postwar rehabilitation was weakening; alcoholism, drug addiction and crime were growing; and the penetration of the stereotypes of mass culture alien to us, which bred vulgarity and low tastes and brought about ideological barrenness, increased.

Party guidance was relaxed, and initiative lost in some of the vital social processes. Everybody started noticing the stagnation among the leadership and the violation of the natural process of change there. At a certain stage this made for a poorer performance by the Politburo and the Secretariat of the CPSU Central Committee, by the government and throughout the entire Central Committee and the Party apparatus, for that matter.

Political flirtation and mass distribution of awards, titles and bonuses often replaced genuine concern for the people, for their living and working conditions, for a favorable social atmosphere. An atmosphere emerged of "everything goes," and fewer and fewer demands were made on discipline and responsibility. Attempts were made to cover it all up with pompous campaigns and undertakings and celebrations of numerous anniversaries centrally and locally. The world of day-to-day realities and the world of feigned prosperity were diverging more and more.

By saying all this I want to make the reader understand that the energy for revolutionary change has been accumulating amid our people and in the Party for some time. And the ideas of perestroika have been prompted not just by pragmatic interests and considerations but also by our troubled conscience, by the indomitable commitment to ideals which we inherited from the Revolution and as a result of a theoretical quest which gave us a better knowledge of society and reinforced our determination to go ahead . . .

WE HAVE NO READY-MADE FORMULAS

Politics is the art of the possible. Beyond the limits of the possible begins adventurism. It is for this reason that we appraise our possibilities carefully and soberly and map out our tasks taking this into consideration. Taught by bitter experience, we do not run ahead of ourselves on our chosen path, but take account of the evident realities of our country.

The greatest difficulty in our restructuring effort lies in our thinking, which has been molded over the past years. Everyone, from General Secretary to worker, has to alter this thinking. And this is understandable, for many of us were formed as individuals and lived in conditions when the old order existed. We have to overcome our own conservatism. Most of us adhere to correct political and ideological principles. But there is a substantial distance between a correct stand and its realization.

It sometimes even happens that during the discussion of an issue in the Politburo we seem to draw substantiated conclusions and take innovative decisions, but when it comes to choosing methods for implementing them, we end up trying to use old methods to accomplish new tasks.

In politics and ideology we are seeking to revive the living spirit of Leninism. Many decades of being mesmerized by dogma, by a rule-book approach have had their effect. Today we want to inject a genuinely creative spirit into our theoretical work. This is difficult, but it must be done. Creative thought seems to be consolidating.

We realize that there is no guarantee against mistakes, the worst of which would be to do nothing out of fear of making one. We know the mistake of doing nothing from our own experience. Many of our troubles derive from it. Our opponents in the West have noticed this weakness, which was particularly manifest in the late seventies and early eighties, and were on the verge of consigning the Soviet Union to the "ash-heap of history." But their requiem was clearly premature . . .

We are living through no ordinary period. People of the older generation are comparing the present revolutionary atmosphere with that of the first few years after the October Revolution or with the times of the Great Patriotic War. But my generation can draw a parallel with the period of the postwar recovery. We are now far more sober and realistic. So the enthusiasm and revolutionary self-sacrifice that increasingly distinguish the political mood of the Soviet people are all the more valuable and fruitful.

2. Chernobyl: A Victim's Account

The dramatic and terrible accident at the Chernobyl nuclear power station in April 1986 led to a great deal of questioning and soul-searching on the part of Soviet authorities and ordinary citizens alike. The lack of built-in safety devices, the environmental threat, and the incapacity of Soviet medicine to deal with the crisis have all been the subject of intense scrutiny—a public airing of a disaster that could not have occurred prior to 1985. The following report appeared in the government newspaper Izvestia *in June 1989. Since then, evidence has grown that the damage from Chernobyl was much greater than anyone realized at first. Pripyat is a small town very close to the Chernobyl plant, and April 26 was the day after the accident.*

"I am Valery Fyodorovich Zosimov. I am 34 years old. I am writing to you for the first time. No, I'm not a compulsive writer. I just want to tell you that for us—those who worked at Chernobyl—it's obvious: People are suffering and dying, quietly and alone so far—middle-aged and elderly people as well as young people, so far mostly men . . .

"I was born in Kirovograd Province. I came to Pripyat in 1976 with my wife Antonina; she was 18 then and I was 21. I was helping to build the Chernobyl Atomic Power Station . . .

From Zosimov, V., "Confessions of a Chernobyl Victim," *Izvestia* (June 18, 1989). In *Current Digest of the Soviet Press* 41 (July 1989): 31–32.

"[On April 26, 1986] I went to Kiev early in the morning, about 5 a.m., to meet my family. I was coming back in a privately owned car. They only let us go as far as Kopachi; it's not far from Pripyat, and the station is right nearby. A captain with a walkie-talkie gave us permission to leave the car in Kopachi and go home to Pripyat on foot. And so we went. My 10-year-old daughter, my wife and I. Ahead of us and behind us other people were walking too; from Kopachi you could see the ruined fourth power generating unit. At the place where the power line intersects the road there was a long trail of graphite-laden smoke. I brushed from my jacket the soft, black flakes that were falling on us. It was night when we got home. (Later, most of the forest along that same road was declared contaminated and chopped down—it was considered dangerous! What was it like when I walked past with my family?)

"Then, on the 27th, I tried to ride to work on my bicycle. A serviceman wearing a respirator pointed at my temple with his hand and twirled his finger. He mumbled that there was a lot of contamination where I was headed. I went back home and on the way I met my supervisor. He said: Take your family and get out, but leave your address. By that time I was already working at the station, as an inspector in the technical monitoring bureau. V. Kravtsov, our acting supervisor, said: 'Unfortunately, there's nothing for us to do now. But when the time comes to restore the whole facility we'll be badly needed.'

"I believed that wholeheartedly and proved to be a fool.

"I returned to work on June 30. Between the evacuation and the time that I actually got involved in cleaning up the aftermath of the accident, I got caught up on my work at the institute . . .

"Our tours of duty began on June 30. We built a dividing wall between the third and fourth power generating units, a storage container for spent nuclear fuel and a covered passageway, and we worked on repairing the first and second power generating units and restoring the third. In the summer and the fall, we were almost too tired to stand. But we joked a lot, and there was practically no ill humor.

"By fall, however, chronic headaches showed up. People's blood pressure was jumping up and down. 'Cosmetic measures' helped at first. Then it got harder. You could feel your health slipping away. You needed to leave, but where could you go? Your strength was abandoning you. Nobody believed the lies any more; we laughed at the doctors' assurances that we were fine, but we kept on working. And once a month we had a laugh over the 'official tally' of the dose each of us had received. Even basic arithmetic wouldn't let you take seriously the numbers we were shown.

"Time passed; life went on. Then, in January of this year, a pre-infarction condition forced me—as it did many others—into a hospital bed. I was taken from Zeleny Mys to Slavutich in an ambulance. At first I couldn't walk, but then it eased up a little. Then I got sick all over: My bronchial tubes, stomach and intestines burned, my head ached, my blood pressure went up and down again, and I was nauseous. A month in the hospital and a month at a sanatorium. I barely got home before I was back in Hospital No. 25. There I was told: We can't admit you again—this is a complicated problem! You'll have to deal with the medical-disability commission. I went to the city commission for the area where I lived. I obtained another admission order—this time for the Radiology Center in Kiev. They had a hard time finding a place for me; it took a lot of coaxing.

"Once the rounds were made by a professor and doctor of science—a former military man. He was in a big hurry. He asked me what dose I'd had. I knew I'd been exposed, but officially, it was as if I hadn't been. He said: 'You're such a young man but you're so sick. Come on now, get better!' I want to, of course, but tell me how to do it.

"Another two weeks or so went by. The professor made rounds again. 'How's it going?' I said: 'Badly.' The professor turned to my attending physician, Ye. Matova, and said: 'You've kept him too long; get him ready for discharge. His illness has nothing to do with radiation.' Matova answered him: 'What's that got to do with it? Let's get him into a little bit better condition!' Two hours after that conversation, for the first time in the four months I'd been gravely ill, I got the feeling, as I was talking to Viktor Aleksandrovich Sushko, a pulmonary specialist, that I was talking to a real professional and an honest man to boot. He did a bronchoscopy on me and said: Your bronchial tubes also need serious treatment. And not even three hours had passed since they were insisting on discharging me.

"I'm in bad shape now. In this condition, I'll scarcely last more than a year. It's hard to be a condemned man. And it's doubly hard when you're condemned by those who were supposed to protect you . . . On every corner we talk about a state based on the rule of law, yet we can't protect ourselves (from the state?) in the social realm. We don't know how to do it. But if we keep quiet about it today, tomorrow it will be too late to raise our voices.

"I'm certainly not the sort of guy who makes it into the history books. I'm just one of the little people, one who maybe made some tiny contribution to cleaning up the aftermath of the accident at the Chernobyl Atomic Power Station that I helped build. But it's not just me. I'm only a symptom of a major problem that has to be solved, whether we like it or not, and solved without delay . . ."

3. The Environment

Pollution of the environment is an international problem. The Soviet Union and the other nations of Eastern Europe only recently began to discuss it openly, however. The accident at the nuclear power plant at Chernobyl was

Abridged from Razin, S., "Mailman Vasilyev's Bomb," *Komsomolskaya Pravda* (March 15, 1988). In *The Glasnost Reader.* Edited by J. Eisen, 171–74. New York: New American Library, 1990.

a dramatic example of environmental pollution, but other forms of pollution existed long before Chernobyl. Indeed, environmental issues continue to be very important in the nationalist movements within the former Soviet Union, as they are throughout Eastern Europe. The following story in the March 15, 1988 edition of the newspaper Komsomolskaya Pravda *describes another environmental hazard, toxic fumes from a biochemical plant in the town of Kirishi, near Leningrad (St. Petersburg).*

Kirishi is a young city which has grown rapidly on the bank of the Volkhov, and now it is reminiscent of a coiled spring that could explode at any moment. Opposition—overt, fierce—to the departmental apparatus by 60,000 inhabitants has been going on here for nearly a year.

Mailman Vasilyev plays as big a part in the story as do the leaders of the Ministry of the Medical and Microbiological Industry. As far as Volodya is concerned, perhaps, it all began when he, a 26-year-old correspondence course student, hardened by his hobby of winter sailing, had this strange cough which was getting worse and keeping him awake at night.

Having suffered night after night, he went to the hospital. And he was horrified to see the faces of the children in the corridor. Swollen eyes and red blotches, like burns, on cheeks, necks, and hands. What was going on? The intensive care department was chockablock, asthmatics everywhere were having attacks . . .

Vasilyev wondered where the wind was coming from. He remembered very well when the people of Kirishi began to have trouble breathing—following the ahead-of-schedule startup of the protein-vitamin concentrates plant. Incidence of bronchial asthma increased by a factor of 35! But why? Why indeed was the second phase of the plant launched in 1982 and why was the ambulance service unable to keep up with all the calls?

Vasilyev did not keep the appointment with the doctor. He dashed off to the plant. That's it! The sharp, unpleasant smell hit him in the face. The purification equipment was clogged up and the scrubbers cleaning the exhaust system had been cut off with welding apparatus. The treacherous cloud had again descended on the city. [Letters to the ministry were ignored.]

At that moment the city was like a coiled spring. There had been many empty promises before. But this ministerial reply amazed everyone by its savage indifference. At the very time there had been an accident at the plant: In two months or so another eight children had died, although, at first, they had been diagnosed as having "acute respiratory disease."

The spring exploded last May. The people of Kirishi poured into the Pioneer Center where, behind closed doors, they discussed the emergency situation in the city. "I am not indifferent to the fate of Kirishi! I got my party card here! I promise that there will not be a single molecule of protein in the air!" Minister V. Bykov almost shouted at the audience. "We don't believe you!" the people packing the gangways right up to the platform loudly declared. It was time for a rally. The action group which had formed around mailman Vasilyev set about organizing it. The action group also included engineers, doctors, and workers.

On 1 June, Child Protection Day, the rally was attended by 12,000 Kirishi locals. Without disguising their tears, people talked of their unhappiness, about how they used to go there to do all-union shock work, on Komsomol passes, and how they used to rejoice as the building progressed. Now they had all signed a petition against the poison plant . . .

Plant discharges had been damaging people's health for 12 years. A very powerful allergen had been hitting the city at the rate of 2 metric tons a day. How many Kirishi locals had suffered? And how much longer would they have to suffer?

"More than one generation, perhaps. The trouble is that the weakened organism is now susceptible to other harmful factors, and we have more than enough of them too," V. Yesinovskiy, chief doctor at the Kirishi Rayon hospital, explained the situation. He had figures, facts, and tables. But this frankness would cost him dear.

How many invalids are there in the city as a result of the biochemical plant? Around 100, doctors claim. And another 4,000 or so are suffering from allergies which have a nasty tendency to get worse with time. Whether the statistics are complete no one knows. Local doctors have no specific means of diagnosis. It exists abroad. We do not produce it here. But without it, it is impossible to distinguish a mycogenic allergy caused by plant discharges from an ordinary one. Moreover, as Vasilyev found, medicines are also in horrifically short supply.

4. Yeltsin on Gorbachev

Among the political figures who emerged in the wake of the Gorbachev "revolution," Boris Yeltsin was perhaps the most charismatic. Originally a supporter of Gorbachev, he came to feel that more drastic reforms were necessary, and from his position as president of the Russian Republic, Yeltsin became the leading spokesman of the radicals, advocating rapid transition to a market economy and an increased measure of political pluralism. In the following excerpt from his 1989 autobiography Against the Grain, *Yeltsin analyzed and evaluated Gorbachev's record after four years in power.*

I believe that when Gorbachev first came to power there were few people in the country who realized what a heavy burden was awaiting him. Indeed, I doubt whether he himself fully understood what a disastrous legacy he was inheriting.

From Yeltsin, B., *Against the Grain*, 139–42. New York: Summit Books, 1990.

What he has achieved will, of course, go down in the history of mankind. I do not like high-sounding phrases, yet everything that Gorbachev has initiated deserves such praise. He could have gone on just as Brezhnev and Chernenko did before him. I estimate that the country's natural resources and the people's patience would have outlasted his lifetime, long enough for him to have lived the well-fed and happy life of the leader of a totalitarian state. He could have draped himself with orders and medals; the people would have hymned him in verse and song, which is always enjoyable. Yet Gorbachev chose to go another way. He started by climbing a mountain whose summit is not even visible. It is somewhere up in the clouds and no one knows how the ascent will end: Will we all be swept away by an avalanche or will this Everest be conquered?

I have sometimes wondered why he ever decided to launch the process of change. Was it because he is still relatively young, and he detests the lies and hypocrisy that have almost totally destroyed our society? Was it because he sensed that there was still a chance to make one last effort to break free of the past and become a civilized country? I cannot find an answer to these questions. I would like to believe that one day he will tell us about the trials and tribulations that assailed him in April 1985.

The chief problem in his launching of *perestroika* was that he was practically alone, surrounded by the authors and impresarios of Brezhnev's "era of stagnation," who were determined to ensure the indestructibility of the old order of things. After a while, it became easier for him, and then he himself began to lag behind events. But at that all-important first moment of his reforming initiative, he operated with amazing finesse. He didn't frighten the old mafia of the party apparat, which retained its power for a long time and might easily have eaten any general secretary alive without so much as a hiccup. One after another he neatly pensioned off the members of the old Brezhnev-Chernenko team, and very soon he had gathered around him his own men, with whose help he could make any decision that was necessary.

He was to have even greater successes abroad, although the circumstances were rather more propitious for him there; after Brezhnev, any leader of the Soviet Union who could even speak normally was regarded as a hero. Even so, that was not all there was to it. Gorbachev is quite popular abroad, but whenever I see how well he is treated in foreign countries, I cannot help feeling sorry for him because he has to come back to a country torn apart by problems and contradictions. Back home, no one is going to shout at him in ecstasy, "Misha!" Life here is too stern a business for that sort of thing.

But in 1985, people had faith in Gorbachev as a politician who was a realist, and they accepted his foreign policy based on "new thinking." Everyone realized that to go on living and working as we had done for so many years was simply impossible. It would have been national suicide. A big step had been taken in the right direction, although, of course, it was a revolution from above. Such revolutions inevitably turn against the bureaucratic apparat if it is unable to keep the popular initiative within bounds. And that apparat started to resist *perestroika*, to slow it down and fight against it, with the result that it has effectively skidded to a half. What is more, I'm afraid it has turned out that the concept of *perestroika* was not properly thought through. To a large degree it appeared to be represented only by a selection of new, fine-sounding slogans and appeals.

When I read Gorbachev's book *Perestroika*, I thought I would find in it an answer to the question of how he sees our way forward, but somehow the book did not give me the impression of conceptual wholeness. It is not clear how he sees the overall restructuring of our house, nor from which materials he plans to rebuild it, nor which set of drawings he is using. The main trouble with Gorbachev is that he has never worked out a systematic, long-term strategy. There are only slogans. It is amazing to think that more than four years have passed since April 1985, when *perestroika* was proclaimed. Somehow this period is referred to everywhere as "the new beginning," "the initial stage," and "the first steps." Yet in actual fact, four years is a long time. In the United States it is the length of a presidential term, and in those four years a president must do as much as he can of what he promised to do, insofar as he is able. If the country has not moved forward in that time, another president is elected to replace him. Under President Reagan a number of improvements took place, and he was reelected. He turned out not to be such a simpleton as we had been led to believe—although several sore spots remained, which he was unable to cure in eight years. Nevertheless, the major improvements, especially in the American economy, were there for all to see.

With us, on the other hand, the situation has grown so critical over the past four years that today we are afraid of what tomorrow may bring. In particular, the state of the economy is catastrophic. There Gorbachev's chief weakness—his fear of taking the decisive but difficult steps that are needed—has been fully revealed.

5. Yeltsin on Party Privileges

After the Revolution, the Soviet political elite gradually accumulated a system of privileges not available to ordinary citizens. Those who held certain positions possessed not only power but access to a variety of material comforts. The reluctance of party officials to give up those privileges was a significant factor in opposition to Gorbachev's attempts at reform. Boris Yeltsin was among the most outspoken in describing and denouncing such privileges. In the following excerpt from his autobiography Yeltsin offers an

Abridged from Yeltsin, B., *Against the Grain*. 156–61, 164–65. New York: Summit Books, 1990.

explanation for Gorbachev's failure to attack the privileges. It is worth noting that in 1989, when this was written, Yeltsin did not question that the party would continue to be the main power in Soviet society.

A party mechanism run by full-time salaried officials is necessary but not in such overblown proportions as at present. It needs to be drastically reduced in size. It should be staffed by the best brains in the party, in order that it may analyze any situation and determine clear paths for future development. This is particularly important when one takes into account the role that the party plays in our society. Has a single source of conflict ever been foreseen and predicted, has a single crisis ever been constantly and correctly resolved? Any such serious problem quickly reaches a stage of apparent insolubility, then an apparently ad hoc and invariably wrong solution is applied.

Think of all the words that were uttered about the story of the secret protocols to the Molotov-Ribbentrop pact* spread by the bourgeois propagandists. How many times did Gorbachev have to say that it was all a pack of lies? Yet it was obvious to any sensible person that it was pointless to go on denying what everybody has long known to be true. Then, after a while, we admit that yes, the secret protocols do exist. But how much respect and credibility have we lost for behaving with such woodenheaded obstinacy?

These are just a few examples of the way the Central Committee works, issuing its orders and instructions to the country. But I repeat: The apparat as such is not at fault. It is simply that the party leadership is obsequious, obedient, and unchanging. An intelligent, independent-minded official of the Central Committee is a combination of words so paradoxical that one's tongue cannot even utter them.

Obsequiousness and obedience are rewarded in turn by privilege: special hospitals, special vacation retreats, the excellent Central Committee canteen, the equally excellent service for home delivery of groceries and other goods, the Kremlin telephone system, the free transportation. The higher you climb up the professional ladder, the more comforts surround you and the harder and more painful it is to lose them. Therefore the more obedient and dependable you become. It has all been most carefully devised: A section chief does not have a personal car, but he has the right to order one from the Central Committee car pool for himself and his immediate staff. The deputy head of a department already has his personal Volga,** while the head has another and better Volga, fitted with a car phone.

But if you have climbed all the way to the top of the establishment pyramid, then it's full communism! And it turns out that there was no need of the world revolution, maximum labor productivity, and universal harmony in

---

*The Nazi-Soviet Pact of 1939.
**A fancy Soviet car.

order to have reached that ultimate, blissful state as prophesied by Karl Marx. It is perfectly possible to attain it in one particular country—for one particular group of people.

In using the word "communism," I am not exaggerating. It is not simply a metaphor for an overbright Communist future: "From each according to his abilities, to each according to his needs." And so it is for those at the top of the party pyramid. I have already mentioned their abilities, which, alas, are not outstanding. But their needs! Their needs are so great that so far it has only been possible to create real communism for a couple of dozen people— communism is created for them by the ninth directorate of the KGB, and this all-powerful directorate can do anything. The life of a party leader is beneath its unsleeping, all-seeing eye, and it satisfies his every whim. A dacha behind a high green fence encircling spacious grounds alongside the Moscow River, with a garden, tennis courts, and playing fields, a bodyguard under every window and an alarm system. Even at my level as a candidate member of the Politburo, my domestic staff consisted of three cooks, three waitresses, a housemaid, and a gardener with his own team of assistant gardeners. Long accustomed to doing everything with our own hands, we simply didn't know what to do with ourselves. And surprisingly, all this luxury was incapable of producing either comfort or convenience. What warmth can there be in a marble-lined house?

It was almost impossible to meet anybody or do anything in the ordinary normal way. If you wanted to go to the cinema, the theater, a museum, indeed any public place, a whole squad of heavies was sent there in advance. They would check and cordon off the whole place, and only then could you go yourself. But the dacha had its own cinema, and every Friday, Saturday, and Sunday a projectionist would arrive, complete with a selection of films.

As for medical treatment, the medicines and equipment are all imported, all of them the last word in scientific research and technology. The rooms in the Kremlin hospital are huge suites, also surrounded by luxury: porcelain, crystal, carpets, and chandeliers. Afraid of taking responsibility, an individual physician never makes an independent decision, and diagnoses and treatments are invariably agreed upon by a group of five to ten doctors, sometimes including the most highly qualified specialists . . .

The Kremlin ration, a special allocation of normally unobtainable products, is paid for by the top echelon at half its normal price, and it consists of the highest-quality foods. In Moscow, a total of some forty thousand people enjoy the privilege of these special rations, in various categories of quantity and quality. There are whole sections of GUM—the huge department store that faces the Kremlin across Red Square—closed to the public and specially reserved for the highest of the elite, while for officials a rung or two lower on the ladder there are other special shops. And so on down the scale, all organized by rank. All are called "special": special workshops, special dry cleaners, special polyclinics, special hospitals, special houses, special services. What a cynical use of the word! A specialist is supposed to be someone who has a particular training or talent. There was a time when a highly skilled craftsman really was a specialist. Nowadays in our country the word "special" has a specific meaning, of which we are all too well aware. It is applied to the excellent food products that are prepared in special kitchens and are subjected to special medical tests; to the medicines packed in several layers of wrapping paper and guaranteed safe by the signatures of several doctors (only medicine certified in this way can be given to the Kremlin elite). How many such special people are there, one wonders, pampered by the system even in what seem like the most insignificant details?

When the elite want to go on vacation, they can choose virtually any place in the warm south. There is bound to be a special dacha there. For the rest of the year these dachas are empty. There are other opportunities to go on leave too, because a two-week winter holiday supplements the summer break. Excellent sports facilities exist for "special" use only, for example on the Lenin Hills—indoor and outdoor tennis courts, a large swimming pool, and a sauna. Then there are the personal airplanes, an IL-62 or a TU-134 in which a Central Committee secretary, a candidate member, or a full member of the Politburo flies alone, except for his bodyguard and the cabin crew.

The joke is that none of these riches belong to those who enjoy the special privileges. All these marvelous things—dachas, rations, a stretch of seaside fenced off from everyone else—belong to the system. And just as the system has given them, so can it take them away. It is an idea of pure genius. A man—Ivanov, say, or Petrov—climbs his way up the career ladder, and the system gives him one class of special privileges. Then, as he rises higher, another class. The higher he goes, the more special are the delights handed out to him. Soon Ivanov begins to think he is an important person. He eats what ordinary mortals only dream of, takes his holidays in places where the proletariat are not even allowed to come near the surrounding fence. And stupid Ivanov doesn't realize that it is not *he* who is being thus favored by the position he occupies, and that if he suddenly stops serving the system faithfully, Petrov or somebody else will instantly be put in his place. Within this system nothing belongs to the individual. Stalin cunningly brought this machinery to such a state of perfection that even the wives of his immediate colleagues did not belong to them. They, too, belonged to the system. The system could take those wives away and imprison them, just as Stalin imprisoned the wives of Kalinin and Molotov, and neither man dared to utter so much as a squeak of protest.

Times have changed, but the essence of the system remains the same. As before, a wide selection of perks is being handed out to the position that a person occupies, but each "gift"—from a soft armchair with its numbered metal tag on up to the bottle of normally unavailable medicine stamped "safe" by the fourth directorate of the KGB—bears the seal of the system. This is so the individual (who, as before, is no more than a little cog in the machine) will never forget to whom all this really belongs . . .

It may be a somewhat controversial opinion of mine, but I do believe that *perestroika* would not have ground to a halt, despite the tactical mistakes that have been made, if only Gorbachev had been able to get rid of his reluctance to deal with the question of the leadership's privileges—if he himself had renounced all those completely useless, though pleasant, customary perquisites; if he had not built a new house for himself on the Lenin Hills and a new dacha outside Moscow; if he had not had his dacha at Pitsunda rebuilt and then an ultramodern one put up at Thorosin in the Crimea. And then, to cap it all, at the Congress of People's Deputies he announced with pathos that he has no personal dacha. Doesn't he realize how hypocritical that sounded? Everything might have happened differently had the people known all this, because they would have lost faith in his slogans and appeals. Without faith even the best and most enlightened changes in our society will be impossible to accomplish. And when people know about the blatant social inequality that persists, they see that their leader is doing nothing to correct the elite's shameless appropriation of luxuries paid for from the public purse, then the last droplets of the faith will evaporate.

Why has Gorbachev been unable to change this? I believe the fault lies in his basic cast of character. He likes to live well, in comfort and luxury. In this he is helped by his wife. She, unfortunately, is unaware of how keenly and jealously millions of Soviet people follow her appearances in the media. She wants to be on view, to play a noticeable part in the life of the country. No doubt in a rich, prosperous, contented society that would be accepted as natural and normal—but not in our country, at least not at this time . . .

Of course, our establishment cannot run away and hide. The moment will come when they will have to give up their private dachas and answer to the people for having hung on to their privileges tooth and nail. Even now some of them are starting to pay the price for their former "establishment" status. The massive defeat at the polls suffered by party and government officials who stood for election is the first warning bell for them. They are now being forced to take steps to satisfy the demands of the voters. But they make concessions reluctantly and grudgingly; they are so wedded to their privileges that every possible contrivance, including bald lies and sheer deception, is employed by them. They will, in fact, do anything to slow down the process of reform . . .

As I write in late 1989, I still don't know the outcome of the commission that was set up to investigate the matter of undeserved privileges. The second Congress of People's Deputies did not debate the topic either. I suspect, though, that there will be no more of this shameless practice. We will give up—I hope forever—the system of reserving minor luxuries for a bureaucratic caste and adopt the civilized method, where the only yardstick for material acquisitions will be the honestly earned ruble. I greatly hope this is so.

6. In Defense of Coca-Cola

While reactionaries decried the liberalization of the Gorbachev regime and the accompanying increase of Western influence, others believed that the Soviet Union could benefit from such influence, even in the form of hamburgers or soft drinks. Such disagreement on the value of cultural intrusion was reminiscent of the mid-nineteenth century debate between Slavophiles and Westerners. The following editorial by Alexander Ivanov, "In Plain Sight of Pushkin," appeared in Moscow News *in 1990.*

Our "patriots" now have some new "eccentricity." According to them, if one's back is to the monument to Pushkin (on the square of the same name), one can clearly see large advertisement for Coca-Cola.

"Help!" scream the "patriots"—"it's an insult to one of Russia's sacred places!"

How interesting! That nine million Muscovites, plus four million guests have to daily rush from one empty shop to another—not to buy, but to find a bit to eat or drink . . . that's not an insult. But the advertisement of a nice drink is!

What's it all about? The thing is that were Russian kvas being advertised instead of Coca-Cola, everything would be OK, but it's a foreign beverage that's being advertised.

This is where the root of all evil is. Again it smells of "not ours," alien, contra-indicated for everything primordial.

The thought is being nurtured that nobody is any authority for us. Let the whole world do as it likes, but Russia is following its own "special road." It pains me to read such words. What an ill omen. Is this our fate—all people are ordinary, but we're "special" . . . is it true that "what Russians consider useful, infidels consider death"? Then why do the "infidels" feel so good and we feel so bad? Maybe, we've overlooked something?

Addressing the 2nd Congress of People's Deputies writer Vasily Belov said: "Speaking about the current economic programme, I want to ask: why is orientation towards Western technology so persistent? Don't we have our own industry? Are we short of gifted engineers and technicians, or do we lack the necessary aptitude?

From Ivanov, Alexander, from *Moscow News* (November 1990): 4.

"That's enough, Comrade Abalkin, we have all this. As though you've forgotten about your internal material and spiritual reserves . . ."

So, "we have everything . . ." If that's true, then why don't we have anything? Why apart from oil, gas, timber, furs and gold do we not or almost not export anything to the world market? But nobody wants to buy, even at a cheap price, so what's the result of our "labour heroism"?

Although these questions are not addressed to me, I'm not Leonid Abalkin [a top economic adviser]. I want to ask the well-known writer: indeed, why aren't such computers made in Vologda so as to arouse envy in the Japanese? Maybe aptitude alone is not enough?

We are lagging behind, my dear colleagues, hopelessly lagging behind in what world progress rests on—technology. We shall not catch up with them by ourselves. It can be put roughly and simply: either we try to enter the world community, or . . . I don't even want to think about what'll happen.

Therefore, one feels sorry for the campaign being conducted intensively by different movements—from circles close to the Pamyat society [extreme Russian nationalists] to the United Workers Front—directed practically against any cooperation with advanced Western and Eastern countries. The plans to create the so-called free economic zones arouse particular fury. "We'll not give an inch of our soil!" Blood-curdling shrieks are heard from all sides. A letter from a woman who lives in the Far East was read over TV: better let the devil take it, but not them . . .

Who's "them"?

The Marshall Plan from overseas came to ruined postwar Europe shaken by shortage, inflation and disruption. Our propaganda at that time gloated over this, saying that Europe is the backyard of the USA. Europe is a colony of Uncle Sam . . .

Well? All the countries of Europe are there, the sovereignty of none of them is violated, their economies flourish and the populations thrive. Of course, undoubtedly, they too have problems, but—to put it more delicately—theirs are of a different quality. They are racking their heads over where to sell and we—whom to get from?

For the present, huge lines in the same Pushkin Square have a great desire to enter McDonald's restaurant. Quick, nice, clean, tasty, no nitrates and no rudeness . . . Are all those in the queue really traitors to sacred Russia, blood-sucking cooperators, rootless cosmopolitans and masons? If so, then their number is too great . . .

The menu includes the world famous Big Macs, Hamburgers, Cheeseburgers and the very same Coca-Cola.

Had Alexander Pushkin been alive (it is common knowledge that he liked French wine), I think he would no doubt have tasted the American beverage. And after eating at McDonald's, he would surely and—unpatriotically—say in French: "Merci!"

He was a clever man, educated and with broad outlook.

7. The Disillusioned Farmer

After five years, Gorbachev's attempts at economic perestroika *appeared to have made very little progress. The difficulty of transforming a command economy into a market economy was overwhelming, leading many Soviet citizens to wonder whether they weren't better off in some ways under the old system. Some who honestly attempted to take initiative found themselves confronted with problems, most often in the form of dishonesty and corruption. Letters to newspaper editors like the following, published in* Moscow News *in 1990, became commonplace.*

My story is straightforward. When the Party called on the people to start perestroika and change their ways, I acted on this call. My husband and I bought a house in the country, borrowed money and built a modern pig farm. I could fatten up to 300 pigs a year. As part of an agreement with the local state farm, I delivered the first four tons of pork. But the farm did not keep its side of the bargain. Deliveries of fodder were erratic and the vet didn't seem to want to be involved. The state farm also insisted on buying my pork at a very low price, so I was left with meagre profits.

I learned a lot on the open market: whose palms should be greased, the size of bribes. You can't simply hire a stall in the market, all of them seem to be booked. You have to pay the meat chopper 10–25 roubles a pig to get a place at the stall. And you also have to bribe the vet. If not, he will say your pork is infected. And you have to bribe the management.

Selling at the market pays: pork gets snapped up at 5–6 roubles a kilo. But selling on the market won't do for me. You spend the day selling pork and the night cutting it. This leaves no time for sleep. I can't sell a hundred pigs single-handed, and I can't find an honest middleman. Honesty is hard to come by nowadays. I saw people of the Russian Union of Consumers' Societies selling meat purchased by the state in Australia and New Zealand. The Union people had bought the meat at 2 roubles a kilo and were selling it at the market for 5–6 roubles. The meat wasn't being sold in state-run shops, so you had to pay through the nose at the market. Many line their pockets using this stratagem, . . . [and the law turns] a blind eye.

After six months of toil I produced 14 tons of pork. An official from the Moscow regional consumers' society, Comrade Lentsi, lavished praises on me saying I had produced more than anyone in the region. But he made a helpless gesture as soon as it came to our right to buy a truck. My husband told him: "The desire to buy a truck is no whim. We need one to deliver fodder and pigs." The reply was that only 150 trucks out of 3,000 will be allocated to private

Abridged from Popkova, Nataliya. "The Admission of a Farmer Who Gave Up." *Moscow News* (28 January 1990): 7.

farmers by the Moscow Regional Executive Committee. So this means that no matter how I toil, the truck will be sold to someone else who can pull more strings. Well, I gave up and the farm is now empty.

It pains me to read reports about the opening of new shops—they have nothing to sell. We could have fed the country, but we cannot ram through the wall of bureaucrats, profiteers and grafters. They exploit the people and drag the country down, in order to then be in charge of handing out ration cards.

What am I to strive for if my country does not need my talent? Should I regard myself as a failure and devote myself to running the house and raising my kids? But what can I teach them, what ideals can I pass on to them?

8. Censorship

While there were notable periods in both tsarist and Soviet Russia that were free from censorship, there also were periods in which censorship severely restricted artists and writers, including the Stalin and Brezhnev eras. After 1985, the list of censored works decreased dramatically, but as the following 1989 article by New York Times *correspondent Bill Keller suggests, the censorship tradition hadn't died completely. It should be noted that the legislation referred to near the end of the article was indeed passed, resulting in a freer press.*

THE LIFE OF A SOVIET CENSOR

MOSCOW, July 17—Suppose an inquisitive Soviet reporter were to unearth evidence that a member of the Communist Party Politburo had a mistress. Could he publish it?

Vladimir A. Boldyrev, the chief censor of the Soviet Union, ponders the question for a long time. A very long time.

"Well, I think the answer is, yes, we are now approaching the stage where personal details can be made public that it was not customary to publish before," he replied at last.

Then he added, with a nervous laugh that suggested that the verdict was not final, "I hope this is just a hypothetical question."

Mr. Boldyrev is the keeper of a shrinking but still formidable catalogue of what the press cannot write, the publishing houses cannot publish, the movies cannot show, the libraries cannot put on public display, and the post office cannot deliver.

In his three years as chairman of Glavlit—the Administration for the

---

Abridged from Keller, B., "The Life of a Soviet Censor: Anything Goes? Not Just Yet." *New York Times*, 17 July 1989.

Protection of State Secrets in the Press—Mr. Boldyrev boasts that he has cut the list by half, lifting the ban on such diverse secrets as the works of Aleksandr Solzhenitsyn, the bunnies of *Playboy* magazine, and the crime rate.

Indeed, it is difficult to extract from Mr. Boldyrev exactly what is forbidden anymore in the Soviet Union, in part because the boundary is moving so fast and in part because the idea of censorship has become so unfashionable in the day of glasnost that even the censor in chief finds the subject a bit distasteful.

"In the classical sense, it is no longer really correct to call us censors," he insisted in an interview at his office midway between the Kremlin and the K.G.B. headquarters. "Today we do not impose limits of a purely political or ideological character, which was one of our duties before . . ."

Mr. Boldyrev said most of the thick catalogue of forbidden themes—a document that is itself restricted to a narrow circle of editors and publishers—consists of military and industrial secrets.

Glavlit's clout is such that it has occasionally overruled the Defense Ministry on what constitutes a secret, Mr. Boldyrev said, although it has never found occasion to overrule the K.G.B., the state security police . . .

Despite his disclaimer about politics and ideology, Glavlit is also empowered to decide that hostile literature poses a danger to the state.

Mr. Boldyrev said Glavlit ruled last year that the works of Mr. Solzhenitsyn, the fiercely anti-Communist Russian living in exile in Vermont, were no longer a threat. Mr. Solzhenitsyn's epic labor camp memoir, *The Gulag Archipelago*, is to be excerpted next month in the magazine *Novy Mir*, and a publishing house has announced plans to publish seven volumes of selected Solzhenitsyn works.

"Regarding Solzhenitsyn, all debates are over," the censor said. "We released all of his works from the closed archives, and our publishing houses have the right to publish them—of course, without violating the copyright."

Mr. Boldyrev said the vast bulk of writing by émigrés and exiles, once banned automatically regardless of their content, have now been removed from the closed archives of libraries, and the rest are to be reviewed by the end of the year.

The liberated writers include some of the bitterest critics of Soviet authority, among them such émigré novelists as Vladimir N. Voinovich, Vladimir Maximov—who once damned Communism as "an evil ideology"—and Viktor Nekrasov, and the non-émigré Vasily Grossman, whose thinly fictionalized attack on Lenin, "Forever Flowing," was published last month in the magazine *Oktyabr.*

The books written by Trotsky before he was expelled from the country as a Bolshevik heretic are now open, but what he wrote in exile is still under review.

Also locked away are foreign works that Glavlit feels might "undermine" Soviet power or outrage public sensibilities.

Mein Kampf, the Hitler manifesto widely studied in other countries as a model of political pathology, is here banned as an offense to memories of the Great Patriotic War Against Fascism.

"I think it will eventually be published, but first we have to live through a certain period of time to absorb what is being done today," Mr. Boldyrev said of the book. "It would be wrong to overfeed the public."

The limits of contemporary writing are murkier.

"If some paper wants to publish a call to arms to overthrow the authorities, we will not allow it to be published," he said.

And what about a scathing satire of President Mikhail S. Gorbachev? Not likely, Mr. Boldyrev said.

"This affects not only the prestige of our country, but perestroika itself," he said. "If we trample on the leader of perestroika, how can we make any progress? . . ."

Mr. Boldyrev estimates that about half of the information dispensed for public consumption in the Soviet Union is reviewed in advance by Glavlit's agents. The rest—including reprints of literary classics, many local and regional newspapers of scant circulation, certain reference works, and publications with a demonstrated devotion to self-censorship—do not undergo prior review, but are spot-checked.

Periodicals that suddenly develop a free spirit may find themselves back under Glavlit's wing. That happened this year to *Twentieth Century and Peace*, a long-quiescent little magazine that fell into the hands of a free-thinking editor and began publishing critiques of the K.G.B.

Mr. Boldyrev explained to the disbelieving editors that the publication had been leashed because it wrote about disarmament, raising the risk that it would disclose some privileged detail of a Soviet negotiating position.

The reins on the press may be loosened further when the new legislature approves a long-awaited law on the rights and responsibilities of the press. But legislators say the new law is unlikely to curtail Glavlit's authority seriously or to permit a truly independent press. Mr. Boldyrev is not worried about job security.

"The system of protecting secrets was created by people who are not completely unreasonable," he said. "It was built up over time, and it has its rationale."

9. Perestroika: The Writers' Response

Russian artists and writers have long been the source of insightful comments on society, and this tradition continues, as filmmakers, play-

Excerpted from Natalya B. Ivanova, "Poetry in the Age of Perestroika and Glasnost," in Abraham Brumberg, ed., *Chronicle of Revolution*. New York: Pantheon, 1990. Translation by Josephine Woll. 217, 225, 227.

wrights, artists, musicians, novelists, and poets all strive to interpret the extraordinary changes that began in 1985. Among them are the three contemporary poets whose works follow, Alexander Kushner, Vladimir Kornilov, and Nonna Slepakova. In Kushner's lines the reader senses the excitement and joy of the period, while Kornilov's verses suggest the difficulties that accompany freedom. Slepakova's lines, from her poem "Rush Hour," are also pessimistic, focusing on the day-to-day hardships that, for ordinary citizens, marked the era of perestroika.

Suddenly a clear day, a sudden unexpected ray,
Like a tender word in a dark quarrel.
Nowhere, nowhere such a sun,
So longed for midst the gloom and sleep!
. . . Suddenly, a bright hour in history, so sparing
Of gentle glance and long indulgences.
Suddenly—a loud laugh in an empty square
And a shaft of light, playing tag.

Alexander Kushner

I'm not ready for freedom—
I'm hardly to blame.
Since I've been at the factory
There's been nought by that name.

. . . .

What is it, then—freedom?
A pleasure-dome's bequest?
Or putting yourself last,
After all the rest?

Happiness or its lack,
Shedding envy and conceit,
Throwing open your soul,
Not wanting to cheat?

Oceans of sweat,
Workloads that kill—
But lack of freedom is
Heavier still.

For years I have waited,
Waited aching and scared.
Freedom's finally come—
And I'm not prepared.

Vladimir Kornilov

RUSH HOUR

What's falling isn't snow, isn't rain,
Easier to die by rope than a bullet in the brain.

Dank greed, sweat, shaking . . .
And life squeezed out through a dropper
Between mealy spuds costing a copper
And costly private baking.

We make our slippery and crooked way
Through the meager joys of NEP's new day
Whatever we dream is just dumb,
Freedom's forced on us, newness won't come.

We rage at each sign that we're right,
Hear our own words with familiar fright . . .
Pushed into heaven itself with the shove
That we know from the coppers we love.

Nonna Slepakova

10. Rewriting History

One of the most important facets of glasnost *was the gradual emergence of a more truthful history of the Soviet period, together with a more open discussion of the tragedies that accompanied collectivization, Stalin's purges, and the mistakes made in World War II. At the same time, however, there remained the temptation to remove from the record names and materials that continued to be viewed as negative, such as those from the "stagnant" Brezhnev era. Thus the old policy of falsification dies hard, as can be seen from the following letter from a puzzled librarian to the newspaper* Izvestia *in August 1989. V.V. Grishin and M.A. Suslov were members of the Politburo under Brezhnev.*

Just recently we, the employees of city public libraries, were summoned to a special seminar and, after being told that these were the instructions of higher authorities, were ordered to remove from our collections the works of Brezhnev, Grishin, Suslov, Chernenko and a number of other authors, as well as all the political and economic literature published prior to March 1985, as material that is outdated and no longer relevant. It was recommended that we remove the documents of the 22nd through the 26th Party Congresses from our shelves and tell any patrons who ask for them that they are currently in use.

From Zavgorodnyaya, I., "New Blank Spots," *Izvestia* (August 17, 1989). In *The Glasnost Reader.* Edited by J. Eisen, 89. New York: New American Library, 1990.

Doesn't this mean that, while granting access to the archival documents of 50 years ago, we are creating new "blank spots" in our most recent history?

11. Opposition to Reform

Stalin, the "cult of personality" he built and what is now called the "command administrative system" that he created, came under attack by the proponents of reform. He and that system were described as without merit. Not everyone agreed. In March 1988, there appeared in the newspaper Sovietskaya Rossia *a long and dramatic letter from a chemistry teacher in Leningrad, Nina Andreeva. She questioned the negative approach to the Soviet past and to Stalin on the grounds that it was psychologically harmful to the country's youth, who had been brought up to believe in the values of Soviet socialism. Andreeva's letter illustrates that in the Soviet Union of the late 1980s a person's view of the past and particularly his or her attitude toward Stalin were closely tied to that person's political position. Following the letter's appearance, it became the subject of much publicity and public discussion. Andreeva subsequently founded a conservative political society called "Unity for Leninism and Communist Ideals." When asked in 1990 what slogan best summed things up for her, she replied, "Socialism or death!"*

I decided to write this letter after a great deal of thought. I am a chemist, and I teach at the Leningrad Soviet Technological Institute in Leningrad. Like many others, I am an adviser for a group of students. In our days, after a period of social apathy and intellectual dependence, students are gradually beginning to be charged with the energy of revolutionary changes . . .

What a wide range of topics is being discussed! A multiparty system, freedom of religious propaganda, leaving the country to live abroad, the right to a broad discussion of sexual problems in the press, the need for the decentralization of the management of culture, the abolition of compulsory military service—Among students, a particularly large number of arguments are about the country's past . . .

It's very gratifying, of course, that even "technos" [students at the technical institute] have a lively interest in theoretical problems of the social sciences. But too many things have turned up that I cannot accept, that I cannot agree with. The constant harping on "terrorism," "the people's political servility," "uninspired social vegetating," "our spiritual slavery," "universal fear," "the entrenched rule of louts"—It is from these mere threads that the history of the period of the transition to socialism in our country is often woven. Therefore, it comes as no surprise, for example, that in some students nihilistic views are intensifying, and ideological confusion, a dislocation of

---

Abridged from Andreeva, N., "I Can't Forgo Principles," [Letter to the editor] *Sovietskaya Rossia* (March 1988). In *Current Digest of the Soviet Press* 40 (April 1988): 1–5.

political reference points and even ideological omnivorousness are appearing. Sometimes one hears assertions that it is time to call to account the Communists who supposedly "dehumanized" the country's life after 1917 . . .

In talking with students and pondering crucial problems with them, I automatically come to the conclusion that a good many distortions and one-sided views have piled up in our country, notions that obviously need to be corrected. I want to devote special attention to some of these things.

Take the question of the place of J. V. Stalin in our country's history. It is with his name that the entire obsession with critical attacks is associated, an obsession that, in my opinion, has to do not so much with the historical personality itself as with the whole extremely complex transitional era—an era linked with the unparalleled exploit of an entire generation of Soviet people who today are gradually retiring from active labor, political and public activity. Industrialization, collectivization and the cultural revolution, which brought our country into the ranks of the great world powers, are being forcibly squeezed into the "personality cult" formula. All these things are being questioned. Things have reached a point at which insistent demands for "repentance" are being made on "Stalinists" (and one can assign to their number whomever one wishes). Praise is being lavished on novels and films that lynch the era of tempestuous changes, which is presented as a "tragedy of peoples."

Let me note at the outset that neither I nor the members of my family have any relationship to Stalin or his entourage, retainers or extollers. My father was a worker in the Leningrad port, and my mother was a mechanic at the Kirov Plant. My older brother worked there, too. He, my father and my sister were killed in battles against the Hitlerites. One of my relatives was repressed and was rehabilitated after the 20th Party Congress. Together with all Soviet people, I share the anger and indignation over the large-scale repressions that took place in the 1930s and 1940s through the fault of the Party and state leadership of that time. But common sense resolutely protests the monochromatic coloring of contradictory events that has now begun to prevail in certain press organs.

I support the Party's call to uphold the honor and dignity of the trailblazers of socialism. I think that it is from these Party and class positions that we should assess the historical role of all Party and state leaders, including Stalin . . .

From long and frank discussions with young people, we draw the conclusion that the attacks on the state of the dictatorship of the proletariat and on the leaders of our country at that time have not only political, ideological and moral causes but also their own social substratum. There are quite a few people who have a stake in broadening the staging area of these attacks, and not just on the other side of our borders. Along with the professional anticommunists in the West, who long ago chose the supposedly democratic slogan of "anti-Stalinism," there live and thrive the descendants of the classes overthrown by the October Revolution, by no means all of whom have been able to forget the material and social losses of their forebears . . .

It is the champions of "left-liberal socialism" who are shaping the tendency to falsify the history of socialism. They suggest to us that in the country's past only the mistakes and crimes are real, in doing so keeping quiet about the supreme achievements of the past and the present. Laying claim to complete historical truth, they substitute scholastic ethical categories for social and political criteria of the development of society. I would very much like to understand: Who needs, and why, to have every prominent leader of the Party Central Committee and the Soviet government compromised after he leaves office and discredited in connection with his actual or supposed mistakes and miscalculations, made while solving some very complex problems on roads uncharted by history? Where did we get this passion for squandering the prestige and dignity of the leaders of the world's first socialist country?

12. Ethnic Problems in the Disintegrating Soviet Union

The breakup of the Soviet Union was enormously complicated by ethnic issues, dominant among which was the presence of substantial numbers of ethnic minorities within each of the republics (see table at the end of Chapter 1). Substantial Russian minorities exist in many non-Russian republics. The minorities were very concerned about their future if they chose to remain, and many were opting to return to the Russian Republic. The following article from October 1990 describes the problem in the central Asian republics, likening the situation to that which existed in Africa following the withdrawal of the European colonial powers.

It is not without bitter irony that they call themselves internal émigrés. They patiently stand in long lines at freight stations to get shipping containers for their household belongings. In Dushanbe, Frunze and Tashkent, the sign-up list for these notorious containers extends into April and May of next year. That's how long people still have to wait, in a state of uncertainty and alarm, as they strive to leave at last—no, not for America or Israel but for another Soviet republic. Last year the number of indigenous residents

---

Abridged from Pulatov, Timor, "We will catch up with and surpass Angola!" Moskovskiye novosti (October 1990). In *Current Digest of the Soviet Press* 41 (November 1990): 11.

who left Uzbekistan reached 94,000, and according to preliminary estimates, the number of people emigrating from Central Asia this year will exceed 200,000.

Who are these people, and why do they have such an irrepressible desire to leave? After all, many of them were born here . . . The bulk of the people are being driven out by uncertainty about the future and by fear . . . They can't sort out the true intentions of the new parties and movements, and they are afraid that people might come to power who would implement in practice the slogan, "Turkestan for the Turks!"

All the major plants, power stations, oil fields, coal and ore mines, railroads, airline routes and communications lines built during the years of Soviet power in Central Asia are still operated mainly by engineers, technicians and highly skilled workers from industrial centers in Russia, the Ukraine and Belorussia. They were lured here by good pay, housing and executive posts. The indigenous population was assigned its traditional place in agriculture, small-scale trade and cottage industry, as well as in the *nomenklatura* of the command system.

But now highly skilled specialists of nonindigenous nationalities are no longer enticed by either the sunny area itself, the good pay or the housing. At the Syr-Darya State Regional Power Station, Uzbekistan's largest, which many shop and shift foremen, leading specialists and technicians have left, today there is nobody to operate two 300,000-kilowatt generating units. Homes empty every day in the settlement of Nuristan, built for construction workers who came in to build one of Central Asia's largest state regional power stations. Specialists are leaving the republic's chemical-industry center, Navoi, and the Angren coal region. Tashkent's ambulance service is operating at half-strength due to the departure of doctors. Last year Uzbekistan lost more than 30,000 specialists with a higher education; their average age was 22–30, and they constituted the most energetic and able-bodied segment of the population . . .

The departing specialists' place under the southern sun is being taken by drifters and vagrants, who are attracted by the warm climate and the possibility of living in Tashkent's numerous public gardens and squares, in cellars and in attics without any conflicts with the police. The nonindigenous population is becoming more and more lumpenized. The number of robbers, prostitutes and drug addicts is increasing, which is making the local residents even more dissatisfied with "the Russians."

The government of Uzbekistan recently decided to offer more training in technical specialties to members of the indigenous population through night-school and correspondence courses. But it will take 10 years to train indigenous specialists to replace those who are leaving. To do this it will be necessary for the whole society to become imbued with "technological thinking." Ahead lies a painful break with feudal consciousness, which, "bypassing capitalism," has entered into the socialist "way of life." Despite all its industriousness, zeal and other positive qualities, our almost entirely agricultural population will need at least three generations to enter the technological world.

Not just our own experience, but also the experience of Asian and African countries where the industrial infrastructure was laid by Western countries according to classical imperialist patterns, shows what ruinous consequences a rapid breaking of ties between a mother country and its colonies is fraught with. The mass departure from Angola of specialists from European countries in the first two or three years after that country's declaration of independence in 1976 led to a threefold drop in industrial and agricultural production, bringing the country, which had been at an average level of development for those times, to the brink of total ruin.

The same thing happened in Mozambique, Ghana, the Congo, Uganda and Mali. Instead of the building of a fitting new life under their newly acquired "independence," there began in these countries many long years of clan struggle for power between various groups like the Popular Movement for the Liberation of Angola and the National Union for the Total Independence of Angola, struggle which brought the peoples untold suffering, all against the backdrop of a sharp decline in production, mass unemployment and poverty.

It is no accident that I am drawing parallels between third-world countries and the Central Asian republics. At the present rate of migration, complex production facilities in Central Asia will feel a catastrophic shortage of specialists and highly skilled workers in just two or three years. This will lead to a sharp decline in business activity, an increase in poverty, and an "Angolization" of all aspects of life.

This forecast, though rather gloomy, is the most likely one. But I am confident that we residents of Central Asia, true to the ideals of civic duty and national accord, have enough common sense to prevent such a dramatic turn of events.

13. Bush on Gorbachev

On May 31, 1990, President George Bush welcomed Soviet President Mikhail Gorbachev on the south lawn of the White House to initiate a three-day summit meeting. The tone of Bush's welcoming remarks, as well as his choice of words, illustrated the extent to which the United States supported Gorbachev's efforts at reform, while still expressing concern over the issue of sovereignty for the Baltic republics. Bush's endorsement of the Soviet leader also reflected American public opinion: The term Gorbymania made its appearance following Time *magazine's selection of Gorbachev as "Man of the Decade" in January 1990. (Compare with Reading 16, p. 279.)*

Abridged from "Bush and Gorbachev Toasts at Dinner." *New York Times*, 1 June 1990, A7.

Friends and distinguished guests, welcome to all of you, especially our guest from the Soviet Union. It is my great honor to welcome to the White House the president of the Soviet Union, Mikhail Gorbachev.

Mr. President, just over a year ago I said that the United States wanted to move beyond containment in its relations with the Soviet Union toward a new era, an era of enduring cooperation.

When we last met in Malta, we agreed to accelerate our efforts on a full range of issues. Today differences remain, of course, but in the short six months since the Malta summit we have made encouraging progress, and I want this summit to take us further still, and I know that this is your view as well, Mr. President.

We have seen a world of change this past year and now, on the horizon, we see what just one short year ago seemed a distant dream, a continent truly divided East and West has begun to heal with the dawn of self-determination and democracy.

In Germany, where the wall once stood, a nation moves toward unity and peace and freedom. And in the other nations of the most heavily militarized continent on Earth, at last we see the long era of confrontation giving way to the prospect of enduring cooperation in a Europe whole and free.

Mr. President, you deserve great credit for your part in these transforming events. I salute you as well for the process of change you've brought to your own country.

So let us expand this new spirit of cooperation, not merely to resolve disputes between us, but to build a solid foundation for peace, prosperity and stability around the world.

In that same spirit, Mr. President, let me quote the words of one of your nation's great minds, one of the world's great men in this or any age, Andrei Sakharov.

Fourteen years ago, he wrote, "I am convinced that guaranteed political and civil rights for people the world over are also guarantees of international security, economic and social progress."

Sakharov knew that lasting peace and progress are inseparable from freedom, that nations will only be fully safe when all people are fully free.

And we in the U.S. applaud the new course the Soviet Union has chosen. We see the spirited debate in the Congress of People's Deputies, in the Soviet press, among the Soviet people.

We know about the difficult economic reforms that are necessary to breathe new vigor into the Soviet economy and, as I've said many times before, we want to see *perestroika* succeed.

Mr. President, I firmly believe, as you have said, that there is no turning back from the path you have chosen. Since our meeting in Malta, we have reached agreements in important areas, each one proof that when mutual respect prevails, progress is possible.

14. The Coup That Failed

On August 19, 1991, with Mikhail Gorbachev on vacation in the Crimea, Vice-President Gennady Yanayev and several of his hard-line comrades announced that Gorbachev had resigned from power and that they had set up a "State Committee for the State of Emergency in the USSR." Gorbachev was detained, and troops and tanks appeared on the streets of Moscow. The Russian Republic's parliament building, nicknamed the "White House," was surrounded. But the leaders of the coup had not anticipated any popular opposition. These impressions of the failed coup were written by S. V. Panin, a young Russian physician. They convey the confusion, as well as the important role played by communication in those events. We have preserved the exact words of his English-language account to the greatest extent possible.

On the evening of the 18th of August 1991, I went to bed and remember sleeping like a log despite the fact that Monday was coming. Most of my lab's personnel were on vacation and I had little to do there if anything at all. Father woke me up at 8:30 the next morning with a contemptuous remark, "Sleeping, eh? Perhaps you'll be sleeping when the sky falls too?" A sleepy question: "What the hell's going on?" "Nothing really, it's a military coup in the country." I jumped up like a ball and rushed to the bathroom. In the following hour I was in the full course of the events: TV was numb as a fish playing solemn music; the military, the KGB, and some other old men claimed on the radio that they were the saviors of the country and the whole nation, that Gorbachev had resigned, that all democratic achievements were false, filthy, and against the people and therefore abolished. Mom lay in bed staring at the ceiling and repeating, "We're lost. God almighty, we're lost indeed." Radio Liberty [a station that broadcasts into Russia, in Russian, from western Europe] was the only source of information.

I gulped down a cup of coffee and went to the lab. All of a sudden everyone was at the spot. We all listened to another dose of gibberish on the radio from "The State Committee on the State of Emergency:" the communist bandits had always liked various committees. My boss felt irritated, said that it was all over for at least another five years—"the Americans won't give me the visa" (he had been invited to the U.S.), "the devil with everything. I'm leaving for my *dacha*, I'll call in a week"—and he left rather abruptly. The women discussed the matter and came to the conclusion that, all in all, the whole thing didn't bother them very much and not a single fool would go to the barricades. "Perhaps you will?" they asked me mockingly. I didn't realize the gravity of the situation yet and returned home.

Mom felt down. Her face was pale, she hadn't touched any food, was embracing Kissinger [the cat] automatically, and kept on repeating: "We're lost, they will get us." She was close to the truth; a week later we learned that the KGB had ordered 200,000 pairs of handcuffs from metalwork plants in Novgorod and had been going to arrest people—even the camps in the far north and Siberia were prepared, enlarged, and mended up. I switched on the television. Yanayev, the temporary head of government, declared, hands trembling (we found out later he had downed half a bottle of cognac), that Gorbachev was ill. Ill? He was fine the other day! Curfew hour? Troops in the cities?

I felt violet clouds of terror streaming from the room's corners and forming under the ceiling—I felt fear. They had thrown out the elected government! At this moment Dad returned home from his office and brought a leaflet with an appeal from Boris Yeltsin to the peoples of Russia: Do not obey the mutinous "committee," general strike, everyone to the defense of the legally elected government at the White House. Dad felt ill and stayed at home. Mom got dressed and we went to Kutuzovsky Prospect. We got on a trolleybus and it delivered us to the Ukraine Hotel [across the Moscow River from the White House]. It went no further: the bridge was blocked by a barricade. Next to the hotel stood a tank. It was a huge ironclad vehicle reminding one of CNN reports on the Gulf War. A very big specimen, with a gun no less than seven meters long. Groups of people were streaming through the barricade. It was constructed of two trolleybuses and fixed with iron pipes, concrete slabs, and iron barrels. A number of tanks stood under the bridge. Everywhere groups of people drew together to exchange information: anger, hatred, and contempt for commies and the KGB were unanimous. I suddenly found out there was a great number of people of my own mentality. We all were in absolute agreement. Soldiers and officers stood near the armored vehicles. Many civilians were talking to them—not in vain as it turned out later. The heavy tank near the bus stop suddenly growled, clanked its caterpillars, blew a cloud of acrid blue smoke, and started moving along Kutuzovsky Prospect [avenue leading from the southwest to the Kalininsky Bridge] away from the bridge. As we crossed the bridge, we bumped into another barricade—actually there were two on the bridge alone. I think these two barricades were the first to be erected.

The day of the 19th of August 1991 was cloudy and misty and wet. It was getting dark early. Near the White House everything was in a terrible mess. The crowd was dark, consisting of very different people of various ages and sexes, dressed in all possible ways. No one knew what to do actually. Rumors spread in all directions. The feelings of alarm and fear, and the total lack of information created a dreadful anxiety. One certain idea prevailed: troops were on their way to the White House to take it by storm and to kill and arrest members of the Russian government and all those gathered there. Paratroopers were expected from the air. Many foreigners were present. They were clicking their cameras and videos, obviously enjoying themselves in every possible way, not understanding anything at all, as usual. I climbed over the barricade in front of the building. The mob was dense and absolutely out of its wits: everyone was shouting, people rushed from one entrance of the White House

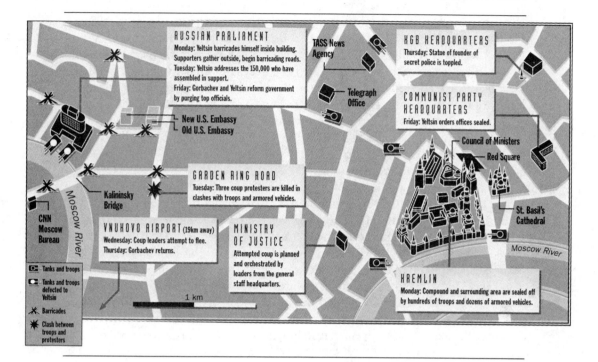

to another. Leaflets were dropped occasionally in huge heaps on the people's heads right out of the windows. Some young men, clad in uniform and armed with machine guns, guarded the main entrance. The atmosphere of dread and uncertainty was suffocating.

All of a sudden I felt I had come here not for Yeltsin, nor for some government, however legal it was, nor even for democracy, but for my own self. If the White House fell, my prolonged journey in a northeasterly direction would become inevitable. No one would protect you if that happened.

I joined some boys constructing the barricade near the White House. Buses, stones, pipes, gates, wheels, and various trash were used for construction. If the junta had had wits enough, they would have attacked during this first evening—the barricades were weak and not many people had gathered, just a few hundred. At ten o'clock in the evening we heard the address of Yeltsin and other government leaders through a loudspeaker. The president of the Russian parliament, Ruslan Khasbulatov, spoke quietly and reassuringly—the first reassuring word since the start of the coup. He said that the leaders of the junta were criminals who were trying to overthrow the legally-elected government and to do away with Gorbachev and democratic reforms. Gorbachev was under arrest in the Crimea at his villa (at dawn, the rumor spread that Gorby had been assassinated). Khasbulatov also said that the coup would be crushed, and the mutineers would be punished with all severity. The Russian government was making attempts to repair its connection to other parts of the country; all significant communication centers were then in the hands of the mutineers. He also appealed to all Muscovites to defend the White House and not to quarrel with the soldiers and officers because they were citizens, too. He told us not to bring and display weapons—if the necessity arose, weapons would be distributed. He added that Yeltsin would address people every hour through a loudspeaker but that he could not appear on the balcony. Part of the Russian KGB had remained loyal to the government of Russia and had found marksmen with long range guns on the roof of the Ukraine Hotel and another nearby building, hunting for Yeltsin and government members. They had been arrested and their guns confiscated.

By eleven P.M., a column of light tanks was spotted moving towards the White House along the river. Several tanks tried to pass under the bridge by the Ukraine Hotel, but could not. The tanks were surrounded by people who began talking with the soldiers and officers. Young people would climb upon the tanks and turrets waving Russian flags. They gave the soldiers cigarettes, beverages, and food. Many old people were there, too. The soldiers and officers were very embarrassed and felt awkward. They said they had been obeying orders. They had been awakened at night unexpectedly and the senior officers had explained nothing to them (very possible as far as I remember from my own army experience). Aleksandr Rutskoi, a member of parliament and head of the Russian Democratic Party, left the White House and joined the talks. He read the soldiers and officers the appeal of Yeltsin to the Russian army: Those who did not obey the junta's orders would not be punished; their orders were illegal.

After two hours of such talks, the wet and troubled defenders of the White House were struck by a shout: "The Russian soldiers and officers of Tomanskoya Armored Corps are loyal to the government of Russia! Their tanks will defend the White House!" The joy was enormous. For the first time in Soviet history, part of the Soviet troops joined their people against the communists. I was a direct eyewitness of the event. We felt no rain. It was tremendous. We all rushed to the newly constructed barricade and in a short while a passage was made for the tanks to come closer to the building. There were only four of them, but it didn't matter. It was a miracle. That was the first moment everyone felt the coup might not succeed. The soldiers were embraced from all sides and the tank near the White House was surrounded by hundreds of exultant people. About six o'clock in the morning, I went home. I found Dad in a great worry. Such was the first night of the coup for me.

Recollecting now the events of that first night, I realize that the situation was very tense. The number of people was very small for real defense, and everything was disorganized; the actions of people were chaotic and at times contradictory. One barricade was erected on one side and taken down on the other—no wonder, since there were no lights and it was as dark as the inside of a man's stomach. There were also dangerous quarrels with the officers and soldiers in the tanks. That was the beginning of the defense, and it was not without casualties. A boy on top of a tank was waving a Russian banner and was pushed clumsily by his friends to the ground and cut his forehead badly. Many (especially teenagers, there were lots of them) were just having a good time, as were the foreigners. I saw two teenagers, a boy and a girl, embracing each other and kissing tenderly time and again. Then the girl said, "I'm tired of swinging here, let's go closer to the barricades, it's more fun there." Maybe I'm growing old and cease to understand things.

Early in the morning, on the 20th of August 1991, I turned on the television and found there the swine muzzle of General Kalinin, head of the Moscow garrison. This particular pig addressed the Muscovites: "The State Committee on the State of Emergency is maintaining law and order throughout the country. Boris Yeltsin will be arrested for his anticonstitutional activities. Last night, small bands of gangsters, criminals, businessmen [businessmen are criminals in communist propaganda] and other trash, drunk and on drugs up to their ears, tried to attack loyal Soviet soldiers on duty in defense of law and order and the constitution of the USSR. Provocative shots were made by the enemies of the Soviet people. As the head of the Moscow garrison I impose a curfew hour. Anyone caught in the street after eleven o'clock P.M. will be arrested and put into custody." And then solemn music began again.

I opened up the operation block of the television and switched to the seventh channel. CNN was there! It was a relief to see Sheryl Atkinson and Bobbie Battista and the embarrassed faces of Bush and Dick Cheney and to know that there were normal people somewhere on earth. Bush claimed he would never recognize a false committee and ordered suspension of help to the Soviet Union. The world supported Yeltsin and the Russian government! The bloody KGB puppets—Saddam Hussein, Arafat, and Qadaffi—supported the mutineers. The CNN reporters stayed for three days on top of a tall building opposite the Ukraine Hotel.

To stay at home was impossible. I felt free again. Not shaved as usual (I'm in a Mickey Rourke style), I put on my raincoat, fixed my kitchen battle-axe for chopping meat to the inner loop under my coat, and left for the barricades. The movement of traffic along Kutuzovsky Prospect existed no more. I had to get there on foot. Passing Pizza Hut, I saw a long line of fancy-dressed young men awaiting the restaurant's opening with their girlfriends. Coup or no coup, it was all the same to them. But hundreds of people were streaming through the barricades. Another six tanks had joined the Russian government. The number of defenders had grown considerably—it now amounted to several thousand. The day was misty, but the sun was shining through the haze that hung over the disturbed city. Rumors were now replaced by authentic information. Loudspeakers reported the news every hour. People exchanged news heard on Radio Liberty and the Russian Democratic Radio, which had managed to get on the air. A group of people gathered around me as I told them the news I had heard on CNN. The position of Bush was cheered; Hussein was cursed and mocked.

At noon, a tremendous meeting was called on the side of the White House opposite its main entrance. There are no high buildings on this side and therefore no reason to be afraid of marksmen. At this point, there must have been fifty thousand people. People were everywhere, even on top of the trees. Yeltsin said he would not retreat, the coup would be crushed, and the mutineers would be brought to trial. Eduard Shevardnadze and the well-known former KGB General Oleg Kalugin also spoke. All in all the whole event was very emotional; people grew more active. Zeal and aggressiveness (in a positive sense) emerged. There were many shouts of "Down with communists!" and "The junta should be brought to trial!" A lot of inscriptions big and small appeared on the walls of the White House and those of nearby buildings. By the end of the meeting it was announced that defense groups were being formed and all those willing to join were welcome. I joined a group constructing a barricade near the American Embassy. An American in a blue shirt was pushing a Toyota to reinforce the barricade. I asked him whether he didn't feel sorry for his car. "No," he said, "not at all. It's for the sake of democracy."

Later I went to my lab and collected all kinds of bandages, medicine, surgical instruments, everything I could. Returning to the White House, I joined a group of five other physicians in a bus under a flag with a red cross. All were volunteers and came from various hospitals and even from the emergency services. At least we would be capable of granting some auxiliary help in the case of severe wounds, before the wounded could be treated properly in a hospital. We learned that several big city hospitals had been getting ready to admit many wounded. The fear and uncertainty were gone; everyone was busy doing something.

The sun shone through the mist and a golden haze hung over the city. The buildings looked dim and menacing against it. We had many things to do. Many old people in the crowd felt sick and fainted, others had their hands bruised, some suffered from headaches, and we had one case of acute pancreatitis. We would stuff aspirin tablets into open mouths every now and then. Closer to the evening, it started raining again. Fires were burning everywhere. People were spitting on the curfew hour. When darkness fell, the situation grew very tense. It was announced that the attack of paratroops and special troops was expected at any moment. Women were told to leave the White House. The guards inside proclaimed they would die, "sword in hand." Rutskoi addressed the people on the barricades, telling them they would be the first victims and they should be ready. Yeltsin, Gavril Popov [the major of Moscow], and some others were hidden in the White House vaults. Around midnight we diluted some alcohol with water and drank for "war spirits." By that time it was raining very hard. The whole area was covered with umbrellas, and sheets of plastic on wooden poles. People were hiding, but not leaving. The area around the White House was lit with floodlights fixed on several buildings and the parliament building itself. The guards inside needed light to shoot accurately.

At about one o'clock in the morning, I got out of the bus and saw a white stripe across the sky—and heard the sound of a shot. Then shooting broke out in several places simultaneously, and we heard the sound of roaring engines. The attack had begun. The most intense shooting was in the vicinity of Kutuzovsky Prospect. The people on the barricades assembled in thick formations and locked hands to form a living wall. Young men from the defense group broke into a car, collected gasoline in a bucket, and poured it on an advancing tank which then caught fire. The shooting continued for about half an hour and ceased as abruptly as it had begun. Rumors came that there were dozens of wounded and about ten people killed. Two hours later we learned that several tanks had broken through the living wall of protesting people, and started ramming the barricade. They were met with incendiary bottles [Molotov cocktails] and one vehicle caught fire. The soldiers started shooting in the air. Crowds of people advanced upon them, calling on them to stop fire. How could they shoot their own people? The soldiers lowered their arms and fled in various directions; the tanks retreated. But three lives were taken. One of the young men had climbed upon a tank (he was an Afghanistan veteran) and covered it with his cloak. A gun barrel stuck out of the tank and he was shot on the spot. Another one tried to haul his body away from the tank, but the machine made a reverse movement and he was crushed by the tank's caterpillars. His body was maimed so badly that at the funeral his coffin was not opened. A third person was killed by a roaming bullet through his head. But the peaceful people had stopped the soldiers. Their victory had cost three lives.

By four o'clock in the morning a second attack was expected. It was announced that a detachment of the KGB special corps would launch a ground offensive. But it never came. We were now blue from the rain, cold, shooting, and lack of sleep for two days. We felt numb to the threat. The night grew less dim and signs of dawn appeared. The rain slackened.

Only later did we learn that a division had been refusing to attack the White House since the 19th of August and on Wednesday morning, the head of the KGB Vladimir Kryuchkov and Defense Minister Dmitri Yazov realized that their troops and special detachments were refusing to act against a legal government. The men of one detachment had been given five months' salary on the 18th of August, but even they realized that it was no joke to slay common citizens, wipe out the legal authorities, and suffer heavy casualties in close-quarters' combat inside the White House. The very night when we stood wet on the barricades, several generals had openly refused to obey their orders.

At eleven o'clock the next morning, August 21, it was announced that the mutineers had fled the city, and that the troops were leaving Moscow. Yeltsin issued a statement calling for the arrest of the junta leaders. One businessman said: "The communists used to say that the last night of Russian capitalism was frosty; now we can say in our turn that the last day of communist rule will be rainy!" Tremendous laughter broke out. By the middle of the day, it was clear that the victory of democracy was near. Many of those who had not dared to come before came to swell the crowd. That is only natural—any donkey is ready to hoof a dead lion. Enormous mountains of food had been brought to the barricades. Food was cooked right there on field stoves and people with dishes covered with cakes, buns, and hamburgers walked through the crowds and anyone could take anything he wanted. At ten o'clock in the evening Yeltsin ordered the Russian KGB to arrest the junta leaders. By three A.M. they had all been arrested. I said goodbye to my companions and went home past exultant crowds of people, campfires, and barricades.

There is nothing much to be added. Two days later a magnificent mourning ceremony and funeral for the three dead boys took place. Millions of people took part in the funeral. Of the many thousand defenders of democracy only these three souls were taken by death. Undoubtedly they were very clear, innocent, and the most beautiful ones. They are now at the threshold of the Creator begging His mercy for their poor devastated and robbed country. I guess in a short while they will become three more saints of the Russian Church. That is only reasonable.

15. Moscow Women

Most Soviet women have full-time jobs. They work for personal satisfaction and also out of financial necessity. These 1978 interviews with Moscow women done by two Swedish women provide a glimpse of how Soviet families lived. They underline the effects of the continuing housing shortage and the difficulty of combining work and family life. The situation for Soviet women remains much the same in the early 1990s.

Lida is a short, solid woman, pale and without makeup. She has a boyish haircut and is wearing a faded sweater past its prime, brown slacks of coarse wool, and heavy shoes. She looks tired and worn.

Tell us about yourself.

I'm already thirty-one years old. Some years ago I started to work as a chambermaid. I work between nine and six.

What did you do before?

I worked on geological expeditions, traveling all over the country. During summers I worked outdoors the whole time, and in winter I lived in a small room on the site. We made geological charts and did a lot of other things. Sometimes the work was very heavy, but I enjoyed it a lot. I kept on meeting new people, going to new places. It was an interesting life. But you get tired of that, too. I wanted to have children, and I had to create another life for myself, so I got a job in Moscow.

Abridged from Hansson, C., and Liden, Karen, *Moscow Women*, 158–61. New York: Pantheon, 1983.

How do you live now?

I have a room in a communal apartment.* Of course I'd like to have a place of my own, but there's absolutely no chance of that. It's a fairly large room—15 square meters. Only my son and I live there.

Before that I lived with my mother. But there's a law here that states that single parents have a right to a single room, so after a while I got this one.

Do you have your son in a day-care center?

No, he's only two and a half, so he's in a nursery. He spends the entire week there. I leave him on Monday morning and pick him up on Friday evening.

Is he happy there?

Yes, he likes it a lot. There are toys, other children, things that a kid needs. The staff is good and caring. But of course it's hard to see so little of him. I miss him. He spends his days with strangers, and when he comes home he seems to want to be back with them. People who aren't even related to him seem closer to him than I am.

He doesn't behave like a real son; sometimes he uses the polite form of address with me.** But in general things are all right. I'd never be able to bring him home every day.

What time do you come home from work?

I don't leave work until six, which means that the earliest I get home is at seven. At least three times a week I have to stop and shop on the way home, and since that's the time the crowds are the worst, it often takes at least an hour. Most of the time I don't get home until eight.

Do you manage to have any free time?

Hardly. I have to cook and wash and do things like that at night. But I do have a couple of hobbies. One is the theater. I'm part of an amateur group. It consists of people who are interested in the theater, both students and workers. We rehearse four times a week—Monday, Wednesday, and Saturday nights and all of Sunday. When we're about to perform we work as much as we can bear. Right now we're working on a piece by Mayakovsky.*** It's a lot of fun.

My second hobby is sculpting in wood. I collect pieces of wood in the forest and sculpt figures out of them. I usually do that late at night . . . [In answer to the question as to whether or not she was divorced, Lida answered, "I was never married. I wanted to have a child, not a family. I'm not the kind of woman who fits easily into a marriage."]

---

*Soviet experts estimate that 20 to 25 percent of the population live in communal apartments where several families share the same bathroom and kitchen facilities.

**The Russian language has both a polite and an informal form of address, unlike English. Family members normally use the informal form.

***Vladimir Mayakovsky (1893–1930), leading Russian futurist poet. Chapter 5, See Reading 2.

[Lyuba]

I'm an artist, thirty-two years old. I was married once before and have a son from that marriage. I was twenty-one when we got married, and I already had the baby. We were divorced when I was twenty-five. Now I'm married for the second time—six months ago.

Many people get divorced very early here. Why do you think that's so?

We know so little about life when we marry; we become independent so late. Almost without exception young people are dependent on their parents to help out economically. The money problem becomes especially acute if a couple has a child and the woman has to stop working. Here a family can't possibly live on one salary. Never! Well, perhaps two people can live on the man's salary, but with a child it's impossible. And it almost never happens that a young person can have her own apartment which she can take care of herself. Newly married couples have to wait a long time to get their own apartment and have to live with their parents in the meantime. If the parents have means, they can buy into a cooperative and the young people can move in after a year or two. But sometimes they have to live with their parents for ten years, or perhaps all their lives.

Very often young people divorce just after they've moved away from their parents. Before they moved they were still like chidlren, and only when they start living by themselves do they notice that they're very different from each other and that they can't live together. Or if the parents don't like their daughter-in-law or son-in-law, there always seems to be a way of making the children divorce . . .

[Nadezhda Pavolovna, 48, is a university professor and party member. She has done well. Like many successful American women, she does not think there are special obstacles to a woman's success.]

Your profession has obviously always been very important to you.

Definitely! When I was fifteen I never thought of just having children and a home and a husband. Never! I felt that kind of thinking was beneath a woman's dignity. I had a long correspondence with my future husband about woman's role in society. How I let myself go in those letters! My husband confessed several years later that he was more interested in the way I ended the letters than in the whole women's debate. But I took the whole thing very seriously!

Is work still the most important thing for you?

The most important thing for me is . . . our country. Of course there are people who express their dissatisfaction nowadays with . . . well, politics. But they underline even more clearly what this country, what the Soviet Union has done for me. When I compare my life with Mama's . . . then I know. Everything I've attempted has seemed to be so easy. My studies went smoothly, my career also. It was probably the right place, the right time, the right profession.

But the children . . . I was often sad that I didn't have more.

Tears come to her eyes, but she quickly composes herself while she blows her nose. "This ought not to be taped!" she laughs. Then she cries again and says, "My third child was stillborn."

Her daughter consoles her, and Nadezhda Pavolovna is soon laughing again and saying to her daughter, "Hurry up so that I can be a grandmother instead!" We laugh together and then move on to a completely different question.

What does equality between men and women mean to you?

My own situation is one of total equality. If one of us does a particular chore in our home, the other will reciprocate some other time. But heavy physical work is hard for a woman, so my husband takes care of the furnace. It's a dirty job and . . . it isn't my cup of tea. I always do the laundry. That's the way we've divided up the chores.

I think that all this talk about equality is something they invented in big cities. There it can obviously become a gigantic problem for a couple to decide who is going to clean an apartment floor which consists of a few pitiful square meters. Our house is ten by twelve meters, and there's never a question about who's going to clean the floors. I do that. My husband makes the fires. He digs up the garden. I do the planting . . .

[Natasha and Yura are students with a small child.]

I'll be twenty-two in May. Right after attending school in Sverdlovsk in the Urals, I came to the University of Moscow. That was four years ago. I'm a student at the faculty of law and will graduate this year. I specialize in criminal law. At first I was interested only in juvenile crime, but gradually I've become interested in all forms of crime. I'm especially interested in the social context of crime.

What does your husband do?

He's majoring in mathematics. We'll graduate at the same time, and then we'll be moving to Akademgorodok.*

Have you lived here since you got married?

No. Actually, we could have had a room at the university. Neither Yura nor I have relatives in Moscow, so we really don't have any place to live here. We lived at the university until we got married, and it wouldn't have been too difficult to get a room in a two-room apartment there. That would have meant a small private room with shower, toilet, and coat closet shared with the neighbors, and a large communal kitchen—there's one on every floor. But we were tired of living in student rooms. There are always people milling around. And then it was a question of finances. Neither he nor I get much help from home.

---

*A suburb of Novosibirsk in Siberia, where the Siberian section of the Soviet Union's Academy of Science is located. Akademgorodok is populated almost exclusively by scholars and students who work at the university. The standard of education and research is considered very high.

Mama is a pediatrician, but she doesn't make terribly much—no more than 120 rubles per month, or maybe 130 if she works overtime at night. She sends me money, but I try to make her stop. Basically, we live on what we earn . . . [At the official exchange rate, .8 ruble = $1.00]

But there are several people living in the apartment, aren't there?

Of course. We considered this when we chose Yura's job. We found a spot where we had friends—some of our classmates live here too—Yura's brother and one of his friends. The three of them arranged to live together. It has its good and bad sides, since I'm the only woman—the others aren't married, so I end up doing the cooking for everybody.

Of course they help with the shopping, but it's still a lot of work. On the other hand it's nice to be the only woman in the kitchen. I can iron and wash and cook when I want to, and there aren't any conflicts. In communal kitchens there are often four women scurrying around, and that creates problems. So in a way I'm lucky.

How long have you lived here?

Not very long. Before this Yura worked as a superintendent in another place. But we were only given an apartment in the basement and it wasn't very suitable for small children. When the baby was really little, things worked out well because we had a small yard where we could put his carriage. But the room was too small and the corridor so drafty that he couldn't play there, and I couldn't keep him in his bed and playpen all day. But we had warm water, and that made things much easier.

You don't have any hot water here?

No, and no bathroom. It's a big problem. I have to heat water for the dishes and the wash. Fortunately there's a public bath not far from here that we use. But we bathe the baby at home and have to heat the water. And the kitchen! Sometimes I visit one of Yura's brothers who lives in a new suburb, and I bathe the baby there. They have a bathroom and a kitchen that are tiny but clean and bright—they're completely white. But this place is horrible!

Where is the baby during the day?

He's with us—as he's always been. Since we don't have anyone else to take care of him, we take turns.

Right before he was born I went home to my mother. I ended up staying there for three months. Because he wasn't very strong and had a little trouble eating when he was born, we don't want to put him in a nursery yet.

Will he go later?

Yes, next year.

Do you think most people think nurseries are a good solution?

No, for the most part people place children in them out of necessity. There are some good ones, especially those connected to factories and institutions; there you don't have to worry about your children. But for the most part nurseries are very bad; the staff is usually very inexperienced and untrained, and turnover is constant. They get minimal wages, the job is taxing, and the groups are far too large—twelve to fifteen children per adult. The children are constantly catching cold because they're always running around in wet diapers. If we were paid for the whole year after having a baby, most women would probably take advantage of it.

16. Shortages

Unfortunately, perestroika *did not alleviate the economic hardship experienced by the ordinary Soviet citizen. On the contrary, at the end of six years of* perestroika, *living conditions for most Soviets were worse than ever, a situation that many blamed on the restructuring policy itself. The author of the following letter to* Izvestia *ponders this problem, blaming much of it on middlemen who buy goods cheaply at a state store and resell them at a cooperative at a much higher price. By 1992, shortages were worse.*

We are patient people, that is well known. But is it really necessary to test our patience so stubbornly and for so long? Could there be another option?

What prompted me to write was my distress at what I heard while waiting in line at the Barnaul Central Department Store. The thing is that since August soap, laundry detergent, toothpaste, and many other things have not been on sale in Barnaul's Stores. The same is true, I have heard, in other cities, but does that make it any easier for us?

On 24 November I stood in a line from 1600 to 1800 hours—there was not enough toothpaste, so I had to wait again from 1500 to 1740 the next day. I bought three tubes of toothpaste and three bars of soap. However, my good fortune was overshadowed. In the time I spent waiting in line, I heard a great many unflattering things from the purchasers about our economic policy. What upset me was that they were mainly berating restructuring. As if it was to blame for everything! I tried to change their minds, but they told me: The lack of goods is created by the trade workers: The "flea market" sells soap, toothpaste, shampoo, and so forth at three times the price, and the people waiting in this enormous line are not going to sell things at the "flea market," it all comes from the stores and from the people who fail to control them properly.

I could not rest for what I had heard. It is upsetting to hear people blaming everything on restructuring. No doubt difficulties are inevitable at the start of anything complex and new. But how much can you take? And why is it all at our expense, at the expense of people who live very modestly?

I went to the "Merkuriy" cooperative. Not long ago the "Svezhest" store used to be there, where they always sold many different kinds of soap, laundry

---

From Kalmykova, S., "Thoughts While Waiting in Line" [Letter to the editor], *Izvestia* (Feb. 3, 1989). In *The Glasnost Review.* Edited by J. Eisen, 352–54. New York: New American Library, 1990.

detergent, and so forth. Now it is all different at "Merkuriy." It is nicer and . . . more expensive. There, they were selling cotton panty hose at R13. I bought exactly the same panty hose in Moscow in July at a store on Gorkiy Street for R2. When I asked who makes the panty hose, the girl dropped her eyes and answered: "A cooperative" . . . They also sell ordinary boots there for R167. In Moscow they are R70–80.

It is no better at the "flea market." Here there really is everything, but the prices . . . Shampoo at R5–8, rabbit-fur hats—R50, boots—R100–200, lipstick—R5–10, and so forth.

After all I had seen, I wondered: What is going on?

I have been living in Barnaul since 1963. I have never once seen either rabbit-fur hats or felt boots on sale in the stores, but the "flea market" is always full of them.

So it has nothing to do with restructuring. We expect it to resolve rapidly problems that have been accumulating for years. No doubt it is necessary to step up monitoring of the trade in shortage goods and to take a close look at the cooperatives. But we also need more substantial, purely economic measures that would enable ordinary people to draw breath, so to speak, and provide their families with essentials. Otherwise people will get angry in the end, and no talk about restructuring, no bright prospects will make any impression on them. Some people might regard this as a consumerist approach. But is that all that concern for consumers is?

17. Jokes and Fables: Social Commentary Soviet-Style

Vladimir Bukovsky, author of an autobiographical journey through the Gulag Archipelago, To Build a Castle *(New York: Viking Press, 1977) and an incisive commentator on the Soviet world, has suggested that someone ought to put up a monument to the political joke, a form of creative expression that was especially enjoyed in the Soviet Union. These jokes often express people's opinions of events and are told and retold, embroidered, refurbished, and brought out for new occasions. The same holds true for fables which, though not usually humorous, contain the same sort of incisiveness. What follows is just a small sampling of the thousands of jokes and stories told throughout the Soviet Union, many of which are still told today.*

STALIN ERA JOKES

A party activist was making his periodic check-up on the farms in his district. He stopped a peasant in his field, and asked about the potato crop. "There has

---

Retold by Janet Vaillant

never been a crop to equal this, thanks to the glorious plan of our leaders," the peasant answered. "If we were to place all our potatoes in a pile, they would stretch to the very feet of God." The activist became angry: "You know there is no God." "Ah," said the peasant, "But there are no potatoes either."

Some time ago, an American and a Russian were discussing the merits of their leaders. The Americans said that Herbert Hoover was a greater man than Stalin, because he put into effect Prohibition and taught the Americans not to drink. "That's nothing," replied the boastful Russian, "Stalin taught us not to eat."

KHRUSHCHEV JOKES

Khrushchev often spoke of the fact that the USSR would soon catch up with and surpass the United States. The following story was told: A Moscow class was studying the United States and the teacher asked a student: "Iurii, what is the United States like?" Iurii replied, as he had been taught: "The United States is a capitalist country which has millions of people unemployed and starving." And now, continued the teacher, "What is the goal of the Soviet Union?" Iurii answered, "To catch up with the United States."

Khrushchev also spoke of the fact that soon the Soviet people would enter the era of true socialism. Two Soviet citizens were talking about how near they were to socialism. One observed, "The party told me that socialism is on the horizon. I wasn't sure what the word horizon meant, so I looked it up in the dictionary. I now see what they meant. The horizon is an imaginary line which moves further away from you as you approach it."

FROM THE BREZHNEV ERA

After the successful Apollo-Soyuz joint Soviet-American space flight, Brezhnev called in the cosmonauts to congratulate them. Then he continued: "The Americans are winning the space race. We must accomplish something to surpass them. They have landed someone on the moon, so we in the Politburo have decided to send you to land on the sun." The cosmonauts let out a groan, "But Comrade Brezhnev, we'll be burned alive!" "Fools, do you think we haven't thought of that problem? Don't worry. We've planned it so that you can complete your landing at night."

In the year 2001, a boy asks his grandfather: "Grandfather, what does the word 'queue' mean?" "Well, my boy, back in 1975 there wasn't enough meat for everyone, so people had to wait in queues, one behind the other, to buy a piece of meat. Does that explain it to you?" "Yes," replied the boy, "But what does the word 'meat' mean?"

A husband came home and found his wife in the arms of another man. He was understandably furious. "You wretch," he shouted, "This is how you spend your afternoon, when all the good wives are out at the corner store standing in line to get the lemons which have just come in."

A man walking down a Moscow street spat on the curb. A voice behind him whispered, "Please, this is no place to talk politics."

On election day, a group of workers was escorted to the polls by a party activist, handed an envelope, and told to put it into the ballot box. One worker was curious so he opened his envelope to see what was inside. "What are you doing?" called out the activist. "I'd just like to find out for whom I'm voting," answered the worker. "You fool—don't you know that this is a secret ballot?"

Two old friends were talking on a Moscow street. Sergei said, "Tell me Ivan, you are a wise man, do you think that there will be a war?" "Certainly not," replied Ivan, "but there will be such a struggle for peace that not a stone will be left standing."

What is the tallest building in Moscow? The Lubianka (KGB building). From there, you can see Magadan, Siberia.

A human rights activist was being interrogated by the KGB. He began to cite his rights under the Soviet Constitution. The KGB officer listened for a little while and then wearily interrupted him: "Please, we're having a serious conversation."

A nurse at a kindergarten tells the children: "In the Soviet Union the workers live a happy life, they have everything, and everything belongs to them. Their children have plenty of food and toys." Little Vanechka bursts into tears: "I want to go to the Soviet Union."

Four archeologists on a dig outside of Cairo found a mummy. They took it back to Moscow and worked for some time to identify it without success, so they took it to the KGB. Two days later they went to the KGB and were told, "It's Ramses IV." "How did you find out?" they asked. "He told us."

FROM THE GLASNOST ERA

After Gorbachev came to power, and people were increasingly free to say what they really thought, the number of political jokes told greatly declined. As the problems of daily life increased, however, jokes began to make a comeback, illustrating the role of humor in helping Russians to express their frustrations and making a difficult life bearable.

Two earnest young men were having a conversation in front of the Supreme Soviet building about the best provisions for the new Soviet Constitution. "What we need," one said excitedly, "is a constitution something like Sweden's." "It won't work here," his friend said. "Why not?" "We don't have enough Swedes."

A prominent Soviet trade official went to England on a business trip and refused to return. A few months later, one of his former school friends was in England and went to see him. "Tell me, I don't understand it. How could you betray your convictions? You always did so well on all your exams in history, the history of the Communist party of the Soviet Union, and scientific communism." His friend answered, "I didn't betray my convictions. On exams they asked me what Marx and Lenin thought. They never asked me what I thought."

Soviet entrepreneur: "Have you heard the latest about our new cooperative and its joint venture?"
"No, what's happening?"
Soviet entrepreneur: "Give me ten rubles and I'll tell you."

It is well-known that workers often steal material from the factories where they work. Every day a Russian worker left his factory pushing a wheelbarrow full of straw. Every day, the guard halted him and searched carefully through the straw, but he found nothing. After several months of this, the guard said to the worker, "I am being transferred far away from here, so you can talk freely to me now. What have you been stealing?" "Wheelbarrows," confessed the worker.

What did Stalin construct in our country? Nothing.
What did Khrushchev build in our country? Nothing.
What did Brezhnev construct? Nothing.
So what is there for Gorbachev to restructure?

What can you buy with the old ruble?
Nothing.
And for the new one?
Ten times more.

A son is talking with his mother:
I don't want to go to school any more.
Why?
You know, Petrov will again insult me. Vinitsin will throw a textbook at me, Vasiliev will trip me with his foot. I'm not going.
My dear, you have to go. First of all, you're already forty years old, and second, you're the director of the school.

Ivan: You know, there are two possible ways to get out of this mess our country is in, a realistic one and an unrealistic one. The realistic one is that a spaceship from Mars will come and the Martians will solve all our problems.
Fedor: And the unrealistic way?
Ivan: We Russians will solve them ourselves.

A SHORT COURSE IN SOVIET HISTORY

Lenin, Stalin, Khrushchev, Brezhnev, and Gorbachev found themselves together on a train speeding across Siberia. It abruptly stopped. Lenin said, "Don't worry," and stepped out to talk with the engineers, raised the consciousness of the driver, and the train began to move forward again. Unfortunately it soon stopped again. This time, Stalin stepped forward, went up to the driver, and shot him. Once again, the train began to move slowly forward. But once again it stopped. It was Khrushchev's turn. He went up to the engine, talked the situation over with the men in it, and came up with a solution: Everyone was to get out of the train, pull up the track over which they had passed, and lay new track ahead of the train so that it would be able to go forward. Alas, this proved only a harebrained scheme and temporary solution, for the train halted once more. Comrade Brezhnev talked the situation over with his advisers, and hit on another solution: He ordered that the shades be pulled down in the railroad car in which they were riding and that everyone pretend that the train was still moving forward. Gorbachev then got his turn. He threw open the shades and shouted, "Look everyone, the train has stopped."

A RUSSIAN FABLE

In addition to jokes, Russian culture includes a fondness for anecdotes and fables. These can be humorous, but they are almost always poignant. The following is one such fable, well-known in Russia, and sometimes told by analysts to dramatize the deep-seated collectivist egalitarianism and lack of individual initiative in Russian culture.

A Russian peasant who has no cow but envies his cow-owning neighbor is offered three wishes by a magic bird. The peasant ponders his wish, and tells the bird that he would like to be equal to his neighbor; to that end, he asks the bird to kill his neighbor's cow. In response, the bird suggests a more constructive option: that he simply give the farmer a cow to make him equal to his neighbor that way. The farmer replies, "No, thank you. Having a cow of my own would mean more work. I'd rather be equal to my neighbor by having you kill his cow."

Chapter Eight

FROM RUSSIA TO USSR AND BEYOND

As they look back at the history of the Soviet Union, historians often discuss the question of continuity and change. In what ways did the Soviet Union differ from tsarist Russia? How many cultural and political traditions were carried on, at least among the Russians? To what extent will traditional practices determine the future? It is impossible to answer these questions once and for all, but the effort to do so provides an effective way to review the Russian and Soviet past.

Those who stress continuity between the tsarist past and the Soviet period see many things that remained much the same. The Soviet government, like that of the tsars, was very highly centralized, militaristic, authoritarian, and dominated by the Russians. The bureaucracy held great power in both systems. Those who stress similarities in the two periods also point out that censorship existed under the tsars as it did in the Soviet Union, both regimes supported a powerful secret police, opposition was interpreted as disloyalty or even treason, and the law was a weak reed when the winds of political expediency began to blow. The Soviet government, even more than that of the tsars, tried to control both the political and spiritual life of its people. Marxist ideology, like the Christian Orthodoxy of old, served the state as the single approved guide for spiritual life. Marxism-Leninism also helped to reinforce such traditional Russian attitudes as distrust of the individual and suspicion of outsiders. Disorder and disagreement were still feared as a danger to group survival, and home and family were prized as a refuge from the state.

Those who stress continuity also point out that the Soviet Union, like the empire before it, extended its reach when strong, and its leaders remembered that when weak, the country had suffered terribly from the invasions of its neighbors. Leaders of the Soviet Union, as those of the empire, looked upon their Western neighbors with a mixture of fear and admiration. They seemed unsure whether they should imitate the West or whether their own traditions offered them special moral and spiritual advantages upon which to build their society.

Mikhail Gorbachev set out to change many of these attitudes and policies. His approach, however, offers historians another opportunity to stress the persistence of certain features of the past. For them, Gorbachev's efforts to reform society from above recall those of Peter the Great, Catherine, and Alexander II, an entire tradition of reforming tsars. Gorbachev tried to introduce democracy by decree but found it difficult to create institutions— independent courts, a strong legal system, or even an effective legislature— that could withstand executive pressure. There were tsars before him who created local self-governing institutions, pushed for legal reform, and established a central elected, representative assembly. In the past, these reform efforts failed for many reasons, including the loss of the leader's nerve, the economic and social backwardness of the people, and a general inability to understand or accept the inconveniences and confusion of democratic decision-making. Such comparisons suggest the possibility that Gorbachev merely set in motion yet another effort to imitate the West and to reform society in order to "catch up," an effort that would inevitably encounter resistance, and may result in a reactionary return to more traditional and authoritarian ways.

Historians who stress change, however, have pointed out that old Russia and its peasant village society have been transformed. The Soviet Union became a well-educated, industrial, and urban society, militarily stronger than its neighbors. Its elite no longer spoke a language different from that of the people, as did the French- and German-speaking courts of eighteenth and nineteenth century Russia. On the contrary, the Soviet government successfully mobilized its peoples to carry out a coordinated state policy, assuring them that their interests and those of the state were identical.

Unlike the tsars' governments, which had neither the desire nor the capacity to transform society, the Soviet party-state attempted to create a new type of man. This party-state, with its capacity to direct the work of all social groups—from the elite to the poorest farm worker, and from the villages near Moscow to the cities of Uzbekistan—created a relationship between the leaders and the led quite different from anything achieved by the tsars. Gorbachev's reforms also differed from those of the authoritarian tsars because he tolerated compromise, the development of a free press, and, most significant of all, allowed initiative to pass from the central government to other social groups. When the people and the provinces began to make demands, the central government tried, though timidly and often unsuccessfully, to meet them. Finally, the level of education created by the Soviet regime and the explosion of communications technology make it unlikely that the country could again be cut off from the rest of the world by any leader. Economic success and international exchange are interrelated, and are prerequisites for any country that seeks to be respected as a major power.

There is yet a third school of thought that sees continuity not between Soviet Russia and the westward-looking court and elite of the eighteenth and nineteenth centuries, but between many Soviet attitudes and behavior and those of the village and court of Old Russia. These historians argue that Lenin's genius for organization and Stalin's ruthless use of force closed Peter the Great's window on the West, uprooted the westward-looking intelligentsia, and set Russia on a course that combined certain traits of early Russian society with a completely new type of political organization: the party-state. For historians from this school of thought, Gorbachev fits the role of westernizer; the reformers that of the westward-looking court. Like earlier westernizers, they must struggle against the survival of the ancient traditions of conservatism, collectivism, and the people's habit of offering allegiance to a strong, authoritarian leader.

To draw up a true balance sheet of continuity and change is, of course, impossible. There is no doubt that the tsars' empire has been transformed. It is just as sure that many Soviet and Russian attitudes and patterns of behavior—especially those that puzzle outsiders most—are akin to those of traditional Russia.

As in all countries, experience determines what people desire and what they fear, what seems familiar and acceptable, and what seems alien or frightening, as well as what makes a government feel secure or threatened. The habits of centuries do not change overnight or on command. They are acquired over a long period of time as part of a particular historical experience, and their roots go deep. Under Lenin and Stalin, the Soviet regime made an attempt to change those habits, an effort in scale and comprehensiveness that is virtually unprecedented in history. Nonetheless, the regime had to build on the traditions of the Russian empire even as it tried to escape them. New Soviet institutions and attitudes were combined with those of the Russian empire in such a way as to create a synthesis that endured for more than seventy years. The Gorbachev regime first challenged and then destroyed that synthesis. Today the peoples of the former Soviet Union are attempting to create a new balance between old traditions and new institutions that will enable them to live normally and peacefully in a world where national differences can be respected and tolerated.

APPENDIX

GLOSSARY

Akhmatova. Anna Akhmatova, one of the greatest Russian poets, founded the Acmeist literary movement. She died in 1966.

Andropov. Yuri Andropov succeeded Brezhnev as general secretary of the CPSU in 1982 and assumed the Soviet presidency the following year. He remained in power for only fifteen months, dying in early 1984.

Antichrist (or anti-Christ) In Christian tradition, a Satanic force who misleads his followers with a claim to be the true Christ. The world ends in battle between followers of Christ and those of the Antichrist.

Apparat The organization of full-time workers for the Communist party. The individual was called an *apparatchik*.

Artel. A cooperative association of Russian craftsmen.

Autocrat. Ivan the Great was the first Russian ruler to assume this title formally, in the late fifteenth century. At that time, it meant a ruler independent of any foreign power. His successor, Ivan the Terrible, interpreted it to mean the unlimited (and arbitrary) power of the monarch over his people, and this interpretation became traditional with later tsars.

Avant-garde. A French phrase meaning "in the forefront," often applied to artists, musicians, and writers who are considered ahead of their time.

Black Hundreds. Reactionary political groups of the early twentieth century who supported autocracy and antisemitism. Under the slogan "Save Russia," they organized pogroms against Jews and terroristic activities against liberal and radical groups. Nicholas II publicly thanked them for their support.

Bourgeois. Term coined by Karl Marx for a member of the bourgeoisie, or property-owning middle class, comprised of businessmen and factory owners. A capitalist.

Bourgeois nationalist. Pejorative term given by Bolsheviks, and later the Communist party, to anyone who seems to put local interests above those of the party or the centralized Soviet government.

Boyar. A member of the privileged aristocratic class, summoned to advise the princes of Kievan Rus'.

Bulgakov. Mikhail Bulgakov (1891–1940) was a major Soviet writer whose posthumous fame stemmed from the 1960s publication of four novels, of which one in particular, *The Master and Margarita*, has been widely acclaimed.

Capitalist imperialism. A phrase used by Soviet and other Marxist-Leninists to signify their belief that countries with free enterprise market economies, by their very nature, tend to extend their rule over other peoples.

Chernenko. Konstantin Chernenko succeeded Andropov as general secretary of the CPSU in 1984 and accomplished little before his death barely thirteen months later.

Collective. Group. In Soviet language, the collective was the source of real value—be it the collective of factory, school, or nation. Individuals were expected always to serve the interests of the collective.

Cominform. The Communist Information Bureau, established in 1947 to encourage cooperation among the Eastern European communist parties.

Comintern. The Communist International. Established in 1919 as an organization to coordinate activities of communist parties around the world, in fact directed from Moscow. Abolished in 1943 as a gesture of Allied solidarity.

Commune (mir). The peasant community of imperial Russia. The *mir* regulated its own internal affairs and was collectively responsible for paying its taxes.

Constantinople. Capital of the Byzantine Empire from the fourth century. The city fell to the Turks in the fifteenth century. They renamed it Istanbul, although Europeans continued to refer to it as Constantinople.

Cossack. Frontiersman and warrior-horseman. Cossacks were descended from Tatar groups and fugitive serfs who established self-governing communities in southern Russia and Ukraine in the sixteenth and seventeenth centuries. Originally allowed considerable independence in return for military service, they gradually lost their autonomy as tsarist power increased. Following the Revolution, most Cossacks either fled or were collectivized.

CPSU Central Committee. In theory the second most important organ in the CPSU, elected by and responsible to the Party Congress. The Central Committee, with some four hundred members, used to meet twice each year, delegating policy-making between its brief sessions to the Politburo.

Daniel. Yuli Daniel, a Russian writer, with Andrei Sinyavsky, was arrested in 1965 for publishing "anti-Soviet" works abroad without permission. Their subsequent trial and imprisonment did much to start the human rights movement.

Democratic centralism. The principle of Communist party organization developed by Lenin according to which factions within the party are outlawed and all decisions of higher organizations are binding on lower ones. Once a decision was made, it had to be carried out without further discussion.

Democratic socialism. In Soviet usage, a term first used by Lenin to describe socialism that has been corrupted by liberal, bourgeois principles and is therefore both wrong and dangerous.

Demokratizatsiya. "Democratization," a term applied to the political reform occurring in the USSR after 1985 that gave more opportunities to the people to participate in governing themselves.

Disiatin (dessiatine). A Russian unit of land area equal to 2.7 acres.

Dissident. Beginning in the 1960s, individuals who participated in activities of which the Soviet government disapproved were called dissidents. Such activities included religious worship, the defense of human rights or writing and publishing works that were considered anti-Soviet.

Druzhina. Russian collective noun that means friends. Prince's retinue or bodyguard in Kievan Rus'.

Duma. Word means thought or thinking, and by extension advice or counsel. In the early twentieth century the tsar created an elected State Council called the Duma.

Five Year Plan. Soviet planners used to set economic plans for five year intervals.

Fortress of Saint Peter and Saint Paul. In imperial Russia, the chief prison for political offenders.

"Gendarme of Europe." "Gendarme" is the French word for policeman. After 1815, the more reactionary European rulers assumed the duty of policing the continent in order to rid it of revolutionary activity.

General secretary. The general secretary of the Central Committee of the CPSU was, since Stalin's time, the political leader of both party and country.

German quarter. That section of Moscow in which, at the time of Peter the Great, most foreigners lived, so-called because Germans were the most numerous and prominent among the foreigners.

Glasnost. One of Gorbachev's chief policies after 1985. Literally "giving voice," this word has come to mean openness, and signifies allowing a greater freedom of expression.

Gosplan. The state planning commission in the Soviet Union. It designed central economic plans.

Great power messianism. An accusation leveled by the Soviet leadership at the major Western powers, claiming that those countries were guilty of forcing other, smaller ones to follow them and espouse their cause.

Gubernia. An administrative subdivision, roughly equivalent to a province, introduced by Peter the Great and abolished by the Soviets in 1923.

Harriman. Averell Harriman was an American businessman/statesman whose first visit to Russia was in 1899, when Nicholas was tsar. Between then and 1983, the year of his final visit, he was much involved in Soviet-American affairs. He spent more time with Stalin than any other American and negotiated a limited test-ban treaty with Khrushchev.

Human rights movement. A movement by a small number of Soviet citizens to pressure the Soviet regime to honor its own Constitution and laws.

Intelligentsia. A Russian word, coined in the mid-19th century, that originally connoted individuals whose education led them to alienation from society and disaffection with the status quo. In contemporary terminology, it refers to those who are not manual laborers, but who are in significant commanding and creative roles in society.

Internationale. The anthem of The International Workingmen's Asociation.

Kaledin-Kornilov band. Kaledin, a Cossack leader, and Kornilov, commander of the Russian army during much of 1917, were both early opponents of the Bolsheviks following the October Revolution.

Kamenev. Lev Kamenev was one of the most important Bolshevik leaders in 1917.

KGB. Acronym, used since 1953, for Komitet Gosudarstvennoi Bezopastnosti, or Committee on State Security. Abolished in 1991.

Kolkhoz. A Soviet collective farm. All land was owned by the collective—the people who lived on the farm. Workers were paid a share of the common produce.

Kollontai. Alexandra. One of the leading female Bolsheviks in 1917 and an outspoken feminist.

Komsomol. The Young Communist League. A selective organization for promising Soviet youth between the ages of 14 and 28.

Konovalov. Alexander Ivanovich Konovalov, was a minister of the Provisional Government in the fall of 1917.

Kuban. A region in the south of Russia, just to the north of the Caucasus Mountains.

Kulak. Word means fist in Russian. Name given to prosperous peasants by the Soviet regime. During the collectivization campaign, poor peasants were encouraged to dispossess the *kulaks,* who were often accused of hoarding grain they did not have, and either forced into collectives or exiled to Siberia.

Kvass. A fermented beverage popular in Russia.

Little Octobrists. The Communist party's organization for school children under age ten.

Marseillaise. The French national anthem, which had originated in the Revolution of 1789, and which was later used by revolutionary groups throughout the world.

Marshall Plan. Named for General George C. Marshall. A program of economic aid to war-torn Europe, initiated in 1947 by the Truman administration. It was offered also to the USSR, but Stalin refused it.

Nevsky Prospekt. The premier avenue of St. Petersburg.

Nomenklatura. A list of important positions for which party approval was needed before a person could be appointed.

Pan-Slav. The nineteenth century movement that sought to unite all Slavic peoples for political and cultural ends under the leadership of Russia.

Party-minded. Keeping the goals of the Communist party in mind as a standard for thought and action.

Party-state. A term sometimes used to describe the Soviet state system. Party and state institutions were virtually fused, with the party playing the leading role.

Pasternak. Boris Pasternak, 1890–1960, author of the novel *Dr. Zhivago*, and an outstanding poet of the Soviet period. He received the Nobel Prize for literature in 1957, but was forced to renounce it.

Peoples democracy. Term used by Soviets to describe those countries of Eastern Europe with Communist party rule. These same countries were often called Soviet satellites by Americans.

Perestroika. Literally "restructuring," this term originally referred to Gorbachev's plans for economic reform, but it was also more loosely applied to all of Gorbachev's policies and to Gorbachev's "revolution" in a general sense.

Peterhof. Location of one of the great imperial palaces on the Gulf of Finland, a short distance from St. Petersburg.

Pise. A building material, somewhat akin to stucco.

Pogrom. An organized persecution and/or attack on a minority group, often the Jews.

Politburo. The small executive committee of the Communist Party Central Committee. The most powerful group in the Soviet Union.

Presidium. An executive committee, as for example the Presidium of the Supreme Soviet, which was elected by the Supreme Soviet and served as its executive committee. In 1917, the term referred to the small group of men who were most influential in the Petrograd Soviet's leadership.

Pud (pood). A Russian unit of weight, equal to about 36 pounds.

Red Director. The state-appointed factory manager of the 1920s.

Revolutionary legality. The principle of law that follows Lenin's precept that "the health of the Revolution is the highest law."

Riazan. A region in Russia southeast of Moscow, on the Volga River.

R.S. Bolsheviks. Russian Soviet Bolsheviks, as Lenin's party was known at the time.

Ruble. The basic monetary unit in Russia since the fourteenth century.

Russification. A program, begun in the Imperial Period, to promote Russian culture and the use of the Russian language in non-Russian parts of the empire.

Sakharov. Andrei Sakharov first gained prominence as a physicist and father of the Soviet hydrogen bomb. He later became a prominent member of the human rights movement. Awarded the Nobel Peace Prize in 1975, sentenced to exile in the city of Gorky in 1980, released in 1987, he was at the time of his death in 1989 a member of the Congress of Peoples' Deputies. Much admired, he never compromised his principles.

SALT I and II. Strategic Arms Limitation Treaties. These were agreements to limit strategic weapons systems, signed in 1972 and 1979, respectively.

Samizdat. Literally, self-publishing. A term that was used for typed or mimeographed manuscripts, circulated among friends, which could not pass state censorship.

Satellite. Term given by Western observers to those countries of Eastern Europe that had Communist party governments and followed the directives of the Soviet Union.

Scientific socialism. Soviet term, used by Lenin to indicate the proper form of socialism that is in accord with the laws of history.

Second economy. An unofficial, spontaneous economy, generally tolerated in the USSR, because the official economy did not satisfy the people's needs.

Secretariat of the Central Committee. A small, centralized organization of full-time party workers that directed the work of the party apparat and Soviet society as a whole.

Serfdom. The institutionalized arrangement in which most Russian serfs were, until 1861, bound to a landlord's estate and prohibited from moving by a decree dating from 1649.

Shliapnikov. A.G. Shliapnikov was an early member and leader of the Bolshevik Party.

Show trials. In the 1920s and 1930s, public trials of so-called spies and saboteurs received wide publicity and were used to explain hardships, warn others, and justify the need for discipline and vigilance.

Sinyavsky. See Daniel.

Slavophiles. Group of nineteenth century Russians who believed that Russia had unique qualities that made it basically different from western Europe, and that those qualities should be preserved.

Smolny Institute. A former girls' school in St. Petersburg, Smolny became the headquarters for the defense of Petrograd in 1917. The Military-Revolutionary Committee of the Petrograd Soviet was housed there.

Socialist realism. A literary principle introduced by Stalin, whereby literature had to portray the world as the party wished it to be, and provide instructive and easily understandable models for readers.

Solidarity. The workers' movement started by Lech Walesa in Poland in 1980 that pressed for reform.

Solzhenitsyn. Alexander Solzhenitsyn is a writer who was expelled from the Soviet Union in 1974 following publication abroad of his monumental survey of the Stalinist forced labor system that he christened the Gulag Archipelago. He has resided in Vermont since 1976, and his works are now being made available in the former USSR.

Soviet. Russian word for council. Elected councils at all levels of the government of the USSR were known as soviets.

Soviet Academy of Sciences. This body was responsible to the Council of Ministers for most of the USSR's scientific research and leadership, carried out in over two hundred institutes. Originally founded as the Imperial Academy by Peter the Great, its current name was adopted in 1925.

Sovkhoz. A Soviet state farm. All land was owned by the state and the workers of the land were paid salary.

State socialism. An economic system in which all property is owned by the state.

Steppe. The prairie grasslands of the southern portions of the former Soviet Union.

Supreme Soviet. The top elected government council, charged by the Soviet Constitution with the making of laws.

Taiga. The great forests of northern Russia, consisting largely of coniferous trees but including some deciduous species such as birch and aspen as well.

Third World. A phrase used in the industrial nations to indicate the less economically developed parts of the world.

Totalitarian. Adjective applied to a political regime such as Hitler's Germany or Stalin's Russia, in which a single mass party promotes an official ideology through a monopoly of control of communication and armed force and through a system of terroristic police control.

Tsarskoye selo. "Tsar's Village," site of one of the tsar's palaces fifteen miles south of St. Petersburg.

Tsvetaeva. Marina Tsvetaeva was a major Russian poet until her suicide in 1941.

Tundra. A region of cold desert in extreme northern and southern latitudes, including much of northern Siberia, characterized by poor soil and limited plant life.

Uezd. An administrative district in imperial Russia roughtly equivalent to a county.

Vanguard party. The term used by Lenin to refer to his party, which is ahead of the working class in its understanding of the revolutionary process.

Veche. Town council, particularly important in early Novgorod and Pskov.

Volost. The smallest administrative division in rural imperial Russia, comprising several villages.

Walesa. Lech Walesa founded the workers' Solidarity movement in Poland in 1980 and was elected president of that country in December, 1990.

Young Pioneers. In the USSR, the organization for young people aged 10 to 15.

THE ROMANOV DYNASTY

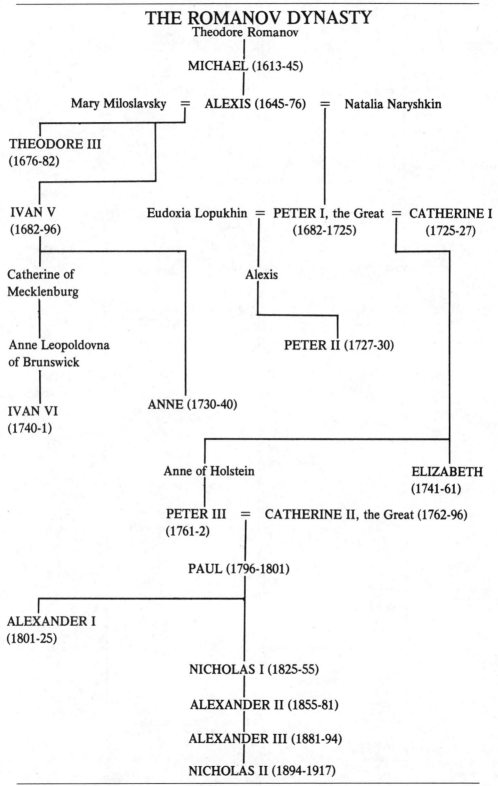

Theodore Romanov

MICHAEL (1613-45)

Mary Miloslavsky = ALEXIS (1645-76) = Natalia Naryshkin

THEODORE III
(1676-82)

IVAN V
(1682-96)

Eudoxia Lopukhin = PETER I, the Great = CATHERINE I
(1682-1725)   (1725-27)

Catherine of
Mecklenburg

Alexis

Anne Leopoldovna
of Brunswick

PETER II (1727-30)

IVAN VI
(1740-1)

ANNE (1730-40)

Anne of Holstein

ELIZABETH
(1741-61)

PETER III = CATHERINE II, the Great (1762-96)
(1761-2)

PAUL (1796-1801)

ALEXANDER I
(1801-25)

NICHOLAS I (1825-55)

ALEXANDER II (1855-81)

ALEXANDER III (1881-94)

NICHOLAS II (1894-1917)

Capitalized names are those of rulers. Dates refer to years of rule.

Chronology of Russian and Soviet History to 1985

With Significant Western Dates as Reference

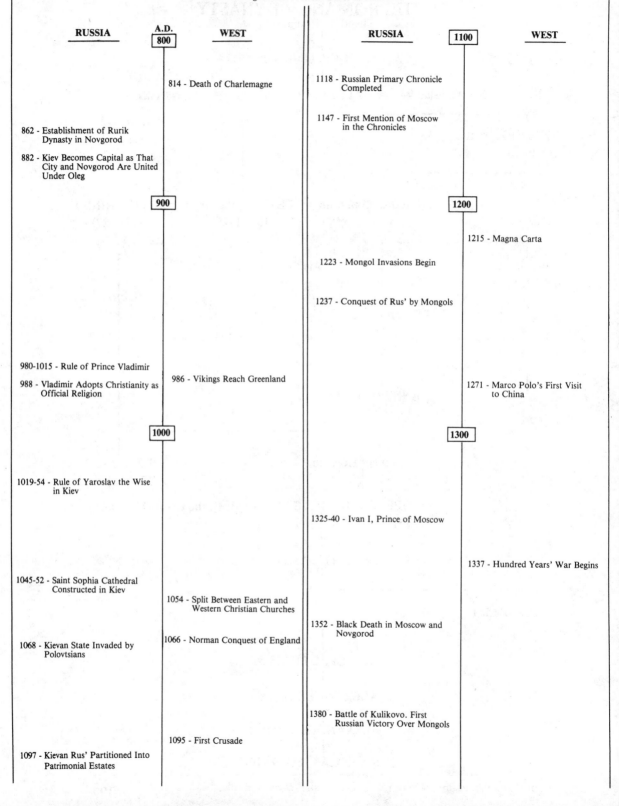

	A.D. 800			1100	
RUSSIA		**WEST**	**RUSSIA**		**WEST**

814 - Death of Charlemagne

1118 - Russian Primary Chronicle Completed

1147 - First Mention of Moscow in the Chronicles

862 - Establishment of Rurik Dynasty in Novgorod

882 - Kiev Becomes Capital as That City and Novgorod Are United Under Oleg

900

1200

1215 - Magna Carta

1223 - Mongol Invasions Begin

1237 - Conquest of Rus' by Mongols

980-1015 - Rule of Prince Vladimir

988 - Vladimir Adopts Christianity as Official Religion

986 - Vikings Reach Greenland

1271 - Marco Polo's First Visit to China

1000

1300

1019-54 - Rule of Yaroslav the Wise in Kiev

1325-40 - Ivan I, Prince of Moscow

1337 - Hundred Years' War Begins

1045-52 - Saint Sophia Cathedral Constructed in Kiev

1054 - Split Between Eastern and Western Christian Churches

1352 - Black Death in Moscow and Novgorod

1068 - Kievan State Invaded by Polovtsians

1066 - Norman Conquest of England

1380 - Battle of Kulikovo. First Russian Victory Over Mongols

1095 - First Crusade

1097 - Kievan Rus' Partitioned Into Patrimonial Estates

RUSSIA	**1400**	WEST	RUSSIA	**1700**	WEST
			1707 - St. Petersburg Replaces Moscow as Capital		
		1453 - Constantinople Falls to Ottoman Turks	1709 - Battle of Poltava. Decisive Victory Over Sweden		
1462-1505 - Rule of Ivan III, the Great			1721 - Great Northern War With Sweden Ends		
			1725 - Death of Peter the Great		
1480 - Mongol Rule Overthrown By Ivan III			1741-62 - Rule of Empress Elizabeth		
1487 - Novgorod *Veche* Bell Removed to Moscow			1762 - Catherine the Great Gains Throne by Coup d'Etat		
		1492 - Columbus Discovers America	1773 - Pugachev Rebellion		
			1785 - Charter of the Nobility		1776 - American Declaration of Independence
			1795 - Final Partition of Poland		1789 - French Revolution Begins
			1796 - Death of Catherine the Great		
	1500			**1800**	
			1801 - Alexander I Becomes Tsar		1803 - Louisiana Purchase
1533-84 - Rule of Ivan IV, the Terrible		1517 - Martin Luther's 95 Theses. Beginning of Protestant Reformation	1812 - Napoleon Invades Russia and is Repulsed		1815 - Battle of Waterloo. Exile of Napoleon
1547 - Ivan IV Assumes Title of Tsar			1825 - Alexander Succeeded by Nicholas I. Decembrist Revolt		
1553 - The Englishman Richard Chancellor Discovers Sea Route to Russia Around North Cape			1837 - First Russian Railroad		
			1854-56 - Crimean War v. France and England		1848 - Marx Publishes *Communist Manifesto*
		1562-1603 - Reign of Elizabeth I in England	1855-81 - Rule of Alexander II		1861 - U.S. Purchases Alaska
1565-84 - Ivan IV's Reign of Terror			1861 - Emancipation of Serfs		1861-65 - U.S. Civil War
1587-98 - Boris Godunov Acts as Regent			1881-94 - Rule of Alexander III		1871 - Bismarck Unites Germany
		1588 - Spanish Armada	1891 - Trans-Siberian Railway Begun		
1598-1613 - "Time of Troubles"			1894-1917 - Rule of Nicholas II		1898 - Spanish-American War
	1600			**1900**	
		1607 - Founding of Jamestown	1903 - Lenin Forms Bolshevik Party		
1613 - Michael Romanov Named Tsar. Beginning of Romanov Dynasty			1904-05 - Russo-Japanese War		
			1905 - Year of Revolutionary Violence		
		1618-48 - Thirty Years' War in Central Europe	1914-18 - World War I		
		1620 - Pilgrims Found Plymouth	1917 - Russian Revolution. End of Romanov Dynasty. Bolsheviks Take Power		1917 - U.S. Enters World War I
					1918 - U.S. and Other Countries Intervene in Russian Civil War
1637 - First Russian Explorers Reach Pacific Ocean			1918-21 - Civil War		
			1924 - Death of Lenin		
			1928-53 - Rule by Joseph Stalin		
1649 - Decree Issued Tying Serfs to Land			1936-39 - The Purges		1933 - U.S. Recognizes U.S.S.R.
1650 - Town of Okhotsk in Eastern Siberia Founded			1941-45 - The Great Patriotic War		1941-45 - U.S. in World War II
			1956-64 - Khrushchev in Power		1950-53 - Korean War
		1661 - Louis XIV Takes Throne in France	1960 - Sino-Soviet Split		1961 - Berlin Wall
		1688 - England's "Glorious Revolution"	1964-82 - Brezhnev in Power		1962 - Cuban Missile Crisis
			1974 - Solzhenitsyn Expelled From USSR		1962-75 - Viet Nam War
1689 - Peter the Great Becomes Tsar			1979 - SALT II Agreement		1977 - U.S. & U.S.S.R. Sign SALT I Agreement
			1979 - Invasion of Afghanistan		
			1982-84 - Yuri Andropov in Power		1980 - U.S. Boycotts Moscow Olympics
1697-98 - The "Grand Embassy"			1984 - Chernenko in Power		
			1985 - Gorbachev Assumes Control		1980 - Ronald Reagan Becomes U.S. President

KEY EVENTS OF THE GORBACHEV ERA

1985

March	Mikhail Gorbachev named general secretary of the Communist party, following death of Chernenko.
July	Eduard Shevardnadze, proponent of reform, named foreign minister, replacing hard-liner Andrei Gromyko, who had held the position since 1957.
November	The first U.S.-Soviet summit meeting since 1979: Gorbachev and Reagan meet in Geneva.

1986

February	The Twenty-Seventh Congress of the CPSU. Gorbachev describes crisis facing Soviet society for first time, calls for *perestroika*.
March	Policy of *glasnost* officially adopted.
April	The Chernobyl nuclear disaster.
December	Dissident physicist Andrei Sakharov released from political exile in Gorky.
	Conservative leaders, led by Yegor Ligachev, begin to agitate against *glasnost*.

1987

June	Multicandidate elections (to local soviets) held for first time.
November	Gorbachev launches attack on Stalin, opening way for examination and revision of Soviet history.
December	Washington summit: Gorbachev and Reagan sign treaty eliminating short and medium range missiles.

1988

February	First nationalist demonstrations break out in Armenia, directed against Azerbaijan.
March	Soviet troops sent to put down ethnic violence between Muslim Azerbaijanis and Christian Armenians.
June	Gorbachev proposes sweeping constitutional changes, including greater power to governmental institutions, a new parliament, and a new, more powerful presidency. Gorbachev's own power increased.
	Russian Orthodox Church celebrates millenium: the one-thousandth anniversary of Christianity in Russia. This with Kremlin support.
September	Shake-up in the Kremlin. Gromyko and other conservatives out of power.

| October | Supreme Soviet confirms Gorbachev as president. Kremlin shake-up continues: now all but two attained power under Gorbachev. |
| December | At United Nations, Gorbachev announces unilateral cuts in conventional Soviet armed forces. |

1989

February	Soviets complete withdrawal of forces from Afghanistan.
March	Elections to new Soviet parliament, the Congress of People's Deputies. This is the first nationwide multicandidate election since 1917. Results show deep dissatisfaction with status quo.
April	Soviet troops put down nationalist rally in Georgia with force; 19 killed.
	Gorbachev forces resignation of political opponents in Politburo and Central Committee.
May	Congress of People's Deputies meets for first time, elects Gorbachev president, with greater power than before.
	Soviet forces begin to leave Eastern Europe.
July	Massive wildcat strikes by coal miners, protesting low pay and poor living conditions.
November	Popular revolutions in Eastern Europe. Berlin Wall torn down.
December	Malta summit meeting. Presidents Gorbachev and Bush proclaim end of Cold War.

1990

January	Renewed hostilities between Azerbaijanis and Armenians; Soviet troops again sent in to quell violence.
February	Large prodemocracy rally in Moscow.
March	Lithuania proclaims its independence. Moscow replies with economic blockade. Estonia also takes steps toward independence.
	Congress of People's Deputies repeals Communist party's monopoly of political power.
May	Gorbachev and Kremlin leaders jeered during holiday celebrations in Moscow on May 1.
	Latvia declares "transition to independence."
July	Boris Yeltsin, spokesman for reform, resigns from Communist party.

December	Conservatives announce dissatisfaction with deteriorating conditions in USSR, pressure Gorbachev to slow reforms. Shevardnadze resigns as foreign minister, warning of an impending dictatorship. Gorbachev picks conservatives Gennadi Yanayev and Valentin Pavlov as vice president and premier.

1991

February	Gorbachev calls himself a "dedicated Communist" and chastises radicals.
April	Warsaw Pact terminated.
June	Boris Yeltsin wins free popular election as president of the Russian Republic in landslide victory.
	KGB head Vladimir Kryuchkov warns of danger in further liberal reforms.
July	Shevardnadze quits Communist party, founds movement for democratic reform.
	Communist party conservatives call on military to save the country.
	Gorbachev reaches agreement with heads of ten republics on a new union treaty that would give republics much greater autonomy.
	At party conference, Gorbachev renounces Marxist-Leninist theories.
August	Liberal Gorbachev adviser Alexander Yakovlev resigns, warns of forthcoming coup.
	Vice President Yanayev and hard-line associates announce state of emergency and place Gorbachev under house arrest in right-wing coup d'etat, which fails after three days. Boris Yeltsin emerges as hero of opposition to the coup.
September	Congress of People's Deputies approves sweeping transfer of power to the Soviet republics, creates interim political structure. State Council established as executive committee to handle foreign policy, security, and law enforcement.
	State Council recognizes independence of three Baltic republics.
October	Eight of twelve remaining republics sign treaty of economic union. Ukraine and three others boycott.
November	Russian Parliament grants Yeltsin sweeping powers to institute economic reform.
	Under international pressure, Ukraine and Moldavia sign treaty of economic union.

Gorbachev proposal to form Union of Sovereign States rejected by seven republics.

December   In referendum, Ukrainians overwhelmingly vote for independence.

The three Slavic republics form Commonwealth of Independent States. Gorbachev denounces this move, threatens to resign.

By the 21st, eleven republics have joined the Commonwealth.

On the 25th, the USSR is formally disbanded and Gorbachev resigns.

ACKNOWLEDGMENTS

"Peoples of the USSR" from "1989 Soviet Census: Preliminary Results" by Elizabeth Talbot. "The Arrival of Rurik" and "The Baptism of Vladimir" from "The Primary Chronicle," *Harvard Studies in Philology and Literature,* Vol. XII by Samuel Cross, translator, © 1930 by the President and Fellows of Harvard College, reprinted by permission of the Harvard University Press. "Boris and Gleb," "The Sack of Riazan" and "The Time of Troubles" abridged from *Medieval Russia's Epics, Chronicles and Tales,* © 1963 by Serge A. Zenkovsky. Reprinted by permission of the publisher, E.P. Dutton Inc. "The Russian Peasant Community" from "Russian Political Culture" by Edward L. Keenan, © 1975 by Edward L. Keenan. "The Maiden Tsar" reprinted from *Russian Fairy Tales* by Alexander Afanas'ev, translated by Nobert Guterman. © 1945 by Pantheon Books, Inc. and renewed 1975 by Random House, Inc. Reprinted by permission of Pantheon Books, a Division of Random House, Inc. "Seventeenth Century Moscow" and "The Building of St. Petersburg" reprinted by permission of Faber and Faber Ltd. from *Palmyra of the North: The First Days of St. Petersburg* by Christopher Marsden. "Riddles" from *Riddles of the Russian People: A Collection of Riddles, Parables and Puzzles,* collected by D. Sadovnikov, trans. with an Introduction by Ann C. Bigelow (Ann Arbor, MI: Ardis, © 1986). Reprinted by permission of Ardis Publishers. "Resistance to Peter: Ruthless Razoring" from *Seven Britons in Imperial Russia, 1698–1812* by Peter Putnam, editor, © 1952, © renewed 1980 by Princeton University Press, excerpt pages 38–39 reprinted by permission of Princeton University Press. "Alexander Pushkin: The Bronze Horseman" from *Alexander Pushkin: Collected Narrative and Lyrical Poetry* by Walter Arndt, translator, © 1984 by Ardis Publishers. "Anna's Ice Palace" from *The Three Empresses* by Phillip Longworth, © 1972 by Constable & Co., Ltd. "The Pugachev Rebellion" abridged from *Imperial Russia: A Source Book, 1700–1917* by B. Dmytryshyn. © Hinsdale, The Dryden Press, 1974. "Napoleon Enters Moscow" abridged from *Eyewitness to History* by J. Carey, ed., New York: Avon, 1988. "A Frenchman's View of Autocracy" abridged from *Journey For Our Time: The Russian Journals of the Marquis de Custine* by Phyllis Penn Kohler, editor & translator, Chicago: Regnery Gateway, 1951. "Leo Tolstoy: A Morning of a Landed Proprietor" abridged from *Childhood, Boyhood, Youth, The Incursion, A Landed Proprietor, The Cossacks, Sevastopol* by Leo Tolstoy, translated and edited by Leo Wiener, Boston, 1904. "Mikhail Lermontov: Prediction" from *The Origin of Russian Communism* by Nicolas Berdyaev, © 1960, University of Michigan Press. "Alexander Herzen: Thoughts on the Peasant Community" reprinted from *The Russian Tradition* by T. Szamuely. ©1974 by McGraw-Hill. "Ivan Turgenev: The Nihilist" reprinted from *Fathers and Sons* by Ivan Turgenev, translated by Barbara Makanowitsky. Translation copyright © 1959 by Bantam Books, a division of Bantam Doubleday Dell Publishing Group, Inc., all rights reserved. "Ivan Turgenev: The Revolutionist's Promise" from "The Threshold" *The Underground Press of the People's Will* by Ivan Turgenev, 1883. "Siberian Exiles on the Road" abridged from "Siberia" *Siberia and the Exile System,* Vol. 1 by George Kennan, New York: Praeger, 1891. "Sergei Witte: A Proposal for Russia's Industrialization" reprinted from "A Secret Memorandum of Sergei Witte on the Industrialization of Imperial Russia" in *Journal of Modern History,* Vol. 26, March, 1954. © 1954 by The University of Chicago Press. "Justification for Imperial Expansion" from *A Source Book For Russian History,* Vol. 3 by G. Vernadsky, et al, translators, © 1972 Yale University Press. "The Worker's Life Under the Last Tsar" from *La Vie Quotidienne en Russie au Temps du Dernier Tsar (Daily Life in Russia Under the Last Tsar)* by Henri Troyat, © 1959, 1961 by Hachette. "Vladimir Ilyich Lenin: The Organization of the Party" abridged from "What Is To Be Done?" *Collected Works,* Vol. 5 by V.I. Lenin, Moscow: Foreign Languages Publishing House, 1964. "Bloody Sunday" from "Bloody Sunday: St. Petersburg, 22 January, 1905" by G. Gapon in *Eyewitness to History* by J. Carey, ed., New York: Avon, 1988. "The Duma of 1906" abridged from *Russia and Reform* by Bernard Pares, London: Archibald Constable & Co., Ltd., 1907. "War Frenzy in St. Petersburg" by S.N. Kurnakov from *Eyewitness to History* by J. Carey, ed., New York: Avon, 1988. "Felix Youssoupoff: The Murder of Rasputin" reprinted from "The Night of the Sixteenth December" from *The End of Rasputin* by Prince Felix Youssoupoff. © 1927 by Doubleday, a division of Bantam Doubleday Dell Publishing Group, Inc. Used by permission of Doubleday and Company, Inc. "Initial Disturbances: A Police Account," "The Mood in the Streets," and "The Provisional Government Proclaims the Revolution" reprinted from *The Russian Provisional*

Government, 1917: Documents, Volume 1, selected and edited by Robert Paul Browder and Alexander F. Kerensky, with the permission of the publishers, Stanford University Press. © 1961 by the Board of Trustees of the Leland Stafford Junior University. "The Petrograd Soviet" and "Lenin's Arrival" reprinted from *The Russian Revolution of 1917: Volume 1* by N.N. Sukhanov. © 1984 by Princeton University Press. Reprinted by permission. "The Revolution as Seen by a Child" and "Dissolution of the Constituent Assembly" reprinted from *The Russian Revolution of 1917: Contemporary Accounts* by Dimitri VonMohrenschildt. © 1971 by Oxford University Press, Inc. Reprinted by permission. "Anarchy in the Countryside" abridged from *Documents of Russian History, 1914–1917* by F. Golder, editor, New York: Stanford University Press, 1927. "Proclamation of the Military-Revolutionary Committee" and "The October Revolution: An Eyewitness Account" from *The Russian Revolution* edited by Robert V. Daniels, © 1972 by Prentice-Hall, Inc., by permission of the author. "The Fall of the Winter Palace" from *Witnesses to the Russian Revolution*, by R. Pethybridge. © 1967. Published by Citadel Press, a division of Lyle Stuart, Inc. "Maxim Gorky: The Gardener" from *Fragments from my Diary* by M. Gorky, New York: Praeger Publishers, 1972, reprinted by permission. "John Reed on Lenin" from *Ten Days That Shook the World* by John Reed, © 1966, Penguin Books. "Alexander Blok: The Twelve" from *The Twelve and Other Poems* by Alexander Blok, translated by John Stallworthy and Peter France, © 1970 by Methuen and Co. "Terrorism: The Cheka," "The Cheka in Action," "The Civil War," and "Victims of the Red Terror" from *Intervention, Civil War and Communism in Russia, 1918* by J. Bunyan, © 1936 by The John Hopkins University Press. "The Peasant's Apology" abridged from *Great Russian Peoples* by G. Gorer and J. Rickman, London: Hutchison & Co., 1949. "Isaac Babel: Prishchepa's Vengeance" reprinted by permission of S.G. Phillips, Inc. from *The Collected Stories of Isaac Babel*, © 1955 by S.G. Phillips, Inc. "Murder of the Royal Family" from *The Last Days of the Romanovs* by G.G. Telberg and R. Wilton, New York: Citadel, 1920. "The Famine of 1921–22" from "Famine in Russia" by Anna Haines, 1922 by permission of the American Friends Service Committee. "The 1920s: Reduction of Class Distinctions" abridged from *Soviet Russia* by W.H. Chamberlin, Boston: Little, Brown, 1930. "Bertrand Russell on Lenin" reprinted from *The Practice and Theory of Bolshevism* by Bertrand Russell. © 1948 by George Allen & Unwin Ltd., London. "Vladimir Mayakovsky: Komsomolskaya" from *Lenin Lives!* by N. Tumarkin, © 1983, Harvard University Press. "Lenin's Testament" from *USSR: A Concise History* by Basil Dmytryshyn, © 1965, 1971, 1978 Charles Scribner's Sons, reprinted with the permission of Charles Scribner's Sons. "Stalin: A Lenin Litany" and "Stalin: How to Deal with Opposition" reprinted from the book *Stalin* edited by T.H. Rigby © 1966. Used by permission of the publisher, Prentice-Hall/A division of Simon & Schuster, Englewood Cliffs, NJ. "Mayakovsky: Americans are Astounded" from *Mayakovsky* by Herber Marshall, translator and editor, © 1965, Dobson Books Ltd. "Katya's Account of Collectivization" from *I Chose Freedom* by Victor Kravchenko, © 1946 Victor Kravchenko, copyright renewed 1974, reprinted with the permission of Charles Scribner's Sons. "John Scott: A Day in Magnitogorsk" from *Behind the Urals* by John Scott, © 1942, The Indiana University Press. "Zoshchenko: Poverty" from *Scenes from the Bathhouse* by Mikhail Zoshchenko, © 1973, The University of Michigan Press. "Ginzburg: Into the Whirlwind of the Purges" excerpts from *Journey into the Whirlwind* by Eugenia S. Ginzburg, © 1967 by Arnoldo Mondadori Editore-Milano; English translation, © 1967 by Harcourt Brace Jovanovich, Inc. Reprinted by permission of Harcourt Brace Jovanovich, Inc. "Stalin's Official History of the Purges" from *History of the Communist Party of the Soviet Union (Bolshevik) Short Course* by Commission of the Central Committee of the C.P.S.U., editor, © 1939 International Publishers Co., Inc. "The Siege of Leningrad" reprinted from *Leningrad 1941: The Blockade* by D.V. Pavlov, by permission of The University of Chicago Press. "A Russian Woman" reprinted from *The Curtain Rises* by Quentin Reynolds. © 1944 by Random House, Inc. and renewed 1972 by James J. Reynolds and Frederick H. Rohlfs, Esq. Reprinted by permission of Random House, Inc. "Soviet War Losses" from *Itogi Vsesoyuznoi Naseleniia*, Central Statistics Bureau, Moscow, 1962. "Stalin in the Late 1940s" abridged excerpts from *Conversations with Stalin* by Milovan Djilas, © 1962 by Harcourt Brace Jovanovich, Inc. Reprinted by permission of the publisher. "Khrushchev's Secret Speech" abridged from "Speech of Nikita Khrushchev Before a Closed Session of the Twentieth Congress of the Communist Party of the Soviet Union on February 25, 1956," Committee Print, Judiciary Committee of the U.S. Senate, 85th Congress, Washington, D.C., 1957. "De-Stalinization and the Cult of Lenin" from "Current Soviet Policies IV," © 1962 Columbia University Press. "Polyakov:

Fireman Prokhorchuk" from "The Story of a Story, or Fireman Prokhorchuk" by Vladimir Polyakov, translated by A. MacAndrew, *Partisan Review*, 1961. "Bukovsky: Dissenters and the KGB" abridged from *To Build a Castle* by Vladimir Bukovsky, translated by Michael Scammell, New York:Viking, 1977. "A Soviet View of U.S. Policy" abridged from "The United States: Will There Be Changes?" by G. Arbatov, *Pravda*, March 1983, *Current Digest of the Soviet Press*, April 1983. "Ronald Reagan: The Evil Empire" abridged from *Speeches of the American Presidents* edited by J. Podell and S. Anzovin, 1988 H.W. Wilson Co. "The Public Bath" from *Russia: The People and the Power* by Robert G. Kaiser, © 1976 Robert G. Kaiser, reprinted with the permission of Atheneum Publishers. "Car Owners' Woes" abridged from V. Petrov and V. Yakovlev, *Sovetskaya Rossio*, October, 1981, "Once Again About Automotive Service," *Current Digest of the Soviet Press*, Vol. 33, No. 52. "Clothes" from Glants, Musya. Interview with Janet Vaillant. Cambridge, Massachusetts, 29 September 1990. "The Soviet People's Court" from *Justice in Moscow* by George Feifer, © 1964 by George Feifer, reprinted by permission of Literistic, Ltd. "Soviet Medical Training under Stalin and Brezhnev" abridged from *Russian Doctor* by V. Golya Khovsky, New York:St. Martin's, 1984. "The Intourist Guide" from "Is It Easy To Be a Guide with Intourist?" *Moscow News* No. 8, 1990. "Gorbachev of Perestroika" abridged from *Perestroika: New Thinking for Our Country and the World* by M. Gorbachev, New York:HarperCollins, 1987. "Chernobyl: A Victim's Account" from "Confessions of a Chernobyl Victim" by V. Zosimov, *Izvestia* (June 18, 1989), *Current Digest of the Soviet Press* Vol. 41. "The Environment" abridged from "Mailman Vesilyev's Bomb" by S. Razin, *Komsomolskaya Pravda* (March 15, 1988), *The Glasnost Reader*, New York:New American Library, 1990. "Yeltsin on Gorbachev" and "Yeltsin on Party Privileges" from *Against the Grain* by B. Yeltsin, New York: Summit Books, 1990. "In Defense of Coca-Cola" from *Moscow News* by Alexander Ivanov, November, 1990. "The Disillusioned Farmer" from "The Admission of a Farmer Who Gave Up" by Nataliya Popkova, *Moscow News*, 28 January, 1990. "Censorship" abridged from "The Life of a Soviet Censor: Anything Goes? Not Just Yet" by B. Keller, *New York Times*, 17 July, 1989. "Perestroika: The Writers' Response" excerpted from "Poetry in the Age of Perestroika and Glasnost" by Natalya B. Ivanova, *Chronicle of Revolution*, Abraham Brumberg, ed., New York: Pantheon, 1990. Translation by Josephine Woll. "Re-Writing History" from "New Blank Spots" by I. Zavgorodnyaya, *Izvestiya* (August 17, 1989), *The Glasnost Reader* edited by J. Eisen, New York: New American Library, 1990. "Opposition to Reform" abridged from "I Can't Forgo Principles" by N. Andreeva, *Sovetskaya Rossia* (March 13, 1988), *Current Digest of the Soviet Press* Vol. 40, April 1988. "Ethnic Problems in the Disintegrating Soviet Union" abridged from "We will catch up with and surpass Angola!" by Timor Pulatov, *Moskovskiye novosti* (October 1990), *Current Digest of the Soviet Press* 41 (November 1990): 11. "Bush on Gorbachev" abridged from "Bush and Gorbachev Toasts at Dinner," *New York Times*, 1 June 1990. "Moscow Women" abridged from *Moscow Women* by C. Hansson and Karen Liden, New York: Pantheon, 1983. "Shortages" from "Thoughts While Waiting in Line" by S. Kalmykova, *Izvestiya* (Feb. 3, 1989), *The Glasnost Reader* edited by J. Eisen, New York: New American Library, 1990. "The Joke and the Fable: Social Commentary Soviet-style" retold by Janet Vaillant.

ILLUSTRATION ACKNOWLEDGMENTS: William Craft Brumfield, pp. 12, 37, 58; Dow Jones & Co., Inc., *Photo Source: Lael Morgan*, p. xx; John F. Kennedy Library, Boston, Massachusetts, p. 229; MacClancy Collection, pp. 138, 145 (left); 159; New York Public Library, pp. 7, 20, 65, 66, 89, 145 (right), 152; John Richards II, p. 257; Sovfoto, p. 216; Soviet and East European Language and Area Center Program, Harvard University, pp. 210, 227, 228, 282, 288, 292, 296, 297; U.S. Army Photo, 225; Victoria and Albert Museum, London, England, p. 35; AP / Wide World Photos, cover; TASS from SOVFOTO, p. 316; Sovfoto/eastfoto, pp. 321, 323, 325; The Bettmann Archive, p. 335; Reuters/Bettmann, pp. 328, 332, 334; Ken Mowry from *CNN Reports: Seven Days That Shook the World* by Stuart H. Loory and Anne Imse © 1991 Turner Publishing, Inc., p. 369.

INDEX